A GENERATION OF REVOLUTIONARIES

A GENERATION  REVOLUTIONARIES

NIKOLAI CHARUSHIN

and

RUSSIAN POPULISM FROM THE GREAT
REFORMS TO PERESTROIKA

BEN EKLOF
TATIANA SABUROVA

INDIANA UNIVERSITY PRESS

This book is a publication of

Indiana University Press
Office of Scholarly Publishing
Herman B Wells Library 350
1320 East 10th Street
Bloomington, Indiana 47405 USA

iupress.indiana.edu

© 2017 by Ben Eklof and Tatiana Saburova

All rights reserved

No part of this book may be reproduced or utilized in any form or by any means, electronic or mechanical, including photocopying and recording, or by any information storage and retrieval system, without permission in writing from the publisher. The Association of American University Presses' Resolution on Permissions constitutes the only exception to this prohibition.

The paper used in this publication meets the minimum requirements of the American National Standard for Information Sciences—Permanence of Paper for Printed Library Materials, ANSI Z39.48–1992.

Manufactured in the United States of America

Cataloging information is available from the Library of Congress.

ISBN 978-0-253-02981-2 (cloth)
ISBN 978-0-253-03121-1 (paperback)
ISBN 978-0-253-03125-9 (ebook)

1 2 3 4 5   22 21 20 19 18 17

CONTENTS

Preface ix

Introduction: Remembrances of a Distant Past 1
About the Main Heroes of this Book 3
Metanarrative and Biography: Lives Obscure and Less So 5
Generational History and Memory Studies 6
Examining Russian Populism as a Movement 7
A Cooperative Endeavor 10

1 Beginnings: How to Become a Revolutionary 13
In His Own Words 14
Untrammeled Childhoods? 18
School Days in Viatka (1862–1871) 23
Crossing a Societal Threshold: Salon Culture in Viatka 29
Last Days and Departure 33
Searching for the Roots of Radicalism 34

2 The Seventies Generation: Young Revolutionaries and the Chaikovskii Circle 39
The Chaikovskii Circle 39
From Student to Revolutionary 40
Generational Tropes: Youthfulness and a Debt to the People 45
Moral Standards 47
Influences on Young Minds: Chernyshevskii and Pushkin? 52
Lavrov or Bakunin? Polarities in Populist Thought 54
On Constitutions and Lassalle 57
The Impact of the Paris Commune (1871) 59
Overcoming Backwardness and the Zemstvo 61

Book Matters: The Cause of the Book 63
  Learning about the Common People 65
  Diverse Views, Intact Networks 67

3 **The Male Gaze and Female Profile: Marriage, Family, Populism** 73
  The Male Gaze 76
  Self-Portraits 80
  "My Unfailing Partner and Comrade in Life" 83
  "My Lovey, My Dovey": Authenticity, Mutuality, and Joint Commitment 87
  How Joyful It Is to Have Children . . . ! 94
  "Domestic Bothers such as Washing Up and Cleaning" 97
  We Are Like Siamese Twins: Final Partings 99
  "My Husband No Longer Posed an Obstacle" 100
  Uniform Life Scenarios? The "Woman Question" Revisited 105

4 **"Punishment Harsh and Cruel": The Experience of Incarceration (1874–1878)** 111
  Arrests 111
  Prison Memoirs 112
  "A Gray Hospital Robe" 114
  "New Accommodations": Spatial Dimensions of the Cell 115
  "Around Us Reigned the Stultifying Silence of the Grave" 117
  "The Variety of the Menu Selections Was Surprising" 120
  "A Hunger Strike Not for Three to Four Days, but Until the Bitter End" 122
  "Time Dragged on Torturously and Without Purpose" 124
  Meaningful Activities 126
  "I Yearned to See People and Hear Live Voices" 129
  "The Potential for Going Mad Terrified Me" 134
  Escape 136
  "The Great Trial of the 193" 138

5 **Seventeen Years in Siberia: Hard Labor, Exile, and Photography** 145
  "You Are Being Sentenced to Siberia" 145

Perceptions of Siberia 148
The Road 150
At the Kara Place Mines and Prison Colony 152
Charushin and Kononovich: "Even the Jailer Weeps at Times" 160
Life as a Penal Colonist: Nerchinsk (1881–1886) 164
A Revolutionary Turns to Photography 169
"The Call of Our First Homeland Was Stronger Than
   Attachment to the Second One" 180

**6 Return to European Russia: Family Ties, Networks of
Exiles, and the Zemstvo (1895–1905)**   **188**
The Charushin Household: Domesticity and Extended Family 190
Networks of Exiles Renewed and Expanded 196
Zemstvo Ties 199
Book Matters 202
Nikolai Charushin: Fire-Insurance Agent 206
Famine Relief: The All-Zemstvo Organization 210
Encounters with the Peasant World Compared 214
The Zemstvo on the Eve of 1905 216
Founding of a Provincial Newspaper 222
Social Networks in Viatka 223

7 After October: The Downward Spiral of Revolution   **231**
Enter Gorchakov: "Liquidation and Renewal" Policies 232
Yumashev, the Zemstvo Executive Board and
   Its Newspaper *Viatskaia Gazeta* 238
Charushin's Newspaper Under Fire: Kuvshinskaia's Exile 242
Forced Resignation from the Zemstvo 246
The "Urzhum Brothers" and Family Matters 248
The "Saltykov Affair" and Departure from the
   Famine Relief Organization 250
The "Viatka Warlord" Exits: Accountability and the Press 253
In the Aftermath: Looking to the Future 259

8 The Revolution Followed Its Own Scenario (1917–1919)   **269**
The New Order 269
"The Joy Was Short Lived … Anxiety Overtook Me" 271

Viatskaia Rech' and the People's Socialist Party   273
The Peasant Union and the "Old Revolutionary
    and Freedom Fighter"   277
"The Deep Countryside Is Mired in Ignorance"   281
"Everyone Is Fed Up with Empty Phrases and Inaction"   283
Surely Not All of Russia Is Infected with Bolshevism!   287
My Position on the Claimants to Power:
    A Matter of Conscience   291
Incarceration Redux: Repeating the Trials
    and Tribulations of Youth   294
The Revolution Followed Its Own Scenario   297

9 Remembrances of a Distant Past   307
"The Thinning Ranks of the Living Among Us"   307
"I Withdrew Completely From the Arena of Politics":
    The Library as Refuge and Outlet   309
"Your Efforts Were All in Vain": The Turn to Writing Memoirs   317
"I Urge You to Write Down Your Recollections"   320
Collective Autobiography and Traveling Narratives   323
Charushin Lauded and Rewarded   326
Memory Wars   328
"We Need More Bolshevik Vigilance!"   330
"Still, I Am Not Yet Ready to Give Up..."   334

10 In Search of the Real Charushin in the Perestroika Era   344
Emerging from the Dustbin of History   344
Perestroika Memory Wars   349
In Search of the Real Charushin   361

Conclusion   365

Biographical Sketches   373

Selected Bibliography   379

Index   391

PREFACE

THE SCHOLAR of Russian history always needs to address a number of minor but thorny issues pertaining to transliteration, Russian names, and dates. We have used the Library of Congress system, except for proper names or geographic sites that are already familiar to the reader by another spelling. Thus we have Leo Tolstoy instead of Lev Tolstoi, Moscow instead of Moskva, Yakutsk instead of Iakutsk. Since Russian is an inflected language, the endings of proper names will often, but not always, change depending on whether we are talking about males or females—the spelling of surnames usually changes, depending on which gender we are referring to. Likewise, the forms of address people use with each other depend on social hierarchies and degrees of intimacy and are further complicated by the addition of patronymics in polite social discourse. Just in case the reader has managed to grasp all this, the Russian language has added a bewildering number of diminutive versions of names to express degrees of affection for the person on whom the nickname is bestowed. We have tried to avoid inserting Russian words into the text, but a few whose exact translation is difficult or cumbersome, such as *meshchanstvo* (roughly: petty bourgeoisie), kustarnyi sklad (cottage industry warehouse), *uprava* (executive board), *zemstvo* (local self-government council), *kraeved* and *kraevedenie* (local historian and local history), and *gosudarstvennost'* (statism) are unavoidable because they convey a nuance not present in the English-language near-equivalent. Similarly, we have occasionally inserted the word *Chaikovtsy* from the Russian, designating the members of the

Chaikovskii circle. As for the use of italics, to avoid burdening the text any further we note here that all have been added by the authors.

The authors express their gratitude to the following programs and institutions for financial support given during the more than three years they spent on this book: at Indiana University the Office of the Vice President for International Affairs, the College of Arts and Humanities Institute (CAHI),[1] and the Russian and East European Institute (REEI);[2] the Fulbright Program;[3] the Higher School of Economics[4] and the German Historical Institute in Moscow;[5] and the staff at the following archival holdings: RGALI (Moscow), RGIA (St. Petersburg); GAKO, the Herzen Regional Library, the ROSFOTO Museum Exhibition Center, and the Vaznetsov Museum of Fine Arts (Kirov). Padraic Kenney offered helpful insights for our chapter on incarceration. We are especially grateful to Janet Rabinowitch and Larry Holmes, both of whom read most or all of the manuscript at different stages and provided us with sage advice at all times, and to Alex Rabinowitch and Hiro Kuromiya for their unflagging support. We thank the participants at the several sessions of the Midwestern Russian Historians' Workshop (MRHW) who read early versions of several chapters. Finally, we thank Dee Mortenson and Jennika Baines, our able, patient, and supportive editors at Indiana University Press and Charles Clark at Newgen North America for superbly shepherding this manuscript through its final stages.

Abbreviations:
MVD—Ministry of the Interior
OPK—Society of Former Political Prisoners and Exiles
NS—the People's Socialist Party
SR—Socialist Revolutionary Party
Kadet—Constitutional Democratic Party

In our notes, we follow the standard abbreviated conventions for identifying the locations of archival documents: f.—fond (holding); op.—opis' (registry); d.—delo (file), and l.—list (page);
ll.—listy (pages), and ob.—oborot (reverse side of page)

NOTES

1. Faculty Research Travel Grant of the College of Art and Humanities Institute.
2. Faculty Summer Research Fellowship.
3. The Fulbright Senior Scholar Research-Teaching Fellowship and Visiting Scholar Fellowship
4. The Basic Research Program at the National Research University Higher School of Economics (HSE) and a subsidy granted to the HSE by the Government of the Russian Federation for the implementation of the Global Competitiveness Program.
5. Short-term Research Fellowship

A GENERATION OF
REVOLUTIONARIES

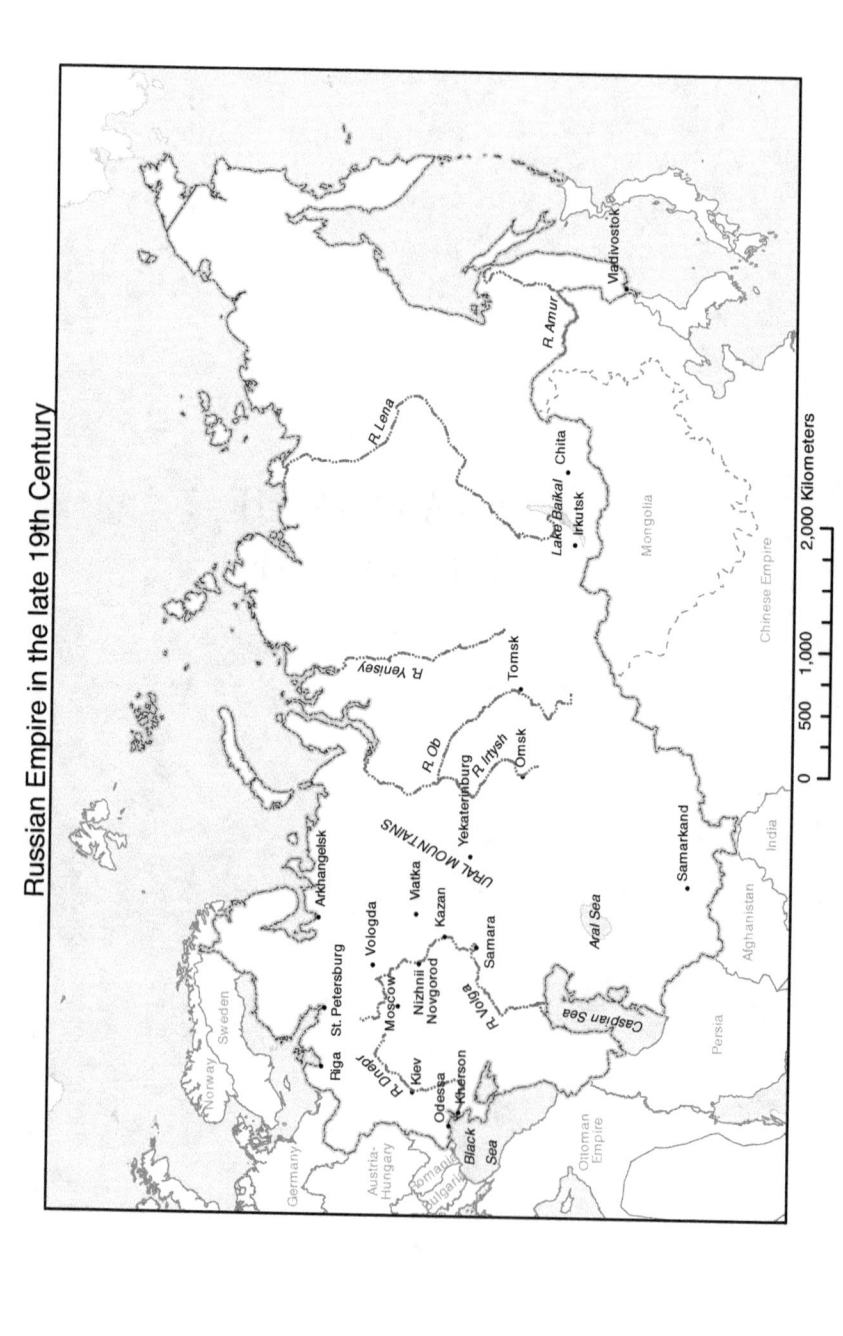

European Russia in the late 19th Century

Introduction

Remembrances of a Distant Past

IN THE MIDDLE of the nineteenth century, after an embarrassing defeat in the Crimean war (1854–1856), the Russian autocracy set about overhauling its fundamental institutions, including serfdom, local government, the judicial system, the military, and education. This period came to known as that of the Great Reforms, and indeed, in its breadth and scope it has few parallels in the modern history of Europe. Yet ecstatic praise of the ruler, Alexander II, was followed by disappointment and disillusionment with the outcomes—for no limits were placed on the powers of the autocracy itself. Even if several of the reforms moved the country forward, much of the nobility and intelligentsia lost faith in the government's ability to address the country's needs and willingness to make government accountable to society or even to listen to public opinion. Some among the nobility petitioned to have the recently established elected local zemstvo institutions serve as the basis for a national parliament, while university students, frustrated by increasingly repressive measures applied to their daily lives, protested, organized into mutual aid circles, or found themselves expelled from their institutions.

Many of them were able to move beyond their own grievances to consider the often-wretched lives of the peasantry and found evidence of such in the vivid depictions of the countryside by the itinerant social commentator Vasilii Bervi-Flerovsky. At the same time, the moral exigency to commit oneself to a larger cause was framed by the exemplary characters depicted in the radical democrat Nikolai Chernyshevskii's wildly popular novel *What Is to Be Done*, as well as by the moral injunctions of Petr Lavrov in his *Historical Letters*. Lavrov insisted that the intelligentsia had received its privileged education only through the exploitation of Russia's enserfed peasantry; in so doing, it had incurred a moral debt to give something back to the people. But how was that debt to be repaid in the constricting environment of the nineteenth-century tsarist autocracy—however limited its actual powers were in comparison to twentieth century police states?

The dramatic story of how operating within a closed political system led young Russians down the path to terrorism has been told often. But in reality, terrorism was an aberration not reflecting the broad contours of the Populism that emerged at the time. So instead of focusing on terrorism in the Russian revolutionary movement, we examine the Chaikovskii circle, a small group that played an outsized role in the emergence and evolution of the Populist movement in the 1870s. We follow the members of this group through their childhoods and education, their moves to St. Petersburg to study at the university, and immersion in what Daniel Brower called the "culture of dissent." We depict the consolidation of their world views and ethical constellations as members of the Chaikovskii circle, and then their arrests, incarcerations, trials, and banishments to Siberia to perform hard labor at a time when the autocracy, itself confronting widespread public discontent over the dismal performance of its armies in the Russo-Turkish War (1877–1878), struggled to discredit the revolutionary youth but ended up only increasing sympathy for their martyrdom.

After decades of exile, during which many of this generation made major cultural contributions to Siberian life, those who could afford to do so returned to European Russia in the 1890s, just as a surge of opposition to the status quo was sweeping through all segments of society, culminating in the powerful but failed revolutions of 1905. This cohort experienced the disarray and disillusionment of the aftermath, but they were also caught up in the vast changes underway in society and culture—the rise of a modern periodical press, emergence of the professions, rapid growth of cooperatives and of a modern rural infrastructure, and heated discussion of the best path forward politically for Russia.

When the February 1917 revolution overthrew the Romanov dynasty, it established the Provisional Government to hold the country together until Russia could extricate itself from World War I and hold genuinely democratic elections. The now-aging seventies generation (as they saw themselves) played active roles at both local and countrywide levels in these endeavors, only to be "swept into the dustbin of history" by the Bolshevik Revolution in October 1917 and the ensuing horrific civil war (1918–1921). Several of those who survived emigrated and spent their remaining years pining for their homeland. Others stayed in Russia and sought to find ways to contribute purposively to the building of a new society in ways that accorded with the convictions they had formed in the aftermath of the Great Reforms era.

ABOUT THE MAIN HEROES OF THIS BOOK

This book tells the story of that group—a generation of revolutionaries—through the lives of Nikolai Charushin, Anna Kuvshinskaia, and their circle of friends. Charushin and Kuvshinskaia were both born in 1851, in Viatka province in the Volga region, 500 miles northeast of Moscow. After completing their secondary schooling in the provincial capital (chapter 1), each went forth to St. Petersburg, where they soon joined the Chaikovskii circle (later called the Big Society for Propaganda) at the birth of the Populist movement. Participation in this group largely defined their future—shaping their political views, convictions, and values as well as their public activities and private lives (chapters 2–3).

Arrested early in 1874 because of his efforts to educate workers, Charushin spent nearly four years in solitary confinement in various places of detention, including the famous Peter-Paul Fortress. Kuvshinskaia was arrested in the same year, and in 1878 both were brought before the judges in the notorious Trial of the 193 (chapter 4). During this period of incarceration, Kuvshinskaia managed to arrange her marriage to an initially reluctant Charushin, something which then allowed her to follow him into exile when he was sentenced to nine years of hard labor followed by forced penal settlement in Siberia. They were to remain in the region for seventeen years; during that time, Charushin became a noted photographer and made a significant cultural contribution to the life of Kiakhta, a prosperous trade entrepot on the border with China (chapter 5).

Upon returning with his family to European Russia in 1895, Charushin found employment in the Viatka provincial zemstvo at a time when that institution was rapidly expanding its activities, soon to become a site of political mobilization as Russia entered the turbulent twentieth century. When the massive 1905 Revolution led to new and liberal press regulations, Charushin founded an oppositionist newspaper, *Viatskaia Rech'*, which the prime minister, Petr Stolypin, called "the most revolutionary provincial newspaper in Russia." While managing their household, Kuvshinskaia played an active role in the affairs of both the newspaper and an independent book cooperative they and their friends had organized. For her role as publisher she was exiled from the province in 1906 and died three years later, in 1909 (chapters 6–7).

Although Charushin had welcomed the 1917 February Revolution, which led to the collapse of the autocracy and a "springtime of freedom" in Russia, he rued the ensuing polarization of the country, recognized the dangers inherent in the Bolshevik takeover of power in October, and took measures to oppose Bolshevism's further spread (chapter 8). Arrested four times over the next two years, he then eschewed all involvement in politics. Attempting to find a new niche in the emerging Soviet political order, he buried himself in the local library doing bibliographic work and joined the newly established Society of Former Political Prisoners and Exiles (OPK). In this decade, too, he set about writing his memoirs, joining other members of the OPK in an effort to preserve the legacy of their movement in an increasingly hostile political environment. The legendary Vera Figner was instrumental in launching the collective effort of memoir writing by Charushin and others that anchors this work. Her contact with Charushin and correspondence with other figures in the Populist movement feature prominently in the book.

Ill and fragile, Charushin retired from the library in 1930, becoming increasingly isolated as the last of his generation passed away, and died in 1937 (chapter 9). His name, like that of many of his peers, was largely forgotten until it was revived locally in his hometown during the memory wars of the Perestroika era (chapter 10).

METANARRATIVE AND BIOGRAPHY: LIVES OBSCURE AND LESS SO

It is one thing to provide a chronology of the lives of two figures; it is quite another to ascribe meaning and find ways to convey the emotional and spiritual tonality of these lives. In order to address that task *A Generation of Revolutionaries* engages with several ongoing conversations in historical studies and specifically in the study of modern Russia. First and foremost is the recent biographical turn.[1]

The new biography employs a variety of approaches in order to provide imaginative reconstructions of lives of people who left scant traces in the historical record[2] or, alternatively, to revisit prominent figures, approaching them with new tools and perspectives.[3] Our work deals with figures neither famous nor obscure, what the German historian Fritz Stern long ago called "second tier" contributors to a country's cultural and political life—people whose names are long forgotten, but who often represented a significant force in society, made a visible contribution, or even (in this case) helped set a metanarrative.

Indeed, Charushin's memoirs are often used by historians of the Russian revolutionary movement, though the diligent reader might need to look closely at the footnotes in such works to find his name. We have used his life and the lives of his network of friends to paint a picture of an entire epoch in Russian history, one full of dramatic, often tragic, and transformative events that had a global impact; to analyze the shifting relationships between the state and society in Russia's regions; to describe an entire generation of revolutionaries, the institutions of incarceration and exile, and the memory wars of the twentieth century—but not only for this. The lives of Charushin and of his family and friends were in and of themselves an independent subject of research as we sought to uncover an individual and group world of lived experience, moral norms, interpersonal relations, and emotions. Individual memories merged with the collective memory of an entire generation; personal convictions, with group platforms; and the vivid love story of Charushin and Kuvshinskaia, their extended family relationships, with gender stereotypes, the "woman question" in Russia, and the dynamics of private versus public. Our access to memoirs, but especially to a private correspondence that has been surprisingly underutilized by most historians of Populism, has allowed us to deal extensively with such questions.

GENERATIONAL HISTORY AND MEMORY STUDIES

Above all, this work draws on generational and memory studies. In the opinion of Stephen Lovell, Russian intellectuals found a powerful source of self-determination and self-identification in the concept of generation, one far more resonant to them than the notions of class, culture, or nationality.[4] Indeed, in the second half of the nineteenth century, Russia was changing rapidly and many of the traditional markers of social identification no longer worked to situate a person in the social structure. Vertical and horizontal social mobility led to the erosion of the previous legally defined estate boundaries (the peasantry, nobility, merchants, *meshchanstvo*, etc.) which the state endeavored to keep intact to preserve the integrity of traditional hierarchies in the empire. The expansion of secondary and higher education created a societal boost for many from the commoner classes who made their way through the schools, a process fueled by the shortage of cadres with professional expertise as the economy evolved. The simultaneous rapid growth in the ranks of the intelligentsia in Russia resulted in a search for new markers of self-identification, new ways of self-expression and of consolidating group solidarity—one of which was "generation."

For the cohort with which the Charushins identified the 1870s were a period of socialization into the ways of society, a time when, having completed their education, they were to begin the process of self-realization in a profession, creating families, establishing active social connections—moving, in short, out of youth and into maturity, and consolidating a new status in society. Yet the process this generation went through was distinctive, and their maturation was conditioned not only by the era of the Great Reforms but, especially, by the experience of incarceration, which cut them off from all contact with the outside world for protracted periods of time and resulted in a sharply different pattern of adaptation.

Most studies of this generation end after the shocking assassination of Alexander II in 1881. This tendency was helped along by the recollections of the Populists themselves, who in their memoirs described the years of their youth—unremarkably—as the best of their lives, which, almost without exception, end after their release from exile. Apparently, they believed that the subsequent two decades, during which they returned to the world outside prison to make substantial contributions to society, were not consequential enough to merit inclusion in their memoirs. We beg to differ. Chapters 6 through 9 are distinct from the earlier ones in that we had to reconstruct this period (1890s–1930s) without the help of their testimony, relying instead on correspondence and other traces of their lives found in archives, both local and central (police reports, gubernatorial archives, zemstvo records, and newspaper clippings).

We treat the recollections of this generation as an integral part of a "collective memory," using the term of one of the founders of memory studies, Maurice Hallbachs, who emphasized the significance of "social frames" to memory. Aleida Assmann argues that one prominent variant of what she instead calls "social" memory is generational memory, which is especially stable, as well as shaped by the social frame, "[G]enerational memory is an important element in the constitution of personal memories, because ... once formed, generational identity cannot change."[5]

Thus, in our approach, generational studies are closely linked with memory studies. We treat the generation of the seventies as a symbolic community reflecting the values and ideals of the Populism of the 1870s. In this image are deeply embedded understandings about the intelligentsia, the people, and political authority and about the past, present, and future of Russia. But beyond this symbolic community, we can find a real community of living and breathing people, united by their experiences over the course of more than a half century, encompassing the aftermath of the Great Reforms, the dynamism and turmoil of the early twentieth century, and the collapse of an entire empire and way of life, as well as the building of a new society and polity from the ruins of the old order.

EXAMINING RUSSIAN POPULISM AS A MOVEMENT

A Generation of Revolutionaries represents, above all, a plea to reorient studies of what was far and away the most popular political movement in Russia in the half century leading up to the Russian Revolution. As a movement, Populism was first studied at the turn of the twentieth century, received a lot of attention in the 1920s, and then again in the 1960s and 1970s. Early on, this generation was portrayed primarily in heroic colors (often in their own memoirs, especially in Sergei Stepniak-Kravchinskii's influential work at the time, *Underground Russia*, and in the equally influential tome by the Siberian traveler George Kennan, *Siberia and the Exile System*.[6] Later, the Populists themselves played a large role in lionizing their own generation, something that is evident when one pages through their memoirs, penned forty to fifty years after the "remarkable epoch of the 1870s." At the same time, Stalinist scholarship was uniformly hostile to this cohort, and it was only in the late Soviet period that a small cluster of fine scholars provided a more sympathetic interpretation of their motivations and deeds.

In the West, after a spate of monographs on Populist figures and the movement as a whole appeared in the 1960s and 1970s—some of which bore the mark of the Cold War, but others of which still have value today—interest died out and remarkably little was written. During that earlier period, some historians turned to the tools of social psychology to explain their views and behavior, and sought their roots of "alienation" and "displacement" from society, often in family dynamics or childhood experience,[7] or as a result of sociocultural and institutional changes underway.[8] Others treated the Populists as naïve and misled youth, acting in a spirit resembling religious exaltation,[9] with little accumulated experience in the real world, and even less in the practice of politics.[10]

Much ink has been spilled in defining this Russian Populism and distinguishing it from other variants, especially the American version, which has often been led by right-wing demagogues.[11] Broadly speaking, it can be argued that Populism represented the interests and needs of the peasantry, who at the turn of the century still made up more than 80 percent of the population of an empire which covered more than one-sixth of the earth's land surface. Put simply, it was an anti-capitalist movement started by those who were disillusioned by bourgeois democracies and parliamentary systems (of the 1848 variant). Its advocates prioritized what we today call "social justice" and believed that the peasant commune, which dominated the rural landscape in Russia, could (suitably altered) serve as the embryo of a just and productive, agrarian-based and locally self-governing socialist society—avoiding the horrors of the early stages of capitalism so graphically described by Marx and Engels. Like most socialists of the time, they believed fervently in democracy but also that without a redistribution of wealth and restrictions on private property, the promises of representative government could not be fulfilled.[12] At the turn of the century neo-Populist theorists advanced far more sophisticated economic and sociological theories to underpin their analysis and vision for Russia, which in recent decades drew the attention of some developmental economists. Populists were—again speaking in today's vocabulary—believers both in communitarian values and in individual self-fulfillment, as well as in gender equality.

Although the organized movement was largely crushed in the two years following the assassination of Alexander II in 1881, revolutionary Populism re-emerged in 1902 as the Socialist Revolutionary (SR) Party, which soon became a powerful force in the politics of the empire. In 1917, during the only free elections in the country's history (up to the Gorbachev era), the SR Party garnered a clear majority of the vote. Charushin himself belonged to the much smaller People's Socialist (NS) Party, which in 1917 had fewer than ten thousand members, 80 percent of whom were intellectuals and professionals—"generals without an army." If it was a party for the people, it was hardly one *by* the people. Yet the connections between the People's Socialist Party and the moderate wings of both the SR and the Marxist parties were strong, especially in the provinces, where rigid party lines were seldom observed.[13]

At the same time, the program of the People's Socialist Party was far closer to the "small deeds" movement that emerged after 1881 and guided the many thousands of teachers, doctors, and agronomists who believed that it would take generations of cultural uplift and service to the people before the peasants and the intelligentsia could together effect a revolution. The Populists therefore engaged in a sustained effort to build both the infrastructure and culture of a new society, even as they were stymied in their efforts to gain control of the political system. In the process, while clinging to a vision of radical social and economic transformation, they became active participants in Russia's blossoming civil society at the turn of the century and developed an evolutionary view (neo-Populism) of how to make that transition.

For that reason, the biographies of Charushin, Kuvshinskaia, and their sizeable network of friends offer fresh perspectives on this powerful movement, which presented an alternative to capitalist models of development but, for reasons beyond its control, never had the opportunity to fulfill its promise. The Populism we are examining was not confined to party activities or even revolutionary practices, but included a large proportion of Russia's rapidly growing population of educated professionals, who through the zemstvo, the burgeoning cooperative movement, and the periodical press set out to transform the country.

Our study also reaches beyond the circle of revolutionaries to examine the extensive networks of friends, family, local politicians, business leaders, philanthropists, and educators (more broadly, the "culture bearers") with whom their lives were intertwined. This allows us to better understand the dynamics of civil society at the time, the relationships between state and society, and the evolution of the society itself in a fraught period of turmoil and upheaval. Thus our story of a rather small revolutionary movement merges with a much larger later project of societal engagement by adherents of a cultural and political program lasting to the end of Imperial Russia and the following decade of Soviet rule.

A COOPERATIVE ENDEAVOR

To write this book, the authors each spent more than three years working in archives in Moscow, St. Petersburg, and Kirov (called Viatka in the nineteenth century) as well as in libraries and manuscript collections in those cities and in New York City (at Columbia University). In St. Petersburg and Moscow, the files we surveyed included official state documents: records of the gendarmes, the Ministry of Interior, the Land Resettlement, Zemstvo, Press Affairs Offices; those of the All-Russian Famine Relief Organization; the records of the St. Petersburg Technological Institute. In Moscow, we spent much time perusing the personal folders of the Russian Populists, including that of Charushin himself. In Kirov, we also examined several branches of the gubernatorial administration, provincial and district zemstvo archival records; the files of the local gymnasia and women's diocesan school; the local gendarmerie and also the library collections.

The authors come from different countries and historiographical traditions, but each has considerable life experience residing in the other's country, is conversant in the other's language, and familiar with the different historiographies. Nevertheless, the process of producing a joint text, first in Russian and then a significantly modified one in English, was laborious, revealing nuances of language and deep if subtly different cultural understandings of words and concepts, as well as differing notions of readership. The degree of empathy we had for the main characters and the causes they espoused also varied, but in the end, we believe this made for balanced and well-considered interpretations. We present this work as a contribution to cross-cultural, transnational scholarship.

NOTES

1. See Hans Renders, Binne de Haan, and Jonne Harmsma, eds., *The Biographical Turn: Lives in History* (Abington, UK: Routledge, 2017).

2. Examples of this trend: Michael Khodarkovsky, *Bitter Choices: Loyalty and Betrayal in the Russian Conquest of the North Caucasus* (Ithaca, NY: Cornell University Press, 2011); Willard Sunderland, *The Baron's Cloak: A History of the Russian Empire in War and Revolution* (Ithaca, NY: Cornell University Press, 2014).

3. Francis W. Wcislo, *Tales of Imperial Russia: The Life and Times of Sergei Witte, 1849–1915* (New York: Oxford University Press, 2011).

4. Stephen Lovell, "From Genealogy to Generation: The Birth of Cohort Thinking in Russia," *Kritika: Explorations in Russian and Eurasian History* 9, no. 3 (2008): 567–594.

5. Aleida Assmann, "Re-framing Memory: Between Individual and Collective Forms of Constructing the Past," in *Performing the Past: Memory, History, and Identity in Modern Europe*, ed. Karin Tilmans, Frank van Vree, and J. M. Winter (Amsterdam: Amsterdam University Press, 2010), 35–50, esp. 41.

6. George Kennan, *Siberia and the Exile System* (1891; repr. New York: Praeger, 1970).

7. Marc Raeff, *Origins of the Russian Intelligentsia: The Eighteenth-Century Nobility* (New York: Harcourt, 1966); Martin K. Malia, *Alexander Herzen and the Birth of Russian Socialism, 1812–1855* (Cambridge, MA: Harvard University Press, 1961).

8. Abbot Gleason, *Young Russia: The Genesis of Russian Radicalism in the 1860s* (New York: Viking, 1980); Daniel R. Brower, *Training the Nihilists: Education and Radicalism in Tsarist Russia* (Ithaca, NY: Cornell University Press, 1975).

9. Alan B. Ulam, *The Bolsheviks: The Intellectual and Political History of the Triumph of Communism in Russia* (New York: Macmillan, 1965).

10. Philip Pomper, *The Russian Revolutionary Intelligentsia. Europe since 1500* (New York: Crowell, 1970).

11. Ghita Ionescu and Ernest Gellner, eds., *Populism: Its Meaning and National Characteristics*, (London: Weidenfeld & Nicolson, 1969).

12. On early Populist ideology (up to 1881), see Andrzej Walicki, *A History of Russian Social Thought from the Enlightenment to Marxism* (Stanford, CA: Stanford University Press, 1979), 222–267. There is an enormous literature on Russian Populism. Foundational works include,

aside from Franco Venturi: Boris Itenberg, *Dvizhenie revoliutsionnogo narodnichestva: Narodnicheskie kruzhki i "khozhdenie v narod" v 70-kh godakh XIX v.* (Moskva: Nauka, 1965); Nikolai Troitskii, *Pervye iz blestiaschei pleiady: Bol'shoe obshchestvo propagandy 1871–1874* (Saratov: Izdatel'stvo Saratovskogo universiteta, 1991). For the wave of interest in Populism in the 1960s and 1970s, see Philip Pomper, *The Russian Revolutionary Intelligentsia* (Wheeling, IL: H. Davidson, 1993); and especially on the Chaikovskii circle, see Reginald Zelnik, "Populists and Workers: The First Encounter between Populist Students and Industrial Workers in St. Petersburg, 1871–1874," *Soviet Studies* 24, no. 2 (1972): 251–269; and Martin A. Miller, "Ideological Conflicts in Russian Populism: The Revolutionary Manifestoes of the Chaikovskii circle, 1869–1875," *Slavic Review* 29, no. 1 (1970): 1–21. Much recent work concentrates primarily on the links between Populism and either terror or religion. See Susan K. Morrissey, "Terrorism, Modernity, and the Question of Origins," *Kritika: Explorations in Russian and Eurasian History* 12, no. 1 (Winter 2011): 215–226; Claudia Verhoeven, *The Odd Man Karakozov: Imperial Russia, Modernity and the Birth of Terrorism* (Ithaca, NY: Cornell University Press, 2009). For surveys of Soviet-era Russian-language historiography, see Nikolai Troitskii, *Russkoe revoliutsionnoe narodnichestvo 1870-ikh godov (istorii temy)* (Saratov: Izdatel'stvo Saratovskogo universiteta, 2003). For an early study of nonrevolutionary Populism, see Richard Wortman, *The Crisis of Russian Populism* (Cambridge: Cambridge University Press, 1967). For the period immediately following 1881, see Derek Offord, *The Russian Revolutionary Movement in the 1880s* (Cambridge: Cambridge University Press, 1986).

13. Recently, Populism has again drawn the attention of historians, primarily exploring gender, religion, and terrorism. A few new biographies have been published, but as a rule, these rely almost exclusively on the subject's own memoirs or examine the topic primarily through the lens of gender or terrorism.

Beginnings

How to Become a Revolutionary

Life was an unending holiday.

—Nikolai Chaikovskii, "Detskie gody," 1926

When, in 1888, Lev Tikhomirov, once a member of the terrorist organization the People's Will, published his notorious letter "Why I Am No Longer a Revolutionary," it had a profoundly unsettling impact on his former comrades. Decades later, in the early Soviet era, they continued to ask each other if he had ever really been a revolutionary and why they themselves had turned from that path. At this time, Vera Figner was commissioned to do a volume in the *Granat Encyclopedia*, a collection of autobiographical sketches by participants in the movement that had led to the overthrow of the tsarist autocracy. She set about this task with aplomb, and succeeded in putting together forty-four contributions, among which was an entry by Nikolai Charushin.

Figner, an icon of the Populist movement, believed that a revolutionary identity—which she equated with moral principles—was rooted in one of three elements to be found in childhood or adolescence: deep emotionality; a transformative, traumatic event forcing one to re-evaluate one's life; or sustained and purposeful reading. Figner encouraged her contributors to think along these lines when considering their own childhoods and some did. Osip Aptekman, for example, wrote that his father was subjected to a beating because he had refused to take off his cap in homage to an officer being quartered in his home. Aptekman wrote that he relived this experience repeatedly, and that it had left him with an "unshakeable hatred of violence inflicted on people and empathy for the downtrodden and humiliated."[1] Others, however, responded differently. Even a cursory familiarity with the memoirs written by Populists will convince the reader that there was no single scenario defining the pathway to a revolutionary consciousness. Of the thirty autobiographical essays by men contributed to the *Granat Encyclopedia*, nine make no mention of childhood whatsoever. The remainder follow a variety of scripts. Likewise, a study by Valentin Sergeev of the childhood experiences of the Populist revolutionaries born in Viatka province, from where Nikolai Charushin himself originated, could find no uniform pattern in their upbringings.[2]

Roughly at this time, Figner also began to entreat Charushin to write a full volume of memoirs about his life leading up to and following his participation in the Chaikovskii circle, his incarceration, and then the years in exile. After some reluctance, Charushin complied. These memoirs provide one of the pillars of this narrative and analysis of his life. Yet they, along with the briefer contributions to the Granat volume, were written in response to a script provided by Figner in the context of the "memory wars" ongoing in the early soviet era in a heated political atmosphere, and became part of a collective narrative put together through the joint efforts of an aging group of tightly knit Populists and former conspirators. We will return frequently to the process by which this collective narrative was constructed and consider why these aging Populists insisted on being identified as revolutionaries, despite their reluctance to embrace violence and their subsequent immersion in civil society. Here we examine Charushin's narration of his childhood, and the search for why he and others took the improbable step of becoming revolutionaries.

IN HIS OWN WORDS

Charushin, in contrast to many others writing under Figner's watchful eye, devoted considerable space in his recollections to his childhood. Despite his extensive correspondence with Figner on the subject, however, we find nothing there resembling the "formative triad" or "transformative scenes" that supposedly shape one's identity. Charushin himself found nothing distinctive about his experiences. Why, then, did he become a revolutionary? Consider how, toward the end of a very long life, he related the story of his childhood.

Charushin was born into a large, stable, and respected provincial family in Orlov, a district town in Viatka province, situated on the Viatka River, not far from the provincial capital itself. His father was an employee of the state, rising to the status of titular counselor, seventh on the civil service Table of Ranks, and bestowing on the family the status of hereditary nobility. His mother, Ekaterina L'vovna (née Iufereva) was the daughter of a prosperous merchant. Although this merchant's fortunes had declined, one of his sons (Charushin's uncle on his mother's side, Ivan L'vovich Iuferev) continued, after the untimely death of Charushin's father to provide the family with lodgings in a solid building (today it is a bank). Charushin had six siblings: one brother (Victor) died early; two went on to successful careers. Ivan, a prominent and still-celebrated architect in Viatka, thrived in both the Imperial and Soviet periods; Arkadii was a high-ranking bureaucrat in the important Resettlement Office at a time when the government was concerned with both promoting and regulating peasant migration. His sisters married solid citizens whose lives were entangled with the adult career of our protagonist. Judging by their actions and their correspondence, this was a family characterized by mutual love and respect, support, and involvement in each other's lives, sometimes at considerable risk to themselves.

In his own telling, Charushin's early childhood was happy. He describes his boyhood as boisterous and largely carefree. His early years resembled those of Lenin: growing up in a close-knit, comfortable family, with an energetic and resourceful mother and a father who held a respectable position in the provincial bureaucracy, conferring nobility status on the family. Indeed, Charushin's vivid descriptions portray a boy enthusiastically engaged in play, both indoors and outdoors. His depictions of his adventures on the wide Viatka River, which was a hundred yards or so from his home, and its tributary the Vorob'ikha, are positively lyrical:

> In the spring when the river flooded, the creek running through our garden also flooded, providing us the opportunity, once we had grown just a bit, to launch our small boats right from our garden and float right out to

the Viatka. From there we sometimes boldly set out to cross the river, at that time reaching 5–6 *versts* in width and flooding the pine grove on the far side. It was terrifying to be out on our little rowboat in the middle of a river with its banks overflowing, but what joy we had when we reached the other side and floated along the shady alleys formed by the rows of flooded pine groves, come alive with the song and din of birds.[3]

But, unlike Lenin, who was also from in the Volga region but whose early years were spent in a highly cultured household, surrounded by books, Charushin had very little exposure to the printed word. There were only two or three books in the house in all, and the houses of neighboring families and friends were also devoid of reading material. Secular books were spurned; the only religious texts were the Gospels and *Lives of the Saints*. "Even the Bible itself was sometimes frowned upon," he wrote. "People would say, for example, that whoever took to reading it would inevitably lose his sanity."[4] In general, religion played little role in this family. His father was more or less indifferent to Orthodoxy. To be sure, his mother was a devout believer, faithful churchgoer, and observer of Lent who encouraged her children to follow her example. According to Charushin, "[S]he had some impact on the girls in the family, but virtually none on the boys, most likely because the ritualistic practices by which religion was presented held little appeal to us."[5]

The family, and Orlov in general, seemed insulated from the outside world. Although Alexander I had stopped there during his travels in 1824, it seemed that the national dramas of war and political change that were occurring soon after Charushin's birth passed this sleepy district town by. There were no newspapers, and even an event as impactful for the country as the Crimean War "passed us by without affecting anyone." No news of the decisive battles, no word of the siege of Sevastopol circulated by print or word of mouth, "and all of this seemed of little concern... it was as if we had nothing to do with those events."[6] The town seemed to exist outside the stream of history. The most memorable episode Charushin could recall from his childhood was the fuss surrounding the expectation of seeing a comet and the anticipation of a resulting catastrophe.

The absence of books, newspapers, and connections of any sort with the outside world was of little import. Little did it bother young Nikolai.

His life, winter and summer, was too full of activities more pleasing to a rambunctious young boy:

> We children were little perturbed since we had not yet acquired a taste for reading. Unhindered by our parents we—and especially the boys—lived a full existence, spending most summers and winters outdoors. In the winters, we so were caught up in sledding downhill that we often returned home suffering from frostbitten hands or toes. Summer was an especially rich time, since we could fish, boat, cross to the other side of the river in search of mushrooms and berries, or carry out pirating raids on neighboring orchards when the cherries had ripened—stolen berries were always much tastier! But the loudest and most fun-filled times were when whole gangs of neighboring children congregated to play games until late in the evening.[7]

Nor—also unlike Lenin, who won a gold medal for his academic achievements—did school put a wrinkle in Charushin's seemingly carefree existence. At the age of seven or eight (he was not sure) he was sent to the town's church parish school, where he boarded with a dozen or so other local boys in a ramshackle and crowded space. He was taught how to read based on the old alphabet method, and like his peers considered the exercise an obligation imposed by parents, which could only be endured.[8]

In fact, his indifference to schooling and attraction to the fun and games offered by the natural world at times got him into trouble:

> I had no interest in my studies; during the fall and winter I more or less tolerated school, but as summer approached the natural world exerted an irrepressible pull in contrast to my tedious and burdensome studies. So, heading off for school, I took a detour along my beloved river which, being always in sight, always exerted a pull on me. Forgetting all about my studies, I didn't show my face for two weeks, spending all my time at the river or on the far shore, returning home only after the school day had ended.[9]

Eventually, he was caught and suffered an exemplary punishment. He finally completed his stay at the parish school in 1861 ("by the skin of his teeth"), only to be enrolled next in the local district elementary school, to which he went even more reluctantly, since the inspector there was dreaded because of his frequent resort to the rod. But his stay there was short. Responding (in his description) to the currents of the Great

Reforms era emphasizing the importance of a meaningful education, his parents pulled him out of that school and began preparing him instead to take the entrance exams to the gymnasium in Viatka. At this tender age, his feelings about making this step were naturally ambivalent: on the one hand, the thought of going to "the big city" was exciting; on the other hand, it scared him: "I had to say goodbye to the people I love and to everything that was dear to my heart, to all that had made my childhood such a rich experience."[10]

On the eve of his departure, as he himself noted, this young fellow was little different from who he had been when he had begun his schooling three years earlier completely free of any intellectual strivings. School, he insisted, had not stimulated his curiosity in any way. As he put it, if someone had asked him at the time what he wanted to be when he grew up, he would mostly likely have answered, "the police chief!" It was the imposing uniform, and the fact that he was at the top on the town's ladder of power, that impressed him most. So far, we have a rather delightful portrait of an untrammeled childhood, of a youth whose first years were unmarked by the deep emotional experiences or the signature episodes that, according to Vera Figner, resulted in a moral awakening that eventually led to a revolutionary consciousness. Instead, we seem to have a Russian Tom Sawyer: carefree, mischievous, viewing books and schooling as interfering with his education in the great outdoors. It does seem likely that living in a close-knit family that maintained healthy, lifelong, emotional ties did give Charushin good reason to look back at his early childhood with fond nostalgia.

UNTRAMMELED CHILDHOODS?

We find a similar description of an untrammeled and carefree childhood in the memoirs of Nikolai Chaikovskii, a seminal figure in the Populist movement, whose colorful life was intermittently connected with Charushin's. Chaikovskii also grew up in Viatka and remembered a cloudless childhood: a well-kept, sunlit home, time spent playing in the yard, strolling the streets, trips with his father on the Viatka River, an attentive and loving mother. He even describes his father's loss of employment and forced departure from Viatka to a village in a distant district as an adventure rather than a catastrophe. "Looking back at the entire course of my early years, two things can't be denied: their incomparable joy and luminosity as well as a warm and special love for my surroundings; and secondly, the feeling that life was an unending holiday."[11]

The Populist Alexander Pribylev wrote of his childhood in the small provincial town Kamyshlov in similar tones. Despite the early death of his mother, those years "were spent in the "cradle of Nature, unrestricted by any limitations or pedantry, and leaving us with the memory of a gentle, beautiful and dreamy period."[12] Mikhail Sazhin (who would later marry one of Vera Figner's sisters) wrote, "My thirteenth year passed by without any reading except for the textbooks required in school. Summers and winters, we spent on the streets, in the courtyards, in the orchard, playing ball or card games ... flying kites or whatever with the neighborhood gang."[13]

Gender considerations must also be addressed when examining the autobiographical texts. Research published decades ago identified a distinct tradition of women's autobiographical works and specified the gendered aspects of the genre as a whole.[14] Yet, of the many such gendered aspects of content, style, and temporal structure that have been pointed out by scholars such as Estelle Jelinek and Hilde Hoogenboom, the only one readily identifiable in the most prominent memoir by a Populist woman, Vera Figner, is a distinctive emotionality. Even that observation must be qualified—for it pertained only to her early years, which were in fact not unlike Charushin's.[15] Her autobiography offers a similarly vivid portrait of a childhood spent in Kazan province. She describes her first impressions, her relations with her parents, and the family situation in general. Despite the task she had set for herself of uncovering revolutionary beginnings, her descriptions of her childhood are vibrant and emotionally resonant, in contrast to the later accounts of her activities as a member of the People's Will; these become a political chronicle devoid of any subjective experience, in which her internal world completely vanishes from the narrative. Writing to Figner, in 1922, after having read her memoirs, Ekaterina Kuskova calls attention to just this:

> Your childhood, your father and mother, your school—all that is new. I was familiar with the superficial facts but your own interpretation of this interval was an eye-opener. And for that reason, these chapters are full

of life. You see before you, almost as in life, the surrounding forest, the stern father, all those schoolmarms and you, the captious prankster—the girl who lived through all this. Then, around age twenty-four, the onset of a new stage. The style of your writing and the underlying spirit changes abruptly. The texture of life is covered over by a shroud/cloak made up of programs, decisions, all these external developments, however important they may have been, lacking subjectivity, the psychological. The human being, the ordinary things that make up the person, feelings—love, friendship, attachments, all of that which was so evident in the atmosphere of nannies and family, somehow gets buried, disappears. Was this on purpose or did it just turn out that way? To put it another way, *did revolutionary activity really bring an end to daily life?*[16]

It may be that an answer to Kuskova's query can be found in Figner's stated intent to find the childhood origins of a revolutionary personality in profound emotionality, in the search for firm moral principles—hence the coloration of the first part of her memoirs. Moreover, in writing of her childhood she relied exclusively on the deeply personal impressions lodged in her memory, whereas her writings about the People's Will period rested on archival documents that became available to her only after 1917. It is also indisputable that she wrote the latter part with an eye to the political environment of the Soviet era as much as through the filter of memory. Writing of childhood, she could express herself freely and rely on literary models as well.

Where does this brief foray leave us in terms of assessing the veracity of the Populists' accounts of their childhoods? We have seen that despite strong encouragement by Figner to seek out elements of the formative triad of deep feeling, formative episodes, and purposeful reading in order to "read the evolution of [his] path backwards into childhood," Charushin's account tells of a happy and stable childhood. In fact, his narration, and those of several of his peers, conforms more to a different mythology. Andrew Wachtel, in his influential study of autobiographical accounts of childhood, has identified a "specifically Russian conception of childhood."[17] This mythology originated in Leo Tolstoy's hugely influential and paradigmatic "pseudo-autobiographical" account (1852) of his own happy childhood, a "myth developed and canonized not in fiction but in autobiography." Was it the case that when Charushin, his friends, and other members of Russia's educated classes sat down to write their life stories, they "recalled childhood, consciously or unconsciously, through the filter of Tolstoy's work?"[18]

Aside from mythmaking, there are reasons to question the accuracy of some aspects of Charushin's account of his childhood surroundings. For example, his depiction of the sleepy town of Orlov has little in common with the thriving commercial market town and cultural center that emerges from the historical record. The record does not show a town entirely devoid of contact with the outside world or culture, but rather one that is modestly thriving. Despite the poor soil and harsh climate there, the town founded in the fifteenth century had prospered because of its location on two major trade routes: by land from Moscow to Siberia, and by boat to Velikii Ustiug and Arkhangelsk to the north, Charushin himself mentions Orlov's status as a commercial hub, and remembers seeing wagons laden with grain and other commodities making their way to Arkhangelsk, receiving in exchange products of the sea. There were two seasonal markets (local trade, of course) in March and November. Merchants willing to contribute some of their wealth to the betterment of the community had built many stone buildings in the eighteenth and early nineteenth centuries. There was a library and a museum, and it was the only district town with a hospital. There was a church parish school and one for girls, as well as a district school, and plans for more.[19]

One wonders, too, why a family purportedly indifferent to education went to such great lengths to make sure the boys in the family received an education, which allowed Nikolai, but also Ivan and then Arkadii, to advance in the world. To be sure, with the Great Reforms came a realization among the nobility that developing professional expertise was a key to success in a changing world. Nikolai was the first to be sent to Viatka to enroll in a secondary school, and he was followed by his brothers. As he notes, however, despite his sister Julia's earnest pleadings to be allowed to follow her brothers, Charushin's parents did not see need for a girl to advance her education, especially since it involved substantial financial outlays, not to mention removal from parental supervision and the loss of a needed hand in the household economy.

Charushin's omission of any mention of the peasantry is also noteworthy. Here, his memoirs differ sharply from those of other members of the Viatka intelligentsia—"cultural bearers," such as Ivan Krasnoperov,

Nikolai Blinov, Petr Golubev, who were to play a major role in the transformation of provincial culture and society in the latter decades of the nineteenth century. These figures, well-known outside Viatka province, wrote of growing up and playing with peasant youth and of being intimately familiar with the life of the peasant household and village. The same can be said of the early lives of local revolutionaries from the *meshchanstvo* (loosely: "the petty bourgeoisie") or of members of the clergy such as Anna Iakimova, Mikhail Borodin (and, most likely, Anna Kuvshinskaia), not to mention students of peasant origins, such as Stepan Khalturin and others.[20] Such writers often claimed that it was these childhood friendships and easy access to village household life that later added passion and immediacy to their radical convictions, as they learned of (or took part in gathering) zemstvo statistics on taxation, diet, and crop yields and were exposed to the political tracts that inspired their generation.

Yet here we run into a different issue—one of collective memory. After all, looking back to the 1920s, the Populists sought to highlight their empathy for the sufferings of the people at this early stage in their lives—and this led them, perhaps unwittingly, to exaggerate the degree of contact with peasants they actually experienced. On the other hand, despite Charushin's rather modest origins in a family of the provincial service nobility, it is probably true that his first contact with the Russian peasantry, unlike many others in his local cohort, came first from books, as we will see shortly.

In short, while Charushin's singular lack of mention of exposure to the local peasantry makes sense (and other Populists' accounts of their exposure may well be overstated) the historical record runs somewhat counter to Charushin's narrative of boyhood isolation from the outside world and a culture entirely hostile to books and secular learning There may be a simple explanation: perhaps he was so preoccupied with the boisterous activities he engaged in with his brothers and friends that elements of culture surrounding him simply went unnoticed, and were thus omitted in his later depictions of the town. It is a matter of conjecture what the balance between myth and actuality was. Yet we believe that his childhood narration has a ring of what Lydia Ginzburg famously called authenticity (*ustanovka na podlinnost'*) to it.[21] At the very least, turning to his recollections allows us—with due consideration of the limitations of the genre—to visualize the time and place in which he grew up and to understand his own genuine perceptions of his past.

SCHOOL DAYS IN VIATKA (1862-1871)

In August of 1862, his father escorted Charushin to the provincial capital, Viatka, to be with him as he took the entrance exams and to find him secure lodging. On the way there, stopping at a posting station to change horses, Nikolai, by a bizarre coincidence, met his future bride, Anna Kuvshinskaia, for the first time:

> While the change of horses was taking pace, another team swept into the postal station. In the carriage we could see a frightened and sobbing boy and girl of about my age accompanied by a drunken, bawling soldier. A brief interrogation established that these were the children of a priest by the name of Kuvshinskii from the village of Kokshaga in Iaransk district adjacent to Orlov, on their way to Viatka [where both of them were to continue their educations]. The soldier had evidently been instructed to accompany them on this long and somewhat dangerous route, but along the way had taken to drink and lost all self-control. Our father took charge, telling the soldier to stay behind, and for the children's carriage to join us. This completely unexpected turn of events certainly entertained us.[22]

Such a melodramatic scenario might well evoke a raised eyebrow in the reader—but in fact, though Charushin had ample opportunities to exaggerate the rich drama and turmoil of his life, in his memoirs he instead tends to be laconic and understated about personal matters. In any event, the episode set the stage for what was to be undoubtedly the most meaningful and fulfilling relationship of his life.

Much of this life would unfold in Viatka (see Figures 1.1, 1.2).[23] In the middle of the nineteenth century, this ancient town, once part of the holdings of the medieval city-state Novgorod, and then called Khlynov, was still primarily an administrative center, with a population of 15,000 (increasing to 23,000 in 1897 and 43,000 in 1914). In a province with only a small number of landholding nobles (clustered in two southern districts), the town population comprised primarily bureaucrats, merchants, and artisans; there was little manufacturing or commerce. What economic

FIGURE 1.1.

Viatka, 1900s, by Sergei Lobovikov.
© Vasnetsov Museum of Fine Arts, Kirov.

life there was centered on small-scale enterprises, handicraft industries, and the peasant barter-and-haggle trade.

As for cultural life, in his memoirs Alexander Herzen, exiled to Viatka in the 1830s famously described it as a backwater. But by the 1860s things were changing. Cultural life centered around the public library, a salon culture revolving around a small number of intelligentsia families and, after 1867, a brief but very energetic spell of zemstvo activity. By the early 1860s, the city also had three secondary schools, all of which also both experienced and contributed to the currents of change unleashed by the Great Reforms. Charushin, after moving to Viatka to enroll in the gymnasium, was touched by all three of these sources of cultural and political change, but not at once. He sat in on sessions of the zemstvo assembly, was profoundly influenced by gatherings at the Farmakovskii household, and, after a rather slow start, immersed himself in the "obligatory" reading list that shaped an entire generation.

FIGURE 1.2.

Viatka, 1900s, by Sergei Lobovikov.
© Vasnetsov Museum of Fine Arts, Kirov.

Here, we take special note of this first mention of the local library. Charushin writes that in the 1860s it was "a genuine site of culture with a collection of books, journals and newspapers rather substantial for the time and which welcomed students along with the adult population. It had its own solid building which was well furnished and comfortable; the number of subscribers was considerable, and lovers of reading eagerly frequented the premises."[24] Charushin's mention of the library was no accident, for by the time he wrote these words, in the 1920s, the Herzen State Library had become one of the country's larger repositories of books, and it boasted a vibrant local history section, which Charushin himself directed.

As for Imperial Russia's secondary schools, they still await a modern historian who is capable of examining their dynamics from a comparative perspective.[25] They have been largely portrayed as seedbeds of revolution, as generation after generation of students rebelled against the harsh discipline and sterile curriculum, or, in recent years, by Russian historians as repositories of all that was good in Imperial Russia.[26] Yet such schools also produced several generations of civil servants, military leaders, and prominent figures engaged in business and commerce. As J. Alfred Rieber noted in a seminal article some time ago, "In the Russian lycées and gymnasiums... future bureaucrats and radicals rubbed shoulders. It would be a mistake to perceive them as representing two sharply defined antagonistic camps. They were exposed to the same ideas... [h]ow many bureaucrats concealed a radical past, or at the very least harbored sympathies for ideas they had absorbed as youths?"[27] Certainly, after the accession to the throne of Alexander II notable changes occurred in the classrooms of many secondary schools.

In Viatka, three such schools were functioning in 1859 (a men's gymnasium, a diocesan school for boys, and one for girls, an *uchilishche*, offering the first four classes of the gymnasium—and soon to be converted that status). In each were a number of teachers who sought to instill a love of learning and critical perspectives in their students, ran their classes as "discussion groups" and maintained informal relations with their students. Based on his own experience, Charushin recalled, "Under the influence of new ideas, especially about education, which were current at this time, the straitjacket regime which had prevailed earlier was now replaced by a new and more humane way. The rod was put aside and some teachers, even if in most cases they were the same people, genuinely altered their relationships with their pupils, while others were forced to go along with the new currents."[28]

After matriculating, the ten-year-old Nikolai was homesick and lonely, but gradually he became acclimatized to life away from Orlov and made friends among his peers. Yet the new and tolerant educational environment ushered in by the new era in Russia initially did not stand him in good stead. He continues, "Life was much easier and school no longer frightened us. We learned how to make our way and get our work done to one degree or another, but were not inspired by it all." Indifferent to his studies in the first years, he not only "wasn't inspired" but didn't "get his work done"[29] and was forced to repeat the third year in the school. This caused him considerable shame, given his recognition that his parents had made considerable sacrifices to ensure his education. But it took outside intervention to change his ways; it was only after being seen in a tavern by a relative, and being relocated from one boarding house to a quieter one, that he began seriously to refocus.

In December 1866, in his fifth year of study,[30] Charushin was summoned to meet with Matvei Sintsov, a doctor from Orlov who would become the chair of the provincial zemstvo board the following year, and who was later singled out by Charushin's newspaper *Viatskaia Rech'* as one of the three most important figures occupying that position in the half-century following the founding of the zemstvo. But this meeting was of a different and catastrophic sort: Sintsov brought news of the sudden death of Charushin's father. He was serving at that time as assistant to the regional official in charge of peasant affairs and had been making the rounds of the villages, when his carriage struck a deep pothole in the road and he was tossed out of his carriage. A heavy-set man, he hit the ground hard, lost consciousness, and never recovered. The young Nikolai was stunned and so distraught that later he could not recall how he made his way home to Orlov, some fifty kilometers from Viatka. He arrived there to discover that the family's bereavement had been aggravated by the local gendarmes' decision to remove the body from its place of rest in the local church in order to perform an autopsy, required because he had been carrying out his official duties at the time of his accident. Charushin's mother, having recently given birth, managed nevertheless to muster the energy to press the authorities to release her husband's remains for a proper burial without performing the autopsy.

Apollon Ivanovich Charushin had been a benevolent and good-humored, if somewhat disengaged, presence in the children's lives, and his death came as a profound shock to the family, leaving them with no savings or sources of revenue; Charushin writes that a protracted search of the house for cash turned up all of three to five rubles. For some time, it was only the financial assistance of a guardian angel in their lives, his uncle Ivan Iuferev, that allowed the family not only to continue living in the house that he owned, but also to keep the earnings from renting out to the treasury the second floor of that dwelling as well as the income earned from a mill he owned. These small sums kept the family afloat—if barely—and at first, it was not at all clear whether the oldest son would be able to return to his studies in Viatka. He did do so, but recounted that from that point on he lived a penurious existence (although this account of his situation was to become a bone of contention in the Perestroika era. See chapter 10).

Later, reflecting on his years as a *gimnazist*, he describes the straitjacket regime he had encountered. The phrase he uses, *futliarnyi rezhim*, is revealing, for it is a reference to Chekhov's classic short story ("The Man in a Hard Case," or *futliar*), written in 1898, long after Charushin had completed his schooling. "Chekhov's story tells of an obsessive-compulsive school teacher in a highly regimented classroom. Were Charushin's memories of his school years filtered through literature and other accounts of the Russian gymnasium from the turn of the century, most of them overwhelmingly negative? Only partly so it seems, for he also speaks admiringly of his history teacher Iakov Rozhdestvenskii, who actively encouraged open discussions, which sometimes went well beyond the official curriculum. Likewise, he praises his teacher of mathematics and physics and the natural sciences, who had rigorous standards, but was not politically oriented. He was not alone: the Populist Solomon Chudnovskii begins his memoirs with a description of his school days and describes in detail two of his teachers, one in history and the other in rhetoric, crediting them for shaping his entire world view.[31] To be sure, Charushin's depiction of various teachers eerily correlates well with the grades he received in their courses: in his fifth year, he received the equivalent of an A in algebra and history; a B in geometry, physics, world history, and rhetoric; and a C in Latin, French, and German. Accordingly, his language teachers are vividly described as dunderheads totally unsuited for teaching, ignorant in their own specialities and privately ridiculed by the pupils.[32]

Charushin also notes that throughout the course of his studies the provincial authorities gave the school considerable autonomy to run its own affairs. The only disciplinary intervention by the governor occurred when pupils strolling the streets of the town encountered that august figure on the streets and in their youthful jauntiness failed to remove their caps or bow to him. The one student whom the governor could later identify from a line-up adamantly refused to give away the names of his co-conspirators. That was the end of the affair—hardly the stuff of revolution.

CROSSING A SOCIETAL THRESHOLD: SALON CULTURE IN VIATKA

Instead, Charushin's gradual political awakening originated outside the classroom. By the fourth class (1866) he was also actively engaged in a small student (male) circle, which together compiled a "program" of common readings, and periodically assembled at the apartment of one them, N. K. Prazdnikov (who would later to become a prominent doctor in Viatka) to discuss characters from the novels of Chernyshevskii and Turgenev, such as Bazarov, Rudin, Rakhmetov. While Charushin notes that the circle was interested in the "critical literature" of the time, he admits that without outside guidance, these gymnasium students made only limited progress in systematizing and clarifying their knowledge, and that the circles ended up being more important for socializing and finding entertainment.[33]

Matters changed in 1868, during his second year in the fifth class (see below), when, at age 16, he was introduced to the locally prominent Farmakovskii family, who maintained a salon that was open to all comers. The head of the Farmakovskii family was the archbishop of the Spasskii Cathedral in Viatka, a zemstvo delegate, and a teacher at the local seminary, an erudite figure. The mother was also well educated and liberal in her views, and it was she who served as the hostess of the salon. Among those frequenting the salon were Sintsov and the notable zemstvo agronomist Vsevolod Zavolzhskii. Politics, the condition of the peasantry, and other timely issues were often discussed. Recalling those days, Charushin wrote that it was there that he first began to be exposed to the wider world, to shed his insularity: "Personally, I owe much to the Farmakovskii household, which opened my eyes to new vistas, and provided me with a wealth of information on a wide range of topics."[34]

It was not all business, however; the youth who gathered at the Farmakovskii household also found ways to socialize and frequently danced and held their own songfests. Two attractive daughters also graced the Farmakovskii household. One daughter eloped with Sintsov, who happened to be married, which temporarily put an end to the gatherings at the household. The other married Zavolzhskii and then enrolled in Medical-Surgical Academy in St. Petersburg, later becoming a doctor. As for Charushin, he confessed that the presence of refined young women at the gatherings initially made him quite uncomfortable. In general, he admits that his circle of friends initially had little interest in the "woman question" and even less respect for the potential of women, and felt little need to include them in political discussions.[35]

Yet it was at the Farmakovskii household, in 1868, six years after his accidental encounter with Anna Kuvshinskaia on the way to enroll in school in Viatka, that he once again made her acquaintance, which soon led to a blossoming friendship, and more. She had recently graduated from the local women's gymnasium and was employed as the *klassnaia dama* (or governess, a teacher entrusted primarily with the "conduct, deportment, and health" of the pupils) at the local diocesan school.[36] Perhaps as a result of his deepening relations with her, his views on women began to change radically. As he tells it, by the end of the decade in Viatka, "the traditional lot of women" no longer satisfied [him or his friends]"; they had become avid feminists standing for "the full equality of women.[37]

When Charushin was in the sixth and seventh classes his circle of social acquaintances grew rapidly as he joined in the affairs of the prosperous Mashkovtsev merchant family.[38] The deceased father, A. I. Mashkovtsev, had been a factory owner and mayor of the town of Orlov until his early death. Two daughters were preparing to enroll in the medical studies courses in St. Petersburg (one of them subsequently married the liberal merchant P. I. Kolotov, who replaced Sintsov as chair of the provincial zemstvo executive board and, like Sintsov, ran afoul of the authorities). The Mashkovtsev home was also a place where students returning from St. Petersburg congregated during their vacations, bringing with them the energy and excitement of that city in heady times, invigorating the household. The head of the household was the uncle of the soon-to-be prominent revolutionary Nikolai Chaikovskii. In his memoirs, Chaikovskii recollected frequent childhood visits to his uncle's household. Chaikovskii's own nephew Leonid Yumashev would, not long before the outbreak of the 1905 Revolution, become the chair of the executive board (*uprava*) of the provincial zemstvo; Charushin would serve in the zemstvo under Yumashev and join him in the leadership of the opposition to the Bolsheviks in 1917. At the turn of the century, one of the younger generation of the Mashkovtsev family would join the staff of Charushin's oppositionist newspaper, *Viatskaia Rech'*.

Such were the entanglements that marked Charushin's life and characterized both provincial society and the revolutionary movement (see chapter 6). His experience with the Farmakovskii and Mashkovtsev households certainly expanded his vistas. At the same time, it revealed a pattern that continued throughout his life, marking his later years in Kiakhta as well as the Viatka years—namely, that he was always able to form and maintain strong ties with prominent individuals from the worlds of business, local government, insurance, and the arts, moving in a world where people with oppositionist views mixed freely with merchants, clergymen, professionals, and civil servants. Far from his radical views separating him from the "normal" world, he remained immersed in it. This would serve him well.

In 1869, Charushin moved into what he called a "dormitory," a shared living arrangement with other local students, with the explicit goal of establishing ties with the seminarians, the traditional rivals of gymnasium students, some of whom had ties with radicals in Kazan'. These same students had been connected with Charushin's history teacher, Rozhdestvenskii, mentioned earlier, who had earlier taught at the seminar before being forced out. The latter was in turn connected with another teacher at the seminary, A. A. Krasovskii, one of the local founders of the radical organization Land and Freedom. In turn, one of his students, Krasnoperov had enrolled at Kazan University, and played a prominent role in the famous "Kazan conspiracy." All three of these figures were brought to trial for their role in that matter.[39] In his memoirs, Charushin does not indicate that these new connections had a particularly strong effect on him, but surely, he could not have been entirely oblivious to this milieu.

During his years in school, Charushin had begun to read independently, and the novels of Cervantes, Thackeray, and Dickens revealed to him the "chivalrous and noble" character of their protagonists, but little else that he could recall. Perhaps it was the exposure to the Farmakovskii circle that now turned him to readings addressing social and political issues. Paradoxically, it was a second failure at his exams, at the end of his sixth year (fifth class), that allowed him to do so. It seems that by then he was actually taking his studies seriously and had achieved consistently good grades. But in May, beset with a case of spring fever and once again lured away from his studies by the "boundless field and forest" at home, he had feigned illness so that he could return home early, and missed his exams entirely. He avoided books all summer, but when he returned in August was required pro forma to take the exams. Despite the efforts of two empathetic teachers, he couldn't carry out even simple tasks in geometry and was forced once again to repeat an entire year in all subjects. He found most of his coursework familiar the second time around, and in his free time he now plunged deeply into a reading list that all "politically aware" people were discussing at the time, reading works by Ivan Turgenev, John Stuart Mill, Nikolai Chernyshevskii, Vasilii Bervi-Flerovskii, Nikolai Nekrasov, and others. A virtually identical list can be found in other Populist memoirs, and one wonders whether the entries were in fact a product of the "traveling narrative" constructed later in life by elderly Populists looking back at the past and comparing notes (chapter 9), more than of their individual recollection.

It was at this time that he first turned to the peasantry, but vicariously through writers who were currently popular, such as Pomialovskii and Reshetnikov, who, in his words revealed to him the "zoological" life of the peasantry. Once he left Viatka for St. Petersburg, and joined the Chaikovskii circle, he was instrumental in guiding that group away from "consciousness-raising" sessions to focus instead on establishing ties with worker-peasants. But that was later; now, when the students returned from St. Petersburg, gathered at the Mashkovtsev household, and resolved to carry out a "survey of peasant needs," the project soon collapsed because nobody had the slightest clue how to actually establish contact with the peasants.

Reading certainly made him more politically aware (or "conscious" as the intelligentsia liked to describe themselves, in contrast to the "benighted" masses and their educated peers who took no interest in public affairs). Charushin was undoubtedly moved by the radical critic Chernyshevskii's political martyrdom and refusal to ask for clemency; Bervi-Flerovsky's poignant description of the lamentable conditions of Russia's working people;[40] the poet Nekrasov's depictions of the sacrifices made by the Decembrists in their struggle for political freedom and emancipation of the serfs; the political essays of John Stuart Mills; and by the flamboyant (recently deceased) German socialist Ferdinand Lassalle's attempts to mobilize workers. These stories were now, in his last years of secondary school, lodged in his mind and especially in his heart, but he had hardly formed a coherent view of the polity. Aside from his readings the only clue we have of his shifting priorities comes from his general recollection that by the time he had graduated from the gymnasium, he and his group felt that "our faith in the miracle-working capabilities of the world of (student) circles had been eroded."[41]

LAST DAYS AND DEPARTURE

After nine years of study in Viatka, Charushin finally graduated from the gymnasium, in May 1871. The previous fall he had set his sights on enrolling in the Technological Institute in St. Petersburg, and successfully petitioned the Orlov zemstvo for a 250-ruble annual stipend to allow him to matriculate the following year, without which the family lacked the resources to provide for the twenty-year-old's stay in the capital city.[42] Now his trajectory was clear, his path forward assured. This must have been a great relief to the young man.

In May, joyful at having completing secondary school he decided to linger a few weeks in Viatka. As he put it, "Free as a bird I wanted to be with my friends at time when the pace of life picked up considerably with the return of students from outside."[43] Perhaps he also had a presentiment of the ambivalence he would feel once he actually returned home to Orlov. There, life went on as before, but his mother was clearly apprehensive about his looming departure for St. Petersburg. The family was no longer in desperate financial straits, but it was still difficult to make ends meet, and three boys still needed to be educated. The only real source of income came from the generous uncle, but there was no guarantee that it would last forever. Charushin saw this clearly and also acknowledged his moral debt as the oldest son and his obligation to pitch in, "but given the direction of my thinking and my strivings in general, I had little confidence in my ability to fulfill my obligations."[44] As he put it, this internal conflict caused him no small amount of "moral torture," mitigated only by the only-too-human rationalization that somehow, something would work out.

Back again in Viatka before departing for St. Petersburg, Charushin had received a cautionary note from a former Orlov-born tutor now studying in that city, who advised him to avoid dangerous radical student circles there.[45] However Charushin knew that an old gymnasium schoolmate and close friend, Nikolai Lopatin, was part of just such a circle, and so the warning fell on deaf ears. He left Orlov early in August. The trip to Petersburg from Viatka was an arduous one. He traveled by horse-drawn carriage to Kazan' (about 400 kilometers away) next by boat on the Volga to Nizhnii Novgorod, and then by train, via Moscow on to his final destination.[46] Stopping in Moscow he was struck by this "huge, unique and semi-Asiatic city with it labyrinth of streets, filthy but at the same time immeasurably wealthy—how could it not amaze someone like me from the provinces!"[47] He raced frantically around Moscow, managed to visit the Kremlin, and traveled to the Petrovsky Agronomy Academy—a hotbed of radical activity at the time. There he wandered the nearby park and was shown the grotto where two years earlier the notorious revolutionary Nechaev had murdered the student Ivanov, giving birth both to Dostoevsky's novel *The Possessed* and also, in reaction against the murder, to the Chaikovskii circle. Clearly Charushin was already on a given path; otherwise why would he have chosen an excursion "to memorable revolutionary sites." But who was his guide? He does not tell us. Next was St. Petersburg.

SEARCHING FOR THE ROOTS OF RADICALISM

Vera Figner pointed out that "the human personality is ordinarily configured by almost imperceptible deposits made by other people, by books and by their surroundings. But it sometimes happens that one of these elements forces a profound rupture resulting in the formation of a new identity."[48] Scholars have long sought an explanation for why many young Russians became revolutionaries in the second half of the nineteenth century—and this chapter has only further confounded the question. Mark Raeff located the origins of radicalism in a socio-psychological process of "alienation," which the nobility experienced as early as the middle of the eighteenth century after being released from their obligatory service obligations to the state, but this argument found a formidable opponent in Michael Confino. Daniel Brower traced this development to the dynamics of school politics in the era of the Great Reforms.[49] Especially during the Cold War, theories involving deviational psychology, unhappy childhoods, and arrested development proliferated, and one work even dubbed the 1874 student movement to connect with the peasantry the "children's crusade."[50] A largely discredited formulation saw radicalism as the outgrowth of the supposedly increasingly plebeian origins of university students. Most recently, one historian connects terrorism with the onset of modernity.[51] But the fact remains that many of these students came from stable and privileged backgrounds and could expect to go on to brilliant careers in the military, the bureaucracy, or in the burgeoning professions because the country was experiencing an acute shortage of human capital. Instead, they chose an uncertain route offering little but the likelihood of prison exile and lifelong hardship.

Can we find an answer in the writings of the Populists themselves? In her astute analysis of the body of autobiographical texts composed by revolutionaries of that time, Hoogenboom has noted, "Populist memoirs were mediated by several factors—time, the teleological nature of hindsight, and the process of writing itself—as the Populist writers themselves were aware."[52] Hoogenboom has demonstrated how the requirement of the genre dictated the selection of episodes and how Populists, like other memoirists, rummaged through their childhood recollections in search of developments that determined their later path in life: "They made choices about what to include and exclude, and in the process their lives became less random, more purposeful." Yet Hoogenboom acknowledges that the revolutionaries could seldom answer to their own satisfaction the question of just why they had taken the path that they did.[53]

At the same time, their reading in adolescence, peer circles, observations of life around them, contacts with benevolent and progressive adults—rather than traumas or conflicts—could have imperceptibly planted seeds that were gradually, if only subconsciously, to develop. We should not ignore their influence in shaping his outlook, but this was a work in progress, one that operated at the boundaries of emotion and intellect. In Charushin's own telling, by the time of his departure for St. Petersburg, he may have lost all faith in the ability of the government in St. Petersburg to address the burning issues of the day, yet he himself had only the vaguest of notions of what was to be done. He would soon find out.

NOTES

1. *Deiateli SSSR i revoliutsionnogo dvizheniia v Rossii.* Entsiklopedicheskii slovar' Granat (Moskva: Sovetskaia Entsiklopedia, 1989), 16.
2. Valentin Sergeev, *Raznochintsy-demokraty Viatki* (Kirov: Filial MGEU, 2003), 21–34.
3. Nikolai Charushin, *O dalekom proshlom* (Moskva: Mysl', 1973), 23.
4. Ibid., 26–27.
5. Ibid., 24.
6. Ibid., 26.
7. Ibid., 27.
8. Ibid., 29.
9. Ibid., 30.
10. Ibid., 31.
11. Nikolai Chaikovskii, "Detskie gody," *Golos minuvshego na chuzhoi storone* 1 (1926): 288.
12. *Deiateli SSSR i revoliutsionnogo dvizheniia v Rossii*, 188.
13. Ibid., 209.
14. Mary Ann Mason, *The Equality Trap* (New York: Simon and Schuster, 1988); Sidonie Smith, *A Poetics of Women's Autobiography: Marginality and the Fictions of Self-Representation* (Bloomington: Indiana University Press, 1987); Sidonie Smith, *Subjectivity, Identity, and the Body: Women's Autobiographical Practices in the Twentieth Century* (Bloomington: Indiana University Press, 1993).
15. Estelle Jelinek listed several differences between the writings of men and women in terms of content, style, and temporal structure. According to her, whereas men characteristically focused on the professional sphere and on one's individual contributions to the era and to society, women tended to address private life, family, home, and relationships with others. Jelinek stressed that men's depiction of events were linear and structured; women's tended to be more fragmented and nonsequential. In her opinion, "These discontinuous forms have been important to women because they are analogous to the fragmented, interrupted and formless nature of their lives." Estelle C. Jelinek, *Women's Autobiography: Essays in Criticism* (Bloomington: Indiana University Press, 1980), 19. Likewise, Hoogenboom concluded from her reading of the Populist essays in the *Granat Encyclopedia* that there was a strong link between women's place in the family and society and the formation of their notions of social justice, which in turn defined their directions in life and shaped their recollections of childhood. Hilde Hoogenboom, "Vera Figner and Revolutionary Autobiographies: The Influence of Gender on Genre," in *Women in Russia and Ukraine*, ed. Rosalind Marsh (Cambridge: Cambridge University Press, 1996).
16. *Russkoe Proshloe: Istoriko-Dokumental'nyi Al'manakh* (1993), 4:335–336.
17. Andrew Wachtel, *The Battle for Childhood: Creation of a Russian Myth* (Stanford, CA: Stanford University Press, 1990), 2.
18. Ibid., 4.
19. G. Suvorov, "Gorod Orlov v kontse XVIII—pervoi polovine XIX v.," *Pamiatnaia knizhka Kirovskoi oblasti i kalendar' na 2009 god* (Kirov, 2009), 267–275; N. A. Kolevatov, *Orlov: drevnie goroda Rossii* (Kirov, 1998), 9–18, 25–26.
20. On this, see Sergeev, *Raznochintsy-demokraty Viatki*, 3–20.
21. Lidia Ginzburg, *O psikhologicheskoi proze* (Leningrad: Khudozhestvennaia literatura, 1977).
22. Charushin, *O dalekom proshlom*, 32–33.
23. P. N. Luppov, *Istoriia goroda Viatki* (Kirov: Volgo-Viatskoe knizhnoe izdatel'stvo, 1958), 29–50; *Istoriia goroda Kirova, 1374–1974: Kratkii ocherk* (Kirov: Volgo-Viatskoe knizhnoe

izdatel'stvo, 1974), 16–30; V. A. Berdinskikh, *Istoriia goroda Viatki* (Kirov: Viatskoe knizhnoe izdatel'stvo, 2002), 175–186.

24. Charushin, *O dalekom proshlom*, 90.

25. Robert Anderson, "The Idea of the Secondary School in Nineteenth-Century Europe," *Paedagogica Historica: International Journal of the History of Education* 40 (2004): 1–2, 93–106.

26. Daniel R. Brower, *Training the Nihilists: Education and Radicalism in Tsarist Russia* (Ithaca, NY: Cornell University Press, 1975), 88–94.

27. Alfred J. Rieber, "The Sedimentary Society," in *Between Tsar and People: Educated Society and the Quest for Public Identity in Late Imperial Russia*, ed. E. W. Clowes (Princeton, NJ: Princeton University Press, 1991), 351.

28. Charushin, *O dalekom proshlom*, 45–46.

29. Ibid., 34.

30. Ibid., 38. In his memoirs, he writes he was in the third class. However, since he had enrolled in August of 1862 and repeated his third year, by December 1866, when his father died, he must have been in the fourth class (his fifth year).

31. Solomon Chudnovskii, *Iz davnikh let. Vospominaniia* (Moskva: Izdatel'stvo Vsesoiuznogo Obshchestva Politkatorzhan i Ssyl'noposelentsev, 1934), 7–9.

32. GAKO, f. 205, op. 2, d. 1627, l. 34.

33. Charushin, *O dalekom proshlom*, 41–45.

34. Ibid., 60.

35. Ibid., 42.

36. Charushin described her as the *klassnaia dama*, but this term applied only to teachers filling the same role at the next level of schooling, the gymnasium, where Kuvshinskaia was offered a position after being forced to resign from the diocesan school in 1871.

37. Charushin, *O dalekom proshlom*, 68.

38. On the Mashkovtsev clan, see Mikhail Sudovikov, "Mashkovtsevy. Kuptsy i obshchestvennye deiateli," *Kupechestvo Viatskoe*, ed. Mikhail Sudovikov and Tamara Nikolaeva (Kirov-Viatka: KOGUP, 1999), 15–34.

39. See *Istoriia goroda Kirova*, 60–61.

40. On this volume, see Franco Venturi, *Roots of Revolution: A History of the Populist and Socialist Movements in Nineteenth Century Russia* (New York: Grosset & Dunlap, 1966), 488–495.

41. Charushin, *O dalekom proshlom*, 44–45.

42. GAKO, f. 616, op. 1, d. 499, l. 13. Charushin and Kuvshinskaia had sat through the zemstvo assembly meeting in December 1870 which considered his application. Charushin, *O dalekom proshlom*, 84.

43. Ibid., 86.

44. Ibid., 88.

45. Ibid., 92.

46. Ibid., 92–96.

47. Ibid., 95.

48. Vera Figner, *Zapechatlennyi trud* (Moskva: Mysl', 1964), 1:91.

49. Marc Raeff, *Origins of the Russian Intelligentsia: The Eighteenth-Century Nobility* (New York: Harcourt, 1966); Brower, *Training the Nihilists*.

50. This was the title of a chapter in Avrahm Yarmolinsky, *Road to Revolution: A Century of Russian Radicalism* (Princeton, 1957). See also Anna Geifman, *Thou Shalt Kill: Revolutionary Terrorism in Russia, 1894–1917* (Princeton, NJ: Princeton University Press, 1993).

51. Claudia Verhoeven, *The Odd Man Karakozov: Imperial Russia, Modernity, and the Birth of Terrorism* (Ithaca, NY: Cornell University Press, 2009).

52. Hilde Hoogenboom, "Vera Figner and Revolutionary Autobiographies: The Influence of Gender on Genre," in *Women in Russia and Ukraine*, ed. Rosalind Marsh (Cambridge: Cambridge University Press, 1996), 78.

53. Ibid., 78–79.

The Seventies Generation

Young Revolutionaries and the Chaikovskii Circle

We were neither Lavrovists nor Bakunists, but went our own way.

—Alexandra Kornilova-Moroz to Nikolai Charushin, April 26, 1928

THE CHAIKOVSKII CIRCLE

The Chaikovskii circle, numbering perhaps fifty young men and women in St. Petersburg, and small clusters in half a dozen other cities,[1] sought to reach out, first to students and the intelligentsia and then to factory workers fresh from the countryside. Those who had not been arrested by 1874 joined the Going to the People movement that summer. Some three thousand men and women traveled to the countryside to embed themselves with the peasantry, only to be discouraged by their reception. Two years later the Populist movement coalesced into an organized revolutionary movement (Land and Liberty) seeking to create a broad basis of support among the population, and using the press and the court system to publicize its goals.[2] As repressive measures accelerated, the movement split over what tactics to use in what they regarded as a police state. One branch, the People's Will, with perhaps five hundred committed adherents, devoted itself to terrorism directed at odious political figures and, ultimately, at the tsar himself. It succeeded in assassinating him on March 1, 1881. All in all, between 1873 and 1877, at least 1,600 Populists were arrested (15 percent of whom were women); the total number of "professional revolutionaries" (a new term at the time) is harder to determine.³

The Chaikovskii circle and revolutionary Populism have long interested historians both in Russia and abroad. We seek primarily to approach the topic *through the prism of generational history*—how Charushin and his friends in the Chaikovskii circle constructed a world view colored by events, readings, and interactions. According to Karl Mannheim, a generation as a genuine community comes into being through shared historical experiences.⁴ Equally important is the subjective process by which the members of a generation (or in this case an age cohort) internalize the epoch in which they enter into adulthood and identify specific events as markers in the formation of this generation. Generational identity remained significant for these revolutionaries, who continued to call themselves the "Chaikovtsy" (singular, Chaikovets) throughout their lives) and manifested itself in the collective construction of memoirs in the 1920s. But why? Let us return to the life trajectory of Charushin's life to answer this question.

FROM STUDENT TO REVOLUTIONARY

Charushin's relocation to St. Petersburg, in the summer of 1871, marked the beginning of a new period in his life. He had received a scholarship to continue his education at the Technological Institute. In reality, this scholarship was more like a loan, because after completing their studies, recipients were obliged to work for a set number of years in the zemstvo back home. As it turned out, Charushin never came close to completing his degree, for even in his first year at the university he threw himself entirely into spreading revolutionary propaganda, completely neglecting his studies. The archives have preserved a record of his first two years of academic prowess—or rather lack thereof; on his transcript, next to each of the courses listed is a dash, indicating that he never even took his exams. In November 1872, the Viatka zemstvo wrote to the Technological Institute inquiring about the standing of its scholarship recipient only to learn that he was required to repeat his first year of study. In January,

1873, the zemstvo forwarded 125 rubles to the Institute to enable Charushin to continue his studies, but according to the official record, since he had completely discontinued his academic career, he never received this sum. The university returned the money, and Charushin was expelled from the institution in June 1873.[5] It can't be said that Charushin was the only *viatich* (as those from Viatka called themselves) to follow this path. The provincial zemstvo was constantly taking measures to locate other scholarship recipients who had gone astray. For example, in 1872, it was also trying to establish the current location of one Semen Driagin, who had received a stipend six years previously, but with whom they had lost contact.[6]

In truth, soon after matriculating at the Technological Institute, Charushin realized that he had erred in his choice of an educational institution and that he was far more interested in the social sciences than he was in the natural or hard sciences. Moreover, his notions of the public good and of an active life had little to do with learning a profession and taking up work at some enterprise. Within a month, he had completely dropped his studies. Instead, he sought to join the intelligentsia in its search to politically enlighten the people and to prepare cadres to disseminate propaganda among workers and peasants. It seemed intolerable to stand on the sidelines when so much had been said and written about the inequities of the existing order, the difficult lives of the people, and the need for change. Influenced by radical thinkers at home and abroad, Charushin readily put public need over private want, and dreamed of being part of a large-scale movement that would bring about changes in Russia's political and social structure. In the Chaikovtsy's memoirs, for example, we often find such phrases as "a vibrant and tumultuous time," "young Petersburg was overflowing with energy and life there was intense," "the common level of excitement was continuously growing."[7] The turbulent lives of Petersburg students at the time, the establishment of communes and study circles, fervid discussions about the past and the future—how could Charushin not have been touched by all that was going on! Like many others of his age, he yearned for action.

To the causal onlooker in the early 1870s, Charushin's external appearance (see Figure 2.1)—especially his blue-tinted glasses—would have identified him as a student, or even a nihilist. Sergei Sinegub described

FIGURE 2.1.

Nikolai Charushin, 1870s.

© Russian State Archive of Literature and Art, Moscow.

him as "tall and slender, moving gracefully, with a prominent and sagacious forehead, an imposingly huge red mane of hair and a firm, decisive gaze coming from his blue eyes."[8] Lev Tikhomirov also left behind a rather striking portrait, "tall, emaciated, clean-shaven, but with a huge head of russet-colored hair and wearing huge blue-tinted glasses."[9] Tikhomirov recalls that Charushin looked out at the world with head bent, not through but over the top of his glasses, and spoke in a weak and muffled voice.[10]

Yet the next step—becoming a professional revolutionary—was accompanied by a good measure of inner turmoil. It is difficult to speak with certainty of Charushin's feelings at the time, for both his own memoirs and the portraits of him by those who knew him well describe an emotionally reserved person who avoided elevated speech and preferred practical activity above all. Sinegub wrote that he was "always self-contained, avoiding expansiveness, a severely serious individual, we felt he was a person with a heart and capable of tenderness, but completely averse to sentimentality."¹¹

At the same time, from the memoirs of Charushin's younger brother Arkadii, published in the form of a novelette in 1926, we know that Charushin's decision to devote himself entirely to revolutionary activity did not come easily. After all, a university degree at a time when there was a serious shortage of educated personnel virtually guaranteed employment, social status, and access to the good life. He fretted about his responsibilities to his large family, for he was the oldest son, and his widowed mother fervently hoped that he would be able to help provide his younger siblings with an education. He fully realized that dropping his studies at the institute and joining the revolutionary movement meant that he was subjecting himself to the possibility of arrest and exile to Siberia, which would bring grief to his mother and leave his brothers and sister in a very vulnerable position. Returning home to Orlov for the last time in 1872 (his next visit occurred only after a long exile to Siberia, more than two decades later), he remained there only three weeks instead of the two months he had originally planned. In Arkadii Charushin's thinly fictionalized account, "It seemed that his brother was suffering deeply. On several occasions, he came across him sitting alone, buried in his thoughts. Before him was an open but untouched book; his eyes were fixed far away, and seemed lost in the distance. [Arkadii] didn't dare ask him what was causing this spiritual agony... he understood only that his brother could no longer be close to him, that a vast gulf had emerged between their two worlds, a gulf that made return to the past inconceivable."¹²

However, from this point on, he never seems to have looked back. Taking part in a number of gatherings and student circles (one such self-education circle even met in his apartment) Charushin made many new acquaintances, especially among the tightly knit group of fellow Viatka students in St. Petersburg. Such collectives of students from the same region (*zemliachestva*) played a big role in the student movement and were a key form of the self-organization of students as a whole. But the Viatka *zemliachestvo* would continue to exist for many after its members left the university, functioning as an active social network. Early in the twentieth century, those from Viatka forced into exile by the repressive measures of the provincial authorities turned first to their fellow compatriots (*zemliaki*) residing in St. Petersburg or Moscow in the effort to gain a foothold in a new milieu, find support, and become members of a larger community.

One such fellow Viatich whom Charushin met in St. Petersburg was Nikolai Chaikovskii, a colorful and erratic but ingenuous revolutionary with whom Charushin would maintain contact throughout his life.[13] It was through Chaikovskii that Charushin came into contact with the circle of friends around Mark Natanson and the Kornilova sisters, which had coalesced in 1871 and came to be known in history as the Chaikovskii circle, or the Big Propaganda Society; and its members, as the Chaikovtsy.[14] Chaikovskii himself always objected to the appellation because it implied that he had been the organizer of the group, when in fact, the initiative had come mainly from Natanson. Later, Chaikovskii wrote to Leonid Shishko, also a member of the circle, "Natanson was even then an influential and well-read person; some of prestige rubbed off on me. But I always felt uncomfortable about this, as if walking on stilts, because in fact I had not taken the initiative, and had not the knowledge nor the maturity to lead such a group."[15]

After pursuing the same activities as most other circles of the time—preparing book summaries and holding discussions of topics pertaining to philosophy, history, political economy—the Chaikovskii circle resolved to begin propagating its ideas among students and others in the intelligentsia through the publication and distribution of books in St. Petersburg and especially in the provinces. Political enlightenment and the formation of a cadre of propagandists would, in their mind, lay the groundwork for the transformation of society. Like Petr Lavrov, a leading Populist thinker at the time, the Chaikovtsy believed that the intelligentsia were the driving force of history, but also that a genuine societal transformation required a popular revolution. Consequently, they believed that their primary task for the moment—albeit a long-term one—was education (or in their words "enlightenment"). Chaikovskii recalled, in 1902, "Establishing a cadre of militants from among the best of the student milieu at the time, preparing them for revolutionary activity, having them collectively go to out to the people . . . (then) fostering an intelligentsia from among the people . . . this was at the core of the self-education circles, the *zemliachestva* and other types of communes as well."[16] Seemingly conscious of its role in history, the intelligentsia set about carrying forth widespread propaganda among the people, building to the point where it would itself carry out a social revolution.

What were the roots of the solidarity that held this group together over the course of their lives? What people and books inspired this generation and how did the times shape their identities? Elucidating a collective world view requires at the same time emphasizing the instability of its separate components, for this generation was at a stage of life during which they would normally be becoming socialized in the larger world and searching for a profession. False starts and experimentation were the name of the game, and intense peer-group dynamics shaped the process. Thought and emotion were interwoven in a heightened fashion. As Deborah Hardy wisely advises us in her work on the Populists of that period, they "were emotional and intellectual, rational and irrational, complex and unpredictable."[17] Yet in order to assess the degree to which Charushin's core values and political beliefs about the role the state and the intelligentsia might play in promoting change, how revolution should be pursued, and how the peasantry could be included in the process, we need to examine the sources of their inspiration, the debates within the circle about who—among the plethora of authorities in the diverse world of socialism at this vibrant time—might best address their own search for a way forward, and provide the tropes of their own self-identification. As we noted earlier, the task is made more difficult in that many of the texts available were produced much later in life, forcing us to consider these questions through the prism of memory.

GENERATIONAL TROPES: YOUTHFULNESS AND A DEBT TO THE PEOPLE

The revolutionaries of the 1870s often used the words *youth* and *youthful* to describe themselves, emphasize their status in society, and symbolize the progressive nature of their movement. Revolutionary propaganda, the Going to the People movement (1874), and demonstrations and protests were all attempts at a "youth revolution" in Russia, one that had begun with study circles and student communes seeking to work out a completely new world view and behavioral code for the young. Sergei Kovalik underscored the exclusive youthfulness of the movement, writing in his memoirs, "In the 1870s, eschewing the participation of an older generation inclined to compromise, the youth set out all alone, to resolve all (of Russia's) cursed questions which gave humanity no respite. This generation resolved to take upon its own shoulders the entire burden of rejuvenating the world."[18]

Indeed, primarily because of a surging youth movement, the decade gained the reputation as one of unprecedented renewal of public life. Petr Kropotkin, for example, labeled youth as a distinctive grouping, movers of history. He contrasted Russian youth to its equivalent cohort in Western Europe, emphasizing the former's striving to embody in their own lives the principles of socialism, "Russian youth of that time approached socialism by a completely different path."[19]

Sergei Sinegub conflates the notions of "youth" and "intelligentsia" and in so doing replicates a characteristic descriptor of the latter, one originating with Lavrov's famous notion of bearing a "debt to the people." Sinegub wrote, "For the young of the time its overriding task was to determine what action to take that would be of the greatest benefit to the people, before whom it—the youth of the intelligentsia—stood an as yet unpaid debt."[20] Likewise, Charushin wrote of that time:

> Everywhere there was talk of the sufferings of the people, of rampant poverty and systematic oppression ... of how it was long overdue to open the people's eyes to the roots of this evil and in so doing point to how to extricate themselves from their passive state. Further, it was argued that the primary burden in this great and immediate task rested upon the intelligentsia, who were fully cognizant of the causes of this situation only because that very people, at enormous cost to their own well-being had for centuries provided for the upbringing of the intelligentsia, given them the opportunity to have access to education and the benefits of culture.[21]

Thus, the revolutionaries of the 1870s considered themselves members of the intelligentsia, not least because they also acknowledged their debt to the people and were willing to stand up to the autocracy in the quest to set Russia on a progressive historical path. It was precisely this semantic notion of the intelligentsia that prevailed in Russian society in the second half of the nineteenth century as it was coalescing as a societal stratum.[22]

MORAL STANDARDS

High moral standards are another oft-cited characteristic of the Chaikovskii circle, for whom public service, self-abnegation, comradeship, and courage were bywords. The Soviet historian Nikolai Troitskii, seeking to explain the Chaikovtsy's unprecedented emphasis on living according to a strict ethical code, concluded that it created strong bonds between members of a group that had otherwise cast off all ties to society and could feel adrift in an uncomprehending world.[23] In any event later, remembering their past many referred to this moral code as central to their existence. For example, Alexandra Kornilova-Moroz, reminiscing about student communes and circles of the 1870s, placed mutual aid at the core of that generation's ethics.[24] As for Charushin, in a letter he provided his own list of the characteristic features of the Chaikovskii circle: unlimited self-sacrifice, devotion to the cause, and unconditional honesty.[25] Chaikovskii recalled that one of the members of the circle (Gertsenstein) had been expelled because of his "bombast, womanizing, dishonesty."[26]

The memoir writers attributed this heightened attention given to the moral caliber of the circle's members to the reaction to the notorious Nechaev affair, which had provoked revulsion among many in that generation. Sergei Nechaev was a charismatic young revolutionary who convinced young students that he was the leader of a vast international conspiracy and then murdered one who had uncovered the fabrication. Of peasant origins, Nechaev was also the author of *Catechism of a Revolutionary* in which he advocated that whoever wished to carry out a revolution had to give up on all ties in the outside world, whether family or friends, practice deceit in matters public and private, and live according to a code that recognized no traditional ethical principles. Nechaev was exposed, arrested, and incarcerated, but over time, his charisma was such that he managed to recruit several of his jailers. Textbook treatments of the Russian revolutionary movement often cite Nechaev's catechism as the code by which the movement as a whole subsequently lived and operated. For that reason alone, it is worth reminding readers of the "principles" Nechaev inscribed in the *Catechism*:

> The revolutionary is a doomed man. He has no personal interests, no affairs, no sentiments, attachments, property, not even a name of his own.

Everything in him is absorbed by one exclusive interest, one thought, one passion—the revolution. In the very depth of his being, not merely in word or in deed, he has broken every connection with the social order, and with the whole educated world, with all the laws, appearances and generally accepted conventions and moralities of that world which he considers his ruthless foe. Should he continue to live in it, it will be solely for the purpose of destroying it the more surely.[27]

The Nechaev affair is singled out in the memoirs of our group as the event that most determined its mood and future orientation—but in reaction against his teaching. Charushin recalled that Nechaev's trial provoked intense discussion among group members, who pored over the accounts published in the press. The affair concentrated their attention on moral questions as well as on how their organization should be structured, what its modus vivendi should be. The whole case became a byword for deceit and moral turpitude, and it was immortalized in Dostoevsky's novel *The Possessed*, published first in the "thick" journal *Russkii Vestnik* (*Russian Herald*), although one searches the memoirs of the time in vain for references to the novel or its impact on the group. For the Chaikovtsy, lies were incompatible with revolutionary activity or with "serving the people." In Charushin's accounts of the group's stance toward Nechaev's organization, he constantly reverts to the word "deceit" or its equivalents: "an organization based upon deceit"; "mystification and lies were its common currency"; "blatant and coarse deceit"; "an organization which had as its foundation deceit."[28] In opposition to this his circle juxtaposed trust and probity as its core principles, along with a categorical refusal on the part of Nikolai Chaikovskii to resort to "false currency" in order to meet the group's needs and the determination to cut off all ties with anybody who did so.

In their memoirs, too, they write about each other as being, above all, people of unusual moral purity, the diametrical opposites of those involved in the Nechaev affair. Vasilii Bogucharskii describes the Chaikovtsy and the followers of Nechaev as polar opposites, and calls the former one of the "brightest aspects" of the youth movement of the 1870s, offering many acts of extraordinary moral heroism (*podvizhnichestvo*). He adds effusively, "It is as if from a dank underground one ascends to a sunlit, well-tended meadow."[29] After a lifetime of engagement with revolutionary circles of every stripe, the member of the Chaikovskii circle and renowned future anarchist Prince Kropotkin remembered his group as "ideally pure and morally outstanding."[30] Charushin remembers his own time with the Chaikovskii circle as the "best and most luminous of my life; memories of which were never far from my consciousness wherever I was and whatever the circumstances, helping me deal with whatever tribulations fate sent my way."[31]

Moral quests and the search to define ethical boundaries are, of course, a stage of growing up, and that fact helps explain the heightened attention to such questions when the Chaikovtsy looked back on their earlier lives in their elder years. The literature at that earlier time was also replete with discussions of burning moral issues and how to ethically orient oneself in life, which only further encouraged such questing. But this was not merely a stage for the Chaikovtsy; throughout their entire lives their thinking and behavior were framed in ethical terms. Reflections on what was ethical and what was not in the context of revolutionary organizations and their actions—particularly concerning the use of violence and the justification for resort to deceitful practices in the repressive environment of a police state—retained their urgency in later years.

Later, in the 1920s, the urge to preserve the memory of those who had perished in the struggle against the autocracy (at a time when their legacy was threatened with erasure by the Communist authorities), and the desire to provide exemplary models to shape the outlook and behavior of a new generation growing up in the Soviet era, certainly bore on the construction of the image of the revolutionaries of the 1870s as ideal moral types. It might well be that contemporary circumstances were on Charushin's mind when he contemplated the meaning of the Nechaev affair in his memoirs, "Aware and free people cannot long endure in an atmosphere of deceit and unconditional submission to the will of one person."[32]

So intense was the moral fiber of this group that some have compared these revolutionaries with the early Christians. Sergei Kovalik described them as "bursting with the most stalwart of religious belief in the elevated nature of the mission before them" and "under the influence of faith they were ready to carry out any heroic deed, no matter how daunting."[33] In the opinion of one reputable earlier historian of the Russian intelligentsia, the 1870s saw a fundamental change in the orientation of progressive-thinking individuals. By comparison with the previous decade the new type of *intelligent* was much less deliberate and rationalist, displaying instead a certain type of religiosity in their bearing, actions and even identity.[34] The memoirs of Populists do seem to support this assertion. When a religious worldview was imparted in childhood, it later merged with the ethos of Populism or, more often, provided the language and imagery through which Populist beliefs could be formulated and communicated. Vera Figner, in a particularly vivid passage, wrote:

> Anyone who like me once came under the spell of the image of Christ, of the idea of experiencing humiliation, suffering and death, who in one's youth saw Him as her ideal, and His life as the model of sacrificial love—will understand the state of mind of the recently condemned revolutionary, cast into a living grave for serving the cause of popular emancipation.... Christian ideals, which from early childhood are instilled in all of us, whether consciously or unconsciously, along with the tales of the heroic deeds of believers, lead that condemned person to the joyful realization that the moment has arrived at which the spiritual strength of his love and resolution as a warrior for the ideals he is serving not for his own immediate benefit but for the people, for society and future generations, will be tested.[35]

The quest for moral ideals, a rejection of the crude materialism of the nihilists of the previous decade, and a growing disillusionment with the Orthodox church led to a rethinking of Christianity, the attribution of new meanings to religious symbols, and, especially, the rephrasing of revolutionary ideas in religious terminology. The descriptions one finds in the literature of suffering and redemption have led some recent historians to treat Populism as a full-blown religion, replete with sacrifice, devotion and faith,[36] as a variant of belief concealed in a secularized wrapping.[37] Another historian compares the communal bonds of the Populist revolutionaries with those of the persecuted first Christians; he labels the resort to the language and symbols of the Christian faith a sign of the "religious ambivalence" of this cohort.[38]

Of course, it is possible to find an abundance of Old Testament metaphors, even in the writings of Karl Marx—sometimes his thunderous proclamations make him seem akin to a biblical prophet. Likewise, Irina Paperno has identified multiple religious links in the phraseology, use of metaphors, and even strivings to martyrdom of the Populist idol Chernyshevskii, who was, after all, the son of a priest educated in a seminary.[39] So it is not surprising that the members of the Chaikovskii circle also revealed traces of religion from their family and cultural backgrounds, their schooling, in their efforts to describe their quests in life, their sacrificial behavior, their dedication to a cause, and the "communal spirit" that was central to their identity.

Yet dwelling on these parallels can be misleading, for it ignores the secular ethical roots of the political ideals, which held them together and, more importantly, guided them throughout their lives. Vera Zasulich recalls, with a slightly different twist, reading the Gospels in childhood, "I did not ask for God's intervention; instead I wanted to serve, even save Him. *But four years later I did not believe in God and easily made my farewells with religion* . . . all that remained dear to me was Christ; we never parted, in fact became even closer."[40] Charushin's own memoirs laconically dispute the notion that Populism was a thinly secularized religion: "Authentic religiosity was not instilled in us in childhood, and if the official church had any influence whatsoever, it was a negative one. It was only the Gospels which left an imprint, but not as a divine revelation, rather as a moral doctrine, in many ways corresponding with notions and principles we had appropriated ourselves."[41]

Later in life, little or no trace remained of the youthful exaltation which, dressed up in religious imagery, has misled many historians to describe their activities as a "children's crusade."[42] Returning from exile, the veterans of the Chaikovskii circle showed no interest in the Orthodox revival, Baptist movement, spread of theosophy, or mystical cults that found fertile ground in educated society and among the country's elites after the turn of the century. What remained instead was what had always been at the core of their beliefs: a moral code of solidarity and service based on carefully thought out ethics, not a cult of martyrdom. As Franco Venturi put it, "So powerful was this ethical spirit among the [Chaikovtsy] that it was sometimes expressed in religious terms—a religion which gave a more or less simple symbolic form to their aspirations to purity and total sacrifice. But a religious expression of this kind was always only marginal. The [Chaikovtsy] cannot be described in terms of a political manifesto or of a religious credo."[43]

INFLUENCES ON YOUNG MINDS: CHERNYSHEVSKII AND PUSHKIN?

The seventies generation of revolutionaries drew their inspiration from several sources. Literature and literary criticism exerted a strong influence on the values and outlook of Russian society in the nineteenth century, and literary heroes were often seen to be expressing the spirit of an epoch. For that reason, what one read was always a marker of one's membership in a given generational cohort. As Marina Mogilner has written, "[T]he reading process became an act of political opposition. The world of fiction and poetry, populated by 'real' people and saturated with 'real' feelings became a normative reality, according to whose rules readers belonging to the intelligentsia sought to live."[44] The trope of unavoidable conflict between "fathers and sons," generational change as a symbol of the societal renewal, all this was the common phraseology of the literary journals of the time.[45] It was these readings that shaped the lasting image of the sixties generation in Russia, which in turn opened the way for constituting subsequent "generations" in the history of the Russian intelligentsia.

At the same time, the memoirs stress that books were a substitute for interaction with an older generation whose experiences and ideas were not meaningful for them. Such a fixing of boundaries is also an indispensable part of generational discourse. As Charushin would have it, "Many of us were unsatisfied with the older generation, including those from the intelligentsia who had settled down and made their peace with life, and we marked out broader horizons for ourselves."[46] Many memoirs, including Charushin's own, provide confirmation of this perspective: "We sought in Russian literature not merely a depiction of Russian life, but rather responses to the contemporary world... that could serve as warnings, but especially guideposts in our own lives."[47] The memoirs of that time emphasize the search to emulate literary models, to carry over the behavior of their heroes into their own daily life. With a wry touch, Kornilova-Moroz wrote to Charushin, in 1924, "Our intellectual and moral development proceeded under the influence of Dobroliubov, Pisarev, Chernyshevskii, as well as Lavrov and Flerovskii, *and we subsequently went forth self-sacrificially.*"[48]

Although Nikolai Chernyshevskii[49] is traditionally classified as "the voice of the 1860s generation," those of the 1870s generation also acknowledged the influence of his works, citing his enormous authority, both ideationally and morally. Especially important was his "thick" journal, *The Contemporary*. According to Charushin and others selections from that journal were frequently the subject of group discussions; so close and intense were the discussions that it is reasonable to predicate that these journals merged later with the narratives of their own lives. Chernyshevskii's influence is registered in Charushin's reflections on both public and private matters, his estimation of the people around him, and his life strategies. He wrote of Rakhmetov, the protagonist in Chernyshevskii's most famous novel, *What Is to Be Done*, a fellow who slept on a bed of nails to toughen himself up for the revolution but also lived a life of probity and earnest commitment to a cause, "[His] image was etched into our minds; he loomed large in front of our eyes. When we ourselves were searching for the right path forward in life that figure succored and inspired us to take decisive steps!"[50] In a novel written at the turn of the century, the hero, a revolutionary from the 1870s, talks of how the "half-forgotten shadow of Rakhmetov peered reproachfully at him from the fog of the past," that is, to remind him that he had not lived up to his aspirations of that earlier time.[51]

It was not only the ideas put forth in Chernyshevskii's novel, but also the author himself who inspired such admiration among the Chaikovtsy. He was a writer, but he was also a martyr who had suffered for his convictions. Charushin's recollections of his impact are revealing of just how deep their veneration of him was, "Even by that time Chernyshevskii had assumed the crown of the martyr [he had been exiled to Siberia and had refused offers of clemency], and bore his burden of suffering stoically and with dignity. He had become our mentor in life, whose tragic fate only intensified his allure for us and heightened the attraction of his ideas."[52]

In defining their reading preferences, the men and women of the Chaikovskii circle displayed their preference for verse with a clear social message rather than for form or the beauty of language. Writers of an earlier generation received mixed reviews. Alexander Pushkin was not a favorite poet among Charushin's cohort. In light of the ever-expanding renown of Pushkin's name toward the end of the nineteenth century, the noisy celebrations of his anniversaries, and the virtual immortalization of his image in the twentieth century, our memoirists later felt compelled to explain why back then they had instead revered Lermontov and Nekrasov (the latter, a "people's poet" and the favorite of the seventies generation—rather paradoxically, given his less than exemplary personal life). Charushin recalled:

> Pushkin, with his limpid and melodious verse, so easily remembered and so exquisite, nevertheless had little appeal for us. Lermontov, on the other hand, was more to our liking. It's likely that it was the influence of the young and radical literary critic, Pisarev, who continued to cast a spell on our generation, that shaped our preferences. Without a doubt, it was Nekrasov's works that we read avidly and often memorized word for word. His Populist leanings, his fierce love for the underprivileged and the civic themes of his poetry, toward which we were predisposed, drew us to him.[53]

Even the works of Turgenev, who is often thought of as one of the favorite writers of this generation, were valued primarily for his ability to depict the contemporary state of society, not for his exquisite aesthetics and certainly not for Turgenev's refined ambivalence. The legendary figure of Bazarov, from *Fathers and Sons*, controversial at the time as the embodiment of nihilism, had provoked heated debate when the book was first published (1862) but also a decade later among Charushin's circle of friends. He wrote:

> Some of us were totally receptive [to Bazarov]; others, while acknowledging his strength and integrity of character, and discerning in him a prototype of a dawning new Russia, at the same time believed his portrait was one-sided, lacking in full-blooded civic ideals, and ultimately unsatisfactory. For that reason, even Rudin, (not to mention Insarov and Elena in *On the Eve*), that bearer of new tidings in the desert, and a person incapable of worshipping idols—despite all of his flaws—was far more attractive than Bazarov. This was even more the case after we learned that in an unpublished denouement to the novel the author has Rudin dying on the barricades in Paris.[54]

LAVROV OR BAKUNIN? POLARITIES IN POPULIST THOUGHT

Their selection of readings in philosophy, economics, and politics also served to shape the Chaikovtsies' worldview while serving as a marker of their membership in a revolutionary subculture. Sergei Kovalik recalled that among those readings the most important in shaping their beliefs was Petr Lavrov's *Historical Letters*. According to Kovalik's account, this work "awoke in our inner beings latent feelings that had been set there by our long history, summoning us to pay back our debt to the people for the education we had received. It would be fair to say that this book tutored an entire generation."[55] In truth, although the extent of Lavrov's influence in shaping the views of the Chaikovtsy remains a subject of debate,[56] we certainly can find reflections of his ideas and frequent references to him in their memoirs. Charushin first encountered his work while still enrolled at the gymnasium, at the recommendation of his history teacher Rozhdestvenskii, who led a discussion of the then recently published *Historical Letters*.

The relative importance to the Chaikovtsy of Lavrov and of the colorful and renowned anarchist Mikhail Bakunin has long occupied the attention of historians. Were they "preparationists" committed to arduous work among the peasantry for long decades, or Bakuninist incendiaries who wanted to spark an immediate popular uprising, sweeping away the state along with the ruling classes? According to a future convert to Marxism, Pavel Axelrod, writing in 1923, Bakunin's views certainly had purchase in that circle, "Revolutionary youth felt that Lavrovism led them away from an authentically revolutionary path. Its oft-repeated hesitations pushed into the indeterminate future that very revolution to which we urgently wanted to devote all our efforts. Bakunin's theories better conformed to the mood of young radicals, and seduced us by its unmediated simplicity and its capacity to dispel all our doubts. Quite simply, Bakuninism intoxicated us with its revolutionary phraseology and fiery eloquence."[57] Others have pointed to the draft program put forward, in 1873, by Petr Kropotkin to define the group's philosophy and goals. The mild-mannered Kropotkin was an avid proponent of Bakunin's insurrectionist ideas and insisted that Charushin had shared his views.[58]

But not everybody recalled that Bakunin's views held sway.[59] Mikhail Frolenko later recalled that the Chaikovskii circle had initially examined Bakunin's essays and even organized a group discussion for students. The first meeting was well attended, the second much less so, and nobody showed up for the planned third discussion. According to Frolenko, the Chaikovtsy were not satisfied with their reading of Bakunin, and in the spring of 1874, they set out for the countryside in the Going to the People movement, "having completely forgotten him."[60] In his memoirs Charushin repeatedly asserted that he, like most other Chaikovtsy, had never subscribed to Bakunin's political views, especially on the need to eliminate the state (although when Charushin was arrested in 1874, Bakunin's *The State and Anarchy* was among the books confiscated by the police).[61]

Long after the fact, surviving members of the Chaikovskii circle themselves sought to provide an answer to this question. In 1928, a commemorative gathering was held in Leningrad to mark the fiftieth anniversary of the Trial of the 193, and at one session a debate ensued about Charushin's stated position—namely, that the Chaikovtsy had never resolved the question of allegiance to one view or the other. Charushin did not actually attend that gathering, but, as Kornilova-Moroz wrote to tell him, she had spoken up in support of his stance, namely that "we were neither Lavrovists nor Bakunists, but went our own way."[62] At that time Kornilova-Moroz agreed with Charushin that with the exception of Kropotkin there were no anarchists in the circle and that most of them had only the vaguest notion of what anarchism was all about. Both Soviet and Western historians have come to a similar conclusion. The debates that raged in Switzerland among exiles who were proponents of or the other of the two parties apparently did not find purchase among the Chaikovtsy in St. Petersburg.[63]

All in all, the youth of all those involved and the likelihood that their political views were still not fully formulated; the fluidity of the situation in 1873, when Kropotkin put forward his proposal for a program; the fact that because of the arrests that began to devastate the group at that very time, no program had in fact been adopted; the circumstances in the mid-1920s when many of the memoirs were written and the surviving elderly Populists were being challenged by Communist party militants to justify their earlier ideological positions—all caution us not to make too much of the distinctions argued here.

Yet in terms of Charushin's life story, it is frustrating that we cannot clarify his views on the topic. Throughout his life, he was proud of his status as a revolutionary. Still, as we move into the twentieth century, his views become increasingly evolutionary, and by 1917, he stakes everything on maintaining a robust but reformed state and establishing a constitution legitimated by a popular vote. The evolutionary strand can be found in Lavrov's insistence that large-scale political and social change was possible only with the participation of an enlightened population. But how do we explain Charushin's later statist turn, one endorsed by neo-Populists as well—the belief that only a strong central government (with a popular mandate to be sure) could successfully implement the transition to socialism? Can his fervid denial that he was a supporter of Bakunin simply be a rationalization for his later stances, an attempt to prove that his later views were consistent with those of his youth?[64]

ON CONSTITUTIONS AND LASSALLE

Perhaps an answer to that question can be found in the influence of another figure who was popular at the time. Given the pleiad of European and Russian thinkers (Marx, Proudhon, Darwin, Buckle, and J. S. Mills, on the one hand, and Lavrov, Mikhailovskii, and Chernyshevskii, on the other), we might be forgiven for overlooking the German political activist (and bane of Karl Marx) Ferdinand Lassalle (1825–1864). But his late works, *On Constitutions* and *The Idea of the Working Classes*, were read eagerly by the group. A dashing and charismatic, if contradictory figure in the international socialist movement, Lassalle was the subject of avid discussion and an object of their admiration, although Kornilova-Moroz wrote that both she and Sofia Perovskaia had been impressed more by his style of writing than by what he had to say, and Vera Figner abashedly admitted that as a student abroad she had humiliated herself by confusing Lassalle with the French scientist and scholar Pierre Laplace. No doubt Lassalle's flamboyance played a role. "His passionate eloquence, his ability to make understandable economic issues and his wonderful command of words were powerful and enchanting. I personally at least, cannot recall any other book which I read with such absorption and enthusiasm."[65] Indeed, Lasselle figures prominently in the novels of Spielhagen, which romantically portray him as a chivalrous figure, and it is more than likely that when Charushin first encountered his works as a student in the Viatka gymnasium, he was captivated by the dramatic persona and melodramatic end to Lassalle's life (he died in a duel, defending the honor of a lady friend).

In Charushin's memoirs, however, the talk is entirely about ideas, "I was profoundly impressed by this book and couldn't put it down ... for that reason it depressed me to realize even more acutely that nothing resembling European conditions prevailed here and reinforced the awareness of the ... urgency of the struggle to achieve better political conditions, which in turn would open up a space for exchange of ideas and public activism."[66] Vladimir Debogorii-Mokrievich also later recalled that he observed the strong influence the writings of Lassalle had on members of his generation in defining their views.[67]

Indeed, as Derek Offord has argued for a later decade, Lassalle's notion that socialism could be achieved only with the intervention of the state in the country's economic life, that the state could take upon itself the establishment of workers' collectives to replace capitalism, and could expropriate private land and the means of production to that end—had substantial appeal to the Populists, certainly more than the Marxist version. What this means is that a criticism commonly addressed to Populists—namely, that they were apolitical in their search for economic justice—is not entirely accurate.

Constitutions were another area where Lassalle's writings shaped Populist thought. The historian Troitskii concluded that the Chaikovtsy believed having a constitution without a social revolution would only be harmful because it would serve primarily to consolidate the position of a country's ruling class and divert the people from the revolutionary struggle.[68] Like Lassalle, the Chaikovtsy came to believe that constitutions were indeed meaningful but only when they could be "the expression of the people's will" secured "through the institution of universal suffrage."[69]

Charushin himself had difficulty recalling what the views of the Chaikovtsy were on constitutions and the state in 1873. In 1925, he wrote Kornilova-Moroz asking whether there were statists among their friends. She responded that in fact few in their circle had taken an active interest in the subject. At the same time, she begged to disagree with his opinion that the group put any faith in constitutions. In her mind, the tragic outcome of the Paris Commune had served as an object lesson on the matter,

"We all recognized that we needed to concentrate on workers before the bourgeoisie managed to grab power in its own hands."[70]

The encounter with the works of Lassalle is especially important in understanding the evolution of Charushin's views *over time*. It is quite possible that Charushin's thinking about constitutions changed in the context of the 1905 Revolution; all the more so when he wrote in the 1920s about a gathering at the Tagantsev home, at a time when all traces of a functioning constitutional government had been erased by a militant single-party state and individual freedoms had been severely curtailed.[71] After witnessing those changes in Soviet Russia, what were his private thoughts about the notion that political freedoms would inevitably follow a social revolution? Yet the popularity of Lassalle among the Chaikovtsy also seems to indicate that Charushin's later adherence to statist positions, as well as his determined faith in a Constituent Assembly, were consistent with his earlier views, not something added only based on later experiences.

THE IMPACT OF THE PARIS COMMUNE (1871)

Events, as well as important thinkers and literature, shaped this generation. Perhaps far more important than the epoch of the Great Reforms—were developments in Europe at the time: the polarization of bourgeois liberalism and the socialist working-class movement brought about by the 1848 revolutions; the turbulence within the international socialist movement itself; the unification of Germany and the Franco-Prussian war; and above all, the Paris Commune, which in the minds of the revolutionary Populists was inseparable from their images of the French Revolution of 1789. Both Shishko and Bogucharskii later wrote that the Paris Commune had exerted an enormous influence on the mood of their generation. The latter noted, "When we examine the epoch of the 1870s, we constantly come across signs of the impact of this event on the Russian intelligentsia at that time."[72] Youth circles rejoiced in the re-establishment of a republic in France, and their hopes were pinned on further progress there. To make that point, Bogucharksii cited proclamations that were promulgated calling on sympathizers to respond to the devastating retaliatory measures being taken against the Communards and to carry forth the cause of revolution. Charushin's assessment of the reaction to the events surrounding the Commune was more nuanced. On the one hand, he pointed to the reportage of the Russian press covering the events in France, which provided a highly negative portrait of the Commune and accused it of betraying the country's national interests. On the other hand, in Charushin's telling, the tales of eyewitnesses and other press sources evoked widespread sympathy for the insurgents, especially after the fierce repression of the Commune.

In Viatka, youth groups avidly studied the developments surrounding the Paris Commune. Anna Iakimova recalled in her autobiography that she first heard about the Commune in the summer of 1871, when Charushin himself, then (she remembered) a student at the Technological Institute, returned home to speak to a group of young women students of the local diocesan school organized by Anna Kuvshinskaia. Although Iakimova had either the dates or Charushin's whereabouts wrong,[73] there is little doubt that the session took place, and was replicated elsewhere in the provinces with other participants. For example, in 1936 Vera Figner set about collecting the remembrances of the surviving fellow Populists, to determine how important the Paris Commune was in putting them on the path of revolution.[74] Frolenko wrote that it had been widely discussed in student self-development study groups and "played a huge role in convincing people of the need for revolution and for any righteous (self-respecting), thinking person to join it."[75] Stepniak-Kravchinskii, in his book *Underground Russia*, which was widely circulated in Russia and abroad, also confirmed that the Commune had convinced many of the urgency of acting on behalf of the Russian peasantry, just as many Communards had fought and died in the cause of liberating the French worker (he seems to ignore the fact that it was the French peasantry who served in the army who had so viciously crushed the Paris Commune). He even went so far as to assert that it was precisely the impact of the Paris Commune that "gave birth to the socialist-revolutionary movement of 1872–1874."[76]

But it was an object lesson as much as inspiration that the Paris Commune provided these young people. As the Populists recalled later, they learned from it that the success of a popular uprising depended critically upon the levels of education and political consciousness of the participants themselves. As Charushin put it, "These events [taught us] that the simple fact of establishing a republic is no guarantee its government will work in the interests of the masses themselves, if the latter are politically undeveloped and incapable of knowing how to defend their own interests."[77]

Thus, the response to the Paris Commune reinforced the stance of the Chaikovskii circle toward bourgeois revolutions, the question of political freedom, and its link to social revolution.[78] This combined with the long-standing tradition of cultural uplift among the Russian intelligentsia to cause the circle to emphasize on "the cause of the book," the spread of knowledge, and efforts at propaganda. At the same time the "lessons" taught by the Paris Commune retained their immediacy for the elderly former revolutionaries in the early Soviet era, when they were forced to confront the great disparity between the ideals of their "distant past" (as they labeled the 1870s) and the new realities of the 1920s—including the indifference or even hostility of the peasantry. Others in Russia however, drew different lessons from the Paris Commune, treating it as an example of the crowd psychosis and mob violence that so disturbed liberal social psychologists and their readers after the massive violence of 1905.[79]

OVERCOMING BACKWARDNESS AND THE ZEMSTVO

We have examined the intellectual sources of inspiration and self-identity that defined the world views of the Chaikovskii circle. But other than disillusionment with the outcome of the Emancipation of the serfs, and consternation at the tragedy of the Paris Commune, it was the overall perception of *backwardness* that defined their mission and shaped their search for instruments of change. Describing Viatka province in the 1860s, Charushin later had few good things to say. In fact, he wrote of a rather hopeless state of affairs: the province "had no schools, no medical or agronomical provision, and no roads, and the completely illiterate population remained mired in the life of a primitive people, periodically suffering devastating famines."[80] Judging by the memoirs of the revolutionary Populists of the 1870s, one might even get the impression that the Great Reforms had left no impression on the consciousness of this generation, given the predominance of tropes of backwardness in their descriptions of the time. This condition, in the minds of the revolutionaries of the 1870s, made a social revolution in Russia unthinkable in the near future, and called for a long period of "preparatory" efforts, both educational and propagandistic.

The newly created (1864) zemstvo in Russia seemed to be a natural outlet for the Populist striving to "serve the people," to spread the printed word, and overcome backwardness. The zemstvo was tasked with expanding elementary and secondary education in the provinces of European Russia (other responsibilities included the providing medical services, agricultural and veterinarian aid, road building and other infrastructure projects). How did Charushin regard this institution at the time, and in whose programs were he and others to become deeply immersed later in life?

As elsewhere in European Russia, the convening of the first Viatka provincial zemstvo assembly in 1867 caused a flurry of excitement among the local intelligentsia. Charushin recalls that he and other students had attended its sessions, but it is unlikely at that point he had formulated any clear opinion on the zemstvo's prospects for addressing Russia's backwardness. He writes of the high hopes entertained initially by educated society. But he adds that then the increasing limitations placed by the autocracy on the zemstvo led to a slackening of its energy and the flight of "its most progressive elements," some of whom were subsequently exiled. Some members of the Chaikovskii circle recalled that they had made attempts to establish contact with representatives of the zemstvo, but to no avail. Other Populists recalled being more skeptical of its potential, and all concluded that it was soon effectively hobbled. Charushin concluded, "All of this shook my faith in the cause of the zemstvo over whom the provincial governor loomed like a capricious and arbitrary nanny, insisting on complete obedience from her charges. And this meek and obedient zemstvo, lacking any support from the masses, over time gradually became tightly intertwined with the forces of reaction emanating from the center."[81] Public opinion of the zemstvo, initially highly positive, also changed rapidly beginning in 1868, when criticism of its activities on the part of the liberal and radical periodical press became quite strident. In turn, "criticism leveled by the periodical press soon carried over to the realm of fiction, where the daily affairs and morals of the zemstvo were portrayed in no less gloomy colors."[82]

Given the Populists' isolation and exclusion from society in the 1870s, it is likely that in reality, rather than direct observation, it was the palette drawn by journalists and writers that later shaped their remembrances of the zemstvo. Nevertheless, the institution that in their youth they had dismissed as ineffective came to be a major platform for fulfilling their aspirations for societal change at a later date. Upon release from exile, many of this generation would find employment and the chance for meaningful fulfillment of their aspirations in this institution (chapter 6).

BOOK MATTERS: THE CAUSE OF THE BOOK

Overcoming backwardness and mobilizing for change involved reaching out both to the intelligentsia as a whole and to the working classes. Initially, in 1871–1872 the group pinned its hopes on *knizhnoe delo* ("book matters," or "the cause of the book") by which was meant the publication and distribution of print materials, both legal and illegal. The goal was thereby to promote awareness of the need for social transformation and revolution.

So what books did the circle set about circulating? The lists provided later by Sinegub, Charushin, and Chudnovskii included many of the same books that had earlier shaped their own political world views, but also studies of European revolution by Francois Mignet, Louis Blanc, Thomas Carlyle, and others. The Chaikovtsy worked to establish a network of book distributors linking up Petersburg, Moscow, Odessa, Kherson, Saratov, and other cities—all in all the network involved thirty-eight provinces.[83] In 1873 Charushin traveled to several towns as a "delegate" from the circle to facilitate the distribution of literature. Axelrod recalled Charushin's arrival in Kiev in the spring and again in fall of that year on the way to Odessa, "Organizational ties were created between our circle and revolutionary groups operating in Odessa, Moscow, and Petersburg."[84]

As their efforts unfolded the Chaikovskii gradually became aware that they needed to publish their own books and the circle took advantage of connections in the business community to persuade a book entrepreneur, seller and owner of a printing press to be involved.[85] The first such initiative was to print 2,500 copies of Bervi-Flerovskii's subversive *ABCs of the Social Sciences* (other authors whose works were reprinted included Lassalle, Blanc, Proudhon). Anticipating that the book would be prohibited and seized—as indeed soon happened—the Chaikovtsy first bought up the lion's share of the print run and circulated the books through their own channels; only a small number were actually given over to book stores. All in all, it would be difficult to label these efforts a success, since most of these books were promptly censored, seized and destroyed. A new press law of 1872 gave the Ministry of Interior broad powers to prohibit "harmful books" and the revolutionaries were forced to relocate to Switzerland, where a new printing press was established.

The efforts to spread literature moved beyond the intelligentsia in the period 1873–1874, as the Chaikovtsy began reaching out to the workers' factory milieu and tried to address what they later described as a serious shortage of books suitable for a popular audience. To fill this gap, they themselves took to writing fairy tales, short works of fiction, and poetry. The most successful of these writers were Stepniak-Kravchinskii, Sinegub, Tikhomirov, and Shishko.

Thirty years later, Charushin would return to the "cause of the book" by participating in the work of the Viatka provincial zemstvo book warehouse. And in fact, if we compare the books published and distributed by the Chaikovskii circle in the early 1870s with those promoted at the turn of the century we find some common names, for example, *The Tale of One French Peasant*, by Erckman-Chatrian.[86] According to prosecutorial material collected after his arrest in 1874, Charushin had used this book in his efforts to reach out and politicize workers. At the turn of the century it also appears on a list of the Viatka Book Cooperative—of which Charushin was the titular chairman—scheduled for retranslation and publication. Lenin famously ridiculed those who attempted to reach out to workers through literacy campaigns and cultural uplift, but the nature of these activities could be either evolutionary or revolutionary—or both simultaneously. They also provided a source of continuity in the often-fractured lives of the seventies generation; in Charushin's case *knizhoe delo* would occupy him until the end of this active life.

LEARNING ABOUT THE COMMON PEOPLE

But who were "the common people" whom the Populists sought to instruct through their writings? Many years later, reflecting on the events of these years, Charushin confessed that he and his friends had known very little about the people, "about their experiences in life, their traditions, [we] were unacquainted with their milieu, their psychology and daily life; the little we knew came from books."[87] Among the Chaikovtsy's favorite writers was Bervi-Flerovskii, whose works they actively promoted in the capital cities as well as the provinces. It was his *The Condition of the Working Class in Russia* (1869), based on his peripatetic wanderings across the country that, according to multiple testimonies, aroused their interest in the lives of factory workers and convinced the Populists of the need to recruit them. The Chaikovtsy were fascinated by Bervi-Flerovskii's comparisons with the West, his extensive usage of statistics, and his own personal experiences among the people, which allowed him to vividly portray the situation in different regions of the country. No less intriguing was the author's conviction that Russia had a distinctive historical role to fulfill and that the intelligentsia should be instrumental in bringing about change and achieving societal harmony.[88] Bervi-Flerovsky, it must be added, wrote about "workers" in the sense of "working people," having in mind the peasants as much as if not more than the factory workforce—quite understandably given that Russia was in only an early stage of industrialization at the time the book was written. One section of the book dealt with laborers in the country's highly agricultural region; another with Siberian laborers, and only the third with Russia's industrialized region.

The Chaikovtsy's desire to be closer with the people, to prepare a cadre of propagandists from among the workers' milieu, especially from those workers who still maintained a strong connection with the countryside, led to a serious re-evaluation of their activities. Seeing the workers' striving for education, toward the end of 1871 the circle began to offer lessons in math, geography, chemistry and other subjects, interweaving propaganda with instruction. Initially, only a few members took part, but lessons continued throughout 1872, and in 1873 the decision was taken to make propaganda the first priority. Accordingly, when Charushin set about his travels that year to promote the book trade, he also had the mission of motivating these regional circles to turn to propaganda among worker circles.

Charushin was among the first to make contact with workers in a Petersburg factory; for him and many others of his peers, it was his first experience of direct collaboration with the people, and first chance to observe rather than simply read about the miserable conditions in which the people, on whom they were placing all their hopes for the future, were forced to live. What impression did Charushin have of these Petersburg factory workers? Did he view them simply as peasants living in the city or were they an intermediary stratum situated between the intelligentsia and the people who, because of their education and exposure to urban life might serve as conduit in spreading ideas to the countryside? Or were factory workers a new and distinct social entity capable of exercising its own impact on events? Reginald Zelnik surmised that Sinegub, one of the first to interact with workers, initially viewed them as backward peasants, and instead of discussing factory conditions with them sought to influence them by calling on their religious convictions.[89] But gradually, he and other Populists came to treat workers as potential propagandists for socialism in the village.

The political leanings of Russia's factory workers and their relationship with the intelligentsia was long a heated topic of disagreement among Soviet and Western historians, but cannot be treated here.[90] Yet in order to understand Charushin's skepticism about the Going to the People movement and his later views about the common people's inability to act politically in an informed manner commensurate with their own real interests, his reflections on this first experience with workers are invaluable. Charushin made little distinction between factory workers and the peasant masses as a whole. Oppressed, disenfranchised, they were receptive to discussions about urgent topics, such as land, taxes, and administrative arbitrariness, but displayed limited political consciousness at best. His description of workers closely parallels that given by Sinegub in his memoirs, although the latter also highlights their purported moral qualities: sincerity, rectitude, honesty, and a striving for truth. Such a description might well draw less from sober observation than from a projection of the Chaikovskii circle's own professed values, as well as from persistent tropes about peasant virtues found in intelligentsia discourse at the time.[91]

Returning to the discussion earlier about Charushin's alleged allegiance to Bakuninism, we note that sustained contact with workers only seemed to confirm his preconceptions of the error of Bakunin's ways. This period of engagement with a workers' milieu served to convince Charushin that Bakunin's belief in the innate revolutionary qualities of the masses was an illusion. There was much revolutionary potential in the people, but their lack of education and poor understanding of what socialism was meant that, even among factory workers, the path to a genuine popular revolution would be long and difficult. "We entertained no faith in a popular revolution, much less a successful one, in the near future ... we had no illusions, and drew no comfort on that account," he wrote.[92]

In the 1920s, once again testing the accuracy of his recollections, Charushin sought Kornilova-Moroz's opinion about whether they had believed revolution was imminent. She replied by ridiculing Stepniak-Kravchinskii's portrait of the movement in *Underground Russia*, in which he had written that he and his peers had believed revolution was just over the horizon, "despite all the evidence to the contrary."[93] She retorted, "Even Kravchinskii, the most inclined to exaggeration among us, would never have left for Herzegovina, would not have spent long years along with Dmitrii Klements abroad [if that had been the case]; they never even responded to Natanson's pleas for them to return home."[94] She instead asserted, "Even in the court records we were accused only of trying to foment revolution 'in the more or less distant future.'"[95]

DIVERSE VIEWS, INTACT NETWORKS

Thus, the first half of the 1870s was formational for the political values of that generation of Populists. Still, many issues remained unresolved, to be returned to later in life as they gained experience and knowledge of the world. It is not surprising that their recollections of their positions at the time differ substantially or that historians would also have difficulty in reconstructing them. The absence of a formulated program or any organizational structure, as well as the priority given to moral and ethical foundations instead of doctrinal positions, led to an extraordinary ideological diversity within the Populist movement, and allowed those who sought "their own path" to remain loosely united and personally close. As Mikhail Chernavskii later confessed, his world view remained quite unsettled in the 1870s, and it would require considerable effort and systematic reading on his part to become integrated, a process that was interrupted by his arrest and subsequent exile to Siberia.[96] Perhaps this also explains why at the beginning of the twentieth century, we find former Chaikovtsy in the Socialist Revolutionary Party, but also the People's Socialist and the Social Democratic parties.

At the same time, thanks to the collaborative propaganda activities that took place in the early 1870s a social network was established that held firm even as late as the 1920s, as did an awareness of belonging to a distinct generation. The "young revolutionaries" of the 1870s evolved into the "elder revolutionaries" of the early twentieth century. In part their political views may have changed but their ideals and code of behavior, their commitment to social and political change—indeed their very identities—remained stable. In turn, this was to underlie their determination to defend their legacy once it came under attack in the Soviet era.

NOTES

1. Philip Pomper, *The Russian Revolutionary Intelligentsia*, 2nd ed. (Wheeling, IL: Harlan-Davidson, 1993), 111. This figure does not include a scattered number of adherents in other cities.

2. On the role of the press in forming the public image of the revolutionaries in the 1870s, see Yulia Safronova, *Russkoe obshchestvo v zerkale revoliutsionnogo terrora, 1879–1881 gody* (Moskva: NLO, 2014), 109–151.

3. Franco Venturi considers that number to be an understatement in *Roots of Revolution: A History of the Populist and Socialist Movements in Nineteenth Century Russia* (New York, Grosset & Dunlap, 1966), 595; Norman M. Naimark puts the number of people convicted for their connections to the People's Will later, between 1881 and 1894, at 5,851. Norman M. Naimark, *Terrorists and Social Democrats: The Russian Revolutionary Movement under Alexander III* (Cambridge, MA: Harvard University Press, 1983), 42.

4. Karl Manheim, "Problema pokolenii," *Novoe literaturnoe obozrenie* 2 (1998): 7–47.

5. TsGIA SPb, f. 492, op. 2, d. 2143, 1871, ll. 19, 21–22, 28, 43–45.

6. Ibid., l. 26.

7. Nikolai Charushin, *O dalekom proshlom* (Moskva: Mysl', 1973), 200–202.

8. Sergei Sinegub, *Zapiski chaikovtsa* (Moskva: Molodaia Gvardiia, 1929), 273.

9. Lev Tikhomirov, *Vospominaniia* (Moskva: Gosudarstvennaia publichnaia istoricheskaia biblioteka Rossii, 2003), 92.

10. Ibid.

11. Sinegub, *Zapiski chaikovtsa*, 274.

12. Arkadii Charushin, "Brat'ia Urzhumovy," *Katorga i Ssylka* 1 (1926): 67.

13. On Chaikovskii, see Venturi, *Roots of Revolution*, 469–506.
14. Chaikovskii admitted that the group's name emerged quite accidentally and to a large degree because of his extensive contacts and prominence in the book endeavors of the circle.
15. Chaikovskii to Shishko, July 3, 1902, Columbia University, Rare Book and Manuscript Library, Bakhmeteff Archive, Boris Sapir Papers, box 30.
16. Ibid.
17. Deborah Hardy, *Land and Freedom: The Origins of Russian Terrorism, 1876–1879* (New York: Greenwood Press, 1987), xii.
18. *Revoliutsionery 1870-kh gg. Vospominaniia uchastnikov narodnicheskogo dvizheniia v Peterburge* (Leningrad: Lenizdat, 1986), 154.
19. Ibid.
20. Sinegub, *Zapiski chaikovtsa*, 15.
21. Charushin, *O dalekom proshlom* (1973), 200.
22. Our argument is at odds with the opinion of Nathaniel Knight—namely, that the notion of an "intelligentsia" was forthcoming only in the 1880s, and originated in the conservative periodical press. It is, we acknowledge, entirely possible that wide resort to the term "intelligentsia" by those writing their memoirs in the 1920s was in fact an artifact of later discussions in the circles of the intelligentsia—despite the reams of paper spent on the subject, the question remains open. Nathaniel Knight, "Was the Intelligentsia Part of the Nation? Visions of Society in Post-Emancipation Russia," *Kritika: Explorations in Russian and Eurasian History* 7, no. 4 (2006): 733–758.
23. Nikolai Troitskii, *Bezumstvo khrabrykh. Russkie Revolutsionery i karatel'naia politika tsarizma, 1866–1882* (Moskva: Mysl', 1978), 95.
24. *Revoliutsionery 1870-kh gg. Vospominaniia uchastnikov narodnicheskogo dvizheniia v Peterburge*, 67.
25. Charushin to Kornilova-Moroz, RGALI, f. 1642, op. 1, d. 51, l. 12 ob.
26. Chaikovskii to Shishko, July 3, 1902, Columbia University, Rare Book and Manuscript Library, Bakhmeteff Archive, Boris Sapir Papers, box 30.
27. Cited in Pomper, *Russian Revolutionary Intelligentsia*, 93.
28. Charushin, *O dalekom proshlom* (1973), 100.
29. Vasilii Bogucharskii, *Aktivnoe narodnichestvo semidesiatykh godov* (Moskva: Sabashnikovy 1912), 152.
30. Petr Kropotkin, *Zapiski revolutsionera* (Moskva: Mysl' 1966), 290.
31. Charushin, *O dalekom proshlom* (1973), 226–227.
32. Ibid., 100.
33. *Revoliutsionery 1870-kh gg. Vospominaniia uchastnikov narodnicheskogo dvizheniia v Peterburge*, 175.
34. Dmitrii Ovsianiko-Kulikovskii, "Istoriia russkoi intelligentsii," Sobranie sochinenii 8 (Petersburg: Izdatel'stvo O. Ovsianiko-Kulikovskoi, 1914), 213–224.
35. Vera Figner, *Zapechatlennyi trud* (Moskva: Mysl', 1964), 2:37.
36. L. G. Berezovaia, *Samosoznanie russkoi intelligentsii nachala 20 veka. Dissertatsiia na soiskanie uchenoi stepeni doktora istoricheskikh nauk* (Moskva, typescript, 1994), 51.
37. E. B. Rashkovskii, "Ob odnoi iz sotsial'no-psikhologicheskikh predposylok institutsionalizma v razvivaiushchikhsia stranakh (eshche raz o probleme 'populizma' v stranakh tret'ego mira)," *Obshchestvo, elita i biurokratiia v razvivaiushchikhsia stranakh Vostoka* (Moskva: Nauka, 1974), 1:68–70.
38. Pomper, *Russian Revolutionary Intelligentsia*, 117–118.

39. Irina Paperno, *Semiotika povedeniia: Nikolai Chernyshevskii–chelovek epokhi realizma* (Moskva: NLO, 1996).
40. Vera Zasulich, *Vospominaniia* (Moskva: Vsesoiuznoe obshchestvo politkatorzhan i ssylno-poselentsev, 1931), 14–15.
41. Charushin, *O dalekom proshlom* (1973), 65.
42. Avrahm Yarmolinsky, *Road to Revolution: A Century of Russian Radicalism* (Princeton, NJ: Princeton University Press, 1957), 189–209.
43. Venturi, *Roots of Revolution*, 471–472.
44. Marina Mogil'ner, *Mifologiia 'podpol'nogo cheloveka': Radikal'nyi mikrokosm v Rossii nachala 20 veka kak predmet semioticheskogo analiza* (Moskva: NLO, 1999), 30–31.
45. Nataalia Rodigina, Tatiana Saburova, "Pokolencheskoe izmerenie sotsiokul'turnoi istorii Rossii 19 veka: preemstvennost' i razryvy," *Dialog so vremenem. Al'manakh intellektual'noi istorii* 34 (2011): 138–157.
46. Charushin, *O dalekom proshlom* (1973), 91.
47. Ibid., 42–43.
48. RGALI, f. 1642, op. 1, d. 51, l. 4 ob.
49. Chernyshevskii, long a key figure in the pantheon of "predecessors" of Leninism created by Marxism-Leninism, but long maligned and caricatured by Western scholars, is given sympathetic treatment in a fine chapter by Venturi, *Roots of Revolution*, 129–186. His life is also examined through a semiotic lens by Irina Paperno, *Chernyshevskii and the Age of Realism: A Study in the Semiotics of Behavior* (Stanford, CA: Stanford University Press, 1988).
50. Charushin, *O dalekom proshlom* (1973), 44.
51. Alexander Ertel', "V sumerkakh," *Russkaia mysl'* 2 (1898): 155.
52. Charushin, *O dalekom proshlom* (1973), 63.
53. Ibid., 43.
54. Ibid., 43–44.
55. *Revoliutsionery 1870-kh gg. Vospominaniia uchastnikov narodnicheskogo dvizheniia v Peterburge*, 151.
56. See Nikolai Troitskii, *Pervye iz blestiashchei pleiady. Bol'shoe Obshchestvo Propagandy 1871–1874* (Saratov: Izdatel'stvo Saratovskogo universiteta, 1991), 33; Boris Itenberg, *Dvizhenie revoliutsionnogo narodnichestva. Narodnicheskie kruzhki i 'khozhdenie v narod' v 70-kh godakh 19 veka* (Moskva: Nauka, 1965), 89–90.
57. Pavel Aksel'rod, *Perezhitoe i peredumannoe* (Berlin: Izdatel'stvo Z. Grzhebina, 1923), 111. Axelrod himself describes his own early leanings toward Bakunism more cerebrally: he points to the anarchist's role in the International, to his writings, and to the insufficient militancy of Lavrov's journal *Vpered* (*Forward*).
58. Solomon Chudnovskii and Sergei Sinegub were of the same opinion, recalling later that it was Charushin's enthusiastic comments about Bakunin that had shaped their own opinions.
59. *Byloe* 1 (1907): 308. Earlier, in 1906, upon the publication of Kovalik's memoirs, in which the author asserts that none of the 193 revolutionaries brought to trial in 1878 subscribed to Lavrovism, Chudnovskii sent a response to *Byloe* (where Kovalik's memoirs had appeared in print) insisting that all those brought before the court were "committed Lavrovists with no connection whatsoever to anarchism" and that equating the Populism of the 1870s with Bakunism was simply wrong-headed.
60. RGALI, f. 1185, op. 1, d. 805, l. 78.
61. Charushin rejected Kropotkin's assertion, complained that his friend Sinegub had also made a dyed-in-the-wool anarchist of him in his memoirs, and sought to explain why both

Kovalik and Chudnovskii had taken the same position in their recollections. Charushin felt that perhaps the explanation for their flawed recollections lay in his genuine sympathy for Bakunin as a person, as well as the latter's undeniable credentials as a revolutionary, something that could not be said for Lavrov, who was something of an armchair revolutionary.

62. RGALI, f. 1642, op. 1, d. 51, l. 23 ob.

63. Martin A. Miller, "Ideological Conflicts in Russian Populism: The Revolutionary Manifestoes of the Chaikovskii Circle, 1869–1874," *Slavic Review* 29, no. 1 (1970): 1–21.

64. As Venturi points out, the views of Lavrov himself were evolving in the 1870s; living abroad he was strongly influenced by the debate on this topic in the International, and by the middle of the decade he had begun to ascribe a substantial role to the state in reconstituting the political and social order. Yet by that time Charushin had been confined to solitary confinement for several years and soon would be whisked away to decades of exile in Siberia, and he was hardly likely to be aware of Lavrov's evolving views on the matter. Venturi, *Roots of Revolution*.

65. *Revoliutsionery 1870-kh gg. Vospominaniia uchastnikov narodnicheskogo dvizheniia v Peterburge*, 66.

66. Charushin, *O dalekom proshlom* (1973), 82–83.

67. Vladimir Debogorii-Mokrievich, *Vospominaniia* (St. Petersburg: Svobodnyi Trud, 1906), 77.

68. Troitskii, *Pervye iz blestiashchei pleiady*, 144–145. In fairness, this might have been an ideological tenet of Soviet Marxism with which the author chose not to take issue.

69. Derek Offord, *The Russian Revolutionary Movement in the 1880s* (Cambridge: Cambridge University Press, 1986), 134–135.

70. RGALI, f. 1642, op. 1, d. 51, l. 11.

71. The works of Lassalle were quite likely at the heart of the fervid disagreements among members of that circle at a meeting in December 1871, at which the value of constitutions was discussed and some members argued for "directing their efforts to influencing the government rather than the intelligentsia and the people." Charushin recalled that meeting at the apartment of the well-known professor N. S. Tagantsev, at which several other notable figures of his cohort were present (Dmitrii Klements, Felix Volkhovskii, Nikolai Chaikovskii, Sofia Perovskaia), and where a heated discussion of Lassalle's work "On Constitutions" ensued. The question arose of the prospects for a constitution in Russia, and despite agreeing with Lassalle about the virtue of constitutions, it was concluded that neither the bourgeoisie nor the nobility in Russia were capable of achieving that goal without the muscular participation of the working classes especially—hence the need to propagandize among the people (Charushin, *O dalekom proshlom* (1973), 129–132; Charushin, "Chto bylo na sobranii u professora Tagantseva," *Katorga i Ssylka* 2 (1925), 99–102.

72. Bogucharskii, *Aktivnoe narodnichestvo semidesiatykh godov*, 163.

73. In her essay for the Granat encyclopedia she also recalled that it was specifically Charushin who spoke to Kuvshinskaia's student circle at the diocesan girls' school about the Paris Commune. But there is a discrepancy between Iakimova's and Charushin's accounts concerning the date of this meeting. Charushin wrote that it took place while he was still a pupil at the gymnasium. Thus, in the summer of 1871, when this could have happened, he was not yet enrolled at the Technological Institute in St. Petersburg—so could not have been returning from that city, as Iakimova described it. He enrolled in the fall of 1871 and returned home only the following summer (at which point Kuvshinskaia had been forced out of the diocesan school for her political activities, but moved to the (far more prestigious) women's

gymnasium. It is possible that Iakimova simply conflated her recollections of Charushin's visit to the diocesan school with hearing about the Paris Commune from another source.

74. Svetlana Obolenskaia, "Pis'ma i zametki. Iz arkhiva V.N. Figner," *Voprosy istorii* 5 (1971): 207–209.

75. RGALI, f. 1185, op. 1, d. 805, l. 77.

76. Sergei Stepniak-Kravchinskii, *Podpol'naia Rossiia* (St. Petersburg: V. Vrublevskii, 1906), 8.

77. Charushin, *O dalekom proshlom* (1973), 85.

78. Itenberg, *Dvizhenie revoliutsionnogo narodnichestva*, 128.

79. Daniel Beer, *Renovating Russia: The Human Sciences and the Fate of Liberal Modernity, 1880–1930* (Ithaca, NY: Cornell University Press, 2008), 133–134.

80. Charushin, *O dalekom proshlom* (1973), 62.

81. Ibid. Today, some scholars paint a somewhat more positive picture of the zemstvo's ability to gather information about local conditions and to implement programs that promoted infrastructure, not to mention regional identity. Earlier work, especially the landmark four-volume tome by the Menshevik B. B. Veselovskii (1909–1911), provided a narrative of inertia and inactivity after a brief spurt of energy on the part of most zemstvos but explained it, at least until the 1880s, less as owing to autocratic restriction than to the dominance of the landed nobility in these institutions and their unwillingness to tax themselves for the betterment of society. To be sure, Veselovskii does note that the Viatka provincial zemstvo (one of four of the thirty-four original zemstvos that were, somewhat misleadingly, labeled as "peasant zemstvos") was somewhat exceptional in its initial energetic level of activity, which "carried forth throughout the 1870s only to completely fade by the middle of the 1880s." Boris Veselovskii, *Istoriia zemstva za sorok let* (St. Petersburg: Izdatel'stvo O. Popovoi, 1911), 3:187.

82. Veselovskii, *Istoriia zemstva za sorok let*, 3:199.

83. See *Protsess 193-kh* (Moskva: V. M. Sablin, 1906).

84. Aksel'rod, *Perezhitoe i peredumannoe*, 106.

85. Troitskii, *Pervye iz blestiashchei pleiady*, 118.

86. Emile Erckmann and Alexandre Chatrain were two French writers of historical novels, almost always coauthored. Their works often attacked the Second Empire, monarchism, and militarism; promoted republican values; and were praised by Emile Zola and Victor Hugo. *Histoire d'un paysan* was first published in 1867.

87. Charushin, *O dalekom proshlom* (1973), 125.

88. Derek Offord, "The Contribution of V. V. Bervi-Flerovsky to Russian Populism," *Slavonic and East European Review* 66, no. 2 (1988): 236–251.

89. Reginald E. Zelnik, "Populists and Workers. The First Encounter between Populist Students and Industrial Workers in St. Petersburg, 1871–74," *Soviet Studies* 24, no. 2 (1972): 254.

90. Zelnik, "Populists and Workers," 267–268; Venturi, *Roots of Revolution*, 502, 507–557; Troitskii, *Pervye iz blestiashchei pleiady*, 208.

91. See Cathy A. Frierson, *Peasant Icons: Representations of Rural People in Late Nineteenth Century* (New York: Oxford University Press, 1993).

92. Charushin, *O dalekom proshlom* (1973), 170–171.

93. Stepniak-Kravchinskii, *Podpol'naia Rossiia*, 22.

94. RGALI, f. 1642, op. 1, d. 51, l. 10 ob.

95. Ibid.

96. *Deiateli SSSR i revoliutsionnogo dvizheniia v Rossii*, 297.

The Male Gaze and Female Profile
Marriage, Family, Populism

... my unfailing comrade and partner in life.

—Nikolai Charushin about Anna Kuvshinskaia, *O Dalekom Proshlom*

My thoughts have never been far from you, but because we have both gone through so much tragedy I didn't want to burden you any further and for that reason, even while together, I have felt myself alone.

—Anna Kuvshinskaia to Nikolai Charushin, January 1907

Women in the Russian revolutionary movement are often depicted as nihilists who forsook family and personal fulfillment in order to serve the people, and who were willing to suffer imprisonment or even loss of life for the cause. Some of them have become canonical figures: the "icon of the revolution" Vera Figner; "grandmother of the revolution" Ekaterina Breshko-Breshkovskaia; and Sofia Perovskaia, the daughter of the governor of St. Petersburg, who became a symbol of self-sacrifice and utter devotion to the movement. Western historians in particular have made the themes of suffering and personal sacrifice central to their depictions of the Populist women. Vera Figner was truly a central figure in the Populist movement, and became a centerpiece of its mythology, defining the role of women in the revolutionary movement for years to come. Later, writing to Figner, Anna Kuvshinskaia addressed her as a "treasured, unforgettable, grand Russian woman,"[1] echoing how Figner was perceived by her contemporaries through the idealistic prism of Nekrasov's poetry, which had glorified the sacrifices of the wives of the Decembrists. Biographies of Figner often follow the same trajectory, eliding her actual, multilayered complexity.

In the era of the Great Reforms the "woman question"—determining the place of women in the family and in society—had become an essential element of societal renewal as a whole.[2] Women's striving for higher education, the emergence of a feminist movement, and women's active participation in the oppositionist youth culture and communal organizations all contributed to the shaping of the seventies generation, the revolutionary movement, and the lives of Charushin and Kuvshinskaia. As Richard Stites demonstrated, women revolutionaries of the era played a huge role in the struggle for emancipation even as they, paradoxically, refrained from directly fighting for the rights of women. The explanation for this lies in the fact that the notion of the equality of the sexes spread rapidly among the Russian intelligentsia at that time, something that allowed women to approach the revolutionary struggle (at least theoretically) on equal footing. Moreover, "it was the self-confidence that women silently absorbed from the literature on the woman question which acted as their psychological armament in the revolutionary struggle."[3]

Issues of love and marriage also evolved as women's status in society changed. Discussions of these topics had begun earlier, in the writings of George Sand, Alexander Herzen, Chernyshevskii, and Turgenev, and they were renewed by the seventies generation, which agonized about how to reconcile the personal and the public and to live under a new and rigorous moral code. In Barbara Engel's opinion, the extraordinary impact of Chernyshevskii's (1863) novel *What Is to Be Done* provided concise answers to the "woman question," which defined the mindset of this and subsequent generations and offered a balance between the private and the public, but also gave men the central role in the emancipation of women.[4] Charushin reminisced about reading the novel:

> The new people in this novel, with their novel and humane interpersonal relations, especially as it concerned an intimate and delicate matter such as marriage, could not help but intrigue us. Arranging their personal lives

in a perfectly suitable manner they were also able to exuberantly commit themselves to public affairs—something that we especially valued in them—in a way that allowed them to focus upon the downtrodden in the world, to whom they brought light and knowledge as well as new foundations for their working lives.[5]

The role of instructor and mentor to women purportedly in need of guidance by which men decided how worthy women were of their attention could easily appeal to the masculine sex. Elizabeth Wood points to the "asymmetrical hierarchy" governing relations between men and women at the time, manifest in the description of women as passively waiting for help and men as energetic doers.[6] In reality, women of the seventies generation were already choosing for themselves strategies that did not follow the script mapped out in Chernyshevskii novel. Kornilova recollected, "[His] novel posed for us the question 'what is to be done.' As for Vera Pavlovna [the prostitute who was 'saved' and placed in a women's workshop], she posed no interest to me in my youth even if her actions found many followers. What impressed me most was the self-discipline of Rakhmetov [the hero who slept on a bed of nails to toughen himself]; his influence was much more marked among the best representatives of our generation."[7]

Relations between women were treated as an inseparable part of the code of conduct governing the revolutionary milieu in the 1870s, and several memoirists pointed out that a number of participants were excluded from the Chaikovskii circle for behavior deemed inappropriate. As Kornilova wrote, "[W]omanizers" were scorned, as were "coquettes"; amorous pursuits were considered amusing or vulgar, while the difficult lives of the women in the group with small children evoked compassion, especially those who hadn't managed to earn a degree and acquire a profession before becoming pregnant.

But what really changed in the relations between men and women, their conceptions of each other and of their respective gender roles? Were marriage and family life truly forsaken? How were the personal and the public balanced? Were the life scenarios formulated in literature actually followed by the seventies cohort of young revolutionaries? How did young women of that time visualize their own futures, and how did men see them—what was the Populist "male gaze"?

Here, we discuss not only Charushin and Kuvshinskaia, although in many ways their lives were emblematic of the paths followed by others of their generation, and thus they serve to address many of these questions, but also the individual and family histories of many of this generation, which were inseparable from the history of the societal movement of which they were a part; the fates of individual revolutionaries—both men and women—remained closely connected over many decades. In fact, the telling of the life stories of Charushin and Kuvshinskaia would be difficult without including those with whom their paths were intertwined.

THE MALE GAZE

As we will discover, some relationships grew deep roots, others not so deep, or not at all. After all, both the discursive framework and the realities of marriage were evolving in Russia in the second half of the nineteenth century. What is perhaps harder to grasp is how women combined notions of equality, independence, and a strong sense of personal identity with more traditional notions of femininity and women's domestic role in the household. We can better understand how young male and female revolutionaries of this generation perceived and engaged with each other if we examine the terms they used to describe one another and the meanings they ascribed to various personal attributes. We first examine how terms describing "masculinity" and "femininity" were deployed, and then turn to dress codes, and finally to "domesticity" and understandings of the respective roles of men and women.

As a rule, when men described women they found physically attractive, they also noted their "femininity" and defenselessness. Displaying feelings and emotionality were also connected with femininity and counterposed to masculine reserve and seriousness. For example, in comparing the two Kornilova sisters, Charushin wrote that Liubov' Kornilova was "on top of her undoubted intelligence, a lively and expansive girl, responsive and light-hearted, and because of that easy to be comfortable with. She could make contact with people quickly and easily disposed them to her. . . . Alexandra . . . was always reserved and serious, seemingly even severe; more likely to observe and listen rather than to take part in a discussion, she could be difficult and harsher and in her judgments."[8]

Judging from the comments of those who knew Kuvshinskaia, as well as from a photograph of her from that time (see figure 3.1), she was a beautiful young woman, elegantly dressed and with a fashionable hairdo. Sinegub wrote of her and of Chemodanova: "Their external appearances were such that many aristocratic women would have been jealous."[9] In his recounting of their decisive meeting on July 4, 1878, with Countess Tolstoy (Alexandra Andreevna Tolstaia, 1817–1904, the aunt of the great writer and a maid of honor at the imperial court), hoping to gain her help in winning permission to join their husbands in exile, Charushin explains their success in terms of the impression they made as young, comely, and well-dressed women

FIGURE 3.1.

Anna Kuvshinskaia, late 1860s–early 1870s.

Herzen Regional Library, Kirov.

having little in common with the prevailing image of *nigilistki*, as radical women were called. "[E]nchanted by her conversation with denizens of another world alien to her own, and by their devotion and selfless love, the countess actively took up their cause."[10]

Yet it was not physical beauty alone that drew people to Kuvshinskaia and Chemodanova. The same Countess Tolstoy wrote to Leo Tolstoy of that meeting, "You can't imagine just how strange it was that I was inspired by a special kind of love I felt, especially for one of them ... a remarkable personality despite having wandered from the true path. I can't convey how happy I was."[11] That "remarkable personality was Kuvshinskaia, with whom Countess Tolstoy then struck up a correspondence.

Charushin describes Kuvshinskaia in his memoirs as "modest and serious, always self-possessed, conducting herself with utter simplicity, and somehow effortlessly disposing people in her favor by her attractive looks."[12] "Seriousness" was an attribute commonly encountered in the descriptions at the time, and it characterized the new profile of women as companions. It also reflected women's striving to overcome the stereotypes prevalent, to signal their independence and efforts to be educated and spiritually advanced.

"Modesty" remains among the attributes frequently encountered (especially) in male descriptions of their female companions. This would seem to contradict the stereotypical portrait of women taking part in the revolutionary movement—purportedly rejecting all conventions and norms. But the frequent use of this term in fact indicated that modesty as a traditional female attribute did in fact preserve its positive connotations in male descriptions of their female comrades.[13] This was certainly the case in Charushin's description of Larisa Chemodanova—a lifelong friend and co-revolutionary: "A real beauty, but at the same time modest and serious, with a searching intellect, always working to improve herself."[14]

As for women, their self-descriptions combined "male" and "female" attributes. At the same time, "softness" and "tenderness" remained "female," and "severity" and "firmness" were treated as "male" characteristics. Recalling Sofia Perovskaia, Figner wrote, "By nature she combined feminine softness and male severity. Tender, maternally tender toward the common people, she was demanding and strict when it came to her like-minded comrades, and toward her enemies; toward the state, she could be merciless, something which really disturbed Sukhanov and could not be reconciled with his notion of the ideal woman."[15] Then Figner emphasized, "[S]he was a woman after all: she was easily wounded, physically wounded."[16]

"Weakness" (vulnerability), then, is a female attribute; yet in Populist memoirs we often see women described as mentally stronger than men, firmer, and with more fortitude in working toward their goals. Describing a hunger strike in Shlisselburg, Figner again expresses disillusionment, even irritation, at the men's behavior; they turned out to be less resolute and prematurely ended their participation:

> If their words and intentions were serious, their retreat displayed insufficient fortitude [*muzhestvo*—in Russian the word has a masculine root] to complete the task at hand. Yet my comrades were strong people, the strongest to be found in Russia. Otherwise they wouldn't have acted as they did while free rather than buried in this stone grave. Yes, they were strong people and had to be strong, but, in fact, it was all talk. I was bitterly disheartened and infuriated.[17]

Populist women's ambivalence, seen in the way they represented themselves in their memoirs, has been observed by Elizabeth Woods. She noted that on the one hand they sought to demonstrate their dedication to the cause and readiness to sacrifice themselves, participating side by side with men in the riskiest endeavors. On the other hand, they committed themselves to the "family" of revolutionaries, in terms stereotypically "womanly." According to Woods, this ambivalence stemmed from conflicting desires—not to appear too "feminine" but, at the same time, not to pose a threat to the dominant group (men).[18]

As for Kuvshinskaia, in Charushin's memoirs she always emerges as intrepid, determined, and ready to take the initiative. This is how she appears during her time in Viatka and later in Petersburg, when, determined to join Charushin in exile, she pressed hard to be allowed to marry him, ignoring his own irresolution and apprehensions. She steps forth from these pages exhibiting all the best attributes of masculinity, while he appears relatively indecisive and lacking in confidence. In sketching this contrast, perhaps Charushin wanted to call attention to her praiseworthy attributes, or perhaps this was more a legacy of the generational effort to emphasize women's masculine qualities in order to underscore their equal status.

SELF-PORTRAITS

In their own self-portraits, women focused more on external appearance than on intrinsic character, on visible markers of their political views, overriding those of social origin or wealth. It was necessary to dress simply, modestly, cleanly. For some this stemmed from an inner need; for others it followed a code of etiquette, of observing moral norms, in that extravagance in dress was seen as inappropriate, excessive, and even offensive. Setting as their primary goals in life achieving an education and dedicating themselves to public service, women were also demonstrating their freedom of choice in their external appearance (dress, hairdo, shoes, and eyeglasses) as an element in their struggle for overall equality. Changing their manner of dress was a manifestation of emancipation and a way of expressing their convictions, but at the same time signaled changes in their way of life (formal apparel seemed inappropriate in the university environment, but was also quite uncomfortable for work in laboratories and clinics). Still, at the same time, even while incarcerated, Figner—a noted beauty—paid considerable attention to the way she dressed, to how elegant she looked in a given skirt or outfit.

The effort by women to change their external appearance was part of a drive to achieve equality, but it also reflected the move toward the democratization of dress among revolutionary youth as a whole. The need to be closer to the people was as much a practical imperative while engaged with peasants and workers as it was an ideological formulation. As a rule, in the Going to the People movement propagandists outfitted themselves to be as inconspicuous as possible, seeking to present themselves as artisans or hired workers. At the same time, it seemed morally derelict to spend money on clothing when they were surrounded with such deep-seated poverty, and more appropriate to commit one's available resources entirely to the cause of revolution. For those from humbler backgrounds, who lacked financial support and had also given up the opportunities a university education offered, minimalism and democratic dress were natural choices. On occasion, some of those living in communes went so far as to share clothing and footwear.

But even some of those from more comfortable backgrounds adjusted easily to this apparel code. Alexandra Kornilova, who was from a very prosperous merchant family, wrote, "[In childhood] we were outfitted very simply and taught to avoid extravagance or excessive concern about how we looked."[19] Her descriptions of Sofia Perovskaia emphasize her hair swept back, a modest brown dress with a white collar, giving her the appearance of a gymnasium pupil in a school costume—not at all like the daughter of a governor.[20] Moreover, it is clear that Kornilova felt it important to dispel any notion of Perovskaia as a society lady, seeing in that something reproachful and insulting, violating the ideals of her generation. In so doing, Kornilova was also trying to correct the image of Perovskaia put forth in memoirs by Kropotkin and Kravchinskii, who were not so concerned that she might appear to be a "lady."[21]

Later in life, participating in the construction of a collective remembrance, this generation of revolutionaries sought to fix a unified image of themselves in the historical record. This is apparent as well in Charushin's memoirs when he turns to Perovskaia and evidently feels the need to reinforce his own portrayal of her: "All these stories of how [she] had earlier shone at aristocratic balls ... related in order to enhance her luster ... were of course mistaken, completely out of line with reality."[22] As we will see in chapter 9, in order to achieve that goal, they reviewed each other's texts and often quoted one another without attribution. Still, in the women's memoirs simplicity of dress symbolized earnestness and a rejection of societal privilege; in the men's memoirs simplicity of dress was treated as a symbol of modesty. Once again, Charushin on Perovskaia, "Modest, rarely appearing in polite society, she was strictly self-regimented in life and appearance, but always simply and neatly outfitted, as was her friend Kornilova."[23]

By dressing more like men, women were asserting their equality, and this was noticed by others. As much research demonstrates, fashion plays a major role in the gendering of dress, since it symbolizes the perceived intrinsic attributes of each sex. Thus, by appropriating male style, the women were seen as transgressing the boundaries of their sex.[24] Simultaneously with the appearance of new gender roles and opportunities, women began borrowing elements of men's outfits to function in spheres traditionally limited to males. According to Barbara Engel, those women who donned men's apparel displayed an even greater measure of freedom than those who merely dressed more simply or appeared on the streets unaccompanied.[25]

Donning men's apparel could be intended to provoke, challenge, and symbolize equality, or it could simply be a matter of being comfortable and practical. When Charushin first made the acquaintance of the Chaikovskii circle, he immediately noticed that Kornilova and Perovskaia dressed like men, "I noticed a small, but interesting group of young girls [which might be freely translated as "sweet young things"], reclining along the roadside and dressed in men's blouses and wide trousers."[26] Here we have the unadulterated male gaze, further intrigued by the violation of the societal dress code. Kornilova explained the turn to men's style as follows:

> When evening came the two of us often took strolls in the park during which we engaged in long conversations. Near Lesnoi [the dacha settlement rented by the Chaikovtsy] there were some barracks, and when we encountered soldiers on these solitary paths we were somewhat apprehensive. So we came up with the idea of dressing up more like men. Perovskaia appropriated her brother's wide trousers and simple blouse, and I the jacket and trousers of my cousin. Looking like that we were quite unafraid, since nobody cared to pay any attention to two adolescents.[27]

In Christine Ruane's view, "To display their unhappiness with Russian patriarchy . . . women radicals wore dark, plain woolen frocks, cut their hair short, smoked cigarettes and wore blue glasses, the uniform of women radicals in Europe."[28] But it would be a mistake to assume that wearing men's outfits and blue-tinted glasses, and cutting one's hair short was widespread among women students, even those who were politically active. Kornilova recalled that among those who attended the Alarchinskii courses (provided by liberal professors for women, who were not allowed at the time to actually matriculate in universities) she and her friend Anna Vil'berg stood out for their nihilistic appearance—Kornilova wore men's boots, and Vil'berg had the cropped hair and blue-tinted glasses. Moreover, those who like Kuvshinksaia were enrolled in Medical-Surgical Academy courses were required to wear long skirts and wear their hair appropriately swept back.

Democratized dress codes reflected changes in society and in beliefs at this time in Russia. Certain elements of one's dress came to symbolize political protest, and signified one's alignment with an oppositionist subculture that rejected societal and gendered hierarchies and asserted new values. As Ruane writes, political activists adopted a "uniform," much as those employed by the state or serving in military had their own. Those who were committed to transforming the country and who refused to be reconciled to the status quo made their protests legible "bodily."[29] On the other hand, examining an abundance of photographs as well as memoirs leads one to conclude that despite this rejection of fashion and democratization of dress, women's fashion and dress remained symbolically important and continued to contain traditional elements. Whether it was a minimalist approach to dressing, overall sloppiness of dress, or borrowing elements of what men wore, it all attracted notice, even in revolutionary circles, and was subject to a wide range of interpretations. In truth, many women felt no need at all to express their equal status through costume, for their equality was already manifest in their revolutionary work. More important to such women than rejecting their gender as they saw it, was a desire to demonstrate their democratic views and to cast off all signs of their aristocratic or bourgeois origins and affiliation with the "other" Russia. Thus, if they ascribed to radical beliefs, they were often confronted with the choice of expressing those beliefs through their dress or having access to the education they desired.

"MY UNFAILING PARTNER AND COMRADE IN LIFE"

The life of Anna Kuvshinskaia that is central to this narrative was representative of her generation. Kuvshinskaia was born into the large family of a rural priest in the village of Kokshaga, Iaransk district, Viatka province. What was in store for her as a priest's daughter was to inherit her father's parish, marry a priest, and in so doing, provide him with a coveted place in the diocese. Like other wives and daughters of priests carrying forth the "civilizing mission," she might receive an education in the diocesan school for girls and use that education to work for the cultural uplift of the local population.[30] Or, in the second half of the nineteenth century, she might join many other graduates of these schools (*eparkhialki*) who endeavored to escape the confines of the roles assigned them, fleeing their parents' home in search of a more lustrous and independent future. In Kuvshinskaia's case, though her life took her far away from Kokshaga both physically and spiritually, it was not to escape her origins. As Sinegub explained, "[Kuvshinskaia] rather than cutting off all family ties, retained the warmest relations with her father, mother, and brothers."[31]

In the middle of the century, virtually none of the children of the families of priests in Viatka province received a formal education; but by the close of the century, 51 percent of the sons of church servitors of all ranks were enrolled in secondary schools, primarily the gymnasia. However, this tendency was much less evident in rural areas, where only 11 percent of the sons of the clergy received a secular education.[32] Access to a secular education was far more limited for daughters. According to Laurie Manchester, despite the rapid growth of the humbler diocesan schools for girls and the fact that most priests' daughters were educated in such schools, with only a few making it to the more prestigious and advanced gymnasia, education of any sort was often considered a luxury for the daughters of the clergy, of any rank, but especially of humble village priests.[33] Financial considerations played a role, as did notions of what young women needed to prepare them to be good wives and assistants in tending to the parish.

So it was something of a rarity that Kuvshinskaia was sent off to a women's gymnasium instead of a diocesan school. Upon graduating with honors in 1869, she was offered a teaching position at the Viatka diocesan school. She sought to be a mentor as well as an instructor for her pupils, to broaden their horizons and introduce them to the latest (socially aware) literature and political essays.[34] In the evenings she invited her pupils to gatherings at her apartment, where they discussed their readings as well as conditions in the country and abroad. Self-education circles of this sort were widespread in educational institutions at the time and young women were especially targeted in light of their unequal status in society and official limitations placed upon their schooling. Here, too, the works of Chernyshevskii and of the popular essayists M. L. Mikhailov and N. V. Shelgunov on gender issues came into play.

Kuvshinksaia enjoyed considerable authority and was admired by her charges. In his memoirs—drawing from his wife's recollections—Sinegub notes that Kuvshinskaia was "beloved," and "succeeded in enlightening some of her pupils on the need to serve the people. Upon graduating, some of them tried to arrange their lives according to her convictions, but encountered the harsh despotism of family [patriarchy]."[35] Most likely, the common clerical origins of the teacher and her pupils facilitated the bonds of trust, and Kuvshinskaia served as a role model for what they could achieve in life.

Not surprisingly, the director of the school, who was aware of Kuvshinskaia's influence over her pupils and of her political stances, eventually told the school board that she would submit her resignation if Kuvshinskaia was not let go. Matters might have been settled in Kuvshinskaia's favor, for she was highly respected, but to avoid a scandal, the board offered her a position teaching mathematics at the women's gymnasium—a significant promotion. She worked there for a year before leaving for Petersburg with Charushin.[36]

We can only speculate about what led Kuvshinskaia to relinquish a well-paid and prestigious position to depart for Petersburg to enroll in the medical courses offered women at the Military-Medical Academy—virtually the only higher education institution in the country that offered women medical training at the time. Undoubtedly, she was influenced by the general striving of women of various social origins to gain an education and professional training in a variety of fields, by the ongoing discussion of gender issues in the important thick journals of the time—none of this would have escaped her keen intellect. She had already taken several steps out of the clerical milieu, having received a secular education and taking part in intellectual circles in Viatka. She may have been influenced by students who returned home from Petersburg with tales of its exciting cultural life. Charushin was one of those students, and certainly their evolving relationship played a role; in 1872, they left for the city together. After she had left the authorities decided that she had exerted a baneful influence on her pupils at the gymnasium, and she was forbidden henceforth to engage in teaching. This only increased her resolve to find another profession.

In Petersburg Kuvshinskaia arranged to live in a commune, along with other women attending medical courses for women. She divided her time between coursework and her political activities, soon becoming, like Charushin, a member of the Chaikovskii circle. Kornilova-Moroz later wrote of the significance of these communes for young people, especially for young women of limited means, for they encouraged the sharing of resources and helping one another, often in straitened circumstances.

Moreover, such communes served as a model for prioritizing the common well-being over individual want:

> Making life far more affordable, such communes brought youth together, and in so doing increased the influence of the more mature students upon recent arrivals and facilitated the spread of socialist ideas. At the same time, communes offered an opportunity to implement such ideas in practice, in one's own personal life; to genuinely reject the comforts of the "old world" and to live in conditions like, or even worse than those experienced by factory workers; making no distinction between what is "mine" and what is "yours" and forgoing expenditure on oneself in favor of contributing to the betterment of society.[37]

Kuvshinskaia's relationship with Charushin was clearly evolving, but it remained primarily a companionate rather than intimate connection. Friendship between young men and women was at the time viewed as a manifestation of the equality of the sexes, a recognition of women as "comrades" and "friends" on the same level as friendships among males. Moreover, Charushin considered himself unattractive, and had only slowly become used to the company of women. Influenced by female characters in the novels of Turgenev and Chernyshevskii, he was initially far more comfortable thinking of women, including Kuvshinskaia, in purely platonic terms as comrades and fellow revolutionaries. Further, he wrote, "I made no plans for marriage. I feared that matrimonial life and a family would bind me hand and foot and prevent me from realizing my goals, however I defined them."[38]

But gradually Kuvshinskaia allayed his fears. Charushin summarized their relationship as follows: "Our common concerns brought us together and led to friendship, then love, then marriage."[39] She convinced him that a commonality of views could be the foundation of their relationship, facilitating self-fulfillment for each in civic affairs without limiting either one's freedom. Over time, Charushin came to see that marriage could combine the private and the public, and allow both to serve the people: "[W]e were one in our views and preferences, we shared the same moral code, and all of this allowed us to enjoy our freedom without posing any danger whatsoever to our individual strivings."[40] Then, at some point, it was his turn to reassure her of his feelings for her. While confined to the Peter-Paul Fortress he wrote her (in a letter she apparently never saw): "You still seem to believe that it makes no difference to me where I end up, but that is just not the case. I venture to tell you that being with you means everything for me."⁴¹ Evidently, his natural reserve had given her cause to doubt. Their marriage took place later, in February 1878, and only because of her determined efforts to gain permission to follow him to Siberia.

Their relationship was emblematic of the new conceptions of marriage and the family, something that is evident despite Charushin's reticence in his memoirs with respect to matters concerning his private life, emotions, or tribulations. His reluctance to reveal more intimate parts of his life both reflected his own reserved and shy personality and conformed to the unwritten rules of memoir writing at the time; what was important to share was one's contribution to civic affairs, not one's personal dramas.

Despite this emphasis on comradely relations, we will see in subsequent chapters that during their nearly thirty years together they shared each other's joys and tribulations, supported each other in their endeavors, and sorely missed one another when circumstances pulled them apart. The letters he wrote to her other during her nine months of exile are quite expressive of his emotional ties to her. In the first such letter he confessed, "And so my dear Anya, you are gone, and along with you the spirit of our abode vanished."⁴² Evidently, he saw her as the "guardian of the domestic hearth." Yet Kuvshinskaia responded that it was in fact he who made their home and family what it was, for "when alone I no longer stand out and simply merge into my surroundings."⁴³

"MY LOVEY, MY DOVEY": AUTHENTICITY, MUTUALITY, AND JOINT COMMITMENT

The commune Kuvshinskaia had joined upon moving to Petersburg often served as a refuge for daughters whose fathers were blocking their path to education and a new life, or who had entered into a fictional marriage also to escape parental control. Such fictive marriages were a phenomenon of the 1860s and 1870s and were virtually the only path available to an independent life since traditional conceptions excluded living alone. At the time it was still considered improper for women to be on the street unaccompanied. Moreover, as late as 1914 women had to have the permission of father or husband in order to receive the domestic passport necessary for unimpeded travel or residence within the country.

The relationship between Sinegub and Larisa Chemodanova began with one such fictive marriage, but it, too, evolved into an authentic and lifelong partnership. In his memoirs Sinegub recalled that the Chaikovtsy "considered among their obligations that of liberating those who were suffering for their convictions, whether in exile, prison or domestic confinement, depriving them of the opportunity to serve the popular cause."[44] In terms of revolutionary discourse, the domestic restrictions on women were equated to societal imprisonment, and one sometimes encounters the term "family prison." Young men regarded fictive marriages as a way to "emancipate" women, both narrowly and in terms of their place in society as a whole.

The first part of Sinegub's memoirs, "Fictive Marriage," consisted primarily of the story of his rescue mission for Chemodanova, daughter of a village priest influenced by the currents of the time—most directly by the tutelage of her teacher Kuvshinskaia—and struggling to win her independence. But the history of Sinegub and Chemodanova's fictive marriage is an unusual one, since over time it evolved into a genuine union; the tale of saving a young damsel became, as in novel, a love story.

The voice of Chemodanova herself is quite evident in Sinegub's memoirs. A substantial amount of the text is devoted to describing her life in the parental home, her dreams, and her tribulations. It is likely that she directly contributed to the text, for they were living together in Siberia at the time he wrote, and of course, Sinegub had no way of remembering her childhood.

At the same time, Sinegub memoirs have elements of a classical Russian tale of heroic exploits. He emerges from the pages as a noble knight, fearlessly setting forth on a crusade, experiencing no self-doubt, overcoming sundry obstacles put in his path, finding solutions to seemingly hopeless situations, and demonstrating chivalrous modesty toward his "wife" by concealing his true feelings for her so as not to impinge on her "freedom." Chemodanova appears as the "object" of salvation, possessed of all the attributes of modesty and beauty ascribed to women by the masculine voice. At the same time, she is his peer and a new type of woman, helping him overcome obstacles, actively striving to break away from domestic tyranny and from her parents' plans to find her a spouse not of her own choosing. She is not willing to limit herself to the roles of daughter, wife, and mother and instead reaches out to acquire an education that will allow her to serve the people's needs.

The story of Sinegub's fictive marriage has also come down to us through the memoirs of another Chaikovets, Tikhomirov. In fact, Sinegub quoted Tikhomirov's words as a confirmation of Chemodanova's comeliness; but the two men's accounts differ somewhat in their depiction of Chemodanova's conduct. If in Sinegub's telling Chemodanova emerges as resourceful, clever, bold, and decisive, displaying "masculine" capabilities, in Tikhomirov's interpretation she is more typically "feminine," displaying an amplitude of modesty and even helplessness, to the degree that her behavior simply added to the obstacles the young hero (Sinegub) had to overcome to carry out his mission.

Both men frequently refer to Chemodanova's stunning beauty (see Figure 3.2). Tikhomirov writes, "To say that she was attractive is not enough. Her beauty was of a rare kind worthy of the noble race of the northern

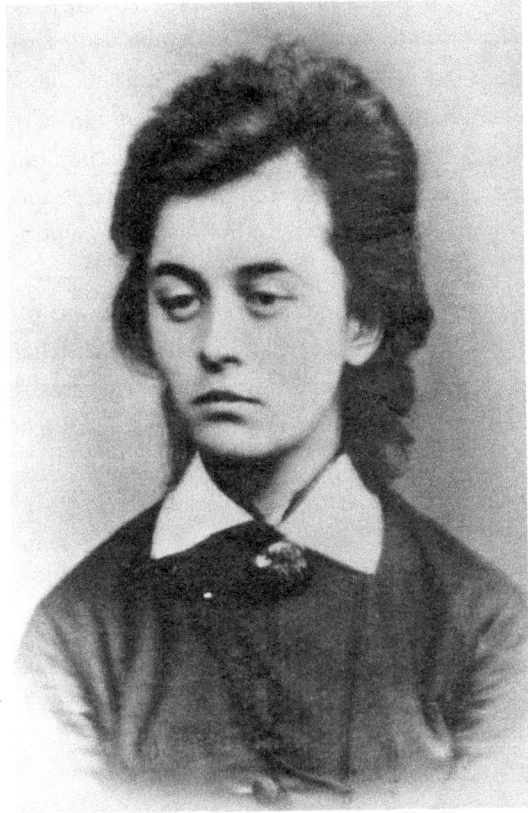

FIGURE 3.2.

Larisa Chemodanova, early 1870s.
Herzen Regional Library, Kirov.

clime, which preserved so well the characteristic of the ancient Slavs. Dark chestnut hair framed her sculptured visage. Her perfectly proportioned features gave her that unflinching boldness characteristic of women with matchless beauty. At the same time her eyes exhibited a stunning, childlike innocence."[45] Sinegub describes his first encounter with Chemodanova, "At the threshold appeared a being of stunning beauty—tall, well-proportioned, pale of complexion and with remarkable eyes."[46] And Charushin labels her a "dreamy beauty."[47] Sinegub does comment that he had been willing to travel to the Viatka countryside to rescue a woman unknown to him regardless of her looks, but the tale of rescuing a beautiful woman is all the more alluring for his subsequent fortitude and restraint in the belief it was improper to divulge his true feelings.

The interactions of Sinegub and Chemodanova at her parents' home prior to the marriage are depicted in terms of enlightening the "female element"; there are discussions of their readings, the situation of the people, and the desirable civic activities to be taken up. Sinegub recalls that they discussed the protagonists in a novel by Friedrich Spielhagen (1829–1911),[48] a very popular author in Russia at the time. Vera Figner wrote of encountering his work, "No novel expanded my horizons more than did this one; he depicted two sharply divided camps: in the one were people of high principles, struggling and suffering, the other—smug, vacuous and living the life of plenty."[49]

Gradually, however, and despite Chemodanova's initially frigid response to him, Sinegub came to realize that he was falling in love with her and confessed that it would have been difficult for a young man to resist such stunning beauty. At the same time, he considered it unacceptable to reveal his true feelings; doing so "would have been a criminal infringement upon her freedom, since legally speaking I was her husband,"[50] and could have taken advantage of that fact. Maintaining his distance from her, Sinegub escorted Chemodanova to Petersburg, where he found her a place in a women's commune. Considering romantic feelings to be trivial compared to working for the good of society, and at the same time placing the public over the private in imitation of the protagonists in Chernyshevskii's *What Is to Be Done?*, Sinegub threw himself into propagandizing workers, hoping to find relief from the feelings now enveloping him.

The love story then becomes one about the growth of authentic feeling; the attachment emerges in the process of cooperative efforts founded on equality of the sexes and a shared commitment to relieve the conditions of the working classes. The couple set out for the countryside to become village teachers, and there they read books to the peasants, held discussions about social justice. Their success in these endeavors brought them even closer: "We hastened to share everything with each other, and now we spent many a good evening in long conversations, planning an ambitious agenda of activities, dreaming about the future happiness of the people, and sharing our vexation at what we found benighted and coarse in them; in the process our love grew deeper and deeper."[51]

It was, in fact, Chemodanova who professed her love to Sinegub, which in turn freed him to express his own emotions, "to do away with the barriers long restraining the vibrant and intense flood of feelings I had been experiencing."[52] Their marriage became the embodiment of an "authentic" conjugal union for their generation. Like Kuvshinskaia, after strenuous efforts to make it possible, Chemodanova followed her husband into hard labor and exile in Siberia. Sinegub wrote one of his poems about (and named after) her, a poem that, incidentally, is written as her own first-person narrative of their story, but at the same time articulates *his* masculine vision of his wife—a companion in a revolutionary struggle initiated by men. This image incorporated a capacity for strong feelings, dedication, a striving to share one's experience, to remain together, and to support one another.

Despite experiencing much hardship and sorrow in Siberia—incarceration, deprivation, the horrors of civil war and the loss of several children—Chemodanova never returned to European Russia. She outlived her husband, who died in 1907, by almost twenty years and was the object of respect and veneration by others of her generation. Kuvshinskaia once wrote her, "In my soul I am often with you. . . . I have never ceased to be amazed by you, my dearly beloved and closest friend: you are a true heroine, a veritable saint. When I think of you, my own illness seems petty."[53] Anna Pribyleva-Korba also regarded Chemodanova an exalted figure for her fortitude: "I have always said . . . that you are one of the most remarkable women ever. . . . After all the blows you have suffered in life, you have somehow preserved a "lightness and vitality of spirit."[54] Charushin remembered Chemodanova as a person who despite the tragedies that fate inflicted upon her retained the ideals and energy of her youth to the very end of life.[55]

The marriage of Dmitrii Klements, though not a fictive one, contained the same elements of authenticity, mutuality, and joint commitment to a cause. His wife was a fellow member of the Chaikovskii circle. The Jewish daughter of a smuggler, Anna Epstein was skilled at moving books and people across borders. Their marriage, however, was kept a secret; Anna's mother knew about her daughter's illegal activities, and even helped her on occasion, but she had also "forced [Anna] to promise that she would never convert to Christianity or marry a 'goy.'"[56]

Epstein studied medicine at the University of Bern in Switzerland, where, mainly because the doors to higher education was closed to them in Russia, an entire colony of women students had congregated. Here, they had the opportunity to organize study groups to discuss politics; one such group was the legendary Fritche circle, of which the Figner sisters were members.[57] Epstein became close with many other revolutionaries and reached out to aid several of them when they ran into difficulties. Zasulich, Deutch, and Morozov all wrote about Epstein in their memoirs, and Kravchinskii used her notes to write one of the chapters of *Underground Russia*, the book that had helped shape the image of Populist revolutionaries at home and abroad.

After Epstein's death in 1895, Klements married Elizaveta Zvereva, a graduate of the Bestuzhev courses for women, the director of the Minusinsk women's gymnasium in Siberia, and his coworker at the Minusinsk museum. Zvereva accompanied him on his natural history and archeological expeditions (for which he became well-known), working as a botanist and ethnographer. Their contemporaries often mentioned their close collegial relationship, common interests, and shared activities. One friend, Ivan Popov, who was also prominent in Siberian affairs, wrote, "A very close friendship and love marked [their] relationship over the course of thirty years."[58] This accords completely with the generation's understanding of marriage as a union based on love, but also collaboration in mutual tasks, with the wife functioning as friend, partner, and helper.

In contrast to the long-standing perception that many of these revolutionaries gave up their private lives in favor of public activism, their private correspondence reveals that their interpersonal relations were characterized by intense attachments, strong emotions, and the open expression of their feelings for one another. The legendary Sergei Kravchinskii, whom Leonid Shishko described in his memoirs as single-mindedly devoted to the revolutionary struggle, was someone "for whom, both in his youth and his maturity, personal life was entirely absorbed into the cause of the people. All of his most dearly held dreams and plans were centered upon the Russian revolutionary movement."[59] Kravchinskii's letters to his wife Fanny, however, reveal him in a completely different light: he suffered greatly when she was absent, dreamed about their reuniting, did everything in his power to have her nearby. He constantly uses terms such as "my sweetheart," "my dearest, "my lovey, my dovey," entreating her to come to him, promising that he would make every effort to make things better for her, confessing that she was his one and only. The prose is rather remarkable for a revolutionary:

> My sweetheart! Why is it you don't want to travel? Are you ashamed, uncomfortable? Or even worse, don't you want me to come to me? Why won't you let me know? After all, my precious, you're not coming here for them, but for me. And you know, the truth is, I also came here for you alone. I want to be able to take you up into the mountains, go on walks with you; it would be so good for you. If you are hesitating because you are uncomfortable with the idea then, really, you must get over it. On the other hand, if you really don't want to come, then so be it, as you wish, for I don't want to make things difficult for you my darling. In that case I will come to you wherever you are. If you like Bern better than Geneva, then let it be Bern. You are my dear, wonderful girl! You are sweeter, dearer than all else in this world! I have no desire to spend the last months of my time abroad without you. Who knows what awaits us in Russia? So, my dear just tell me straight out what is your preference, for you to come to the mountains, or for me to join you in Bern (I can't let myself believe that you are so ill-inclined toward me that you will keep me from seeing your adorable peepers)! Do come, my beloved! It's so good here! On our own, we can escape into the woods and the mountains, nobody will see us, we can kiss and embrace as much as we please. We can go about arm in arm and chat to our heart's content.[60]

The understanding of marriage as founded on mutual love was connected in the revolutionaries' minds with the notions of authentic and real feelings, genuineness and candor, according to the core moral norms of their group. For that reason, Kravchinskii frequently notes in his correspondence that what was most important to him was to love a genuine person, with all of her strengths and shortcomings, not some sort of abstract ideal:

> It would be even more unpleasant if through loving me you were made into somebody worse or better than you are now.... I don't want that, and neither should you, dear one. It's the most unseemly result that love can bring about, because it compels you to spend every moment wondering about one's existence, and always leaves behind a bitter residue in the realization that someone else loves not you, but rather some concocted and painted idol. I don't think of you as some idol or heavenly being, nor do I want you ever to become one; I want you as is, I don't need you "bettering" yourself; just to be that same sweet, exquisite girl whom I have always known... whom I may argue and quarrel with, but all the same love, love, love![61]

In short, according to Kravchinskii, love should not change a person; it should provide the opportunity to remain true to oneself rather than make one better or worse.

HOW JOYFUL IT IS TO HAVE CHILDREN...!

The story of Ekaterina Breshko-Breshkovskaia, who gave up her child because maternity was incompatible with revolutionary struggle, is often presented as emblematic of her entire generation.[62] Yet for many women of this generation of revolutionaries, the issue of whether or not to have children was no simple matter, and maternal impulses remained strong. Chemodanova raised ten children (see Figure 3.3) and lost several of them tragically (one was a casualty of the Russo-Japanese war, another was executed for his role as a terrorist in the Socialist Revolutionary Party, a third perished in the Civil War following the Bolshevik Revolution, and two others—a boy and a girl—committed suicide). Kuvshinskaia had three children, although two died young (her daughter Lydia died,

FIGURE 3.3.

Larisa Chemodanova (Sinegub) and Sergei Sinegub with children, 1890s.
Herzen Regional Library, Kirov.

at age eight, in Siberia, and her older son Leonid died in murky circumstances while on a geological expedition in the Caucasus; her son Vladimir survived—only to end up in Stalin's Gulag). Both women suffered enormously from their losses; Charushin recalls that after the sudden death of their daughter, Kuvshinskaia was long unable to return to a normal life, and even considered his suggestion that she return to European Russia ahead of him but could not bear to leave her husband's side. Charushin himself was no less affected; their friend Ivan Popov later recalled that he had feared for Charushin's well-being, for he appeared "fragile, ill and broken."[63]

Whether in Siberia or after returning to European Russia, their children were central to their lives. After the tragic loss of Leonid in 1903, Kuvshinskaia spent more and more time with her one surviving son, even writing that she was living vicariously through him. Still, she acknowledged that one child was not enough to satisfy her maternal needs. She wrote to Larisa Chemodanova:

> I envy you just one thing—and that is your immortality, living through your children. Oh, what a blessing it is to have children; it's only now, in my declining years that I fully understand this treasure. Volodia—I can't say anything bad about him, but he is, in the first place, only one, and second, he isn't of the same caliber of the two that I lost; and finally, alone he is not enough to exhaust the still unfulfilled maternal feelings I have, the boundless love ... that I feel in my heart. Yes, I was apprehensive about having children when I was young, not because of my own needs, but because I feared not being able to do a good job keeping them fed and healthy.[64]

In 1906, while languishing in exile in Perm' and separated from her home in Viatka, Kuvshinskaia wrote a revealing letter to her husband, "My dear one; I certainly don't have a mother hen mentality; at the same time, I'm unable to live a full-blooded public life simply because there is nothing available here for me to make my own cause. For that reason, I am acutely aware of and pained by all that is missing in my life."[65]

The sizeable families the Sinegubs and the Charushins created were not the norm, for the severe and Spartan conditions the Populists encountered in prison and in exile during their prime child-bearing years severely limited the opportunities to raise children. Sometimes, too, children had to be left behind with relatives so as not to be exposed to danger and ensure they received an education. Yet the examples of Kuvshinskaia and Chemodanova justify skepticism about the notion that Populist women found maternity and revolutionary commitments incompatible. Moreover, it is quite likely that the legendary Breshko-Breshkovskaia left her own child behind fully believing that it was a temporary arrangement, not the permanent separation that it ended up being.[66] Also questionable is the argument made by Jane Good and David R. Jones that the desire to avoid giving birth, combined with virtually no access to contraceptives, led most revolutionary women to choose to remain celibate.[67] In any case, the letters Kuvshinskaia wrote to her husband when she was at loose ends and acutely aware of the separation are revealing of the complexity of gender issues at the time, and caution us that it will not do to make sweeping generalizations about the mindset of revolutionary women, who were pulled in several directions in their lives.

"DOMESTIC BOTHERS SUCH AS WASHING UP AND CLEANING"

In such unions as we have just described, the hearth often remained central to their lives, whether they were in exile in Siberia or had returned to European Russia. As Barbara Engel has shown, by the end of the nineteenth century, a cult of domesticity was strong in Russian society, and women—including Populist revolutionaries—subscribed to the notion of a "women's sphere" in the household.[68] The letters Kuvshinskaia wrote during her exile in Perm' (see chapter 7) reflect her close attention to the smallest details of life back at home. She literally "ran" the household from a distance, keeping track of expenditures, listing food purchases to be made and watching over their preparation, noting what clothes should be sent out to the laundry, and verifying that the house was in good order and clean. She instructed her husband to change the pillowcases, to make sure the socks were darned, and to purchase cabbage to be pickled. She fretted that in her absence Charushin would not be able to cope with the household duties. For his part, Charushin made a point in his letters of reassuring her that he was managing and everything was fine at home, even if, to avoid interfering with the established routines, he was leaving many of the details to their housekeeper. Charushin wrote Kuvshinskaia, "Here everything is tip-top: the (storm) windows are installed, the house plants are doing well and the house is clean, we are well fed.... Katerina (the servant) is excellent; she needs no encouragement to maintain the household just as you would like it. I am quite pleased and wouldn't venture to interfere with the existing regime for fear of confusing matters and throwing her off course."[69] A few days later, he repeats his assurances,[70] and a month later describes the situation in almost the same words, then adds, "I myself don't get involved in the household... and feel any interference would be superfluous. [Katerina] looks forward to your return and says that things are better when the lady is around."[71] The Russian word used for lady, *barynia*, aptly describes Kuvshinskaia's position as head of a privileged household. And she had little faith in Charushin's capabilities in the "domestic sphere." Her response to his assurances? "Sorry, but I have strong doubts about your practicality."[72]

In exile she lived with her recently widowed brother and felt obliged to take over household matters, which were chaotic there, as well. She wrote her husband: "I have so much to look after here; I need to make sure the kitchen is stocked while keeping to a tight budget, and buying cheap items. Of course, everyone's appetites are marvelous and I have to make sure there is enough to go around without exceeding the budget. I've always been a bit that way, but here, I have to run a really tight ship and my earlier tendencies are running wild."[73]

Kuvshinskaia did not limit herself to maintaining household order; she sewed (a skill in keeping with the gendered expectations of the time, taught as a part of a woman's formal education). In one letter, she writes that she has made four shirts for her husband and son and would be sending them home from Perm'. Following up, she later inquired "Why haven't I heard even a peep about my shirts? I so wanted to please you."[74] Her attention to detail and practicality are evident in these letters: "I am sending Volodia a shirt; he might not put it on because one sleeve is longer than the other, but a couple of washings will take care of that, and I advise him to wear it. The remnants of the trousers will serve as shirt patches when needed."[75] Complaining about having to deal with a deaf cook in Perm', who prepared their dishes poorly, Kuvshinskaia made it known that "household trivia like cleaning and washing take up a lot of my time."[76]

Other women from the Chaikovskii circle displayed varying degrees of commitment to household matters. Margaret Maxwell describes how during the Going to the People summer, Vera Zasulich tried but failed to pass herself off in the village as the peasant wife of one of her fellow propagandists. Her efforts at cooking were a disaster, and she had no idea how to manage the household economy.[77] Vera Figner recalls, however, that Liubov Kornilova-Serdiukov "took care of household matters by herself and twice a week there was a big hubbub in the kitchen: all kinds of dishes were boiled, baked or fried up, and then packaged separately in order to be delivered to the prison for those in need of better nourishment."[78]

A woman's ability to manage domestic matters was an attribute considered praiseworthy in the memoirs written by the women of that time—

even if, as in the case of Kuvshinskaia, such managing was sometimes bothersome. Was this truly a reflection of a growing cult of domesticity,[79] or did the attention paid to the possession of such skills perhaps stem from the privileged background of some of these women, who had been brought up with servants tending to their needs, and hence took notice of women who could fend for themselves in the kitchen and elsewhere? For example, Kornilova-Moroz proudly related how on one occasion she managed to make use of the samovar, despite skepticism on the part of the Chaikovtsy men present at the time. Later in their lives, Kuvshinskaia and Chemodanova exchanged letters lamenting the difficulties they encountered managing their households without servants.

WE ARE LIKE SIAMESE TWINS: FINAL PARTINGS

Decades of marriage based on shared convictions, joint endeavors, and of course, rich feelings were shared, together with prison, exile, the loss of children, and repeated attempts to begin life anew. The death of a spouse was, of course, a traumatic experience, and often led to the partner burying herself in work or the lives of their children. In 1906, after almost thirty-five years of marriage, Larisa Chemodanova wrote Kuvshinskaia of her husband: "We are like Siamese twins, we have so grown together that the death of one inexorably leads to the death of the other."[80] A year later, after the passing of Sinegub, she confided, "I didn't think I could outlive [Sergei]; I thought my heart would burst with agony if he died before me, but my heart, inured to tribulation, turned out to be unfeeling... he died yet I live on.... I need to stay alive another couple of years no matter what, to give Vlad and Larisa a chance to grow up."[81]

After the death, in 1931, of Evgenia (Vera Figner's sister), his wife of almost fifty years, Mikhail Sazhin suffered the loss intensely, writing to Figner that given his "dry" character he hadn't expected to experience such a strong emotional reaction: "I had no clue that losing her would be so awful; I weep and weep my heart out. It is the first time in my life that I have experienced such a blow."[82] This, despite the norms of emotional restraint the revolutionary Populists had established for themselves that were so central to their images, which they perceived as masculine, in opposition to feminine emotionality. We recall Sinegub's description of Charushin in his memoirs, writing that the latter was "always restrained, expansiveness was alien to him."[83] Tellingly, Sazhin compared his response to Evgeniia's death with his response to the death of his friend Bakunin, "Bakunin I loved deeply, and his death moved me profoundly, but [her] death was incomparably worse."[84] Such comparisons show just how interwoven were their conceptions of love and friendship, family and comrades.

For Charushin, Kuvshinskaia's death, in 1909, was a tremendous blow, and he sought relief from his pain by committing himself heart and soul to his newspaper, as his close friend and collaborator at the newspaper Vera Tanaevskaia counseled him to do.[85] Eighteen years later, writing to his old friend Ivan Popov, with whom he had shared Siberian exile and whose wife had died in a tragic accident, Charushin drew from his own experience of such a huge loss to console him: "The passage of time, throwing yourself into work, and fortitude—that's the only medicine for such personal catastrophes."[86]

"MY HUSBAND NO LONGER POSED AN OBSTACLE"

By no means were all the marriages between the Populists "until death do we part." Marriages could be dissolved as well as contracted, and as often as not, the issues leading to a parting stemmed from the partners' differences in belief and conflicting life choices made under the aegis of "serving the people." As a rule, the person who initiated the parting of ways was the woman who, wanting to move beyond the confines of traditional gender roles and to find self-realization in public or professional activities, had concluded that family life and revolutionary struggle were incompatible.

Not all fictive marriages evolved into close and lasting relationships. Vera Kornilova, the oldest of the several sisters who were all prominent in the Chaikovskii circle, under the influence of her brother[87] began to read radical literature, and within a year after completing her studies at the Elizavetinskii institute began to change her appearance and take an interest in the "woman question." It was soon afterward that she joined the Chaikovskii circle. Her father, the prosperous merchant, had never objected to his daughters' education or restricted their freedom, but according to her sister Alexandra, Vera "had no interest in leading a bourgeois life in her father's home," and instead entered into a fictive marriage with N. A. Griboedov (a friend of Kropotkin, Kravchinskii, and others and the treasurer of the Chaikovskii circle). But instead of moving in with Griboedov, Vera took up residence with two friends from the medical courses who had also concluded fictive marriages. Yet another sister, Liubov' Kornilova, initially followed a similar path, studying at the institute, taking the Alarchinskie courses, joining the Chaikovskii circle, and then marrying one of its members, Anatolii Serdiukov. After the majority of the Chaikovtsy had been arrested, Liubov Serdiukova delivered food and books to the prison, in so doing becoming the first to perform the relief services of a "Red Cross" for political prisoners. But when making these deliveries, as Figner noted, she made no distinction among prisoners; her husband received no more or less than others. Their marriage was not a happy one: Serdiukov was arrested several times for spreading propaganda among Petersburg factory workers, and twice incarcerated in a mental hospital (after being declared "unfit" for trial), exiled to Tver', in 1878, after which he ended his own life. Liubov' Serdiukova was exiled to Siberia in 1880, where she married again; this time to a teacher in a secondary school.

Anna Pribyleva-Korba's trajectory is instructive, if complicated. Educated at home, she was well-read and bookish in her youth, and first found her place in the world at the Alarchinskii Courses in Petersburg. There she made the acquaintance of Kornilova and Perovskaia. But she had also married early: her first husband was a citizen of Switzerland, a stockbroker, accountant, and insurance agent who supported her every endeavor and did everything in his power to keep them together—to no avail. She confessed in her autobiography—written at the invitation of Vera Figner—that despite concerted efforts to make her marriage work, she finally made the decision to give her all to "underground Russia." She left for the front during the Russo-Turkish War to serve as a nurse and returned to participate in the People's Will.

Contemplating the reasons for the breakup of her marriage, Korba blamed it on the incompatibility of their personalities, something that was manifest in their conflicting positions, strivings, and values. The thought of divorce had frightened her, and she feared for her husband's well-being if she left him, but she was even more fearful that she would never realize her wish for self-fulfillment or make any contribution to society. She felt obligated in her recollections to dwell upon her husband, who did have a difficult time after they parted, something for which she blamed herself: "Again I struggled with the thought of tossing everything else aside and returning to help him, but then I went through the same agonies of reflection. Instead, to escape these tormenting thoughts I threw myself into my work... how could I return to the family hearth again? It just could never be. Whoever had begun to serve her country can never again give her all, her every thought and every moment to any single person."[88]

For her role in the assassination of Alexander II, Anna Korba was sentenced in 1883 to twenty years of hard labor at Kara and then to enforced settlement in Siberia. There, after her marriage to V. F. Korba was officially dissolved in 1894, she married another member of the People's Will, A. V. Pribylev. It was his second marriage as well; the first had also been to a collaborator in the People's Will, R. L. Grossman, who, in order to be able to marry him, had converted from Judaism to Orthodoxy. Pribylev and Grossman were tried along with Korba and likewise sentenced to hard labor—he for fifteen years and she for four, but while in exile their relationship had fallen apart. Sent to the far north, in Yakutia, after completing her term of hard labor, in 1885, Grossman began a common-law marriage with another exile (by the name of Tiutchev); her official marriage to Pribylev was ended in 1893.

We find no such agonizing or second thoughts about her divorce in Vera Figner's memoirs. After completing her schooling at a residential institute for girls of the nobility, at age eighteen, she stepped out into the world and eventually married A. V. Filippov, a criminal investigator and the son of a noble landowner whose property was adjacent to her family's property in Kazan' province. She had met him at a society ball in Kazan', and after some initial fluster, she gradually become absorbed in the fast-paced life of high society and he became her cavalier. So as to be close to her family, he requested a transfer from the capital of the province to a site near a Figner family estate in Tetiushi district, and they were married in less than a year. She recalled that "he shared my views and supported my plans. We read books together, and were united in my decision to matriculate in the university."[89]

Figner's husband supported her wishes to gain a higher education, even tutored her in algebra and geometry—we often encounter in the memoirs instances where the male, having received a university education, then tutors a young woman who is hoping to pursue the same path. Figner than persuaded her husband to give up his career as a criminal investigator, primarily because she found the work offensive, but also so that he could follow her to Switzerland, where both would pursue a degree in medicine. In 1872, the two, accompanied by her sister Lydia, departed for the university in Zurich. Like many of her contemporaries, Figner considered marriage to be a partnership, in which common values and like-minded purposes led to joint endeavors for the common good.

But in Zurich, instead of the anticipated collaboration and merging of the minds, the two grew apart. Figner explained this as the result of finding themselves in a new environment with new acquaintances, so different from what they had known in Russia: "As soon as my husband and I came into contact with a crowd of new people and came face to face with new issues our differences emerged: he gravitated toward an older and more conservative group, while I went quite in the other direction. Whenever there was a gathering, and whatever question arose, we found ourselves on opposite sides."[90]

Generational differences are obvious here, but Figner's memoirs also note her husband's condescending attitude toward the women's circles that had formed in Zurich and toward feminist leanings in general. It seems that her growing independence and radicalization did not fit with his views on marriage. Although Filippov could quite genuinely support her drive to be educated and to pursue an independent career, he was nevertheless a loyal subject of the Empire, and after his return home and divorce, he rejoined the Ministry of the Interior (MVD) (the subsequent criminal judgments against Figner had no impact on his career). In short, their seeming commonality of views had been largely an illusion, and for the revolutionary generation such a radical divergence in perspectives clashed with the notion of marriage as a partnership of like-minded individuals sharing basic goals.

Growing suspicion of the radicalization of women studying medicine in Zurich led the Russian government to order them home; otherwise, even with a degree from Switzerland, they would not be certified to practice their profession in Russia once they returned, Instead, Figner moved to Bern to continue her studies, immersed herself in a revolutionary milieu, and became fully estranged from her Filippov: "At that time I was virtually free, since my husband had returned to Russia to take up the post of secretary of the circuit court in Kazan'."[91] But despite her proclaimed willingness to cut off all ties with him in favor of the revolution, she confessed in her memoirs that she wasn't yet prepared to follow the example of those who had dropped their studies at the university and returned home to promote the cause. She wrote: "I was still bound by family ties and the desire to find a suitable program; that desire was bolstered by the entreaties of my mother, who had been dismayed by Lydia's departure from the university."[92]

In the spring of 1875, Figner sent her husband a message spurning his financial aid and asking him to terminate all connection with her. When in the fall of that year she had to decide whether or not to return to Russia to join the revolutionary movement, the issue for her was not one of politics versus family, but rather whether or not she should finish her education, be certified as a doctor and able to take up a profession, or plunge into dangerous underground activities. As she wrote, laconically, "My husband no longer posed an obstacle to me."[93] In general, we find in her memoirs a revealing presentation of marriage as limiting individual freedom ("relations were fastened/tied up/attached," "I was already almost free," "posed no obstacles").

Divorce proceedings were concluded in 1876, and Figner reinstated her maiden name. She later described the divorce and passing the exam to become a midwife the two benchmarks marking the end of that period of her life, "By November, 1876, all my practical concerns had been addressed; I bid a firm farewell to my past and at the age of twenty-four my entire life was now devoted to the party of revolution in Russia."[94]

Some marriages were initially fictive, but thrived; others were authentic from the start; and still others collapsed because of conflicting views or life trajectories, but one fit well into the messiness of life by combining all of these attributes. Liudmila Aleksandrova (Vol'kenshtein) was sentenced along with Vera Figner after the assassination of Alexander II to a long term of solitary confinement in the Schlisselburg Fortress, and her marriage doesn't fit into any neat category. She was betrothed only one year after graduating from the gymnasium; her husband Alexander Vol'kenshtein was a graduate of the medical faculty at Kiev University, an active participant in the Chaikovskii circle, a member of Land and Freedom (1876), and employed as a zemstvo doctor. The story of her divorce, in 1878, is a bit murky. He was brought to trial (the Trial of the 193), exonerated, then went to the front during the Russo-Turkish War (Pribyleva-Korba writes of meeting with him there). Liudmila later wrote that it was she who had initiated the divorce from Vol'kenstein in order to devote herself entirely to the revolutionary cause, despite having given birth to a son a year previously. After thirteen years of incarceration in Shlisselburg, she was sent to compulsory resettlement on Sakhalin Island in the Far East; soon afterward she was joined there by her former husband, who had left his second wife in order to be with her. Evidently, according to Lydia Dan, Figner considered her good friend Vol'kenstein fortunate in that after all those years in Shlisselburg, she managed to reunite with a son who had grown up without her and with a former husband, both of whom she had seemingly lost. Figner told Dan, "of course [her husband] was undeserving of her, being a very ordinary person, although he knew how to say just the right thing, to utter a kind word just when it was most needed."⁹⁵

UNIFORM LIFE SCENARIOS? THE "WOMAN QUESTION" REVISITED

The moral norms derived from common readings established notions about the family and marriage but did not result in uniform life scenarios. Moreover, the conception of women as comrades in the revolutionary struggle equally sharing all tasks, dangers, and difficulties often coexisted with notions of women as wives, mothers, and heads of households, complementing rather than contradicting their revolutionary identities. The understanding of equality at that time in Russia did not exclude acknowledgment of what were seen as biologically determined distinctive roles of women and did not imply the leveling of all spheres of life—in that, it resembled European social feminism of the early post–World War II period.

As historians have long noted, for the Populists the "woman question" did not stand alone but merged with the goal of political and social revolution, surviving as a topic to be addressed "the day after" that revolution. Women who joined the revolutionary movement put aside the "woman question," and at one point or another, their professional ambitions were subordinated to their political activities.[96] Moreover, the men in the Chaikovskii circle took for granted the notions of equality and mutual responsibility in personal relations—even if they did not always live up to these ideals.[97] In this, they can be distinguished from the generation of the sixties, when women played a distinctly subordinate role.[98]

At the same time, outside the parameters of the revolutionary movement, women continued to be seen as their husband's helpers, playing a subsidiary role in the home and at work. As Kuvshinskaia wrote her husband late in life, "I am ashamed to admit that I am a nobody. It's obvious that in my lifetime I have become accustomed to playing the role of second fiddle—left alone everything falls apart, and how!"[99] Even though the revolutionaries who frequented their home viewed her politics rather than Charushin's as the more militant; even though she was highly active in the book publishing cooperative founded in Viatka at the turn of the century; and even though the staff at the newspaper Charushin had founded (*Viatskaia Rech'*) emphasized her prominent role in its daily operations—she still regarded herself as secondary to him in public affairs.

Most of the memoirs written by Populists indeed create the impression that they had relinquished all claims to a private life in favor of the cause. In so doing, women sought to create an image for future generations of a generation dedicated solely to the struggle for freedom. Moreover, the themes of intimacy and marriage are passed over in their correspondence, only further compounding this presentation of self. As Barbara Engel put it, women paid dearly for aspiring to the high moral ideals of the 1870s generation and for achieving equality in the revolutionary struggle. The ideal which they embodied excluded sexuality.[100] Correspondingly, the theme of self-sacrifice came to be central in works describing women's role in the revolutionary movement.[101]

Without completely rejecting this side of their lives, we emphasize an equally important aspect—their desire in real life to have close relationships, families, and even children, their private emotions, attachments, and valuing of domestic comforts—that is, everything traditionally connected with the "domestic sphere." Women sought to establish a presence in the "male sphere" of professional and societal activity; like men, many managed to combine family and public activism in their lives. Of course, others had their lives cut short and never had the chance to do so, had they desired it. For those who were fortunate enough to live full lives, domesticity was highly treasured and only grew in importance as they grew older. Perhaps too, it was those who found it impossible to combine the public and the private and found self-realization solely in revolutionary activity who, in search of vindication—whether to themselves or in public—gave rise to the narrative of self-sacrifice.

NOTES

1. RGALI, f. 1185, op. 1, d. 818, l. 1.
2. См.: Barbara Alpern. Engel, *Breaking the Ties That Bound: The Politics of Marital Strife in Late Imperial Russia* (Ithaca, NY: Cornell University Press, 2011), 313–315.; Elisabeth Wood, "The Woman Question in Russia: Contradictions and Ambivalence," in *A Companion to Russian History*, ed. Abbott Gleason (Chichester, UK: Wiley-Blackwell, 2009), 353–367. Richard Stites, *The Women's Liberation Movement in Russia: Feminism, Nihilism, and Bolshevism, 1860–1930* (Princeton, NJ: Princeton University Press, 1978), 29–63; Christine Johanson, *Women's Struggle for Higher Education in Russia, 1855–1900* (Kingston, Ontario: McGill-Queen's University Press, 1987), 9–19.
3. Stites, *Women's Liberation Movement in Russia*, 153.
4. Barbara A. Engel, "Women, the Family and Public Life," in *The Cambridge History of Russia*, 3 vols., ed. Dominic Lieven (Cambridge: Cambridge University Press, 2006): 2:316.
5. Nikolai Charushin, *O dalekom proshlom* (Moskva: Mysl', 1973), 44.
6. Wood, "Woman Question in Russia," in Gleason, *Companion to Russian History*, 357–358.
7. *Deiateli SSSR i revoliutsionnogo dvizheniia v Rossii* (Moskva: Sovetskaia Entsiklopediia, 1989), 118–119.
8. Nikolai Charushin, *O dalekom proshlom. Kruzhok chaikovtsev. Iz vospominanii o revoliutsionnom dvizhenii 1870-kh gg.* (Moskva: Izdatel'stvo Obshchestva Politkatorzhan, 1926), 95.
9. Sergei Sinegub, *Zapiski chaikovtsa* (Moskva: Molodaia Gvardiia, 1929), 235.
10. Charushin, *O dalekom proshlom* (1973), 273.
11. L. N. Tolstoy and A. A. Tolstaia, *Perepiska (1857–1903)* (Moskva: Nauka, 2011), 369.
12. Charushin, *O dalekom proshlom* (1926), 53.
13. Barbara Engel similarly includes "modesty" among the most characteristic gendered markers of normative female behavior. See Engel, *Breaking the Ties That Bound*, 46.
14. Charushin, *O dalekom proshlom* (1926), 104.
15. Vera Figner, *Zapechatlennyi trud* (Moskva: Mysl', 1964) 1:276—277. Here Figner is referring not to the chronicler of the 1917 Revolution, Nikolai Sukhanov, but to a fellow member of the People's Will—also named Nikolai (1851–1882)—executed after the assassination of Alexander II.

16. Ibid., 279.
17. Ibid., 273.
18. Wood, "Woman Question in Russia," in Gleason, *Companion to Russian History*, 359.
19. *Deiateli SSSR i revoliutsionnogo dvizheniia v Rossii*, 115.
20. Alexandra Kornilova-Moroz, Perovskaia i kruzhok chaikovtsev, *Revoliutsionery 1870-kh gg. Vospominaniia uchastnikov narodnicheskogo dvizheniia v Peterburge* (Leningrad: Lenizdat, 1986), 56. Likewise, Kornilova's portrait of Sofia Leshern seeks to dissociate her entirely from her roots as the daughter of a general.
21. Ibid., 60—61.
22. Charushin, *O dalekom proshlom* (1926), 96.
23. Ibid.
24. See Christine Ruane, *The Empire's New Clothes: A History of the Russian Fashion Industry, 1700–1917* (New Haven, CT: Yale University Press, 2009), 12.
25. Engel, "Women, the Family and Public Life," in Lieven, *Cambridge History of Russia*, 316.
26. Charushin, *O dalekom proshlom* (1926), 79.
27. Kornilova-Moroz, Perovskaia i kruzhok chaikovtsev, *Revoliutsionery 1870-kh gg*, 63.
28. Ruane, *Empire's New Clothes*, 155.
29. Christine Ruane, "Subjects into Citizens: the Politics of Clothing in Imperial Russia," *Fashioning the Body Politic: Dress, Gender, Citizenship*, ed. Wendy Parkins (Oxford: Berg, 2002), 58.
30. Laure Manchester, "Gender and Social Estate as National Identity: The Wives and Daughters of Orthodox Clergymen as Civilizing Agents in Imperial Russia," *Journal of Modern History* 83, no. 1 (2011): 48—77.
31. Sinegub, *Zapiski chaikovtsa*, 235.
32. A. Skutnev, "Sotsial'naia mobil'nost' prikhodskogo dukhovenstva v Viatskoi eparkhii v seredine XIX—nachale XX v.," *Voprosy Istorii* 11 (2007): 147.
33. Manchester, "Gender and Social Estate as National Identity," 61.
34. Kuvshinskaia's position as *nastavnitsa*, sometimes translated as "governess," put her in charge of the conduct and deportment of her charges rather than of their classroom instruction. However, we beg to disagree with Barbara Engel when she describes this position as a lowly and subordinate one, which one would agree to take up solely because of dire need. See Barbara A. Engel, "Women as Revolutionaries: The Russian Populists," in *Becoming Visible: Women in European History*, ed. Renate Bridenthal and Claudia Koonz (Boston: Houghton Mifflin, 1977), 351. When, in August 1871, Kuvshinskaia's political activities became obvious, the director of the school had to go to the school board with the ultimatum "either she goes or I do." The board gave Kuvshinskaia a favorable recommendation and helped her obtain a position as a teacher at the local gymnasium, a significant promotion.
35. Sinegub, *Zapiski chaikovtsa*, 18. Kuvshinskaia found Sinegub's memoirs to be "cold" in relation to her and even wrote his wife, Larisa Chemodanova, about it, "[Y]ou know, my dear, it was painful to read [his] memoirs in *Russkaia mysl'*; he seemed so frosty when it came to me. Is that really the case? If so, you can't change the past and the thought distresses me." (RGALI, f. 1291, op. 1, d. 38, l. 8).
36. GAKO, f. 221, op. 1, d. 17, l. 27—28.
37. Kornilova-Moroz, "Perovskaia i kruzhok chaikovtsev," 67.
38. Charushin, *O dalekom proshlom* (1926), 67.
39. Ibid., 21.
40. *Deiateli SSSR i revoliutsionnogo dvizheniia v Rossii*, 287.

41. Cited in Valentin Sergeev, *Platony i Nevtony Viatskoi zemli: Istoriko-Kraevedcheskie Ocherki* (Kirov, n.p., 2006), 75.
42. Charushin to Kuvshinskaia, September 10, 1906, RGALI, f. 1642, op. 1, d. 108, l. 1.
43. Kuvshinskaia to Charushin, September 14, 1906, RGALI, f. 1642, op. 1, d. 79, l. 8.
44. Sinegub, *Zapiski chaikovtsa*, 19.
45. *V podpol'e* (St. Petersburg: Drug Naroda, 1907), 11.
46. Sinegub, *Zapiski chaikovtsa*, 58.
47. Charushin, *O dalekom proshlom* (1926), 54.
48. The novels of Spielhagen, which usually centered around the events and aftermath of the 1848 revolutions, were popular in Russia. The theme of the grandeur of the ideas inspiring those revolutions and the ideals of liberty, equality, and fraternity embedded in the novels were combined with reflections on a country's perception of and comments on the moral qualities of revolutionaries, the role of the people, and of heroes in history. Spielhagen's heroes were ordinarily of aristocratic origin but with democratic inclinations, and thus could find no suitable place in society, though some were solitary freedom fighters. All of his works were listed in the private library of N. I. Vershinin in Viatka in 1871. As late as 1934, among the books Charushin sent to his hospitalized second wife, Olga Koshkareva, were the work of Spielhagen—testimony to that author's lasting influence upon him.
49. Figner, *Zapechatlennyi trud*, 1:91. In her memoirs Figner wrote of the novel *In Reih' und Glied*, translated into Russian and very popular in Russia. Ferdinand Lassalle was depicted as Leo in this novel.
50. Sinegub, *Zapiski chaikovtsa*, 93.
51. Ibid.
52. Ibid.
53. Kuvshinskaia to Chemodanova, July 17, 1908, RGALI, f. 1291, op. 1, d. 38, l. 1. Suffering from leukemia at the time, Kuvshinskaia was herself less than six months away from dying.
54. Pribyleva-Korba to Chemodanova, June 25, RGALI, f. 1291, op. 1, d. 32, l. 9.
55. Charushin, *O dalekom proshlom* (1926), 54.
56. Vera Zasulich, *Vospominaniia* (Moskva: Izdatel'stvo Obshchestva Politkatorzhan, 1931), 81.
57. Cathy Porter, *Fathers and Daughters: Russian Women in Revolution* (London: Virago Quartet Books, 1976), 139–140.
58. Dmitrii Klements, *Iz proshlogo. Vospominaniia* (Leningrad: Kolos, 1925), 62.
59. Leonid Shishko, *S.M. Kravchinskii i kruzhok chaikovtsev (Iz vospominanii i zametok starogo narodnika)* (St. Petersburg: V. Raspopov, 1906), 44.
60. Columbia University, Rare Book and Manuscript Library, Bakhmeteff Archive, Sergei Mikhailovich Kravchinskii Papers, box 1.
61. Ibid.
62. Margaret Maxwell, *Narodniki Women: Russian Women Who Sacrificed Themselves for the Dream of Freedom* (New York: Pergamon, 1990), 132; Porter, *Fathers and Daughters*, 201.
63. Ivan Popov, *Minuvshee i perezhitoe. Sibir' i emigratsiia. Vospominaniia za 50 let.* (Leningrad: Kolos, 1924), 95.
64. Kuvshinskaia to Chemodanova, n.d., RGALI, f. 1642, op. 1. d. 38, l. 11 ob.
65. Kuvshinskaia to Charushin, April 28, 1907, RGALI, f. 1642, op. 1. d. 79, l. 63—63 ob.
66. Jane E. Good, *Babushka: The Life of the Russian Revolutionary Ekaterina K. Breshko-Breshkovskaia (1844–1934)*, ed. David R. Jones (Newtonville, MA: Oriental Research Partners, 1991), 45.

67. Ibid., 41.
68. Engel, *Breaking the Ties that Bound*, 157–200.
69. Charushin to Kuvshinskaia, September 18, 1906, RGALI, f. 1642, op. 1, d. 108, l. 2.
70. Charushin to Kuvshinskaia, September 21, 1906, RGALI, f. 1642, op. 1, d. 108, l. 5.
71. Ibid.
72. Kuvshinskaia to Charushin, January 19, 1907, RGALI, f. 1642, op. 1, d. 79, l. 41.
73. Kuvshinskaia to Charushin, October 6, 1906, RGALI, f. 1642, op. 1, d. 79, l. 16 ob.
74. Kuvshinskaia to Charushin, February 22, 1907, RGALI, f. 1642, op. 1, d. 79, l. 48 ob.
75. Kuvshinskaia to Charushin, October 7, 1906, RGALI, f. 1642, op. 1, d. 79, l. 18 ob.
76. Kuvshinskaia to Charushin, October 1, 1906, RGALI, f. 1642, op. 1, d. 79, l.13.
77. Maxwell, *Narodniki Women*, 27.
78. "Narodnaia Volia," accessed February 10, 2014, http://narodnaya-volya.ru/Person/kornilova.php.
79. Engel, *Breaking the Ties That Bound*, 160–166.
80. Chemodanova to Kuvshinskaia, November 24, 1906, RGALI, f. 1642, op. 1, d. 105, l. 1 ob.
81. Ibid., November 15, 1907, l. 5 ob.–6.
82. Sazhin to Figner, November 22, 1931, RGALI, f. 1185, op. 1, d. 707, l. 11.
83. Sinegub, *Zapiski chaikovtsa*, 274.
84. Sazhin to Figner, November 22, 1931, RGALI, f. 1185, op. 1, d. 707, l. 11.
85. Tanaevskaia to Charushin, January 29, 1909, RGALI, f. 1642, op. 1, d. 73, l. 14 ob.
86. Charushin to Popov, July 17, 1927, RGALI, f. 408, op. 1, d. 114, l. 2.
87. The influence of older brothers is often noted in memoirs in two ways: connected with the student movement, they introduce their sisters to the "wider world" of education and politics, encouraging them to move beyond the boundaries of family life; and serving as models to be emulated.
88. *Deiateli SSSR i revoliutsionnogo dvizheniia v Rossii*, 204.
89. Figner, *Zapechatlennyi trud*, 1:104.
90. Ibid., 122.
91. Ibid., 127.
92. Ibid., 127–128.
93. Ibid., 132.
94. Ibid., 136.
95. Lidia Dan, "Iz vstrech s V. N. Figner," Inter-University Project on the History of the Menshevik Movement (typescript: New York, August 1961), 11. Figner wrote an entry about Vol'kenstein in a collective volume about the denizens of Shlisselburg.
96. Engel, *Mothers and Daughters*, 125.
97. Stites, *Women's Liberation Movement in Russia*, chapter 5.
98. Engel, "Women as Revolutionaries," in Bridenthal and Koonz, *Becoming Visible: Women in European History*, 357–360.
99 Kuvshinskaia to Charushin, October 6, 1906, RGALI, f. 1642, op. 1, d. 79, l. 15 ob.
100. Engel, *Mothers and Daughters*, 125.
101. See Maxwell, *Narodniki Women*.

"Punishment Harsh and Cruel"

The Experience of Incarceration (1874–1878)

ARRESTS

Toward the end of 1873, the Chaikovtsy began to find themselves under arrest. Charushin himself was arrested early in January 1874,[1] as were other members of the circle who were spreading propaganda among factory workers or engaged in publishing and disseminating illegal literature, along with the thousands who participated in the Going to the People movement in the summer of 1874. Most of the arrested would spend three or four years incarcerated and awaiting trial. The outcome of these events was undoubtedly the most spectacular trial in the history of the Russian Empire to date: the Trial of the 193 (the number who were targeted for trail among the more than four thousand initially arrested).

The young revolutionaries—for the most part yesterday's students—now suddenly found themselves in jail. As Charushin wrote in his characteristically terse manner: "At that time my period of strict solitary confinement began, lasting almost four years without interruption by visitations or letters until my trial."[2] Of course, many of them had been aware of the possibility of arrest, hard labor, and exile, and had expressed willingness to sacrifice their lives for the common good, but few of them really had any real understanding of what it meant to be incarcerated, and the experience marked them for the rest of their lives. Most of them were only just then entering full-blooded adulthood and were still undergoing fundamental processes of developmental socialization; now they were to experience a prolonged period of solitary confinement, one of the most difficult of psychological trials. They were to learn a new mode of (clandestine) communication with their peers and to encounter the full powers of the state. For many, this period engendered a painful testing and rethinking of their values; for others, it provided an education in life.

Some historians, especially during the Cold War, emphasized the contrast between Tsarist and Soviet treatment of political prisoners, suggesting that those of Charushin's generation were treated with kid gloves in comparison. Other historians have also noted that George Kennan's hugely influential work on Siberian prisons was produced without any awareness or study of the exceptionally harsh conditions prevailing elsewhere in the world, including in American prisons. An impartial comparative examination of prison conditions is certainly useful, but it should not be allowed to obscure the lived experience and subjective responses to incarceration of an entire generation as they entered their adult years or to negate the value of examining their descriptions through the filter of memory.

Indeed, those imprisoned by the Tsarist regime truly experienced many travails and harsh, humiliating treatment. Some broke under the strain of these tribulations and some went mad or committed suicide.[3] Memories of the physical and emotional trauma haunted those who survived those years long after they were released back into society, remained vivid in their consciousness and shaped their future lives. Vera Figner said it all when, a few years after being released after two decades of solitary confinement, she confided to a friend, "You can't erase twenty years of your life during which I experienced more than at any other time; for me Shlisselburg always looms in the background; I can't disown it, I don't want to cast it off, nor could I if I wished to."[4]

PRISON MEMOIRS

The Populist's memoirs understandably dwell upon the experience of imprisonment. These memoirs began to appear in the early twentieth century, when the 1905 Revolution made it possible to publish such works and stimulated a good deal of interest in the life stories of those who had been involved in the country's "liberation movement" (as it was called). Those who had been incarcerated—often quite soon after being released—wanted to share their painful experiences, emphasize the sacrifices they had made for the cause, and underscore their own forbearance and courage, but also to record the contribution Populism had made to the struggle against autocracy.

Memoirs written in the 1920s pursued the same goals, but now within the context of a somewhat altered historical narrative and in a changed political environment that was increasingly hostile to any notion of preserving the legacy of Populism for future generations. There can be little doubt that the building of Soviet prisons and especially the incarceration of some Populists of the seventies generation weighed heavily on the minds of these older revolutionaries. Charushin was arrested four times between 1917 and 1919, released only in response to petitions citing his past service to the revolution; in his memoirs one can read between the lines to find comparisons between the past and the present.

In general, the Populist memoirs entered into a long literary tradition and a metanarrative going back to the Decembrists, including Dostoevsky, and extending far beyond Charushin's lifetime. At the same time, if treated with care these memoirs allow us to reconstruct the revolutionaries' temporal and spatial perceptions of incarceration, learn how they adapted to the circumstances, and discern the contextual specificities of imprisonment for political crimes in Russia at a particular moment in time.

It is important to keep these two polarities in mind: a rather fixed metanarrative and the changing environment of prison life in Russia. Penal policies and conditions were changing rapidly in the empire throughout the last half-century of its existence. Conditions also frequently differed from site to site. The memoirs of Populists often concerned imprisonment at Shlisselburg Fortress, on Lake Ladoga, near St. Petersburg. Many of the Chaikovskii circle spent time in the Peter-Paul Fortress on a small island in the center of the city, at the Litovskii Fortress (formerly a barracks, built in the late eighteenth century, torn down in the early Soviet era, and usually used for common criminals), and the House of Preliminary Detention.[5] Charushin was initially held at the headquarters of the secret police, and then transferred to the Litovskii Fortress. Later, he was sent to the Peter-Paul Fortress, still later to the House of Preliminary Detention, and was finally sent back to the Peter-Paul Fortress. During the actual trial, in 1877, he was moved yet another time back to the House of Preliminary Detention, and then to the Peter-Paul Fortress again, from where he was finally sent off to exile and hard labor in Siberia. In all, his incarceration before his departure for Siberia lasted from January 1874 until July 1878.

"A GRAY HOSPITAL ROBE"

In the memory of many, their period of incarceration began with a disrobing and change of garb, the results of which stood as external markers of changed status and entry into a different society or even world. Charushin recalled his first day at the Peter-Paul Fortress, "[T]hey undressed and carefully search[ed] me, after which I put on all state-issued garb—underwear, robe and slippers."[6] Solomon Chudnovskii wrote, "[O]nce again a body search, this time more complete and invasive, involving even places I'd rather not mention. They made me completely expose myself, took away my clothes, and then handed over a prison outfit: underwear of decent quality, a capacious robe, and likewise large slippers along with long socks."[7] The implicit analogy with hospital supervision is made explicit in Lev Deutch's account: "The warden ordered me to fully undress right away. The prison guards then examined me closely, then told me to put on prison garb: the underwear, the striped robe just like the one worn in hospitals, and slippers."[8] Sinegub provides a similar description of the procedure, emphasizing his subjugation and forced passivity as an object (having been searched, stripped). At the same time, he preserved a modicum of autonomy by belting the hospital-like robe he was issued with a sash, "not as I was supposed to do it."[9]

Still, in their descriptions, the disrobing and then "investing" in prison garb involved a loss of sense of self, a divesting of all individuality and ownership (of space, time, possessions), everything that distinguished the "I" from the "Other." Sinegub confessed that when he was later transferred to the House of Preliminary Detention, being to choose his own clothing gave him back his identity, "I sat there in my cell dressed in my own outfit, my own underwear rather than what the prison provided; I had my own teapot, cup or mug—I had my own little household economy."[10]

Even more than others, Vera Figner emphasized her perception that under arrest she no longer owned herself; she had been stripped not only of her freedom but also of possession of her own body, "From that point on I no longer asked myself what I would be doing, but what would be done to me."[11] Describing her arrival at Shlisselburg, she recalled how she was disrobed and forced to stand naked while she was carefully examined for distinguishing bodily traits, "Was it painful? No. Was it shameful? No.... I felt indifferent. My spirit had departed my body, gone or perhaps compressed itself into a tiny lump. What remained was only a body, feeling no shame or moral anguish."[12] This passage reveals Figner's coping mechanism of distancing, but also her confidence that though her jailers could take control of her body, she remained in charge of her spirit.

"NEW ACCOMMODATIONS": SPATIAL DIMENSIONS OF THE CELL

In her study of prison memoirs, the Italian scholar Eleanor Canright Chiari appropriates the word "heterotopia," used by Foucault to designate an "alternative space," which in contrast to "utopia," is real and meaningful in everyday practice. In her application heterotopia applies to the prison cell since it is multifunctional in use, different from other spaces but at the same time linked with them.[13]

All the Populist memoirists describe the cells to which they were consigned in detail. At first, the depictions are primarily physical, of a space of specific dimensions, with walls, floors, ceilings of a given material and color, suffused with a distinct light, and containing specific objects. Charushin described his cell at the Peter-Paul Fortress that way, writing that it was "[a] large room with high ceilings, nine to ten steps long and five to six wide, with an asphalt floor and a small semi-circled window with iron bars almost at the level of the ceiling, through which only the upper half of the prison wall and a small patch of the sky were visible."[14] Sinegub's description was virtually identical.[15] Chudnovskii describes a square space, "[T]he cell provided me was substantially larger in width and length than my former abodes—a cell in the Odessa prisons and one in the "holding pen" but with far less light than in either of these places."[16] Almost all the memoirs note that their "new lodgings" were more spacious than those that had allotted to them when they were in preliminary detention. Sinegub in particular noted that the cell in the House of Preliminary Detention had been almost half the size and that its ceilings were much lower than those he later had at the Peter-Paul Fortress. The cramped cell was stuffed with furniture, leaving precious little space to move about, so that "I felt as if I were truly in my grave."[17]

Other prisoners took careful note of the furnishings in their dwellings. Charushin writes, "A cot, a small table and a stool, and then in one corner a wash basin and in the other a slop bucket—such were the contents of my new domicile."[18] In Vladimir Debogorii-Mokrievich's cell in the prison in Kiev were a wooden bed with a straw mattress and pillow, a small wooden table set near the window, a chair and small stove; he, too, remarks, "[S]uch were the furnishings of my new home."[19] Chudnovskii provides a more detailed description of "a bed and a mattress which were not attached to the wall and hence could be moved about during the day at the discretion of the prisoner; a tiny table and stool and a rather primitive water closet... state-issued bedding—sheets, pillow case, towel and blanket—were of decent quality and were changed once a week. In general, if you could overlook the inevitable dampness and the reflected light coming filtered through the bars crossing the windows and so harmful for one's vision, conditions in the prison were quite tolerable."[20] Charushin was also quite struck by the fact that his linen and underwear were replaced weekly.

Descriptions of the cells in the Shlisselburg Fortress differ only in the details. But since the prisoners spent roughly two decades there, cells began fill up with their possessions and with furniture they themselves had built in the prison workshop, and even with flowers on the windowsills (the administration allowed this). Novorusskii described his cell, "At first it was virtually empty, graced only by a small table, an iron bed, a stool and a wash basin, "and absolutely nothing else."[21] Then he was moved to a different building that had fewer cells. Despite this fact, by the end of his term he virtually occupied three separate cells—using one as a bedroom, another as a living room, and the third as a workshop. The furniture in his "living" space consisted of two commodes, shelves, a corner table with drawers, an armchair, and a stool. When he departed the prison Novorusskii took with him some thirty boxes containing the natural science collection he had assembled during his incarceration (he had even managed to build himself two larger steamer chests to hold his possessions).

With the passage of time these cells became their homes, and they themselves came to perceive them as domesticated space. Returning from an interrogation or appearance in front of the court, they breathed a sigh of relief to be "home," to be able to relax after the irritating or exhausting impressions of the "outside world." Novorusskii, recalling his walks in the yard of the Shlisselburg Fortress, noted that while such excursions provided the pleasure of fresh air and exposure to the sun, they also allowed memories of an irretrievable past to creep back in and undermine one's emotional balance so much that returning to one's cell was actually a relief. He quotes from a poem written by Figner, "It seemed easier to breathe / in my suffocating and cramped cell."[22] Despite the seeming contradiction of breathing more easily in a confined space, these lines reflect well the common perception that the cell was one's own, an emotionally inhabited and protected space.

Finally, the cell was not only one's own domesticated space, but also a site of shared experiences. The incarcerated revolutionaries were aware of and often reflected upon those who had come before them and inhabited these cells. By reassuring them of their place in a grander historical endeavor, the link with their predecessors provided compensation for the loss of identity involved in the ritualized disrobing and stripping of individual possessions.

"AROUND US REIGNED THE STULTIFYING SILENCE OF THE GRAVE"

Prominent in the recollections of those who had been incarcerated were the polarities of sound and silence, customary and unanticipated noises, both of which could provoke irritation, psychological unease, and gradually, almost imperceptibly made up an essential component of memory. Charushin recalled, "Around us reigned the stultifying silence of the grave, broken only by the stealthy footsteps of the guards making their rounds every ten to fifteen minutes ... the outside world encroached only in muffled sounds, except that is for the resounding and melancholy pealing of the Peter-Paul church bells every quarter-hour. At noon too, there was the deafening roar of the cannon being fired, a sound which often caught me off guard."[23]

Indeed, the ringing of the church chimes at the Peter-Paul Fortress provoked strong, but differing reactions among the prisoners. It probably didn't help that the hymn "God Save the Tsar" was often the melody played. Chudnovskii wrote of the chimes' "monotonal" sounds acting on his nerves.[24] Sinegub initially liked the chimes, then recalled being strongly agitated, "and this, every hour!" and he claimed that the sounds also drove others to a state resembling hysteria, to the point that they covered their ears in anticipating that "damned sound." After several months, he admitted, the "strange agitation" caused by these chimes faded and that he stopped noticing when they rang out.[25] Novorusskii, by contrast, found something redeeming and uplifting in the chimes, especially as the moment of release approached "even the depressing chiming of the bells in the tower, marking the passage of every quarter hour, like a funeral dirge, was for each novitiate coming under the spell of this music ... like a playful melody. And with the passing of every hour this melody brought with it a firm conviction that freedom and life would triumph."[26]

Upon arriving at the Peter-Paul Fortress, Charushin had initially actually welcomed the silence he encountered, after the unremitting clamor coming out of the sections for the common criminals in the Litovskii Fortress. And judging by his comments above, the pervasive silence seems to have gradually muffled even the ringing out of the hours, at least in his memory, and become oppressive. Deutsch wrote of the petrifying silence in which "all movements took place in silence, without the slightest sound, as if you were in a cemetery for the dead rather than a long-inhabited place."[27] Describing his initial period at the Peter-Paul Fortress, Chudnovskii, in contrast, noted that "within weeks the pervasive silence of the grave ceased to be positively frightening."[28]

Perhaps the most evocative and nuanced description of the silence in these facilities (this time, at the Shlisselburg Fortress) was penned by Vera Figner. Likewise labeling it the "silence of the dead," she called it "that fearsome silence which overcomes a person when he remains alone in the presence of the deceased. Without a word this silence somehow speaks to you, tells you something, reprimands, or even threatens you."²⁹ In her rendition, silence becomes the protagonist in a drama, a presence in the prison exerting a special power and capacity to influence those in residence. She labels silence the most excruciating of instruments of torture, capable of undermining one's nervous system. On the other hand, in the prevailing silence the prisoner's hearing becomes far more sensitive and incapable of bearing even the most ordinary sounds, which come across as piercing and disconcerting, provoking involuntary shrieks or sobbing. Such interruptions "are so intolerable that a person loses all control . . . begins to strike out at anything around him in order to bring the physical suffering to an end."³⁰ Many years after their time at Shlisselburg, she and others found it extremely difficult to tolerate the ordinary sounds of everyday life. Figner described being surrounded by friends engaged in a calm conversation, feeling as if she were a piano on which some madman was pounding away at the keys.

The comparisons to graves or cemeteries seem at odds with the memoirists' descriptions of domesticating their cells over time. But the analogy to a cemetery was evoked not only by the reigning silence, but also by the profound and growing awareness of these young people that their earlier lives had ended; their lives were to be truncated. They were "dead" to their relatives, they could never return to the lives that had just begun, to the dreams they had pursued before entering a prison which they might never leave. Hence the sensation of having been buried alive, or as Charushin put it, "in these grave[s], condemned to inactivity," and then, "my new dwelling was simply a stone grave with a tiny aperture at the top."³¹ In his poetry, Sinegub also sought to recreate the sensation of having been buried alive.³²

Whereas there were regular interruptions of the silence at the Peter-Paul Fortress, by the chimes and by cannon shots, at Shlisselburg a special silence reigned. Figner wrote that this was a silence that "slowly took possession of you, envelopes you, seeps into every pore of your body, your mind, your very soul. . . . And the [unanticipated] sounds! Those awful sounds which erupt without any warning, terrifying you, and then they vanish."³³ Silence had a devastating impact on the psyches of the prisoners: "Premonitions of the future began to wear away at the spirit; in the midst of this overarching silence something just had to happen, you knew it. There was no escaping it, it would happen and be more terrifying than anything you could imagine."³⁴

"THE VARIETY OF THE MENU SELECTIONS WAS SURPRISING"

Discussions of the food offered to the prisoners provide yet another marker of the prison habitat, linking it with home and the kitchen and separating it out at the same time. Charushin confessed that he was struck by the abundance of well-prepared food that was provided—two repasts daily, and three on holidays. Chudnovskii also wrote of the abundance of the offerings at the Peter-Paul Fortress; he remembered having three meals a day ordinarily, and four meals on holidays: "In the mornings and evening[s] we were brought a cup of tea and three sugar cubes along with two buns of white bread. At noon dinner was served, consisting usually of three servings: borsch or other soup with meat; a roast, meatballs, beefsteak or veal—the meat offering varied every day—and something sweet. Around eight in the evening we were also served something with meat."³⁵ Sinegub likewise describes not only abundant, but delicious food.³⁶ The only dissenting voice was that of Deutch, who groused that "although the food there wasn't bad, it was not enough and often delivered cold."³⁷

The food served at the House of Preliminary Detention was far less satisfactory: lunch was cabbage soup and buckwheat groats; breakfast and supper consisted of hot water and bread of inferior quality.³⁸ At the same time, Charushin acknowledged that it was thanks to the simple fare served there that he was healed of the chronic gastritis that he had developed at the Peter-Paul Fortress, despite the rich offerings there. Sinegub's recollections of the food served at the House of Preliminary Detention were similar to those of Charushin, but Sinegub found the food "disgusting"; it gave him heartburn, "which just further depressed me and contributed to my melancholy."³⁹ But he used his personal funds (money that was allowed to brought to him by people on the outside) to improve his diet by paying the cook to cook him special meals or purchasing produce through the guards; he even got a doctor's note allowing him to have wine in his cell.⁴⁰ Of course, assessments of the quality of the food served up in prison depended upon the prisoner's previous experience. For example, Novorusskii noted that the barely tolerable cabbage soup and kasha he ate in Shlisselburg did not bother him since it resembled what he had been served while a seminary student, where "the food was so repulsive that a starving hard labor convict would have turned his nose up at it."[41]

Those who spent long years at Shlisselburg learned how to supplement their diets by using kerosene lamps to prepare their own food. Novorusskii even remembered that later on, he and others gained access to a stove they used to prepare condiments and diversify the menus, thereby managing to avoid the scurvy that had tormented them in their early years there. He also confessed that with his background in chemistry and permission he received to conduct scientific experiments there, he learned how to distill spirits: "I made vodka out of carrots, beets, the roots of bind-weed, a very starchy weed which grew all around us, from treacle, both purchased and our own; sugar, and of course from potatoes, bread and a variety of berries."[42]

Making their own alcohol was probably above all a way of relieving the monotony of their lives and also an adventure of sorts; the memoirs show that the prisoners delighted in any new activity, including those permitted by the administration, whether that was establishing a herbarium or breeding poultry (the latter was something taken up by both Vera Figner and Mikhail Frolenko—who managed to set up a model poultry operation producing up to one hundred chickens in one summer)."[43]

For many the passage of time was marked by the dinner hours; as for the opportunities to purchase produce or receive care packages from the outside, these maintained a sense of contact with the outside world and punctured the feeling of utter isolation. Charushin remembered, "[T]he surreptitious and regular deliveries from the world outside served as testimony that not all was lost, that there were still people out there who could look after those upon whom misfortune had fallen, something that meant a lot to those of us sitting in prison and lifted our spirits... more than the content of the deliveries we were interested in the strangers who brought them to us."[44] Liubov Kornilova and Larisa Chemodanova worked tirelessly to organize aid for the prisoners, sending along personal items, food, and books. As Kornilova's sister remarked that "during visitation days (they) brought along packages for up to twenty prisoners, providing them with fresh linen and homemade cooking."[45]

Along with eating, smoking was another activity associated with home that carried over into prison life. Sinegub recalled that he had earlier given up on that habit but returned to it (on the advice of a friendly gendarme). Cigarettes could be purchased through the guards or by ration (eleven a day was the norm).[46] Deprived of the opportunity to read (his eyeglasses had been taken away), Deutch turned to smoking for relaxation, and it "became my fellow conversationalist and friend—in general it made prisoners feel better, less alone and cast away."[47] Charushin also smoked while imprisoned, but most likely simply as a carry-over from the past, for he didn't make special mention of it. Lev Tikhomirov, on the other hand, recalled that his consumption of cigarettes doubled or even trebled, but then he entirely quit in the hope that an obsession with his unrequited addiction to tobacco would crowd out thoughts about the hopelessness of his situation.[48]

"A HUNGER STRIKE NOT FOR THREE TO FOUR DAYS, BUT UNTIL THE BITTER END"

If food and the rituals surrounding it were prominent in the lives of the incarcerated, hunger strikes were often the only way prisoners had to manifest their discontent. Novorusskii explained that regardless of the consequences to their own health, he and his friends could turn to hunger strikes to address a number of complaints. The frequent resort to hunger strikes in a number of prisons was a weighty argument in favor of the practice, but Novorusskii noted that in most cases the decision to strike was spontaneous, an impulsive rather than reasoned response to accumulated grievances, and triggered by a seemingly random incident. Such, for example, was the cause of hunger strike in Shlisselburg brought on by the decision to remove some of the books in the prison library, a decision which the prisoners treated as a threat to all the hard-won mitigations they had achieved in the prison regime. A hunger strike was capable of achieving results, because the administration feared scandal or even increased attention on the part of higher-ups. As Novorusskii commented, "Most important here, as with any other incident out of the ordinary, [hunger strikes] were unpredictable, and such dramas made the local administration fear for tomorrow. For them as for all bureaucrats, they were above all concerned with predictability and their own safety."⁴⁹

The demonstration of solidarity was key in staging a hunger strike, whether it be individual or collective. The latter were the most difficult to sustain, since the health of the prisoners varied widely and not all could hold up to lengthy deprivation. Because of this the prisoners themselves could be responsible for the death of a comrade. Chudnovskii himself pointed out that when he launched a hunger strike he did so without letting his comrades know, for he didn't want to draw them into a struggle they were not physically able to withstand. Novorusskii also described another hunger strike at Shlisselburg whose initiators had not taken into account the condition of their fellow prisoners. By the eighth day of the strike, the health of one of the participants was rapidly deteriorating, and another tried to commit suicide, and the next day it was decided to call a halt to the strike: "As a result, and as often happened, the strike achieved little, except to irretrievably undermine the health of one prisoner who as result soon passed away. But as one in a chain of circumstances ameliorating the prison regime, it wasn't without consequences."⁵⁰

Vera Figner took a different stance toward that strike to which she devoted an entire chapter in her memoirs. Figner called the tactic of a collective hunger strike a mistake, not primarily because it might result in the loss of her comrades—something she was willing to accept—but because not all of the prisoners had the fortitude or solidarity to carry out such strikes to the very end. She believed that the prisoners were fully aware of the possibility that one of them might perish as a result of the action, but she believed the risk to be justified: "Go on a hunger strike, not for three to four days, but until the bitter end. Let there be one casualty, let there be more, but we will defend the right to have access to books, the only things that brighten up our lives."⁵¹

For Figner, the hunger strike was a bitter experience, not so much because of the physical deprivation, but for the spiritual blow it had delivered. She had expected others to demonstrate the same resolution and solidarity that she was capable of, but it turned out otherwise. She described the decision to terminate the strike as a manifestation of weakness, for it was not worthy of a genuine revolutionary to hesitate in the face of trials. She herself held on for another two days after others had quit, and conceded only after two of her fellow prisoners threatened her with suicide should she herself perish from malnutrition. She was also extremely perturbed by the pressure that put on her, treating it as an infringement upon her free will and spiritual core, "This was moral extortion and made me furious."[52]

Another instance was a hunger strike at the Peter-Paul Fortress during which the participants demanded improvements in their conditions (the right to take walks together and to communicate with their comrades) or transfers to a pre-trial facility, such as the House of Preliminary Detention, where conditions were more liberal—since their guilt had not yet been established. Sinegub devoted an entire chapter of his memoirs to that hunger strike as an example of group solidarity, since the prisoners who had already been sentenced, and who consequently enjoyed certain privileges, had initiated the strike in support of those still under investigation. Explaining the reasons for the hunger strike to the general of the gendarmes, Sinegub said he could not allow himself to eat while others around him went hungry. The participants called off the action after the general promised to accede to the demands of the inmates being held in preliminary detention to be moved to appropriate quarters in a different prison. But they soon learned they had been deceived; instead of being moved to a more liberal pre-trail facility, they were moved to a far worse site within the Peter-Paul Fortress itself.[53] The prisoners contemplated renewing the strike but ultimately could not reach a consensus on the question. Sinegub himself had argued against it, since he had received word of the contemplated assassination of the head of the gendarmes, Mezentsev, by Sergei Kravchinskii in retaliation for his cruel treatment of prisoners and in solidarity with the planned strike. Sinegub opposed acts of terror, and hoped to dissuade Kravchinskii from his plans by convincing him conditions were not in fact so bad in the prison.[54]

"TIME DRAGGED ON TORTUROUSLY AND WITHOUT PURPOSE"

If their experience of space was central in the memoirs of the revolutionaries, no less so was the category of time. For the unfree the passage of time was torturous and quite unlike their experience outside the prison walls. That "other" temporality encountered while incarcerated moved in its own fashion, according to carceral arrangements and the length of the term to which the prisoner was subjected. Charushin recalled that his stay in the Litovskii Fortress, where he spent more than a year, was "monotonous and drawn out," each day replicating the previous one: "Because of its oppressive predictability, time dragged on; on the other hand it seemed as if time flew by. Even after several months in prison, thanks to its repetitiveness, the distance in time from when you were free seemed minimal, despite the fact that your life before prison was now but a vague memory."[55]

The memoirs convey a sense of time slowing down and warping in prison. Chernavskii remembered, "The minutes crept by unbearably slowly . . . minutes, hours, days, months—you look back but see nothing but emptiness; a year seems just like a minute, and a minute like a year."[56] Chudnovskii wrote of solitary confinement in a prison in Odessa as "[those] prolonged, protracted, endless and cruelly vitiating days, months, years."[57] Confined to the House of Preliminary Detention, he prepared himself for a long stay and later recalled, "Time there stretched out into infinity and I stopped keeping track."[58]

Vera Figner entitled the volume of her memoirs devoted to her two decades at Shlisselburg *When the Clock of Life Stopped*. If time passed slowly for those awaiting trial in the Peter-Paul or Litovskii prisons (Charushin was imprisoned three months before he was informed of the charges against him), for those serving a life term in Shlisselburg, time essentially lost all meaning. To cope with the pain of loss, they did their best to erase the past from their memories, but they had no future, and the unchanging present gave them no markers of elapsed time—if anything, it became circular rather than linear. Novorusskii commented, "The almost total lack of notable changes, no matter how severe the regime we endured, made us feel that life had come to a complete standstill. Whether outside our own selves or internally there was nothing by which one could mark the passage of time. It had stopped—or more accurately, it did not exist for us."[59]

Only exacerbating this sense of a temporal void was the enforced inactivity. Combined with the absence of external stimulation, this resulted in quite acute psychological difficulties for a young cohort quite accustomed to a bustling life rich with experiences, excitement and even danger, suffused with intense interpersonal interactions, full of purposeful propagandistic activities and even physical labors. As Sinegub succinctly put it, "[T]he involuntarily idleness tore away at us";⁶⁰ "there were days when I simply couldn't figure out what to do with myself, I was unbearably tired of it all."⁶¹

Inactivity turned the prisoners inward, forcing them to concentrate on their suffering and regrets, causing them, often against their will, to replay the past repeatedly in their minds, which sometimes led to instability and depression. Forced either to lie on their cots or to pace from corner to corner in the cell, at times they lost all sensibility. Charushin wrote that this unhealthy way of spending time drained all his strength, and led to "extreme nervous agitation along with stupefaction."⁶² The monotony and utter meaningless of each passing day were essential attributes of prison life and, as Foucault famously noted, were directed as much at the spirit as at the body of the person. Novorusskii even commented that the enforced idleness led him to dream of being sent off to the mines to do hard labor as a respite from the senseless and demoralizing confinement to the cell.⁶³

MEANINGFUL ACTIVITIES

Unsurprisingly then, the long-term prisoners at Shlisselburg responded enthusiastically when they were provided with the opportunity to engage in crafts, such as carpentry, joinery, book-binding, and horticulture; to set up workshops; and even take special orders for visual aids and other school or museum items. Figner wrote, "We bustled about our work: the joiners and lathe operators planed, sharpened and polished, the book binders made boxes out of cardboard on the side; the nature enthusiasts set up a fantastic herbarium . . . a collection of moss and lichens, water lilies and mushrooms, another one of fruits and seeds; they prepared hundreds of glass plates for dried flowers, gathered up a variety of mountain rocks, minerals, and ores, put together an insect collection, and so on."⁶⁴ In the prison courtyard they created a garden, planted flowers and saplings (sending away for special seeds), built a pathway made of limestone tiles, and regularly made furniture for the cells. Novorusskii called the urge to be productive natural, "our sole means of salvation, bolstering our physical vitality and not allowing us to wither away from immobility and inactivity."[65]

Others took to physical exercise. Sinegub decided to combat the dreariness of his existence brought on by inactivity and the absence of external stimulation by turning to exercise for its own sake. He began a daily regimen, regularly scrubbed his cell and even requested permission to clean other cells. After such labors, his appetite and mood improved, he slept better, and his nerves stabilized. By the time he was moved from the Peter-Paul Fortress to the House of Preliminary Detention, his appearance had also significantly improved, "From a sickly, emaciated and stunted figure with a pasty complexion, listless and eaten up with despair to the point of thoughts of suicide, I had turned into an energetic, almost happy young fellow with a good complexion."[66]

Books offered variety in prison life, and for many reading was the only accessible form of activity. Sinegub remembered that "for almost a year and a half I did nothing but lie in bed until evening reading, while I passed the night pacing from one corner to the other thinking, dreaming, composing poems for myself."[67] For Figner, reading was a distraction from oppressive thoughts and took up time that she would otherwise have spent fretting over her fate, that of her comrades and of their cause. She began studying English, and soon was able to read Thomas Macaulay's *History of England* in the original. She recalled, "Even at the start I energetically took to reading and did so with a pleasure and reward never elsewhere experienced . . . reading was my salvation . . . from the outset of my incarceration it helped to stifle the pain brought on by all sorts of woes of a societal nature."[68]

Charushin likewise remembered that the activity of "reading alone, to which I devoted the better part of my time, saved me from complete stupefaction."[69] But he also admitted that many of the books that had deeply influenced him before his arrest he now found unpalatable. In particular, works by Saltykov-Shchedrin and Gleb Uspensky, whose exposés of Russian life he had avidly devoured, now only further acted on his nerves, exacerbating his already parlous emotional state. Following his initial stay at the Litovskii prison, access to the rich library at the Peter-Paul Fortress offered him an escape from his life in confinement and he took up reading with a gusto. But the longer he languished there without any word about his fate and devoid of any human contact, the less reading satisfied him; it gradually became yet another component of the monotonous prison regime and eventually positively irritated him. "Reading, more reading, and endlessly wandering from corner to corner, nothing else at all!"[70]

At that time, prisoners were not allowed to have on their person writing paraphernalia, which seriously limited their range of activities. Once they were allowed pen and paper, they added note-taking to serious reading, as a means of enhancing what had often been an inadequate education. Such sustained efforts helped fill the time, added meaning to their lives, and helped make up for the truncated schooling many had as a result of following Lavrov's injunction to give it all up and join the people in their struggle for emancipation. Now they were intrigued by the prospect of learning languages, studying the sciences, and pursuing knowledge in general. During his stay in the Peter-Paul prison, Sinegub completed the gymnasium program in mathematics and studied English and French so that he would be able to read works in the original language;[71] he took to reading the classics of Russian historical writing (Kostomarov, Solov'ev, and others), and studied political economy. He later confessed, "Had I remained free, I would never have read as much . . . more importantly I would never have concentrated on the reading in the manner I did, since the lack of other stimuli made reading the only food for thought. Life would not have provided the opportunity . . . which the quiet of solitude and thirst for impressions and events did in prison."[72]

Alexandra Kornilova remembered her time of imprisonment as the most difficult but also most productive in her life, "My health suffered, but attentive, uninterrupted reading allowed me to work out my own worldview."[73] Figner also admitted that before prison her reading had been spotty and unsystematic. The institute for girls of the nobility in Kazan' had lacked a library; at the university in Zurich she had concentrated solely on medicine, and when she served as a paramedic for the zemstvo in the countryside, her efforts had been devoted entirely to health care. As for the time she spent underground, reading was out of the question, "Only in prison . . . could I turn to the subjects which especially interested me: history, political economy, as well as reading everything written by [Herbert] Spencer on biology and psychology."[74] She also recalled being especially fascinated when she learned about the Chautauqua adult education movement founded in 1874 in America[75] and resolved to go beyond mere reading to systematic study of the natural sciences. Her fellow prisoners decided to organize group courses and lectures, which enhanced their knowledge but also provided the satisfaction of intellectual endeavor and exchanges.[76] Many of the friendships formed in these study groups lasted well after release from Shlisselburg.

Being able to have on hand pen and paper led the inmates not only to taking notes on scholarly readings, but also to thoughts of recording their life experiences. Evidently, thinking about their place in history and the wish to be remembered by successive generations began early with this cohort. Sinegub wrote a draft of an autobiographical novelette in prison, which he called "Remembrances of a Distant Past";[77] it was perhaps the first stab at composing a collective narrative of the movement. In 1877, the censors confiscated a note Charushin had written to Kuvshinskaia (and which she evidently never saw) about the need to put together an edited volume of biographies of the prisoners who had perished while in prison or exile, and to find reliable people to carry out this work.[78]

Figner later wrote that all these efforts added spiritual meaning to the lives of the incarcerated, providing them a sense of purpose and connection. But readings, crafts, physical activities, dabbling at memoir writing—none of this could fully replace the real world outside. Instead, it was a survival mechanism, a means of adapting to the cruel realities of incarceration; a "surrogate life," as Chudnovskii called their daily existence, even as he acknowledged the enormous importance of such activities for those pining away in prison.[79]

"I YEARNED TO SEE PEOPLE AND HEAR LIVE VOICES"

The protracted absence of human contact during long periods of solitary confinement was yet another trial for the imprisoned revolutionaries—even the guards were forbidden to speak with them. Charushin, whose friends noted over and over again how reserved and reluctant to share his feelings and impressions he was, nevertheless experienced severe loneliness there and admitted that "he yearned to see people and hear live voices, to share impressions and responses to what they were going through."[80] He later recalled that during his stay at the House of Preliminary Detention, out of desuetude he even began to forget how to pronounce certain words. Figner, remembering her twenty-month pretrial stay in the Peter-Paul Fortress wrote:

> Silence, unending silence... vocal chords weakening, atrophying out of disuse; my voice breaking, fading, changing from a deep contralto to one that was thin, reedy, tremulous, as if after a serious illness; words stumbled out of my mouth in bursts. Along with the disruption of my speech organs, my psyche underwent changes: I began to crave silence. Except for when absolutely necessary I just wanted to stay quiet (the internal impulse to communicate was gone) so that when I had to speak, actually getting words out required an act of will to overcome my reticence.[81]

Those in solitary confinement in the Peter-Paul Fortress nevertheless devised ways to communicate despite every effort by the prison administration to prevent it. They quickly mastered the prison tap code and began to share information about prison goings-on and simply chat with each other. Charushin remembered that he initially had no opportunity to communicate, for in both the Litovskii and the Peter-Paul prisons the adjacent cells had been empty. After he was relocated to the House of Preliminary Detention, where the walls happened to convey sound marvelously, he was able to take part in the life of the prison, doing so at first haltingly, but then with full command of the (Cyrillic) tap code.[82] For Sinegub, being able to communicate this way revived him, helping him to overcome his profound loneliness and to be connected with others, so that "life became much fuller."[83] He even attributed improved sleep and appetite to this new development. We see the same situation in Shlisselburg. Novorusskii remembered that he would tap away for hours on end; another convict managed to tap out the entire political program of the Social Democratic Party. Novorusskii "spent twilight time tapping" with Vera Figner, especially when the weather was cloudy and the light murky in the cells, making reading impossible.[84]

Another form of communication in the House of Preliminary Detention were the "clubs" created through utilization of the sewage pipes: "A prisoner would position himself next to the toilet seat, summon those above or below him in their cells, and carry on a conversation sometimes for hours on end."[85] Novorusskii wrote about using such "water closet clubs," but admitted that despite their strong desire to communicate, "I can't say we were terribly enthused about this type of telephone. There were long stretches when I simply couldn't do it; after all it wasn't all that easy to overcome one's squeamishness, and it was only the dire circumstances and crying need for human contact that made one ignore the conditions involved. Some in fact just refrained, almost never resorting to communicating with their close friends by utilizing these odiferous pipes."[86] Charushin also testified that he rarely utilized this method of maintaining contact, finding it "exhausting."[87]

Describing life in the House of Preliminary Detention, Charushin wrote: "Constant tapping took place openly, club meetings went on without interruption, and sometimes the common criminals and even the prison guards carried messages."[88] After a lengthy period of solitary confinement, Charushin eagerly sought to compensate for the lack of human contact, although as he had noted, tapping could hardly be called full-blooded interaction. But he soon realized that he had become so unused to being around people that even this communication exhausted him and acted upon his nerves and that he actually was "happy when he was once again left on his own."[89] Alexandra Kornilova experienced the same roller coaster of emotional reactions, writing later that "after the total silence . . . prevailing in the [Peter-Paul] Fortress, initially the code tapping and club conversations through the water-closet as well as noise in general wore me out."[90]

Later, during the Trial of the 193, Charushin, despite his joy at being reunited with friends, soon "began to yearn to be returned to his cell and be on his own once again. Apparently, the serving of human interaction provided me was simply too large to be properly digested at the time."[91] He wondered if he would ever be able to return to his former self and function in society. Later, Vera Figner had an identical reaction during her own trial: "After the silence and solitude of the Peter-Paul Fortress any change of circumstances was intolerable. Bewildered at the sight of my comrades, overstimulated by the propinquity and voices of other living people and by the light of the chandeliers in the evening, I was unable to sit through even a single session and retreated to my cell to give my frayed nerves a breather."[92]

Letters were another mode of communication. A lively exchange of them took place in the House of Preliminary Detention, facilitated by common criminals and even jailers recruited as mail carriers, who did it sometimes for money and sometimes out of sympathy for the prisoners' cause. Several of the inmates also noted that ropes were extended across the length of the outside walls, used to transfer books, letters, food, and clothing from one cell to another.[93] Notes were written and exchanged in person as well. Charushin recalled hiding notes for Kuvshinskaia in the ankle of his boots, since prisoners in the House of Preliminary Detention were allowed to wear their own clothing and footwear.[94] This exchange of letters continued until he was returned to the Peter-Paul Fortress, where a whole packet of letters was discovered during a body search and taken from him. Later, to his surprise, he was taken aback to be reminded by the gendarmes of the content of one of these notes, even though it was completely innocent politically speaking, if embarrassingly intimate, especially for the reticent Charushin.

Prisoners were also officially permitted to exchange letters with family members, but the letters were always examined by the prison authorities, which made it psychologically difficult to write them. Charushin admitted that he could not force himself to write "letters of an intimate nature that would be opened and read by the gendarmes, who might smack their chops at what they read or in perusing my words be able to divine my state of mind. With such thoughts, I lost the aptitude to put pen to paper; because of this in the entire four years I spent in preliminary detention I never wrote anyone a single line."[95]

Contrary to the widespread perception of a conflict between fathers and sons, the majority of the Populists maintained firm bonds and warm relations with their parents, regardless of political views. Another time Charushin was searched, a letter was found from his mother asking him in what university he had enrolled and conveying news about other relatives.[96] At the same time, in 1913, almost a decade after her release, Figner reread the letters she had written from the Peter-Paul Fortress and Shlisselburg and confessed to her sister that they had "provoked a strange reaction—that they were something forced, artificial. I was bored reading them, and it took me two tries before I could actually stick with it. I finally did so, and noticed that from 1884 they became livelier—as if I stopped holding back and a genuine note begins to show through. It was the censorship which held us back from expressing ourselves and robbed us of our personality."[97] More than this, several prisoners sought to prevent their families from learning about their dismal fates, preferring to keep them in the dark rather than cause them distress.

But for others, meetings with relatives were highly valued. Kuvshinskaia, who herself spent considerable time in confinement, managed to arrange meetings with Charushin based on her status as his fiancée. The meetings relieved the monotony of prison life, brought information and fresh impressions, provided emotional support, and made the prisoners feel alive. Charushin recalled, "We came alive during these brief but always joyful meetings, paid no heed to the future, shared our stories of what had happened in the intervening years, what we knew about others, and our opinions about the coming trials and how we should conduct in front of the court."[98] Sinegub confessed that he lived for his meetings every Friday with Larisa Chemodanova. Yet a note from him to her has been preserved in which he, despite the huge meaning her visits had for him, cautioned against her coming, fearing for her well-being, "No-no, sweetheart, I am prepared to endure the acute pain of separation no matter how long if only you will be alive and well!"[99]

Visitations were allowed only with the presence of jailers, but in his memoirs Sinegub describes his meetings with Chemodanova as if they were alone, perhaps also because those observing them did keep their distance: "We were seated on a small couch, tightly embraced one another and were able to kiss. I could kiss her as much as I wanted, kiss and stroke the hand of my wife . . . and we conversed about what we were reading, about those close to us."[100]

Kissing was undoubtedly pleasurable in and of itself, but also served the utilitarian purpose of conveying written messages through the act, something widely practiced. The rules governing visitations were eventually changed so that meetings were allowed only when prisoner and visitor were separated by two window bars; all physical contact was forbidden. This became yet another source of punishment and tribulation; Figner recalled bitterly, "On several occasions I was stopped from kissing the hand of my mother. Once during an especially difficult time for me, I entreated the attendant to allow me to stroke her, to put my lips to her little warm hand. No luck! The rules wouldn't allow it."[101]

Charushin's reticence, in contrast to Sinegub's open declarations of his boundless love for his wife and the vital importance of their physical contact, can be explained by differences in temperament but also by circumstances. He and Kuvshinskaia were not yet married. More than that, he was actively trying to discourage her from binding her life to his, for he considered his life to be over, with no prospects for a future.

At the same time, he considered his sole meeting with his brother Arkadii to be among the most important events of his four years in confinement, for it caused him a good deal of emotional turbulence and provoked a flood of family memories. After the meeting, Charushin struggled mightily to restore his emotional balance and settle back in to his daily existence.[102] This meeting in the Peter-Paul Fortress was also of great significance for Arkadii, who had long fought for permission to see his brother. Not long afterward Arkadii wrote a novelette fictionalizing the meeting and the events leading up to it, a work that remained unpublished during his lifetime. It was discovered by his brother when he was collecting Arkadii's belongings after his death in 1922 and published in the journal *Katorga i Ssylka (Hard Labor and Exile)*.[103] The younger brother, despite his somewhat different political views, his determination to receive a university education and gain a career, wrote lovingly and admiringly of Nikolai, confined to the formidable Peter-Paul Fortress. During a three-hour wait for the meeting to happen, Arkadii became acutely aware of the foreboding silence in the prison and the feeling of entrapment created by the stone walls. By contrast to the pallid, oppressive surroundings, his brother emerges as his old self, free of the "kingdom of the dead"; "his russet beard sprinkled with gold twinkled in the gloom; and now he caught sight of the open, joyous smile visible under his mustache . . . his reflective and profound gaze focused upon [Arkadii] . . . his enduring love shone through."[104] The effort made by Arkadii to see the older brother whom he had revered since childhood was only the first in a series of interventions, but it was the one Nikolai would never forget.

"THE POTENTIAL FOR GOING MAD TERRIFIED ME"

The dreary monotony of daily life, inactivity, lack of external stimulation, and confined space—despite the best efforts of the prisoners to combat the effect of prison realities, all of this took their toll on the prisoners' psyches. All of those who later wrote about it spoke of fear of going mad or having psychotic episodes. Charushin noted, "At times I even began to fear the worst—insanity. Death, for which I had long prepared, was not imminent, but the potential for losing my mind terrified me";[105] and "the slightest trifle irritated me, my nerves were totally frayed."[106] Chernavskii's memoirs tell of others who did lose their minds and how that led him to fear for himself, "I developed a deep-seated and unremitting anxiety, and began to watch myself... without recognizing it, the diffuse fear of insanity was gradually crowded out by an equally diffuse fear of the appearance before me of my own double."[107] Chudnovskii observed that many around him suffered hallucinations to the point of delirium; the slightest untoward event or noise could produce mass psychosis. Tales they shared about the jailors' torture or humiliations of other prisoners taxed their already overwrought imaginations and exacerbated their fears. Chudnovskii described an incident when upon hearing shouting he lost self-control and began to experience a split personality, "[S]hortly afterward I found myself next to the door, took to frantically stomping and kicking with my feet, desperately pummeled the door with my hands, a book, my entire body (corpus). 'Gu-ar-d, Gu-ard!' I yelled, but in somebody else's voice. 'Prosecutor, pro-sec-ut-or, I demand the prosecutor, summon him now!' screamed the inner 'I' to the dismay of the outer 'I.'"[108]

All the prisoners were aware of being constantly watched in their cells and of their total lack of privacy, since the doors to their cells were fitted with peepholes through which the attendant could always look. Charushin recalled, "Two eyes were fixed upon you. At first this amused, then irritated, and finally infuriated me."[109] Sinegub was also annoyed at seeing the two eyes of the guard, whom he considered to be especially stupid. Many prisoners spit at the "eyes," tried to stuff a book in the peephole or yelled at their guard. Novorusskii, comparing his stays in the Peter-Paul Fortress and Shlisselburg, noted that surveillance at the latter had been constant, almost every minute of the day, and was therefore far more onerous, "And it drove us crazy at first! It made you think that they did this not so much for surveillance as to get under our skin, so that the prisoner wouldn't think even for a minute that he was a free man."[110] He recalled that after a year or so he resigned himself to this constant surveillance and began to look on the "spying" with indifference; others, however, continued to be profoundly upset and agitated by this unceremonious observation. It was even more difficult for the women to endure, and at Shlisselburg, they won the privilege of covering the peephole with a piece of cloth as decency demanded.

The memoirists often referred to cases of insanity as corroboration of the sacrifices their comrades had made of their lives. Young Populists who had experienced the hardships, strict regimes, and abysmal conditions of the central prisons and had no clue as to what their fates would be were sometimes unable to hold up under the psychological and emotional stress. Some of them committed suicide, seeing it as an escape from an intolerable life, or while experiencing severe depression they were unable to overcome despite their best efforts. As Chudnovskii wrote, "It certainly took a lot of life-affirming energy and faith in a better future... it called for considerable self-control to find a way to make peace with such oppressive circumstances."[111]

Long years or even decades of solitary confinement in Shlisselburg put all those who had endured them in a precarious psychological state. As Novorusskii observed, the probability of mental disorders was increased by the lack of external stimuli, interpersonal interactions, or other activities—an absence that put the imagination into high gear trying to compensate for the emptiness of their lives. Events from the past crowded into their minds, sometimes so vividly as to become hallucinatory. The hopelessness of their situation brought on thoughts of suicide and maintaining control over their thought processes was a difficult task. Figner confessed that to survive the present she had made every effort to forget her past in order or face utter despair, "For ten years I held my memories at bay—buried them in a grave. Over the course of ten years my mother gradually was lost to me, and I no longer yearned for country, life or freedom. I lost the capacity to love or grieve... my memory was obscured as if by a fine film coating.... But as for myself? Despite this I was alive, even well."[112]

ESCAPE

If many prisoners found ways to adapt while others failed, lost their sanity or even their lives, still others attempted to escape from the House of Preliminary Detention. Among them was Charushin, who took part in one such group effort, recounting the effort in his memoirs.[113] The attempt at flight was a dismal failure. Charushin and the other perpetrators left their cells, descended to the floor below them, wanting to escape through a window they knew did not have bars, but in trying to open the window, they raised a ruckus, which drew the attention of their guards. The prisoners had to return to their cells and promise to raise five hundred rubles to buy the guards' silence. (Charushin somewhat dubiously justifies this bribe as not so much a desire to avoid punishment as to avoid complications for others who might be contemplating escape.)[114]

Two moments in his narrative stand out: the ambivalence he felt toward abandoning his incarcerated comrades, and the role played in the event by his jailers. Charushin explained his decision to attempt an escape (at the urging of Kovalik and Voinaral'skii) by his pessimism about the outcome of his case, the prospect of a slow death in prison, and of course, the lure of regaining his freedom. But he reproached himself for acting egotistically, for being willing to leave his friends behind in violation of the moral code of the Chaikovtsy, which called for solidarity and shared fates, "Possessed by a craving to be free I somehow lost track of the fact that in freeing myself I was shamefully leaving my comrades behind to slowly rot away in prison, something that in a more normal state of mind I could hardly have permitted myself to do."[115] At the same time, Charushin emphasized the striving of the would-be escapees to avoid bringing down repercussions on those among the prison staff who aided in the effort or those who were willing to take money and conceal the episode from the administration in the event of failure. Later, in exile in Siberia, the Chaikovtsy returned to a discussion of escape. Many of them rejected the very idea, not so much because of the exceptionally harsh conditions awaiting them in the taiga and the unlikelihood of making it to populated sites unnoticed, but out of such moral considerations, especially the potential impact on those who remained behind. In fact, when, in 1882, some former Chaikovtsy managed briefly to escape from Kara prison, others did suffer severe consequences.[116]

During their stay at the House of Preliminary Detention several other attempts at flight were made, but none succeeded. Despite the urging of his friends, Charushin took part in none of them, explaining this in his memoirs by the fragility of his health, which had left him unable to contemplate further participation in the revolutionary movement at the time.[117]

He also could not imagine fleeing the country and taking up a life in emigration. Even after being arrested multiple times by the Bolsheviks between 1917 and 1919, he decided to remain in Russia, despite the possibility of further arrests or even execution. In both cases his real motives for avoiding flight were probably complex: he knew no foreign language and had never been abroad, and his health, truly shaky throughout his life, became even more so as he aged. After the revolution, he retired to work in the quiet of the local library. Even now, incarcerated and awaiting trial, he seemed to have lost the strength to sustain interactions with people. He wrote that his nerves were shattered, but that his spirit remained boisterous.[118]

"THE GREAT TRIAL OF THE 193"

On October 18, 1877, Charushin and almost two hundred of his peers were brought before a special session of the Senate to be tried for the dubious crime of "spreading propaganda" before the population.[119] Two other mass trials had been held earlier that year; at one in particular, the Trial of the Fifty, a young woman, Sofia Bardina, had given an eloquent speech in defense of her beliefs, which had made a positive impact upon the population at large. The severe sentences handed out to the defendants in the trial were also met with public opprobrium.

These trials took place at a critical juncture for the autocracy: a combination of policy drift, the declining popularity of Alexander II, and a poorly conducted war against the Ottoman Empire made it vulnerable and anxious to refurbish its public image. At the same time, it was not clear how to deal with the revolutionary movement. The judicial reforms of 1864, which had established public trials by jury, had given the opposition a forum from which to address the public with its program. Since the early 1870s, the government had been rolling back the reform and begun resorting to administrative exile as a means of avoiding the judicial process. More than 3,800 individuals (including witnesses) had been held and interrogated during four years of preliminary detention; scores had died of disease and some had committed suicide or lost their mind. Some reckoning had to take place, and now 193 individuals were brought to trial in a process lasting until January 23, 1878. It was a dramatic affair, for the docket was so crowded it left little room for the guards, never mind the public, although in principle it was an "open" trial. The able defense lawyers[120] petitioned unsuccessfully for a change of venue, after which the majority of the accused refused to take further part in the proceedings, believing it made no sense to make speeches without an audience.

At the same time, the gathering provided a wonderful opportunity for the defendants to congregate, share stories, and support each other after long stretches of isolation, and a diverse group of revolutionaries forged new links and a collective identity. As one historian put it, "the trial was a conference of activists arranged by and paid for by the government."[121] Charushin recalled the "noisy greetings, embraces, queries about health and spirits, and conversations in haste which filled the hall with the constant drone of a beehive."[122] Kornilova wrote of "five days of uninterrupted holiday" during which the accused paid little or no attention to the readings of the charges against them.[123] A decision by the court to divide the accused into seventeen different groups and to bring them separately before the docket led to further protests. Threatened with force, the defendants did appear, only to get themselves kicked out of the courtroom for creating disturbances and insulting the judges. The public, for whom space was now available, stood in long lines in order to see to this spectacle.[124]

And spectacle it was; one revolutionary, Ippolit Myshkin, gave a fiery speech accusing the court of being a "house of ill repute" and the senators of prostituting themselves, since they were selling their souls, not for a piece of bread, but for the sake of rank, medals, and careers.[125] Full records of the proceedings were supposed to be published in the official state newspaper, but in fact only brief summaries appeared. However, the lawyers had hired their own stenographers, and a full account of the trial was soon published in Geneva, Switzerland, and smuggled back into the country.[126] Members of the public who had attended the trial also provided their own oral versions of the proceedings, all to the disadvantage of the prosecution.

The disarray and hesitation among government circles were evident in the verdicts, which ranged from five days in prison to ten years at hard labor. Ten of the defendants, including Charushin and Sinegub, received nine years each; Kuvshinskaia was acquitted, along with the majority of the accused. By releasing so many the government hoped to win over the public by displaying its magnanimity, but in the opinion of Franco Venturi, this was a huge tactical mistake—instead, society wanted an explanation for why hundreds of young people had been held for three to four years in preliminary detention if the charges against them had proven to be unfounded. The confusion of the senators was also manifest in their petition to the tsar requesting that he mitigate the sentences they themselves had imposed—a proposal Alexander II rejected. All in all, Charushin was quite correct in concluding that the authorities, hoping to discredit the Populists, had only aggravated public discontent.[127] Moreover, the public, which previously had known about the revolutionaries only by hearsay, now had had the opportunity to learn about their program. On January 24, 1878, Vera Zasulich walked into the offices of the odious governor of St. Petersburg, Trepov, and shot him point blank. The divided government decided to hand her over to an ordinary court rather than the senatorial committee concerned with political cases. A year later, the jury trying her case acquitted Zasulich, and newspapers praised the decision.

Charushin was one of a group of sixteen who, before departing for exile, signed and left behind a "Testament," providing witness to the durability of their revolutionary beliefs and urging others to pick up the baton and pursue their goals with even more vigor than they themselves had done. As Chudnovskii wrote, "[W]e were confident that such an act would resonate with youth, adding energy and fortitude, and in so doing contribute to the liberation movement."[128] They were determined that their sacrifices not be forgotten—something that they were to take up again much later in their lives.[129]

NOTES

1. According to documents of the Police Department, Charushin was arrested in Petersburg on January 11, 1874, and claimed his name was Petr Zhuravin. A search of his apartment yielded a notebook and two personal letters, as well as one recommending him as a friend of Chaikovskii; a handwritten summons to the people to rise up in protest; and the books *Anarchy and the State*, *The History of the International*, and others, GARF, f. 102, D-3, op. 91, 1893, d. 354, t. 1, ll. 8 ob.–9.

2. *Deiateli SSSR i revoliutsionnogo dvizheniia v Rossii* (Moskva: Sovetskaia Entsiklopediia, 1989), 289.
3. See, for example Sarah Badcock, *A Prison Without Walls? Eastern Siberian Exile in the Last Years of Tsarism*. Oxford: Oxford University Press, 2016.
4. Figner to Novorusskii, November 19/6, 1912, in Vera Figner, *Sobranie sochinenii*, 7 vols., (Moskva: Vsesoiuznoe obshchestvo politkatorzhan i ssylno-poselentsev, 1933), 7:197.
5. On prisons see M. N. Gernet, *Istoriia tsarskoi tiur'my. 1870–1900* (Moskva: Gosudarstvennoe izdatel'stvo iuridicheskoi literatury, 1952).
6. Nikolai Charushin, *O dalekom proshlom* (Moskva: Mysl', 1973), 236.
7. Solomon Chudnovskii, *Iz davnikh let. Vospominaniia* (Moskva: Vsesoiuznoe obshchestvo politkatorzhan i ssylno-poselentsev, 1934), 124.
8. Lev Deich, *16 let v Sibiri* (Zheneva: P. Axelrod, 1905), 37.
9. Sergei Sinegub, *Zapiski chaikovtsa* (Moskva: Molodaia gvardiia, 1929), 136.
10. Ibid., 173.
11. Vera Figner, *Zapechatlennyi trud* (Moskva: Mysl', 1964), 2:3.
12. Ibid., 8–9.
13. Eleanor Canright Chiari, *Undoing Time: The Cultural Memory of an Italian Prison*, Italian Modernities (Oxford; New York: Peter Lang, 2012).
14. Charushin, *O dalekom proshlom* (1973), 236.
15. Sinegub, *Zapiski chaikovtsa*, 137–138.
16. Chudnovskii, *Iz davnikh let*, 124.
17. Sinegub, *Zapiski chaikovtsa*, 172.
18. Charushin, *O dalekom proshlom* (1973), 236.
19. Vladimir Debogorii-Mokrievich, *Vospominaniia* (St. Petersburg: Svobodnyi Trud, 1906), 383.
20. Chudnovskii, *Iz davnikh let*, 124–125.
21. Mikhail Novorusskii, *Zapiski shlissel'burzhtsa (1887–1905)* (Petrograd: Gosudarstvennoe izdatel'stvo, 1920), 30–31.
22. Ibid., 40.
23. Charushin, *O dalekom proshlom* (1973), 237.
24. Chudnovskii, *Iz davnikh let*, 126.
25. Sinegub, *Zapiski chaikovtsa*, 141.
26. Novorusskii, *Zapiski shlissel'burzhtsa*, 240.
27. Deich, *16 let v Sibiri*, 37.
28. Chudnovskii, *Iz davnikh let*, 126.
29. Figner, *Zapechatlennyi trud*, 2: 14.
30. Ibid., 53.
31. Charushin, *O dalekom proshlom* (1973), 240.
32. *Poety-demokraty 1870–1880-kh godov* (Leningrad: Sovetskii pisatel', 1968), http://az.lib.ru/s/sinegub_s_s/text_0020.shtml (accessed June 10, 2015).
33. Figner, *Zapechatlennyi trud*, 2:10.
34. Ibid., 14.
35. Chudnovskii, *Iz davnikh let*, 125.
36. Sinegub, *Zapiski chaikovtsa*, 142.
37. Deich, *16 let v Sibiri*, 37–38.
38. Charushin, *O dalekom proshlom* (1973), 237–241.
39. Sinegub, *Zapiski chaikovtsa*, 173.

40. Ibid.
41. Novorusskii, *Zapiski shlisse'burzhtsa*, 35.
42. Ibid., 125.
43. Ibid., 131–132.
44. Charushin, *O dalekom proshlom* (1973), 234.
45. *Deiateli SSSR i revoliutsionnogo dvizheniia v Rossii*, 123.
46. Sinegub, *Zapiski chaikovtsa*, 142.
47. Deich, *16 let v Sibiri*, 42.
48. *V podpol'e* (Petersburg: Drug Naroda, 1907), 75.
49. Novorusskii, *Zapiski shlissel'burzhtsa*, 157.
50. Ibid., 158.
51. Figner, *Zapechatlennyi trud*, 2:69.
52. Ibid., 74, 70.
53. Sinegub, *Zapiski chaikovtsa*, 215–219.
54. Ibid., 224.
55. Charushin, *O dalekom proshlom* (1973), 235.
56. Mikhail Chernavskii, "Ippolit Nikitich Myshkin (Po vospominaniiam katorzhanina 70-80-kh gg.)," *Katorga i Ssylka* 1, no. 8 (1924): 29.
57. Chudnovskii, *Iz davnikh let*, 102.
58. Ibid., 123.
59. Novorusskii, *Zapiski shlissel'burzhtsa*, 7.
60. Sinegub, *Zapiski chaikovtsa*, 143.
61. Ibid., 175.
62. Charushin, *O dalekom proshlom* (1973), 231.
63. Novorusskii, *Zapiski shlissel'burzhtsa*, 42.
64. Figner, *Zapechatlennyi trud*, 2: 83–84.
65. Novorusskii, *Zapiski shlissel'burzhtsa*, 71.
66. Sinegub, *Zapiski chaikovtsa*, 163–164.
67. Ibid., 143.
68. Figner, *Zapechatlennyi trud*, 1:371–373.
69. Charushin, *O dalekom proshlom* (1973), 238.
70. Ibid., 248.
71. Sinegub, in a letter to his wife, Chemodanova, asked her to find him a French-Russian dictionary, the works of Gustave Le Bon on the social psychology of crowds, of John Tyndall on magnetism, or anything on history in French (IRLI RAN, f. 675, op. 3, d. 37, l. 1 ob.).
72. Sinegub, *Zapiski chaikovtsa*, 165.
73. *Deiateli SSSR i revoliutsionnogo dvizheniia v Rossii*, 123.
74. Figner, *Zapechatlennyi trud*, 1:372.
75. On these courses, see the University of Iowa website: http://www.lib.uiowa.edu/sc/tc/ (accessed June 20, 2016).
76. Figner, *Zapechatlennyi trud*, 2:125.
77. IRLI RAN, f. 675, op. 3, d. 24.
78. GARF, f. 112, op. 2, d. 2468.
79. Chudnovskii, *Iz davnikh let*, 129.
80. Charushin, *O dalekom proshlom* (1973), 238.
81. Figner, *Zapechatlennyi trud*, 1:366.
82. Charushin, *O dalekom proshlom* (1973), 240.

83. Sinegub, *Zapiski chaikovtsa*, 157.
84. Novorusskii, *Zapiski shlissel'burzhtsa*, 74.
85. Charushin, *O dalekom proshlom* (1973), 243. Here and in other memoirs the interested reader can find a detailed description of how this worked.
86. Novorusskii, *Zapiski shlissel'burzhtsa*, 77.
87. Charushin, *O dalekom proshlom* (1973), 243.
88. Ibid., 251.
89. Ibid., 252.
90. *Deiateli SSSR i revoliutsionnogo dvizheniia v Rossii*, 123.
91. Charushin, *O dalekom proshlom* (1973), 263.
92. Figner, *Zapechatlennyi trud*, 1:378.
93. Charushin, *O dalekom proshlom* (1973), 251.
94. Ibid., 253.
95. Ibid., 234.
96. RGALI, f. 1185, op. 1, d. 242, ll. 32–32 ob.
97. GARF, f. 112, op. 2, d. 2469.
98. Charushin, *O dalekom proshlom* (1973), 252–253.
99. IRLI RAN, f. 675, op. 3, d. 37, l. 10b.
100. Sinegub, *Zapiski chaikovtsa*, 144.
101. Figner, *Zapechatlennyi trud*, 1:366.
102. Charushin, *O dalekom proshlom* (1973), 249.
103. Arkadii A. Charushin, "Brat'ia Urzhumovy," *Katorga i Ssylka* 1 (1926): 63–92.
104. Ibid., 92.
105. Charushin, *O dalekom proshlom* (1973), 240.
106. Ibid., 248.
107. Chernavskii, "Ippolit Nikitich Myshkin . . ." 33.
108. Chudnovskii, *Iz davnikh let*, 129–130.
109. Charushin, *O dalekom proshlom* (1973), 237.
110. Novorusskii, *Zapiski shlissel'burzhtsa*, 36.
111. Chudnovskii, *Iz davnikh let*, 130.
112. Figner, *Zapechatlennyi trud*, 2:19.
113. In his memoirs Charushin not only described this failed escape attempt but refuted the accounts of Sinegub and Kovalik. Apparently Kovalik's memoirs, written after Sinegub's, simply repeated the latter's account. But Sinegub had not taken part in the attempt and according to Charushin, he got the details all wrong.
114. Charushin, *O dalekom proshlom* (1973), 246.
115. Ibid., 244.
116. Charushin, *O dalekom proshlom na Kare* (Moskva: Vsesoiuznoe obshchestvo politkatorzhan i ssylno-poselentsev, 1929), 50–51.
117. Charushin, *O dalekom proshlom* (1973), 247.
118. Ibid., 263–264.
119. For summaries of the trial in English, see Avrahm Yarmolinsky, *Road to Revolution: A Century of Russian Radicalism* (Princeton, NJ: Princeton University Press, 1957), 208–209; and Venturi, *Roots of Revolution*, 585–595. The best Russian-language account is Nikolai A. Troitskii, *Tsarskie sudy protiv revoliutsionnoi Rossii* (Saratov: Izdatel'stvo Saratovskogo Universiteta, 1976).

120. On the lawyers, see Charushin, *O dalekom proshlom* (1973), 259–260, 263; Chudnovskii, *Iz davnikh let*, 141; Sinegub, *Zapiski chaikovtsa*, 202. Also Troitskii, *Tsarizm pered sudom progressivnoi obshchestvennosti* (Moskva: Mysl', 1979).
121. Yarmolinsky, *Road to Revolution*, 208.
122. Charushin, *O dalekom proshlom* (1973), 256.
123. *Deiateli SSSR i revoliutsionnogo dvizheniia v Rossii*, 125.
124. Chudnovskii, *Iz davnikh let*, 144.
125. Troitskii calculated that 120 supported the boycott; 73 declined to participate (Troitskii, *Tsarskie sudy protiv revoliutsionnoi Rossii*, 189).
126. Charushin, *O dalekom proshlom* (1973), 264; Venturi, *Roots of Revolution*, 595.
127. Charushin, *O dalekom proshlom* (1973), 271.
128. Ibid., 159.
129. The text of the Testament can be found in Charushin, *O dalekom proshlom* (1973), 276–277.

Seventeen Years in Siberia

Hard Labor, Exile, and Photography

"YOU ARE BEING SENTENCED TO SIBERIA"

After several years of incarceration, several members of the Chaikovskii circle were sentenced to hard labor (*katorga*), to be followed by forced settlement (*poselenie*) in Siberia. Charushin received nine years of hard labor, but with allowance for the four years he had already spent in prison. The term was to be spent in Kara, a string of mining settlements and prisons four thousand miles from St. Petersburg, in the region beyond Lake Baikal (Trans Baikal) several hundred miles southeast of Irkutsk, not far from Nerchinsk to the west and Manchuria to the east. Paradoxically, the sentences were met with relief, for Kara and the hard labor regime in Siberia had a reputation for being much less harsh than the central prisons, especially the one in Khar'kov, where prisoners were treated far more brutally. Moreover, those incarcerated in the central prisons were isolated from their relatives, whereas relatives could petition the authorities for the right to join their loved ones in Siberia.

The participants in the revolutionary movement often write of their joy at reuniting with friends and being free to interact once more, at the prospect of being once again with family members who were ready to accompany them to Siberia. After several years in prison and solitary confinement they felt relatively free on leaving the stone walls of enclosure behind and returning to a familiar world, even if they would soon again be separated from that world by their sentence, their guards, and their

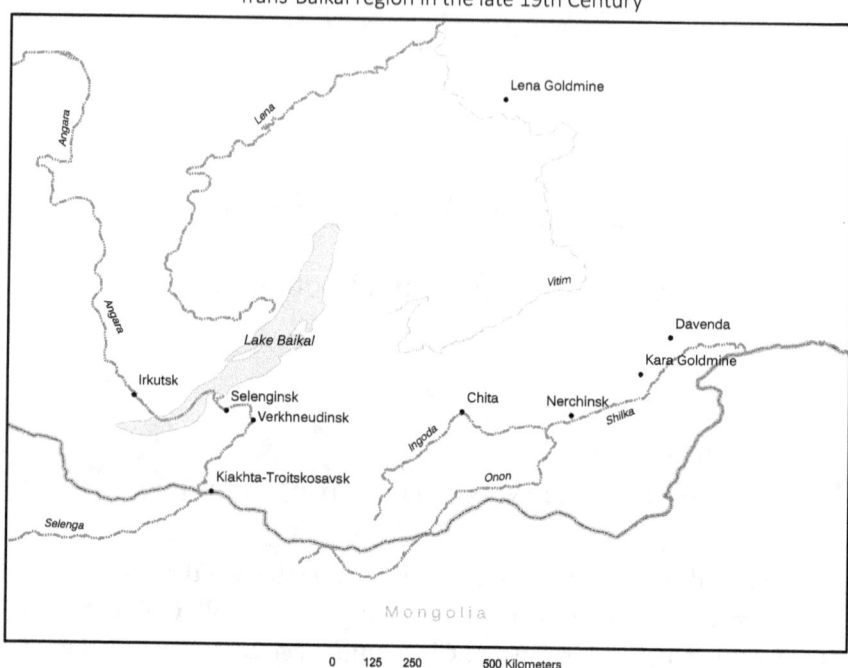

Trans-Baikal region in the late 19th Century

status. Sergei Sinegub wrote of his exhilaration as he stepped onto the special train for prisoners; it meant that he would be seeing his wife and offered the hope that they could be together from that time on, "We were happy beyond belief that walls no longer separated us."[1] Charushin, however, wrote that he had tried to dissuade Kuvshinskaia from joining her fate with his but his entreaties had fallen on deaf ears. It was after gaining an audience with Alexandra Tolstoy that she and Larisa Chemodanova received permission to travel with their husbands.[2]

Yet these reunions with loved ones meant becoming completely isolated from normal society and served as visible markers of their status. They were given to wear standard-issue, visorless caps; shirts and trousers made of course linen; long gray overcoats with yellow diamonds on the back side; foot wrappers and low shoes or slippers; and leather ankle guards and leg fetters (but unlike common criminals, their heads were not shaved on one side).[3] Memoirists inevitably noted the ritual of changing outfits and being fitted for chains, which to them marked a passage out of one stage of their lives and entry into another. Charushin wrote:

> Those first blows of the maul as my leg fetters were riveted, resonating in the empty and gloomy room where those present silently watched as if in the presence of the dead, had a strong impact on me. It was as if something inside of me was breaking, and I was acutely aware of beginning to view that abyss which was growing between my old self and the newly emerging one. Before this ritual had taken place I was still somebody. Now I am a non-entity, shorn of all the rights one takes for granted.[4]

Sinegub also described the ritual of changing clothes and being fitted for leg fetters, emphasizing that the chains were being attached not to a thief or petty criminal but to a youth—not to mention nobleman—suffering away his time in a prison.

By the decision of the courts participants in the revolutionary movement were also deprived of their social status and received that of exiles condemned to hard labor (which ordinarily meant imprisonment). After a certain period of probation (ordinarily one to two years), they were sometimes moved to the status of *vol'naia komanda* (roughly: "free team"), according to which they were relocated to cabins near the prison where they could live with their families, were exempt from hard labor, and received a pittance to use for living expenses, but were also closely monitored. Next, they became penal colonists or settlers (*ssyl'no-poselentsy*) resettled at a location in Siberia outside the hard labor settlements. Still later they could be registered in a local community in Siberia—which once again brought up the issue of their status within the legal estate system, not to mention their sense of identity.

Given the social mobility that was occurring in Russia at the time, how important was their estate status to revolutionaries at the time? After Ivan Popov completed his term of exile, he petitioned to be admitted into the merchant community in order to gain unimpeded freedom of movement that would allow him to travel to St. Petersburg to deal with matters connected with the journal he edited, *Vostochnoe Obozrenie*. Once Charushin's status was changed to that of penal colonist he was ascribed to the *meshchanstvo*;[5] but in 1889 he petitioned to have his status as a nobleman restored in line with an 1883 Imperial Manifesto.[6] His petition was rejected as was a subsequent one submitted on his behalf by Arkadii in 1892.[7] Did the requested status change matter deeply to the exiles or was it simply seen as a practical necessity in order to be free to act and move about as they saw fit? The memoirs don't provide a clear answer to this question.

PERCEPTIONS OF SIBERIA[8]

What lay ahead in Siberia for the exiles? They imagined it to be an enormous, frigid, lifeless, and even hostile space. Their descriptions of the "imagined" Siberia fully corresponded with the stereotypes that were current at the time and endlessly reproduced in the periodical press, including the thick journals read by the educated classes, and textbooks. It was, it seems, so very far away, ferociously cold and inhabited primarily by native populations.[9]

Depending upon the time of year and mode of transportation the road to Siberia could take several months and often provoked a mixed response from those forced to travel it. Many were exhilarated by the vast spaces and wild nature; others could be intimidated by its sparsely settled and seemingly lifeless expanses. Lev Deutsch wrote, "All around I saw empty, dead space; for huge stretches of land we often encountered not a single living being. This absence of all signs of life, coupled with the encroaching cold as we approached the northern regions sometimes had a depressive effect upon our moods. And people actually live in the tundra and taiga! I sometimes had the horrible thought that after many years (in hard labor) I would be transferred to the status of penal colonist and forced to live in such a place, if not worse."[10]

Debogorii-Mokrievich had similar perceptions as he journeyed along the Siberian tract; it was a cold and severe world indeed. He wrote: "I was reminded of the descriptions of the Siberian tundra, the snow-filled winter, snow drifts covering the roads and other horrors, and wondered what awaited me beyond that distant horizon toward which my carriage hurtled me. The Siberia of my best dreams now began to intimidate me. All those exaggerated tales about this so-called 'hostile' region had their impact on me."[11] At the same time, he and others experienced a feeling of emancipation after their long imprisonment. He and others noticed the dense woods and enormous trees, the striking beauty of Siberian rivers and more. Charushin and Sinegub recalled hunting for mushrooms, which were ample around Kara, and seeing abundant fields of oats. All of this reproduced a different stereotype of Siberia already in currency: that of a strikingly beautiful and rich region. Sinegub wrote that exiles often compared its natural beauty with Switzerland; he waxed eloquent in describing "coniferous forests—pines, fir, and spruce in the winter, but redolent of the aroma of pine needles in the spring, and mountain ridges covered by tamarack. On the lower slopes of the mountains and in the valleys shimmering birch trees reached for the sky and aspen leaves quivered endlessly. In the valleys too, as well as along the banks of rivers and streams you come across thick clusters of alder and marvelous copses of birch-cherry bushes."[12]

Like the Russian intelligentsia as a whole, political exiles also viewed Siberia through the lens of the Enlightenment paradigm as a civilizing project awaiting culture bearers. Charushin's narrative of this aspect of his generation's life is revealing:

> The desolate region to which exiles were sent, ruled over by bureaucrats and lacking all signs of spiritual life, or so it seemed to us initially, but at the same time possessing boundless riches, over the years came alive and grew spiritually under the sustained and direct influence of the huge contingent of political exiles spread across the length and breadth of Siberia. This contingent, initially keeping to itself and not deigning to descend from its intellectual heights to the comparatively petty needs and interests of what was an almost primitive world, gradually changed its stance towards it."[13]

In the recollections of former Siberian exiles images of the region's backwardness and primitiveness are crowded out by the tale of cultural and political transformation wrought by their hands. Gradually, the image of a frigid, alien space devoid of life becomes one of a region actively being transformed and familiarized. Exiles find employment with the government and in private companies, and establish newspapers, museums, and libraries and play a major role in local affairs.

If the exiles gradually became acclimatized and engaged with the mostly Russian urban population, that population also came to accept them. This is how Ivan Popov described the reception he and other met in Kiakhta, the tea entrepot on the border with China: "If someone settled down there in the region beyond Lake Baikal and set about making a contribution, then the residents of Kiakhta were quite welcoming despite the potential political risks to themselves. They [the exiles] were held in high regard, for example, Alexei Kuznetsov, who established museums in Nerchinsk and Chita, as well as N. A. Charushin and his wife Anna Dmitrievna, ... S. G. Stakhevich and others."[14]

With the direct participation and sometimes at the initiative of the exiles, intense efforts were made to promote scientific exploration as well as the cultural and educational development of the entirety of this immense region and at the same time in a surreptitious but sustained way to assimilate it to progressive currents in European Russia. Nevertheless, Siberia remains a distinctive space separated geographically and culturally from "Russia," virtually a foreign country. Without a doubt political exiles contributed significantly to the transformation of Siberia. Yet we note that such recollections of their civilizing mission were part and parcel of a larger intelligentsia discourse in which the project of enlightening the people was transferred to an entire region. Narratives, of which there are many, of culture being imposed on a primitive and inert people and land have provoked a skeptical response among postcolonial historians, whether directed at indigenous Siberians or at the transplanted Russian peasantry—and we return to this issue later. As for direct political propaganda as opposed to the advancement of knowledge, Popov recalled that in contrast to a later generation of young Social Democratic exiles, whose focus was entirely upon revolutionary propaganda, "the older generation regarded their forced residence in Siberia as temporary. For them Siberia was a transit station to be abandoned at the first opportunity. Political propaganda ... they saw as harmful, because it might result in pushing back the date of their return to Russia, the only place where genuinely revolutionary work was feasible."[15]

THE ROAD

As a rule those sent to hard labor and exile traveled by train from St. Petersburg via Moscow to Nizhnii Novgorod, and then by steamship or specially designated barges along the Volga and Kama rivers to Kazan' and Perm' near the Ural Mountains. One exile described these barges:

> The barge on which we traveled had been specially fitted out to transport exiles. One section was allotted to the accompanying convoy; another much larger one was for the exiles themselves. Iron bars rose from the sides of the deck and were joined above it in order to ward off escape attempts and gave the barge the appearance of a cage, because of which the prisoners nicknamed it the chicken coop. The name was fitting because the sight of a barge packed with the arrested peering out from behind the bars certainly reminded one of the cages in which poultry were hauled off to market.[16]

From Perm' the exiles traveled by postal horses to Ekaterinburg and Tiumen'; from Tiumen' they traveled, again by barge, to Tomsk, then by carriage using the postal network, all the way to Irkutsk in Eastern Siberia, and then to Lake Baikal and beyond to their final destination. Charushin's group were relatively fortunate; before and after this brief interlude the condemned were forced to travel this vast distance in Siberia from Tomsk almost exclusively by foot. Deutch recalled, "Whether in insufferable heat, the cruel Siberian frost or stormy weather, and despite the notoriously primitive roads, parties of several hundred each would set forth from Tomsk on predetermined days of every week in separate groups made up of 'families' or 'bachelors.' Each party would move from one way station to the next, a distance of roughly 25 to 30 [kilometers], with every third day being one of rest. For many, this snail-like pace had to be endured for months on end under the worst imaginable conditions."[17]

Many of the memoirs contain detailed descriptions of the journey to Siberia, for the arduous and protracted movement from one *étape* (way-station) to another left behind powerful and vivid impressions: of a completely new landscape, of the authorities who were responsible for getting them to their destination, and of the common criminals who often traveled in the same party. The descriptions of the latter figure prominently, both as encounters with the common people and as their first encounters with members of with that distinct criminal subculture, with whom they were subsequently to live cheek by jowl in prison and at hard labor. Although the rule was that the two types of prisoners were to be kept separate, in reality this did not exclude constant interaction; occasionally there were even notorious "exchanges," by which political prisoners paid common criminals to switch identities with them, giving the former the opportunity to escape.

Charushin's party completed the entire journey from St. Petersburg to Kara between July 22 and September 12, 1878. But at Irkutsk, well into the journey, Charushin became seriously ill with typhus and was forced to leave the party. He blamed his illness on his weakened state after years of imprisonment, as well as the conditions during transit, which were ripe for the spread of infectious disease, "The suffocating cells [were] replete with every imaginable miasma, the bunks arranged in two tiers under which exiles also lay shoulder to shoulder, exposing their emaciated bodies to every conceivable parasite which in a frenzy attacked every new arrival."[18]

Charushin was truly ill; at each of the switching stations during the last stages of the journey before reaching Irkutsk he had been transferred in a semi-comatose state from one wagon to another. He was allowed to stay behind in Irkutsk only because of the persistent efforts of his wife, though he was made to remain in chains. His comrades parted from him in Irkutsk believing that they would not see him alive again. Paradoxically however, the illness and brush with death reinvigorated Charushin, who, after his lengthy incarceration, had been seriously depressed. He confessed that "[s]uffering through typhus restored me. I shook off that profound indifference which had settled upon me in the last years of my imprisonment, and was once again energetic and full of joy at being alive."[19]

AT THE KARA PLACE MINES AND PRISON COLONY

The Chaikovtsy were sent together to the Kara hard labor prison. In the early Soviet era, the memoirs of different generations of those sent to Kara were often published in the journal *Katorga i Ssylka* and their having spent time in specific sites of exile became a new source of group identity; at that later date the *Kariytsy* as they were called, formed a distinct subculture among former political prisoners. Other such *zemliachesta* or "regional associations"—the term was reminiscent of the student societies of their earlier days—were organized after 1921 by the newly formed Society of Former Political Prisoners and Exiles.

The Kara hard labor camps were part of a large complex of prisons and settlements distributed along the Kara Valley, from Ust'-Kara to the Amur. It included the Ust'-Kara women's prison, the so-called New Prison and its older predecessor at the Lower Kara, a prison and settlement on the Middle Kara, and yet another prison on the Upper Kara. The prison complex had been established to provide a labor force for the Kara gold mines (and place mines). The Kara settlements were until 1882 the only site to which political prisoners—that is, state criminals—were sent.[20] In the 1880s Kara gained a reputation for its administrative brutality and arbitrary abuse, from which escape, given its remote location in the taiga, was virtually impossible. Political prisoners were well familiar with the notorious "Kara history" connected with mass suicide attempts there in protest against the application of corporal punishment and in solidarity with other prisoners.

But at the time Charushin arrived at Kara, according to another exile, "being sent (there) was considered a great privilege, for the Kara prison was regarded as a republic and 'free space' (*vol'nitsa*, a word ordinarily used to refer to the realm of the Cossacks, who traditionally enjoyed considerable liberties within the Russian Empire), and was looked upon askance by the higher authorities."[21] Charushin, along with Sinegub and Shishko, was sent to the Lower Kara, where the camp administration was also situated, as were the commandant's home, troop barracks along with a large settlement of those serving out their terms in hard labor and those now in the regime of "free command" after their period of probation. The latter were allowed to live in small cabins located nearby, free of the prison regime but under daily supervision.[22]

In 1878–1879 political prisoners in Lower Kara were assigned to live in a guardhouse formerly utilized by officers. There the conditions were considerably better than in the Kara prisons as such. The prisoners were placed two or three to a room (Charushin shared with Shishko and Sinegub) and all shared a kitchen and a common room. Wives of exiles who had voluntarily followed their husbands (Chemodanova, Kuvshinskaia and others) lived separately.[23]

To judge by the memoirs of Sinegub, Charushin and Shishko's life in Kara was not all that difficult, especially in contrast to what was to follow in Kara in the 1880s after the assassination of Alexander II in 1881 and especially when an attempt at escape was uncovered in May 1882—

an episode which remained prominent in the memories of all veterans of Kara. Whatever came next, during their stay the Chaikovtsy were relatively free, could spend their time studying foreign languages and handicrafts, reading and socializing.[24] According to Sinegub, his compatriot Semianovskii devoted his time to reading journals and newspapers, studying English to add to his knowledge of French and German. Because of an eye ailment Shishko was unable to read so Sinegub read to him aloud, also taking advantage of his free time to study French and English. Twice a week the prisoners were allowed conjugal visits, and once a day were taken out for walks.[25]

There was no official canteen for the exiles, so at first they prepared their own meals (Sinegub boasted of how his friends praised him for the soup and meatballs he had prepared), but soon one of the wives (Kviatkovskaia) began to deliver them dinners prepared by a cook. As Charushin recalled: "We were free to interact as we pleased, could occupy ourselves as we were inclined, could organize reading groups, discussion circles, argue to our heart's content, sing or simply banter, especially at the dinner table or at tea time. The number of books and periodicals was adequate, and we didn't hesitate to write letters to relatives and acquaintances, both in Russia and in Siberia."[26]

When he wrote those words in the early Soviet era almost fifty years later the journal *Katorga i Ssylka* was awash with the memoirs of former hard labor prisoners detailing the cruelties of the tsarist penal regime. Among such memoirs were those written by veterans of the Kara penal colony in the 1880s, when political prisoners had been moved into a new, specially built prison to handle a mass influx of prisoners and to enforce a stricter regime. Instead, Charushin confessed that no matter how jarring it might sound, life at Kara after his long stretch of solitary confinement in St. Petersburg had resembled a "well-provided resort" allowing for the recovery of one's physical and spiritual strengths. One wonders if weighing on his mind at the time of writing was a contrast with conditions in the burgeoning system of hard labor camps set up by the Soviet authorities in the 1920s.

Whatever may be the case, the memoirs of Kara composed by Charushin's generation do not echo the trope of "suffering" so many historians of Populism have identified as integral to its narrative. They wrote of their life in common at Kara in glowing terms, as a richly vibrant community with its own unwritten constitution, mores and customs and as an important socializing and educative institution of sorts:

> Several generations of youth passed through the doors of the Kara political prison, and for dozens of those just setting out upon life it was not only a welcoming alma mater (sic), a higher school of personal development and education, but also a public arena in which perhaps for the first time they could establish their first interpersonal relations in a complex individual and societal matrix. For revolutionaries of peasant and working class origins the Kara prison was an authentic university allowing them to complete their schooling and receive a political education.[27]

Indeed, the political prisoners at Kara had the opportunity to organize their affairs in line with the operating principles of *artels* (roughly: work cooperatives, derived from cooperative associations of workers) and communes which were so important for their generation. As long as they did not violate prison regulations, the authorities did not interfere with their daily lives. According to Lev Deutch, the chief organizing principle at Kara was the equality of rights and obligations:

> Whether it concerned produce provided by the system or anything coming from the outside, it all was treated as the common property of the *artel'*. Money was divided as follows: a portion was allocated to improving the diet provided by the authorities, primarily increasing the amount of meat and vegetables available ... another amount was put into a communal fund to be dispensed to those being reclassified as penal colonists, for the purchase of books and periodicals, for medical expenses, and so forth; what remained was divided equally among all members of the *artel'*.[28]

Deutch also describes in detail the way in which chores such as kitchen duty and housecleaning were allocated, the selection of elders, librarians and other positions took place, and the voting procedures for changes in the working constitution occurred.

Such attempts at collective self-organization and societal construction at a micro-level limited by the walls (here: figuratively) of the prison certainly merit our attention. Forced to live and interact within a confined space the political prisoners together worked out rules for successful coexistence and mapped the outlines of a new society. The "Kara Republic" served as a social experiment demonstrating to its participants the joys and perils of building a new society. The irony of course was that this "ideal sodality" within the confines of the prison system was initially designed as a way to ensure their very survival.

All was not perfect of course. The authorities implemented harsh measures on more than a few occasions, resulting in protests which sometimes led to hunger strikes or suicides. There were conflicts among the political prisoners, one shameful incident of misplaced suspicions led to the murder of a member (Uspenskii)—something Charushin later had difficulty addressing in his memoirs (chapter 9). Still, as the exiles themselves noted, compared with the conditions at Shlisselburg and the Peter-Paul Fortress life at Kara was genuinely much better. Moreover, we must not forget that the years of incarceration occurred during the best years of their lives when youthfulness, intense friendships, and a boundless faith in the future provided the resources to bear up to the hardships of incarcerations. As Debogorii-Mokrievich recalled, "The government intensified its repression by sending hundreds of 'unreliables' into exile but these 'unreliables' were in no way fazed or discouraged that they were being shipped out to the far corners of the world. Quite the opposite: we all were buoyant about the future and fervently believed in the successful outcome of our struggle."[29]

For many of those who lived through this period the successful experiment at social equality, at making the *artel'* system, a "constitution," and a "parliament" work robustly, was living proof of the high level of consciousness, intellectual and moral standards and spiritual capacities that separated them from the rest of the population—which they hoped to transfer to society and the people. It reinforced the notion that a revolution must have an ethical as well as a material foundation; it consolidated the ideal image of the revolutionary, and it convinced them of the potential to establish a society based on the principle of equality. One might see these views as self-congratulatory, but such beliefs were harshly tested in years to come, and they provided this generation with the tough moral fiber that allowed them to endure hardships that would have broken many. Overwhelmingly, they continued to live up to the high ethical standards they had set for themselves in the Chaikovskii circle and tested at Kara.

The successful campaign by the tsarist state to destroy Populist organizations after the assassination of Alexander II, the harsh fates individual

Populists endured and their life experiences in general forced them to reassess convictions that in their youth has seem so obvious and clear. A milestone in this process was the famous open letter penned by one of their own, Lev Tikhomirov, once a close friend of Charushin. That letter, "Why I Am No Longer a Revolutionary" (1888), in which the author, writing in exile abroad, explained his conversion to monarchism,[30] was the cause of much consternation and reflection among Tikhomirov's peers and continued to agitate them long afterwards. In his telling Charushin was initially sympathetic to Tikhomirov's quest in exile abroad to rethink the evolving situation in Russia and to reconceptualize his understanding of what was at stake in a revolution. It seems that Charushin had also been pondering his own future life and that of the country as a whole given that the People's Will and their terrorist tactics had exhausted themselves with the assassination of Alexander II in 1881, and that the people remained distant from any thought of revolution. But the conclusions Tikhomirov had drawn (and his sidling up to the autocracy) had evidently shaken Charushin to the core, and seemed to him a betrayal of the convictions of his youth.

At Kara Charushin and his friends made every effort to follow events in European Russia. They discussed the fate of the People's Will movement and agonized over its use of terror as a weapon in the political struggle. Even when they had been incarcerated before being sent into exile, the assassinations attempted by Vera Zasulich and Sergei Stepniak-Kravchinskii (the first, on the life of a particularly harsh prison commandant, a sensational failure; and the second, on the head of the Russian secret police, Mezentsev, a dramatic success) provoked heated debate among the Populists. Considering terrorism a measure of last resort Charushin earnestly hoped it would disappear in Russia with the achievement of basic political freedoms. In his memoirs, he wrote of the danger of a terrorist movement that might emerge operating under the guise of pursuing only lofty political goals. To be sure, when he wrote of this the subsequent political history of Russia surely weighed heavily on Charushin, and his recollections were in fact a condemnation both of the tactics of the Socialist Revolutionary "fighting wing" and the more recent Bolshevik terror in the Civil War as much as they were an effort to reconstruct his views at that earlier time.

In any event, the ethical norms so central to the Populists, self-identity were more important than political calculations when it came to discussions of terror. Their unshakeable faith in the moral qualities of their comrades outside prison led them to believe that the resort to terrorist acts had been forced on them by a repressive police state and were justifiable, even if doubts lingered in their minds. Charushin wrote, "We could not but welcome the turn to open political struggle and consequently—despite our profound revulsion at the thought of murder—to terror, since all other avenues for open political activity had been closed down. But accepting this turn of events was not something that came easily to many of us who struggled profoundly with this decision."[31]

The seventies revolutionaries' arguments about the validity of terror and Russia's future course continued later in exile. Charushin recalled that in Selenginsk, in the Trans-Baikal region, he encountered Breshko-Breshkovskaia, and how it felt like old times as the two talked about all they had been through and suffered, and the frustrations they each felt about the lack of a clear path forward. But, he added, unlike him, she had no qualms whatsoever about the use of terror, in whatever form was available.

Perhaps as important as ethical norms to Charushin's cohort were the linkages they drew between their fate and that of the Decembrists, that small group of aristocrats, many of them veterans of the 1812 campaigns, who a half-century earlier had organized a rebellion against the autocracy, called for a constitution, political freedoms, and the elimination of serfdom. Their uprising was easily crushed in December 1825; hundreds of the rebels were stripped of their civil status and sent into exile in the far reaches of Siberia, where they spent the next quarter century, some with loyal wives who had voluntarily joined them. With the accession to the throne of Alexander II in 1855, some of the survivors had been allowed to return to European Russia, where they were feted by educated society and celebrated for their sacrifices. The wives of these aristocratic martyrs were themselves immortalized in verse by the radical democratic poet and editor Nekrasov, whose lines from *Russian Women* (1872–73)[32] entered the Russian literary canon and were memorized by generations of students. The Decembrists were a constant presence in the collective memories of the Populists' predecessors both in the struggle against the autocracy and in efforts to civilize Siberia during long terms of incarceration. The common experience of hard labor and exile fostered a sense among the Populists of shared fates, all the more so because the Decembrists remained a powerful memory among the people of Siberia as a whole. One might refer here to *lieux de mémoire*, "sites of memory," connected with the Decembrist presence in Siberia and connecting its history with that of European Russia, integrating that region into the larger history of the emancipation struggle, especially given the abundant and lingering traces they had left behind. Charushin felt that the sympathetic reception his generation received from the local population had been shaped by the memory of their earlier experience with "state criminals" as "culture bearers" who had prepared the ground for positive interactions between the two communities.

In their later telling the revolutionaries of the 1870s marched into exile and hard labor intending to pick up where the Decembrists had left off. Popov, for example, begins his recollections of Siberia with quotations from the memoirs and correspondence of the Decembrists, interweaving his text with theirs. In so doing he integrates his own experience with the overall narrative of several generations of exile on the part of the revolutionary intelligentsia: "The old Siberians in general, and especially those who resided in Kiakhta, held dear the histories of the Decembrists and of Alexander Herzen [who was exiled not to Siberia proper, but to Viatka and Perm' just on the European side of the Urals]. Regarding ourselves to be the disciples of the Decembrists we also had learned from Herzen. The two were mingled in our minds and stood in contrast to revolutionaries of a later time by their elevated levels of knowledge and consciousness. To be sure we in Kiakhta sympathized with those later revolutionaries as well, but did not revere them as we did the Decembrists themselves."[33]

The links between Decembrists and Populists were reinforced by the discourse of female sacrifice in both cases. When Kuvshinskaia, Chemodanova and other wives followed their husbands voluntarily into exile, they surely had in mind Nekrasov's ode to the Decembrist women, as did their husbands. Emphasizing the similarity between generations of such women in their memoirs, the Populists were simultaneously contesting a stereotype that had formed of "nihilist women," those who had rejected marriage, children, and all ties with family. Surely, Countess Tolstoy had the Decembrist wives in mind when she wrote, on June 27, 1878, "I left for the city to meet once again with my sweet little *nigilistka* [Kuvshinskaia]. I ran into a jungle of obstacles only finally to learn that she was already in the Litovskii Fortress, awaiting departure for Siberia. I rushed to that place almost without hope of being allowed in, but my name along with my fancy livery opened the door for me, allowing me to meet up with this dear woman, so courageous, self-abnegating and wanting to do good."[34] Sinegub also clearly has the Decembrist women in mind when he describes the impression Kuvshinskaia made upon Countess Tolstoy, "[B]oth of these nihilist wives, young and attractive with a bright future before themselves, focused on one thing alone—to share the dismal fate of their husbands."[35]

Yet while emphasizing their commonalities with the Decembrists and their femininity, the Populists also emphasized the active role women had played in the movement and their higher level of consciousness. In florid prose, in 1927, Vera Figner noted:

> Spiritual beauty retains its aura even with the passage of time, and the enchanting image of the women of the second quarter of the nineteenth century still bears the luster of those remarkable days. Their deprivations, losses and sufferings make them akin to the revolutionary women of a later generations. But for them the incarceration and harsh treatment which descended upon the Decembrists were a shock, undercutting the foundations of their lives. Their own upbringings, habits, milieu and way of life—were all contrary to what the future now had in store for them. But women of the past half century were aware of what the future boded for them, they had consciously prepared for it and felt exaltation at being able to participate in such a noble movement whose bright future they had in their view.[36]

Thus, high morale, strength of character, communal bonds, and the inspiring precedent of the Decembrists and their spouses held the incarcerated Populists together and gave these days of their lives a positive imprint, allowing them years later to write of the "Republic of Kara."

CHARUSHIN AND KONONOVICH: "EVEN THE JAILER WEEPS AT TIMES"

The other position one finds in these memoirs is that the Populists' relative freedom owed much to the actions of individual prison governors.[37] This stance avoided idealizing the system as a whole by identifying specific figures of authority who displayed honesty, propriety and even humane behavior. Thus, in his descriptions of Kara Charushin refers frequently to Colonel Vladimir Kononovich, who facilitated decent conditions and relative freedom to those under his control. Here as elsewhere we come across striking similarities in the memoirs. Sinegub describes Kononovich as follows: "He was a man not yet advanced in years, well proportioned, with a wise, intelligent face, always dressed in a military uniform."[38] In Charushin's account, we read, "This was a tall man, around 40–50, with a military demeanor, a wise and intelligent face, dressed military style."[39] Again, Sinegub: "Kononovich was both a smart and intelligent man, well able to defend his turf as long as it was even possible."[40] And, Charushin, "Kononovich was a smart man, no coward, and able to defend his turf."[41] In order to add weight to the veracity of his portrait of Kononovich Charushin included in his text a long quotation from George Kennan's famous book[42] on the exile system: "Political convicts, honest officers and good citizens everywhere united in declaring that he was a humane, sympathetic and warm-hearted man, as well as a fearless intelligent, and absolutely incorruptible official."[43]

The political exiles made special note of Kononovich's respectful demeanor when interacting with them; he made a point of always using the polite form of the second person when addressing them individually, and addressed them collectively as "gentlemen." When the Charushins arrived at Kara, Kononovich invited them to dinner at his home, where they spent an evening in lively conversation. Charushin recalled that "Kononovich was always a gracious and hospitable host without differentiating according to status; not a single gesture or glance reminded his shackled guest who he was or why he been brought there under his unlimited control."[44] Sinegub added that "Kononovich arranged our affairs such that we felt ourselves to be a more 'cultured' element of Kara society than those (actually performing) hard labor."[45]

The wives of the prisoners also sometimes established cordial relationships with the Kononovich family. Vladimir Kononovich's spouse was thrilled by the opportunities offered to interact with other educated and cultured women, often invited home in order to "cordially interact with people capable of mutual understanding, shared intimacy and who had common spiritual interests."⁴⁶ But unlike Kuvshinskaia, not all prisoners' wives were willing to take part in such intercourse. In particular, Larisa Chemodanova avoided all contact with the Kononovich household, something her husband Sergei Sinegub explained by her principled position that she was willing to associate only with "her own kind" and by the moral qualms about interacting with people with whom one could not be completely open or honest, given the difference in status. In this sense, it was she who most completely adhered to the convictions of the Chaikovskii circle—any disingenuous or deceptive behavior was strictly forbidden.

Kononovich's relationship with the political prisoners and the relatively free regime he established over them must have prompted multiple complaints to St. Petersburg,⁴⁷ but he showed no signs of being daunted by such. Most likely the remoteness and severity of the climate in Kara meant that few qualified applicants were clamoring for his position, and for that reason the higher ups in the capital were willing to look the other way concerning the liberal policies, especially since they had resulted in no serious disturbances. Charushin and Sinegub, however, attribute the security of Kononovich's position to his personal traits; Charushin wrote that "Kononovich was smart, brave, and able to bite back when attacked."⁴⁸ Sinegub used the very same terms in describing Kononovich's survival skills.⁴⁹

Especially important for both Charushin and Sinegub was the way Kononovich handled the situation in late 1880, when a ministerial circular arrived at Kara prohibiting those on hard labor to send or receive correspondence and ordering that all those living outside the prison be returned and put back in chains. Kononovich "invited" them (a revealing term) to his residence to give them the news: "It was a sad gathering this one; during it Kononovich was the most agitated of all, at the end he even lost his poise."⁵⁰ Sinegub confirms this description, "We had to comfort the colonel, brought him some water, found a chair for him."⁵¹ Even more meaningful to them was Kononovich's decision to submit his resignation in connection with the new rules, combined with the distress caused by two incidents of suicide and one of mental breakdown on his watch.

Kononovich spent time in St. Petersburg, and then accepted another posting at a recently established penal colony on Sakhalin Island, famously described by Anton Chekhov after his visit there in the early 1890s. Chekhov provided a similar assessment of Kononovich's personality, recalling him as cultured, well-read, and experienced, "He speaks and writes well and gives the impression of being a genuine and humane individual. I still recall the great pleasure I took at my conversations with him, and how glad I was to hear him . . . repeatedly express how repugnant he found corporal punishment to be."[52] At Kononovich's request, Chekhov later sent him materials for use in primary schools, including sets of textbooks and books for school libraries. Accompanying those materials was a letter from Chekhov stating, "I will never forget your cordiality, hospitality and enlightened engagement."[53] In the Soviet era, writing about his time in Nerchinsk, Charushin devoted an entire chapter to Kononovich, emphasizing his intelligence, tact, and refinement.

Once Charushin had completed his period of probation and was eligible to become a *poselenets*, Kononovich recommended Kuvshinskaia to the director of the Davenda gold mines who was trying to find a teacher for his children; in so doing he ensured that his friends would have money to live on once they were released. Later, after Kononovich was transferred to Nerchinsk (some 200 miles from Kara), he invited Kuvshinskaia to teach his own children, something that not only provided income but also served as the Charushins' introduction to polite society in that city. Charushin recalled that it was Kononovich's offer that had prompted their decision to relocate to that city. Kononovich helped other families as well.[54]

Charushin's new status as a penal colonist rather than a hard-labor convict hardly erased the enormous difference in social standing between him and Kononovich, but it did nevertheless bring about a change in their relationship. Charushin remarked that he was careful not to be presumptuous, and that it was Kononovich who took the first steps. The Charushins began to have dinner with the Kononovich family every Sunday. After a fire (most likely caused by arson) burned down the Kononovichs' home, the family found shelter in the Charushin's lodgings.

Their friendship did not end there. When Charushin was living in Kiakhta at the end of the 1880s, Kononovich helped him gain permission from the authorities in Irkutsk and St. Petersburg to serve as the photographer for an expedition to Mongolia. There may have been another family connection between the two men: at the time Kononovich moved to Sakhalin, Charushin's younger brother Ivan had recently begun working there as the official for the regional government; it is highly likely that the two became acquainted, only further cementing the bonds between the prison commandant and former inmate.[55] There can be no doubt then, that the lives of these two families were intertwined. The unlikely connection between an exiled revolutionary and a high-ranking official in the penal system, one that led both of them to reveal their very human sides, demonstrates, of course, that neither side of the political divide had a monopoly on virtue, but also that the boundaries between state and society could be and were often crossed—something we see more of once Charushin returns to Viatka from exile.

LIFE AS A PENAL COLONIST: NERCHINSK (1881–1886)

According to the records of the Main Prison Administration, on October 21, 1881, "state criminal" Nikolai Charushin was released from hard labor status and assigned to be registered to live in Chita under police supervision.[56] The memoirs tell us that being released from Kara was often an unsettling experience, not only because the prisoners faced an uncertain future, but also because it meant the dissolution of their communal ties and of a stable environment. Moving out into a freer, if still monitored world also brought up the question of how they would earn their livelihoods and provide for themselves and, in Charushin's case, their families (Charushin's and Kuvshinskaia's daughter Lydia had been born in 1880). At Kara, their basic needs had been provided for, sometimes supplemented by relatives in European Russia or by the occasional earnings of their wives who had accompanied them into exile. For example, one of them (Bibergal') gave music lessons to the Kononovich children; Chemodanova taught in a children's orphanage and also gave lessons to the children of the staff at Kara; Uspenskaia worked as a paramedic in the clinic, Kuvshinskaia assisted her and also did embroidery for clients. Released into "free command" at Kara, some of the men had found work: Sinegub kept a garden and experimental field for testing new seeds, fertilizers, or rotation systems at the orphanage; Soiuzov and Shishko practiced carpentry, and Charushin was a record keeper in the mining office. As he recalled, "practically all of us had access to one type of work or another; it paid little, but our needs were minimal and it sufficed."⁵⁷

Virtually all the Chaikovtsy who had spent time at Kara—including Shishko and Sinegub, landed at some point in Chita, where they reconstituted a vibrant community. In the account of his travels in Siberia George Kennan mentions his long conversations with exiles there on whose stories he relied for information about prison and exile. But Charushin never did become registered to live there; instead he ended up at the Davenda gold mines far away, beyond Nerchinsk.⁵⁸ Was Charushin disappointed to be sent so far away from Chita? On the one hand, he described Chita as a town "built exclusively out of wood, tropically hot in the summer and beastly cold in the winter, becoming especially intolerable when the frequent high winds kick up dust storms which tear at the face and blind you. There are no sidewalks and the unfortunate pedestrian sinks deep into the sand as he proceeds."⁵⁹ Yet every time he visited Chita he relished the company of exiles offering him the much-needed opportunity to be with others.

When Charushin and Kuvshinskaia left Kara and moved to Davenda, they were provided with a residence and even domestic help in the person of a Polish exile who was to serve as both cook and nanny. Yet things did not go smoothly. Kuvshinskaia took readily to her familiar pedagogical tasks of instructing children (see Figure 5.1); for Charushin, however, it was the first time in his life he had to "put time in at the office" immersed in tedious bureaucratic paperwork which, in his own words "offered nothing for the mind or the soul."⁶⁰ The lack of opportunity to do engaging work and the absence of his familiar circle of friends from Kara led to an unexpected rough patch in his newly emancipated life. It was here rather than when he was first sent to Kara that he felt himself cut off from his customary world. Describing his life at the mine works, he wrote:

> Work, cards, alcohol and gold made up the daily grind of the employee here. There was no life of the mind and books, journals and newspapers were a rarity. Here in the back of beyond they had seemingly forgotten that Russia existed, lost track of its momentous goings on.... Life at the gold fields plodded on tediously without anything happening.... In the morning—the office, and the rest of the time you didn't know what to do with yourself. The deadening monotony and torpor of life was mitigated

FIGURE 5.1.

Anna Kuvshinskaia, 1880s, Nerchinsk. Herzen Regional Library, Kirov.

by family and books, but it wasn't enough. The need for community and for more meaningful work went unsatisfied.[61]

Charushin's laments replicated much of the intelligentsia's discourse of the nineteenth century: lack of purposeful work, tedium, and enervation, the need for creative endeavors and for doing something useful in society, the notion of public good, and above all, the feeling of distance and separation from the world at large. The only difference now was that it was Siberia, where "[at] the mining settlements we were an alien element."[62]

A year later the Charushins decided to move on to Nerchinsk in the hope of finding a different milieu, new friends, and more meaningful activity. The environs of Nerchinsk contained rich lodes of silver. George Kennan was impressed by what the city—4,600 miles east of St. Petersburg—had to offer, "In point of culture and material prosperity it seems to compare favorably with most East-Siberian towns of its class. It has a bank, two or three schools, a hospital with twenty beds, a library, a museum, a public garden with a fountain and fifty or sixty shops.[63] Aside from Kononovich's presence (and once again, an offer of employment for Kuvshinskaia), Charushin was drawn to the place because the former member of the Nechaev circle and Kara veteran Alexei Kuznetsov also lived there. Charushin and Kuznetsov, despite their common experience at Kara, had never actually met and knew of each other only by word of mouth. That was enough, however. When the Charushins first arrived in Nerchinsk they lodged with the Kuznetsovs. Even after the Charushins found permanent housing, the two families visited each other almost daily. When Kennan arrived in Nerchinsk he met with the two men together, and "during our three days' stay in the town we passed with them many pleasant hours."[64]

Charushin provides a vivid portrait of Kuznetsov in his memoirs, emphasizing his resourcefulness, *joie de vivre*, and ability to maintain contact with a wide circle of acquaintances. He writes that of all those living under the status of *vol'naia komanda* in Kara, Kuznetsov had enjoyed the most liberty. He had taken the initiative to organize an orphanage, a workshop, experimental field, greenhouse and orangery. Eventually he established a library and a museum affiliated with the Russian Geographic Society, and tried his hand at theatrical performances.

Thanks to these friends Charushin found Nerchinsk a more hospitable place than his previous surroundings, but the question of employment—of finding a profession—still loomed large. Teaching did not appeal to him, nor did office work for the government or a private company. It was not merely a question of salary—though earning a living was important, and he was not happy leaving that burden entirely to Kuvshinskaia. There was a crying need for educated people in Siberia; however, Charushin had no professional training (having dropped out of the Technological Institute) and the undiversified economy of Nerchinsk, along with limitations (not always observed) placed on government employment, did not leave him with a lot of options. Charushin wanted to do something creative that also allowed him to work independently. Instead, as he put it, he "even" had to look after domestic matters for a while as his wife provided for the family by giving lessons.

Kuznetsov, whose first employment in Nerchinsk was with the wealthy mine owner Butin thereafter set up his own photo atelier. His example was attractive indeed to Charushin. He saw that Kuznetsov was able to make a living by pursuing something interesting that provided much room for creativity without limiting his freedom. "An artist by nature, and extremely enterprising at the same time, he much preferred the situation of an independent photographer to anything connected with the civil service."[65] Kuznetsov played a crucial role in easing Charushin's way into the "free professions"; he took Charushin under his wing, taught him the rudiments and techniques of the profession, which then led to major changes in his protégé's life, adjustment to a new position in society and soon, yet another relocation to take full advantage of his new skills.

Despite the quickened pace of life in Nerchinsk and gaining a foothold in a new profession, and like several others of his group, Charushin continued to feel at a remove from local society. Even many of those who like Kuznetsov consciously emulated the Decembrist exiles by becoming cultural activists and scientific explorers of the region, felt something missing in their lives. As Mikhail Chernavskii, who left Chita for Nerchinsk in 1886 and spent fourteen years there involved with the Lovers of Music and Literature Society and the Society for the Promotion of Education, wrote, "I wouldn't venture to say that all my work promoting culture was truly a passion."[66]

To be sure, the cultural pace of life in Nerchinsk really blossomed after 1886 just as the Charushins were once again contemplating a relocation; yet something more was going on. Were he and his cohort feeling the absence of the drama that had dominated their earlier years as underground revolutionary conspirators? Did they miss the youthful intensity of their collective efforts to survive and support each other while incarcerated? Most of the political exiles in Siberia continued to interact primarily among themselves, making no sustained effort to connect with local society, whose mundane interests they felt were too distant from their own. Their thoughts and dreams continued to be linked to the European Russia they had left behind which, tellingly, they continued to refer to simply as "Russia," juxtaposing it to "Siberia." As Charushin wrote:

> The entire way of life of the local population, with its uncomplicated and patriarchal world view, had no appeal and we had no notion of how to connect up with it—our interests, views, and tastes completely differed! As

previously and even if only in our thoughts, we continued to live the life and dramas of far-away Russia, something which seemed to mean nothing to the Nerchinsk public. Undoubtedly, we ourselves share a good measure of to blame for being so alienated; we had spent too long, both while free and in prison, putting aside all else and living in our circle of like-minded people single-mindedly devoted to a cause.[67]

These reflections were written long after Charushin had left Siberia, and after he had spent more than a decade in Viatka, working closely with local society through the zemstvo, devoting himself as a newspaper man to mobilizing the public and promoting local activism, and after he had experienced the tumultuous events of 1917–1921. Once again, we may be seeing at work the filter of memory: rather than point the finger at a "humdrum" local society oblivious to the need for revolution, Charushin looked back and saw the exiles' isolation and melancholy as resulting from their own cloistered and exclusive habits of mind. Life had made them reflect on the correctness of the tactics they had chosen, on the relations between the intelligentsia and the society at large, and on the importance of cultural promotion as such. Notable figures such as Alexei Kuznetsov, Dmitri Klements, and Ivan Popov, who had thrived in that environment and left a permanent mark on Siberian society, may have been exceptions. In fact, by the 1920s Charushin saw them in a different light: as carrying out, through different means, the same efforts to transform Russia the members of his circle had earlier pursued by revolutionary tactics. Remembering the life of Klements, who spent most of the remainder of his days pursuing ethnography, geography, and museology (he died in 1914), Charushin noted that the revolutionary movement had lost one of its most capable figures, but "in the end his new endeavors served the same ultimate goals as previously."[68] In his own way, Charushin would go in the same direction.

A REVOLUTIONARY TURNS TO PHOTOGRAPHY

On April 20, 1885, Charushin was notified that the Department of Police had no objection to his opening a photographic studio.[69] But, he wrote, he had had no inclination to compete with Kuznetsov for clients in Nerchinsk (a somewhat puzzling explanation since Kuznetsov had already left the city). He borrowed 800 rubles to purchase equipment, and shortly afterward had to borrow another 500 rubles for supplies. In 1886, he departed for Troitskosavsk, where he rented a house in which to set up his shop. The move was fortuitous, for it soon brought him into sustained contact with a prosperous, sophisticated, and worldly clientele of merchants, without losing contact with fellow exiles (see Figure 5.2). Soon photography would also provide him with an income sufficient to pay off his debts, live modestly, and even save money for an eventual return to European Russia.

Charushin's choice of Troitskosavsk, an administrative and commercial hub situated next to the residential suburb (*sloboda*) of Kiakhta was deliberate, since it offered far more opportunities than he had had in Nerchinsk. "Kiakhta," as the two adjacent settlements are often collectively referred to, was an important transit point in the tea trade with

FIGURE 5.2.

Leonid Zalkind, Nikolai Charushin, Ivan Popov, 1880s.
© Russian State Archive of Literature and Art, Moscow.

China. It was the home of major firms engaged in that business, as well as the residence of the owners of gold mines in the area. In Charushin's descriptions, as in those of another exile, Ivan Popov, Kiakhta was a prospering community that compared favorably with many provincial towns in European Russia. The Kiakhta merchants provided their children with fine educations, purchased books, subscribed to periodicals, arranged concerts, and in general amazed the exiles with the rich cultural life of this distant corner of the Russian Empire. Popov wrote thusly of Kiakhta, "There was much that was distinctive, that surprised and astounded the newcomer: the settlement of millionaires, its inhabitants, their mores and customs.... The culture of a European, the habits of a nomad, the age old, frozen civilization of the Middle Kingdom, shamanism, Taoism, Lamaism, Mohammedism, Christianity, Judaism.... 'Venice of the Sands'—that's what Kiakhta is called in the literature."[70]

Thanks to Popov's ties with Kiakhta society (he was married to the daughter of an influential merchant named Alexei M. Lushnikov), Charushin began taking orders for personal portraits, which quickly turned his photography business profitable, allowing him to pay off the debts he had incurred when he had purchased equipment and photo supplies. Popov described the Kiakhta merchants as millionaires who spent big money on goods from Europe and brought in well-known musicians to give concerts locally. George Kennan, who also happened to be familiar with Lushnikov, also wrote that the Kiakhta merchants were very rich, often seeing (in dollars of that time) $75,000 to $150,000 of straight profit in a given year. So photography in Kiakhta could be a profitable enterprise, indeed.[71]

Charushin's landscape photographs provided one source of his income; they were used on postcards, as illustrations in journals, and purchased by libraries and museums. Later in life, as well as posthumously (see chapter 10), Charushin was accused by Stalinists of unduly prospering at his trade—something purportedly proving his bourgeois inclinations. Charushin himself noted, "I was quite pleased with my new profession. It provided me with complete financial independence and at the same time kept my interest, prompting me to look for new angles and to constantly improve myself.... My income was sizeable."[72] He added that he had no shortage of money, work was abundant, and that he could even manage to put aside savings for his planned return to European Russia.

FIGURE 5.3.

Anna Kuvshinskaia, late 1880s, Kiakhta. Herzen Regional Library, Kirov.

In January 1887 Charushin submitted a request for permission to travel the entire length of Siberia. In March, a bureaucrat dealing with the matter wrote a note requesting a meeting (with whom we don't know) about Charushin, "who has taken up photography in Troitskosavsk" and wants "permission to spend the summer traveling along the banks of the Lena River with his photographic equipment."[73] Permission was granted, and Charushin spent from June to September on the trip. Given the sheer weight and the fragility of his equipment (especially the glass plates needed for his photographs); the rigors of traveling by small craft, carriage, and steamship; the constant need to load and unload barges; and the risk of losing everything at every turn, such road trips were feasible only if there was a real chance of good returns. It was indeed a long and difficult trip, but ultimately rewarding. Charushin made other excursions to take photographs, including a trip to the famed Buddhist temple at Goose Lake Datsan. His series of photographs of the road around Lake Baikal and beyond were collected into a photo album titled *Views of the Trans-Baikal region and of Irkutsk.*

Charushin's photographs of the exploration of Mongolia resulting from his participation in expeditions led by Grigory Potanin, the renowned explorer and Siberian regionalist, were also significant. He had become acquainted with Potanin in 1886 and their friendship quickly blossomed. Charushin knew of the famous explorer—who himself had run afoul of the authorities earlier in life—and was of course eager to make his acquaintance. It seems that Charushin made quite a favorable impression upon Potanin, for on the several occasions that the latter visited Kiakhta, he and his wife stayed with the Charushins and the couples spent much time together.[74] Potanin fit in easily with the local intelligentsia, played an active role in establishing a library and museum there, and even gave a series of lectures. Charushin saw in him the qualities he always valued in the Chaikovtsy: "remarkable modesty, purity of soul, lack of attachment to worldly comforts along with a strength of convictions that not even the harsh realities of Russian life . . . could break.[75]

In turn, Potanin's tales of his travels in Tibet and Mongolia fed Charushin's yearnings to see the world. Charushin wrote to Potanin (most likely early in 1888):

> [T]his summer I'll need to go somewhere to find work and my gaze has fallen upon Urga [today's Ulan Bator]. There's reason to believe that I can find good work there and in the process put together an interesting album of landscapes as well as a collection of *types* [Charushin has in mind the indigenous peoples]. I've heard that you are also thinking of traveling there, which only adds weight to my plans. With your assistance it would be much easier to orient myself in an unfamiliar place. Even more importantly, I could make good use of your direct instructions in the selection of sites to photograph. I presume that for you as an explorer it would be useful to have on hand someone always ready to carry out your wishes in providing you with photographs of views and types.[76]

To travel to Mongolia (which, until 1911, was still part of the Chinese Empire), Charushin needed permission from the authorities. He received the aid of the renowned explorer Semenov-Tian-Shanskii, who often had intervened with the authorities to help exiles with their needs. As Popov commented, "Once again Tian-Shanskii [who held several important posts in the government] had to don his uniform and regalia and make the trip to the Department of Police."⁷⁷ On June 6, 1888, that office received a request from the Eastern Siberia branch of the Imperial Russian Geographic Society to permit Charushin to travel with Potanin as his photographer; the request was approved only three days later, and on June 14, the appropriate papers were issued permitting him to travel to China for up to six weeks "for scientific purposes."⁷⁸

The result of these travels with Potanin was a collection of photographs taken in accordance with the current standards for anthropological and ethnographical photographic work (the correspondence between Potanin and Charushin reveals a discussion of the parameters of photography at the time). In Mongolia Charushin took more than two hundred photographs (see Figures 5.4–5.8). In 1890, Charushin wrote Potanin, "I of course have no objections to producing a phototype album of Siberian landscapes and am ready to do my best."⁷⁹ At the same time he sent Potanin the Mongolia photographs to be part of an exhibition and proposed that they be used as illustrations for an article about the expedition they had taken together to Mongolia.

Charushin was very satisfied with the trip even if the subsequent sale of photographs didn't quite cover his expenditures.⁸⁰ According to Popov's memoirs, the photographs of "Mongolian types" were for Charushin more a research project than a commercial enterprise, not something leading to financial gain. The trip itself, the sensation of freedom, the new impressions—were very important for him. Of equal importance was the acknowledgment by the Academy of Sciences and the Geographic Society that his pictures were of scientific significance. In December 1889, he received a letter from the Eastern Siberian branch of the Imperial Geographic Society expressing gratitude for the eighty photographs he had sent the society and notifying him that these photographs had been forwarded to the society's museum in Irkutsk. "These photographs," the letter said, "at the present time comprise the most valuable component of the museum's collection in terms of numbers, content and technical quality. The Committee considers it its duty to make special mention of the slides with photos representing the various types making up the population of Mongolia. Their conformity with the rules governing anthropological photographic execution fully allow us to label these slides a contribution to science."⁸¹

FIGURE 5.4.

Album "Mongolia" (1889), by Nikolai Charushin.
© ROSPHOTO, Russian State Museum and Exhibition Centre, St. Petersburg.

The natural surroundings are central to the representations of Siberia in the memoirs of exiles, but also in their photography. One summer Charushin traveled along the Udunginsk road (*trakt*), along which tea caravans wended their way through mountains and the taiga from Kiakhta to Lake Baikal. The result of this journey across these "wild, empty, but stunningly beautiful places"[82] was a collection of photographs published in journals and eagerly purchased in Siberia itself. On another occasion, he traveled along the river Selenga to Upper Udinsk (Verkhneudinsk),

FIGURE 5.5.

Album "Mongolia" (1889), by Nikolai Charushin.
© ROSPHOTO, Russian State Museum and Exhibition Centre, St. Petersburg.

spending a month there with his camera. When after seventeen years Charushin returned to his native Viatka in European Russia, he confessed that in addition to all else, his attachment to Siberia stemmed from the bounteous nature, vast expanses and bright sunshine he had witnessed on such trips.[83]

However, the peoples of Siberia drew the attention of political exiles primarily as objects of research. Accordingly, they produced numerous ethnographic works devoted to the Buriats, Yakuts, etc.; organized

FIGURE 5.6.

Album "Mongolia" (1889), by Nikolai Charushin.
© ROSPHOTO, Russian State Museum and Exhibition Centre, St. Petersburg.

FIGURE 5.7.

Album "Mongolia" (1889), by Nikolai Charushin.
© ROSPHOTO, Russian State Museum and Exhibition Centre, St. Petersburg.

FIGURE 5.8.

Album "Mongolia" (1889), by Nikolai Charushin.
© ROSPHOTO, Russian State Museum and Exhibition Centre, St. Petersburg.

ethnography sections at exhibitions; and otherwise pursued their interests. Of course, the indigenous peoples caught their eye primarily as Eastern exoticism; they studied, wrote down their legends and songs, photographed their domiciles and temples, and observed their holidays and rituals—but notably, there is little mention of the peoples of Siberia in the memoirs of political exiles. They remain outside the margins of the Siberia society they describe. "People" (*narod*) for the political exiles meant above all the Russian peasantry with all its distinctive features and the (Russian) workers in the gold mines, but not the indigenous people (*inorodtsy*). Typical of this orientalizing discourse was Charushin's description of his travels in Mongolia, much resembling other exile accounts of travels across Siberia, in which the local population are presented as savages untouched by civilization and their condition is compared with that of childhood—the Enlightenment paradigm of the time (called recapitulation theory or embryological parallelism) by which civilizations progressed from "infancy" to "maturity." Thus, Charushin wrote of Mongolia, "The Mongolians are a poor, extremely primitive people, living in their filthy yurts, devoid of even the most elementary signs of culture."[84]

Charushin's photographs of Mongolians have "museum display" written all over them, for they embody the colonial gaze that defined photographing empire across the globe at the time. It is in the texts accompanying the photos that we glimpse the local inhabitants' responses to the photographer, which sometimes caused him considerable difficulty. This only reinforced his impression of them as uncivilized and governed by superstitions. In his words, "Initially work went painfully slowly. The fact of the matter is that photography was an unprecedented matter in Mongolia and one evoking profound preconceptions. In the Mongolian's mind, anybody who allowed himself to be photographed would lose control over his own soul."[85] Kennan similarly described his fruitless attempts to take photographs of the Chinese, Mongolians, and Buriats, lumping them all under one name: "aborigines." Their fear was so great that as soon as a photographer appeared with his camera, the streets would empty out.[86] Kennan even joked condescendingly that a camera would be a good weapon in the hands of the governor to put down revolts by the local population.

As rewarding as it was, photography did not exhaust his endeavors while in Kiakhta, for while there he also helped establish a library and museum, both of which still stand today. Despite rather daunting red tape and legal restrictions, such libraries were fast becoming part of the cultural landscape in European Russia and Siberia; in the former, the sponsors were typically the zemstvo and local literacy societies (the Kharkov and Viatka zemstvos were leaders). In Siberia, the sponsors were often local merchants working together with the exile community. sometimes with the blessings of the local authorities. According to Popov, in Kiakhta the initiative came from his own and Charushin's families, joined by local teachers and with funding by Lushnikov. Popov worked energetically to promote the idea, was responsible for putting together a basic collection of books, and gained the endorsement of local leaders. With the help of other teachers, Anna Kuvshinskaia organized and catalogued the collection. Charushin and Popov drew up the statute for the library (according to which every reader became a member of its advisory committee, and annual membership fees were set at six rubles). Popov boasted that the statute was the first of its kind in Russia, but Charushin rightly identified the Kharkov library as its precursor. In their memoirs both Charushin and Popov stressed that the establishment of Kiakhta's first library was a collective project.⁸⁷ The library, also reflected a kind of thematic continuity in Charushin's life: from the "book matters" of the Chaikovskii circle, to his participation in the Viatka book cooperative at the turn of the century, and finally, his contribution to Herzen Library matters in Viatka in the early Soviet era.

"THE CALL OF OUR FIRST HOMELAND WAS STRONGER THAN ATTACHMENT TO THE SECOND ONE"

By this time however, despite their immersion in the life of Kiakhta, the Charushins' thoughts were focused on returning home to Viatka. Earlier, unbeknownst to them, Kuvshinskaia's mother had petitioned the empress to allow the family to return, stating that the Charushins had "recognized the errors of their ways," and pointing out that her daughter had gone to Siberia out of loyalty and to honor her commitments to her betrothed. Calling Kuvshinskaia a "misguided daughter," she confessed that as a mother she could not condemn her, and that her long absence was heartbreaking:

> If I could, I would fall on my knees before you and beg you, Your Highness to return my daughter to me, and her to her native land, which she has not seen for ages and for which her heart longs.... I entreat you to return my daughter and her husband home; they have both acknowledged their errors of their way. Their long years of material and moral suffering far away have forced them to look at life more soberly and taught them to distinguish what is truly of worth from the false views of their youth, and if Your Highness would look with favor upon my request, they would return as true and loyal citizens and children of their motherland.⁸⁸

Charushin had also, in 1890, applied for permission to return to Viatka, arguing that he had completed his designated term in exile, but the request was turned down,⁸⁹ as was a similar one in 1892 submitted on his behalf by his brother Arkadii, who pointed to "family circumstances and need to raise their children."⁹⁰ Charushin's memoirs make no mention of his own or his brother's attempts to gain permission to return, perhaps because such appeals for clemency were frowned on by the exiled Populists, who regarded them as signs of weakness or, even worse, of treachery. Vera

Figner was even more adamant; she later wrote that she had felt humiliated and outraged to learn of her mother's efforts on her behalf:

> How could my own mother, my stalwart, courageous mother "pray" for mercy for me? Without shedding a tear and without even a moment of weakness she saw one daughter after another into exile in Siberia and when we parted she gave me her word she would never beg for any special dispensation for me.... I felt degraded in receiving any royal beneficence and who was it that humiliated me? My own beloved, profoundly venerated mother. She humiliated me, but also herself. It was even worse when my comrades comforted me telling me that it was not my fault![91]

Yet the 1890s were a decade during which many of the exiles of Charushin's generation returned to European Russia, both because they had completed their sentences and because of an imperial decree, of April 17, 1891, providing amnesty for some on the occasion of the heir to the throne's (the future Nicholas II) return home through Siberia after an eventful visit to Asia (he had experienced an attempted assassination while in Japan). Popov recalled that 1895–1897 were "years of comings and goings; at no time previously had so many exiles descended upon Irkutsk. For the most part the younger travelers were passing on to the north and the east into exile. As for the "elders" they were returning from exile, and many of them ended up stranded in Irkutsk."[92] In 1895, the Charushins were among those exiles passing through Irkutsk with their families; he spent several days visiting Popov and conversing about days past and present in their lives.

Still, leaving Siberia was not an easy decision, for over the course of seventeen years the Charushins had put down roots there. Three children had been born in the region and they would have to leave behind the grave of their daughter Lydia, who had died in 1888. Charushin would also relinquish a profession and a social network that included fellow exiles but also members of respectable society—as he put it, they had not been alone in the world and "felt themselves almost full-blooded citizens." They and fellow exiles had created an extensive if informal mutual aid society and had collaborated on joint projects. Indeed, many exiles, including those who had gained the right to return to European Russia if they wished, considered Siberia their real home and decided to stay. As Chemodanova later in life wrote Kuvshinskaia, "I am going to remain in Tomsk, where the graves of my husband and child are; where my corner of the world is and where I need to finish bringing up my children. Furthermore, I've become accustomed to life here; the more I read and the more I ask, life seems better here in Tomsk than in some provincial Russian town, and we simply couldn't afford to live in the capital."[93] She remained there for the rest of her days.

Charushin had also become attached to the land itself, "We were drawn to Siberia by the rich natural surroundings, its boundless expanses and bright sunshine, and by the people themselves who were much less beaten down, more aware of their human dignity, and who always treated us kindly. And now we had to relinquish all this and return to that very place that had rejected and shamed us, treating us as an unfit and criminal element, but which also exerted a relentless pull upon us."[94]

That "relentless pull" had several strands. In Siberia, the exile community had closely followed political events in European Russia and were fully aware of the quickening pace of life there. Civil society was becoming more boisterous, the so-called Liberation Movement was emerging within the zemstvo and in the country's newly active professional societies of doctors, teachers, and others whose expertise meant to provide needed services to the population was hindered by a suspicious autocracy. Surely the departure of many of their peers (including Popov, who had left Kiakhta in 1894) had contributed to their decision to leave as well. Finally, the Charushins had friends and, especially, family in Viatka who were ready to help with the move. Ivan had returned from Sakhalin in 1893 to assume the position of official provincial architect; others in the family had made successful inquiries about finding employment for Charushin with the province's progressive zemstvo.

Charushin had to sell his valuable photography equipment and all of his negatives to finance the long journey ahead of him. The profits from the sale enabled his family to do what many others couldn't simply because they lacked the financial resources: move a family and its possessions safely and in reasonable comfort across a vast terrain to return to European Russia. To be sure his failing vision had already caused him to relinquish the profession of photography, but had that not been so the combination of family ties, opportunity, and nostalgia would in any case have justified the extraordinary sacrifices called for. In his words, "[T]he call of our first homeland was stronger than attachment to the second. We decided to return to our dear old Viatka, where we had so many luminous memories of youthful times."[95]

NOTES

1. Sergei Sinegub, *Zapiski chaikovtsa* (Moskva: Molodaia Gvardiia, 1929), 234.
2. Nikolai Charushin, *O dalekom proshlom* (Moskva: Vsesoiuznoe Obshchestvo Politkatorzhan, 1931), 208; A. A. Tolstaia–L. N. Tolstoy. *Perepiska (1857–1903)* (Moskva: Nauka, 2011), 837. See Tatiana Saburova and Ben Eklof, *Druzhba, sem'ia, revoliutsiia: Nikolai Charushin i pokolenie narodnikov 1870-kh godov* (Moskva: Novoe Literaturnoe Obozrenie, 2016), 188–189.
3. George Kennan, *Siberia and the Exile System*, part 1 (New York: Praeger, 1970), 1:370.
4. Charushin, *O dalekom proshlom* (Moskva: Mysl', 1973), 279.
5. The urban *meshchanstvo*, like the nobility, merchants, and peasants, represented a legal category within Russia's official estate or order hierarchy. Economically and culturally, the members of this group (*meshchane*) are variously described as artisans or belonging to the petty bourgeoisie.
6. GARF, f. 102, D-3, op. 91, d. 354, t. 1, 1893, ll. 48–48 ob.
7. Ibid., ll. 64–65.
8. On the general topic of perceptions of Siberia, see Galya Diment and Yuri Slezkine, *Between Heaven and Hell: The Myth of Siberia in Russian Culture* (New York: St. Martin's Press, 1993). On Siberian exile in general several recent works merit attention: Andrew A. Gentes, *Exile to Siberia, 1590–1822* (New York: Palgrave Macmillan, 2008) and Daniel Beer, *House of the Dead: Siberian Exile under the Tsars* (London: Penguin, 2016); Sarah Badcock: *A Prison Without Walls? Eastern Siberian Exile in the Last Years of Tsarism* (Oxford: Oxford University Press, 2016—but none focus upon the period of incarceration of the Chaikovtsy. On official state policies in Siberia, see A.V. Remnev, *Sibir' v imperskoi geografii vlasti XIX-nachala XX vekov* (Omsk: izd. Omskogo gosudarstvennogo universiteta, 2015).
9. See Nataliia Rodigina, *"Drugaia Rossiia." Obraz Sibiri v russkoi zhurnal'noi presse vtoroi poloviny XIX-nachala XX v.* (Novosibirsk: Novosibirskii Gosudarstvennyi Pedagogicheskii Universitet, 2006).
10. Lev Deich, *16 let v Sibiri* (Zheneva: P. Axelrod, 1905), 98.
11. Vladimir Debogorii-Mokrievich, *Vospominaniia* (St. Petersburg: Svobodnyi Trud, 1906), 439–440.
12. Sinegub, *Zapiski chaikovtsa*, 278.
13. Nikolai Charushin, *O dalekom proshlom na Kare* (Moskva: Vsesoiuznoe Obshchestvo Politkatorzhan, 1929), 108–109.
14. Ivan Popov, *Minuvshee i perezhitoe. Sibir' i emigratsiia. Vospominaniia za 50 let* (Leningrad: Kolos, 1924), 45.
15. Ivan Popov, *Zabytye stranitsy: Zapiski redaktora* (Irkutsk: Vostochno-Sibirskoe knizhnoe izdatel'stvo, 1989), 123.
16. Debogorii-Mokrievich, *Vospominaniia*, 431.
17. Deich, *16 let v Sibiri*, 97.
18. Ibid.
19. Charushin, *O dalekom proshlom na Kare*, 15.

20. L. Kler, "Kariiskaia katorga. Ee mesto i rol' v karatel'noi sisteme samoderzhaviia," *Ssyl'nye revoliutsionery v Sibiri* (Irkutsk: Irkutskii Gosudarstvennyi Universitet, 1985), 217–231.

21. Naum Gekker, "Politicheskaia katorga na Kare. Vospominaniia," *Byloe* 9 (1906): 71.

22. According to the criminal statute, sentences were divided into two parts; the first, or trial, period consisted of the time in prison and shackled. Following this was the "rehabilitative period," each year of which served reduced the total sentence by two months. Next, the prisoner was released into a "free unit," or *vol'naia komanda*, where the prisoner could live outside the prison walls and free of constant surveillance but with strict limitations. In December 1880, a decree eliminated the "free unit" option, and those already living outside the prison were forced to return, and were also deprived of right to send and receive correspondence?

23. Charushin, *O dalekom proshlom na Kare*, 24, 27.

24. Those condemned to hard labor never actually worked in the mines, which were depleted by that time, and the closest working sites were too far away to walk to on a daily basis. The Siberian the penal system was thus awash in idle hands, and the prisoners at Kara actually petitioned Kononovich to find them some type of work.

25. Charushin, *O dalekom proshlom na Kare*, 29–31; Sinegub, *Zapiski chaikovtsa*, 269–270, 280–281.

26. Charushin, *O dalekom proshlom na Kare*, 28–29.

27. Gekker, Politicheskaia katorga na Kare, 71.

28. Deich, *16 let v Sibiri*, 153.

29. Debogorii-Mokrievich, *Vospominaniia*, 452.

30. Tikhomirov argued that revolutionaries were too detached from Russia's realities, too bookish and enamored with Western ideas; that instead of focusing on tearing down the political order, they should concentrate on constructive activities—as it was the resort to terrorism that was both morally and politically bankrupt. His qualms about terrorism and especially his argument that only the Russian people themselves could make an authentic revolution were close to Charushin's lifelong views, but his turn to Orthodoxy, nationalism, and monarchism was not. Tikhomirov, Pochemu ia perestal byt' revolutsionerom (Moskva: Vilde, 1895), 10, 13–14, 24–25, 30–33, 38.

31. Charushin, *O dalekom proshlom na Kare*, 55.

32. Anna Biel, "Nikolai Nekrasov's Representation of the Decembrist Women," *Australian Slavonic and East European Studies* 25, no. 1–2 (March 2011): 39–59.

33. Popov, *Minuvshee i perezhitoe. Sibir' i emigratsiia*, 45.

34. A. A. Tolstaia–L. N. Tolstoy. Perepiska, 663.

35. Sinegub, *Zapiski chaikovtsa*, 235.

36. Vera Figner, "Zheny dekabristov," *100-letie vosstaniia dekabristov. Sbornik statei i dokumentov zhurnala Katorga i Ssylka* (Moskva: Vsesoiuznoe Obshchestvo Politkatorzhan, 1927), 229.

37. On this see also Venturi, *Roots of Revolution*, 319–320.

38. Sinegub, *Zapiski chaikovtsa*, 253.

39. Charushin, *O dalekom proshlom na Kare*, 18–19.

40. Sinegub, *Zapiski chaikovtsa*, 256.

41. Charushin, *O dalekom proshlom na Kare*, 38.

42. Helen Hundley, *George Kennan and the Russian Empire. How America's Conscience Became an Enemy of Tsarism* (Washington, DC: Woodrow Wilson Center, 2000). For the history of the translation and publication of this work, see E. I. Melamed, *Dzhordzh Kennan protiv tsarizma* (Moskva, 1981), 60–72.

43. Charushin, *O dalekom proshlom na Kare*, 102; the entire quotation is on pp. 102–104. Charushin draws from one of the several versions of Kennan's work published in 1906; *Kennan, Sibir' i ssylka* (St. Petersburg: Izdanie Raspopova, 1906) but he incorrectly lists the pages cited in the Russian edition as 110–111, whereas the original Russian version has them 210–211. The original English text is in Kennan, *Siberia and the Exile System*, part II, 219 (the wording of the translation differs in these various editions). To protect his informants from repercussions Kennan often cited the testimony of political prisoners without acknowledging them. Charushin was definitely among those from whom he drew his portrait of life in Siberia and the prison conditions there; when the two men met in Nerchinsk, Charushin related his own life story to the author; described conditions at Kara; and in particular, described the circumstances surrounding the suicide of one of the prisoners there, a certain Semianovskii, who had shared lodgings with Charushin (The letter written by Semianovskii is in Kennan papers in NYPL)

44. Charushin, *O dalekom proshlom na Kare*, 19.
45. Sinegub, *Zapiski chaikovtsa*, 275.
46. Ibid., 262.
47. A search in GARF for Kononovich's personal file yielded no results; however, the Department of Gendarmes in Zhitomir, where he lived in retirement, reported to St. Petersburg, in 1905 in the aftermath of large-scale pogroms, that Kononovich had signed a protest letter complaining about the harsh measures taken by the military against the residents of the Jewish quarter. Kononovich, whose name appeared at the top of the list of signatures, was especially indignant at the use of force against innocent citizens (GARF, f. 102, OO II otdelenie, 1905, op. 233a, d. 1350, chast' 27, ll. 49–50 ob.)
48. Charushin, *O dalekom proshlom na Kare*, 38.
49. Sinegub, *Zapiski chaikovtsa*, 256.
50. Charushin, *O dalekom proshlom na Kare*, 72.
51. Sinegub, *Zapiski chaikovtsa*, 287.
52. Anton Chekhov, "Ostrov Sakhalin: (iz putevykh zapisok)," *Polnoe sobranie sochinenii i pisem: v 30 tomakh*, t. 14–15 (Moskva: Nauka, 1978), 60.
53. Chekhov to Kononovich, letter (February 19, 1891), ibid., t.4 (Moskva: Nauka,1975), 178–184.
54. For example, through the intervention of the Countess Alexandra Tolstoy, Kononovich tried to help the daughter of A. V. Armfel'dt, who had been sent to Kara for her revolutionary activities. See *A. A. Tolstaia i L. N. Tolstoy. Perepiska*, 837.
55. By a quirk of fate, Ivan was also present in Sakhalin at the time, working for the government as an architect. In May 1891, Kononovich sent Ivan Charushin to Vladivostok to set up an exhibition on the occasion of the arrival of the heir to the throne on his travels through Asia; for his efforts Ivan received a gold watch with the inscription of the Romanovs (RGIA, f. 796, op. 438, d. 4733, l. 2). For more on Ivan Charushin, see chapter 6.
56. GARF, f. 102, D-3, op. 91, d. 354, t. 1, l. 1.
57. Charushin, *O dalekom proshlom na Kare*, 41.
58. Charushin, *O dalekom proshlom* (1931), 101–102. The Nerchinsk penal district beyond Lake Baikal extended for 200 miles and included twenty mines and seven factories. Apparently, what happened was that, perhaps at the decision of the governor, Charushin was actually assigned to Tataurovo, a small, unattractive settlement near to Chita, about which he wrote "he knew nothing." Instead, Kononovich helped set him up at the Davenda gold mines. Why this was preferable is a mystery, for the mines were far away from the town of Nerchinsk,

an eight-hour drive even today. The most likely explanation is that distant as it was this location offered Charushin a means of employment unavailable in Tataurovo.

59. Ibid., 101.
60. Charushin, *O dalekom proshlom* (1931), 104.
61. Ibid., 104, 106–107.
62. Ibid., 108.
63. Kennan, *Siberia and the Exile System* (1970), 2:322–323.
64. Ibid., 324–325. Kennan described Charushin as a well-educated and considerate person with whom he had the occasion to spend many hours in Nerchinsk: "Sunday morning, November 29, 1885, after bidding good-bye with sincere regrets to Mr. and Mrs. Charushin, whose warm hearts and loveable characters had won our affection and esteem."
65. Charushin, *O dalekom proshlom* (1931), 109–10.
66. *Deiateli SSSR i revoliutsionnogo dvizheniia v Rossii* (Moskva: Sovetskaia Entsiklopediia, 1989), 300.
67. Charushin, *O dalekom proshlom* (1931), 136–137.
68. Ibid., 178.
69. GARF, f. 102, D-3, op. 91, d. 354, t. 1, l. 25a.
70. Popov, *Minuvshee i perezhitoe*, 7–8. Curiously, George Kennan's impressions of Kiakhta differ radically from the vivid portrayals of Popov and Charushin. He depicts Kiakhta as an ordinary Russian provincial town that "does not appear at first sight to be anything more than a large, prosperous village. It contains a greater number of comfortable looking two-story log dwelling houses, . . . and it has two noticeable churches of the Russo-Greek type with white walls and belfries surmounted by colored or gilded domes; but one would never suppose it to be the most important commercial point in Eastern Siberia." Kennan, *Siberia and the Exile System 2* (1970) 2:103–104.
71. Ibid., 104.
72. Charushin, *O dalekom proshlom* (1931), 151.
73. GARF, f. 102, D-3, 1893, op. 91, d. 354, t.1, ll. 31–31 ob.
74. Charushin, *O dalekom proshlom* (1931), 160.
75. Ibid., 161.
76. RGALI, f. 381, op. 1, d. 176, ll. 30–30ob. (undated). Charushin writes that he "eagerly agreed to a proposal on the part of Potanin"; this letter seems to suggest that the initiative came from him instead. See Charushin, *O dalekom proshlom* (1931), 162.
77. Popov, *Minuvshee i perezhitoe*, 251. In one instance, the local governor, Goremykin, recommended that Popov turn to Tian-Shanskii for help with his request to serve as editor of the regional newspaper *Vostochnoe Obozrenie*.
78. GARF, f. 102, D-3, op. 91, d. 354, t. 1, l. 40.
79. RGALI, f. 381, op. 1, d. 176, l. 1.
80. Popov, *Minuvshee i perezhitoe*, 130–31.
81. GARF, f. 102, D-3, 1893, op. 91, d. 354, t.1, ll. 52–52 ob.
82. Charushin, *O dalekom proshlom* (1931), 208.
83. Charushin, *O dalekom proshlom na Kare*, 107.
84. Charushin, *O dalekom proshlom*, (1931), 183.
85. Ibid., 185.
86. George Kennan, *Sibir' i ssylka* (St. Petersburg: Izdatel'stvo Vrublevskogo, 1906), 293.
87. Popov, *Minuvshee i perezhitoe*, 97–98; Charushin, *O dalekom proshlom* (1931), 159.
88. GARF, f. 102, D-3, op. 91, d. 354, t. 1, ll. 2 ob.–3.

89. Ibid., ll. 49–50. The authorities challenged his calculations, arguing that the clock had begun not at the time of his incarceration (1874) but of his sentencing (1878)
90. Ibid., 64–65.
91. Vera Figner, *Zapechatlennyi trud* (Moskva: Mysl', 1964) 2: 206. Charushin called such appeals "moral suicide" and framed his own 1890 petition strictly in legal terms, based upon the expiration of his sentence.
92. Popov, *Minuvshee i perezhitoe*, 262.
93. Chemodanova to Kuvshinskaia, 1907, RGALI, f. 1642, op. 1, d. 105, l. 6.
94. Charushin, *O dalekom proshlom* (1931), 217–218.
95. Ibid., 218.

6

Return to European Russia

Family Ties, Network of Exiles, and the Zemstvo (1895–1905)

> At the time Viatka was a site of accelerated settlement by political exiles; our family home was turned into a political club of sorts where Marxists and Populists freely intermingled.... Many of these exiles set down deep roots in the province and occupied prominent positions in the zemstvo.
>
> —Nikolai Charushin, 1926

The two decades following the Charushins' return to Viatka and leading up to the Russo-Japanese War (1904–1905) and the First Russian Revolution (1905–1907) were dynamic, explosive, and transformative, both for Russia as a whole and for life in its provinces. These events were so massive, momentous, and violent that had they not been superseded a decade later by an even more catastrophic war and revolution they would occupy a significant place in the global history of the twentieth century. Viatka, both city and province, was profoundly shaken by these developments, as were relations between state and society, and the intelligentsia's view on violence, progress, and the people.

The Viatka to which the Charushins returned (see Figure 6.1) was reawakening from a somnolent period caused by the shift in trade routes that had followed the entry of the steamship on Russia's waterways. The reawakening coincided with the arrival of the railroad[1] connecting Viatka, first with Perm' (1899), and then, in 1906, with St. Petersburg, after which

FIGURE 6.1.

Viatka, early 1900s, by Sergei Lobovikov.
© Vasnetsov Museum of Fine Arts, Kirov.

the population grew rapidly and commercial life was reinvigorated.[2] Playing a role in the cultural reawakening were several developments; including the rapid expansion of secondary education; the emergence of the Viatka provincial zemstvo as one of the most progressive and energetic in all European Russia; and, paradoxically the autocracy's decision in 1897, after two decades of hiatus, to once again designate Viatka province as a destination for exiles.

Before departing on that long journey back from eastern Siberia, Charushin had been encouraged by the prospect of finding employment at the end of the trip. As he later wrote, "Our relatives and old friends summoned us, offering hope of employment at the zemstvo";[3] and indeed soon he was working for that institution as a fire-insurance agent. Toward the turn of the century, the local gendarmes decided he was no longer a threat to the status quo, and removed him from active surveillance.[4] During this time (from 1905 until 1908) he also became the official local representative of the All-Russia Zemstvo Famine Relief Commission, responsible for dispersing nearly 300,000 rubles to distressed households experiencing crop failures.[5] He founded an independent newspaper at the end of 1905. As for Kuvshinskaia, with the exception of a brief period when she stepped in to become publisher of that newspaper, formally speaking she played no role in public affairs. However, she retained her firm allegiance to the cause of Populism and behind the scenes shared in Charushin's every endeavor.

THE CHARUSHIN HOUSEHOLD: DOMESTICITY AND EXTENDED FAMILY

First, however, was the matter of finding new lodgings and re-establishing a hearth, something of great importance to the family. Doing so renewed a way of life rich in family ties, humdrum daily concerns, and the material comforts of domesticity that they had experienced in Kiakhta. The Charushins rented the second floor of a home owned by Vasilii Kliucharev, at the time somewhat distant from the center of town.[6] Household and immediate family matters occupied much of their attention. Though they soon employed domestic help, Kuvshinskaia put a lot of energy into household management, and there were two boys, Leonid and Vladimir, whose schooling required looking after.

Viatka provided Charushin with the opportunity to renew links with his family, from whom he had been separated for decades. To begin with, Charushin's young cousin Viacheslav Iuferev (the son of his mother's brother, the family benefactor[7]) found employment with the zemstvo statistical bureau through the intervention of family and was provided a room at his residence. Iuferev, who later wrote his memoirs, left us with us valuable if flawed sketches of his cousins, including two of Charushin's brothers.

As for Charushin's sisters, we know only of Lydia and Yulia. Both were married to prominent local citizens with whom Charushin's life became entangled in sundry ways. Lydia was married to Alexei Lopatin, a hereditary noble serving in the Orlov district court, who was also employed in two different insurance agencies (the Russian Fire Insurance Society and Junker and Co.) and served as treasurer of the Orlov Philanthropic

Society and was delegate to the Orlov district zemstvo. Later, in a period of turmoil, in late 1906 he was also elected to the provincial-level zemstvo executive board, but his elevation to that post was vetoed by the governor. In his memoirs Charushin singles out his brother-in-law's service to the zemstvo in Orlov district, and the activities of that zemstvo as a whole in revitalizing what had been a town in steady decline since the 1870s.[8]

About Charushin's sister Yulia we know little, but she apparently lived a stable bourgeois existence. Iuferev lived in Yulia's household for seven years while attending school and described her "preserving her femininity and elegance well into middle age."[9] Her husband, I. P. Khoroshavin, several years older than she and a "ponderous" individual, was in 1895 the provincial-level zemstvo fire-insurance agent supervising the dozen or so district agents below him and shaping policy in this key area for the entire vast province. The Khoroshavin household included two of his sisters and two children, but few books, and according to Iuferov, they lived a "measured" life.[10] It seems all but certain that it was Khoroshavin who arranged for Charushin to take a position as a fire-insurance agent for the Viatka district zemstvo soon after arriving from Siberia. Khoroshavin went on to serve as provincial secretary in the governor's office, and he is listed in the official provincial handbook in 1901 as "assistant to the records manager."[11] (Soon after, he died; Yulia would remarry). A few years later, in a time of distress, Kuvshinskaia writes her husband telling him to turn to his sister Yulia for help with the household.

Nikolai's younger brother Arkadii (born in 1857), after graduating with a degree in law from St. Petersburg University, in 1883, applied for a civil-service position dealing with peasant affairs in the Tomsk or Tobol'sk provinces but was turned down, most likely because of his connection with radicals (he had been arrested himself in 1880). Although charges against him were not pressed and he was quickly released, the Department of Police recommended that he be kept under close surveillance and not be given a position that would put him in close contact with layers of the population "susceptible to propaganda."[12] Despite this, Arkadii steadily made his way up the civil-service ladder and in 1884 was officially sent to work on peasant resettlement matters in Ufa province; two years later he was sent to Tomsk, in Siberia, as a special envoy (*chinovnik osobykh poruchenii*) for the Land Bureau of the MVD. In 1890 he was transferred to Samara and then to Orenburg provinces, where he gained further expertise on peasant matters. After 1893 Arkadii was stationed in St. Petersburg, working now in the Resettlement Administration (which was also under the Ministry of Interior). He rose to the fourth level (active civil councilor) in the Table of Ranks, which granted him and his family the status of hereditary nobility.[13] During his time of service he made several official trips to the Viatka region, where he undoubtedly met up with his brother; family correspondence indicates a continuing connection.

Arkadii's cousin Iuferev has left a rather unsympathetic portrait of portrait of him:

> When I first met him Arkadii Apollonovich was a died-in-the-wool bureaucrat and reactionary. He subscribed to Suvorov's *New Times* (a conservative newspaper) and read it closely over tea in the morning. When he showed up in Orlov, he put on a show, strutting about in his uniform and conducting himself arrogantly. One of my friends took to calling him "Uncle Minister." In Petersburg Ark[adii] Apoll[onovich] also did his utmost to keep up appearances—when he went to the theater, nothing worse than the parterre was suitable for him.[14]

However, the seemingly dry archival records of the Resettlement Office of the Ministry of Interior offer us a different, far more flattering portrait of Arkadii. In this position he traveled widely across the country to determine what areas were the most promising for relocating needy peasants. He was widely regarded as a leading expert in the field; his reports were reprinted, circulated among the various branches of government, and recommended for use in the field.[15] In recognition of his expertise he was chosen to be chair of the Tenishev Ethnographic Bureau at the turn of the century—an institution well-known to Western scholars for its rich collection of materials on the Russian peasantry. His efforts demonstrate a genuine concern for the welfare of the peasantry but also regard for the needs of the state. Moreover, elsewhere in this volume we have learned of Arkadii's lifelong devotion to his brother: he sought to visit Nikolai in prison, petitioned for termination of his exile and restoration of his noble status, and then later attempted to arrange for Kuvshinskaia's return home to her family from exile. Both J. Alfred Reiber and Peter Holquist have argued that separate ministries in the Russian empire fostered their own distinct ideologies, which were in turn shaped by generational affiliation. In Arkadii's case, he was closer to the Great Reform generation and to his brother's ethical views than to the technocratic mindset that characterized the Resettlement Administration after 1905.[16]

An equally important sibling in this story is Ivan (see Figure 6.2), who was younger than Nikolai by a decade. Iuferev has left an unflattering portrait of this brother as well: "He was not especially intelligent and the breadth of his knowledge was limited to his specialty, architecture. Moreover, he was a slippery individual, a chameleon. Those close to him, especially his relatives, believed him to be a kind and decent person. They were wrong, it was all a guise and in his heart of hearts he was a callous and cold adventurist."[17]

Just how accurate was this depiction? Ivan, who in 1890 had completed his degree in architecture at the Academy of Arts in St. Petersburg chose, for reasons that are unclear, to become the official state architect on the remote island of Sakhalin—at the time a huge penal settlement notori-

FIGURE 6.2.

Ivan Charushin, 1900. Kirov State Archive.

ous for its corruption and violence. He returned to Viatka in 1893 as the provincial architect, and rose to the status of provincial engineer in 1901, in which position he served until 1917.[18] Widowed at an early age, his burden of sorrow was relieved by the governor's wife, who introduced him to his second wife.[19] Ivan's career flourished, if Iuferev is to be believed, partially because of his sycophantic nature, "Though a plebeian by birth,[20] [he] made every effort to circulate among the cream of society.... After arriving in Viatka, he tried to make his way into the governor's close circle and frequented the home of the steamship magnate Tikhon Bulychev.[21] Over the next two decades he designed churches, monumental secondary school buildings, commercial centers, and private residences. Ivan's most lucrative architectural commission was the "palace," built in 1911, for Bulychev, one of the wealthiest and most prominent men in the entire Volga-Kama region, and a prominent figure in government and public circles.[22] On his ample salary Ivan Charushin bought and tastefully remodeled a mansion in Viatka, where he entertained lavishly in his successful search for architectural contracts.

Despite Iuferev's claim, Ivan was well-read and a competent pianist, and his home was a cultural center for the city's elite. According to Ivan's biographer, Nikolai Charushin frequented his younger brother's house and mixed with the society there.[23] Also joining Ivan's household was the family matron, Ekaterina Charushina, who had moved in with Ivan soon after he arrived to help maintain the residence. Ivan flourished under the tsarist regime and also, with major adjustments in the first two decades of Soviet rule; for that reason, Iuferev suggests, he had no convictions. Even so, in 1918 he put his own safety at risk by writing a long letter to the Revolutionary Tribunal appealing for Nikolai's release from his incarceration by the Bolsheviks. Overall, then, the fraternal ties among the brothers were indeed strong and lasting ones.

So how are we to reconcile the unflattering portraits of both Arkadii and Ivan, whom Iuferev saw as officious, careerist toadies, with the far more admirable versions emerging from our narration? How could the two worlds, officialdom and underground Russia, mingle so easily on the level of the family? Iuferev's descriptions are a useful tonic in reminding us that loving and loyal brothers, who on one level shared convictions not fitting well with their official duties, could, once they put on their uniforms, seem and act in ways that were officious, overbearing, and arrogant.[24] Perhaps such behavior and appearances were reflective not so much of individual personalities as of the rules of social hierarchy deeply embedded in what has famously been called an exceptionally complex and multilayered "sedimentary society." Or perhaps we need simply to turn to Ervin Goffman's classic work, *The Presentation of Self in Everyday Life* to understand how and why in modern societies people change their appearance and demeanor to adjust to different settings—without making them hypocrites.

Personal ties also brought Charushin into frequent contact with the world of business, which was rapidly expanding in Viatka early in the twentieth century. The societal networks in Viatka were intricate and hard for the casual observer to follow. At the same time, grasping them is essential if one is to understand just how elaborate the connections between state and society were. For example, it is likely that Ivan's relationship with Bulychev was not merely one of architect and client. In fact, a web of connections linked the Charushins with the Bulychevs. Ivan Charushin served on the board of trustees of the public library; he was joined there by Bulychev's wife, as well as by Iakov Poskrebyshev, the mayor of Viatka.[25] The latter, who later married Bulychev's daughter, was himself the son of a prosperous merchant. Like Charushin, he was connected with an early oppositionist newspaper in Viatka, and as mayor, he promoted liberal agendas. Poskrebyshev's public activities and political views were at several points in his life aligned with those of both Nikolai Charushin and the head of the provincial zemstvo board, Yumashev, whose own life, as we shall see, was also closely entangled with that of Charushin.[26]

In turn, Kuvshinskaia's nine-month exile in Perm' in 1906–1907 was eased by family connections with a prominent merchant there, Nikolai Meshkov. Meshkov had provided the funds crucial for the launching of Charushin's newspaper in 1905, and he continued to contribute sizeable sums later, including a 3,000-ruble donation in 1912. While in Perm', Kuvshinskaia managed to find employment for her recently widowed brother Vladimir through their connections with a local bank officer (a certain S. O. Khlusevich), who along with his wife had also been an activist in the Populist movement and had served time in exile.[27]

Through their personal correspondence we learn of several occasions when their connections in the business world are brought into play to help fellow former exiles find employment. Prince Georgii Kugushev, a member of the fighting wing of the Socialist Revolutionary Party (SR) who was serving as the zemstvo architect for Viatka city[28] (and certainly acquainted with Ivan) wrote Charushin in 1906, soon after loss of his job and expulsion from the province, to request a letter of recommendation in his (ultimately successful) quest to find employment with the prominent insurance firm Salamandra.[29] Subsequently, in Tomsk on assignment for this company he wrote to Charushin again, asking for names of local business magnates who could serve as contacts in his work. Another exile, who was only barely acquainted with Charushin, wrote in 1909 from Siberia asking whether he "might have ties with the commercial and industrial sphere" in Irkutsk who could help his brother, also in exile, to find employment as an accountant or manager.[30] When Charushin lost his job after the 1905 Revolution, Kugushev wrote to him offering to put him in touch with another quite famous Populist, Alexei Pribylev (a member of Land and Liberty), who could "certainly" find him employment in the insurance community in Moscow.[31]

People seemed to have good reason to imagine that Charushin could connect them with potential employers in Tomsk, Irkutsk, Viatka, Moscow, and St. Petersburg. Likewise, he could turn to them for help; for some reason unknown to us, the insurance sector seemed to be a refuge for opposition figures.[32] Even Alexander Peshekhonov, editor of the influential Populist journal *Russkoe bogatstvo*, leader of the neo-Populists and a prominent figure in the Provisional government in 1917, had once worked for an insurance company. If the boundaries between officialdom and society were porous, the same came be said about opposition circles and the business community, for the connections were dense.

NETWORKS OF EXILES RENEWED AND EXPANDED

The cluster of revolutionaries and exiles that had been the center of the Charushins' world before their return to Viatka also maintained robust ties. Scattered correspondence suggests they made an effort to stay in touch, met whenever possible (most often in Moscow or St. Petersburg) and closely followed each other's lives.[33] Here, the tradition of intellectual salons and circles among the provincial intelligentsia carried over from an earlier period of the early twentieth century—though now the social mix was far more inclusive. Although these tea-drinking episodes left little visible trace in the history of social thought in Russia, without them it would be impossible to understand the formation of what Catherine Evtuhov and others have called provincial "cultural nests." Informal interactions and ties of friendship, which then grew into collective public efforts established their own durable space, something maintained even after their departures from Viatka. Such interactions were highly regarded in Charushin's circle and might have reminded them of the 1870s, when students had come together to discuss the burning issues of the day, united in communes, and formed circles and *zemliachestva*.

When the government renewed the practice of sending exiled revolutionaries to Viatka, the list of acquaintances was supplemented by a new generation of oppositionists. The Charushin home became a meeting place for opponents of various stripes, among whom were several young Social Democratic figures:

> At our gatherings disagreements would frequently occur and no common ground could be found, but this did not undermine the amicable relations that existed. Obviously, one such topic was the peasant question. Yet the skepticism which Marxists, who were close to being a majority among Viatka exiles, displayed toward the peasantry, didn't stop them from putting aside their ideological positions and making a serious effort to improve conditions in the countryside. Many of them became long-term residents in the provinces and took up responsible posts in the zemstvo.[34]

And indeed, the home became a meeting place where people of different generations and political orientations to mixed freely and comfortably. In the 1920s, at a time when sharper boundaries had been drawn, a certain N. N. Sokolov wrote to Charushin, "My wife and I often recall just how warmly and open-heartedly both you and your departed Anna Dmitrievna [she had died early in 1909; see chapter 7] welcomed us in your home. Even those doctrinaire [Marxists] and their block-headed disciples, who looked down their noses at the 'retarded' Populists received a warm reception at the home of the old revolutionaries of the seventies."[35]

After 1902, Charushin shared the goals of what was then the newly formed SR Party, but he adamantly refused to adopt a party line. Despite his profound Populist convictions, he became increasingly disturbed by the inter- and intraparty factionalism of the SRs and SDs and the resort to assassination of government officials. For the rest of his life he would stress the *bezpartiinost'* (rising above party affiliation) as well as *ideinost'* (principled nature) of his endeavors.

As for Kuvshinskaia's political convictions, if by the turn of the century Charushin had acquaintances of several political stripes, she, by one account at least, had drawn a line in the sand, spurning those for whom a commitment to social and political change was not primary in their lives. Iuferev, living cheek by jowl with the Charushins and with considerable opportunity to observe her, wrote that she was a very intelligent and good woman who looked after her husband. At the same time, she was "someone who had paid a price for her political convictions; her views on life and people were quite uncompromising... if someone held revolutionary convictions then this was a good person deserving attention, but for average people with no party affiliation she had little respect"[36] (see Figure 6.3).

FIGURE 6.3.

Anna Kuvshinskaia, early 1900s.
© Russian State Archive of
Literature and Art, Moscow.

The portrait drawn here of Kuvshinskaia resembles how Vera Figner seen in the eyes of many of her contemporaries: reserved, stern, and categorical in her judgments. However, a somewhat different picture of Kuvshinskaia emerges from her later correspondence with her husband and friends, as well as in the occasional comments made in passing by others who surrounded her throughout her life. Here she is far more self-doubting, nuanced, troubled by interpersonal conflict, and empathetic to others—willing to extend a helping hand regardless of one's political views. Writing from exile to her husband at a very troubled time in their lives, she reproached herself, "Don't hesitate to say the truth, for it won't add to the shortcomings of which I am already aware in my own personality. The older I get, the worse they are. Well, there is no point in continuing in this vein, but please forgive me for the troubles that I cause you from afar. You are totally involved in your own affairs, bringing you some satisfaction but even more and even worse headaches. And instead of providing your caresses and support from a distance, all I am doing is annoying and upsetting you."[37]

Upon Kuvshinskaia's death, Vera Tanaevskaia, a close friend of the family and fellow political activist, wrote to Charushin about their lengthy correspondence, "Every line she wrote was replete with wisdom and a big heart, both of which encompassed everything and everybody she touched.... Her generosity of spirit was unlimited."[38] Obituraries by her former colleagues at the newspaper also spoke of a woman firm in her convictions, dedicated to the cause, but warmhearted, giving, and vulnerable as well.[39]

ZEMSTVO TIES

If the Charushin household, extended family ties, and their connections with regional and empire-wide networks of exiles formed the core allegiances of their world, then employment with the zemstvo was the key institutional framework and source of income for the next decade (1895–1908). Across European Russia in the period leading up to the Revolution of 1905–1907, provincial zemstvos briefly became sites of opposition, both moderate and radical, to the autocracy, and both delegates and hired employees (the so-called Third Element) made up a large segment of the Liberation Movement during the reign of Nicholas II. Yet these institutions, despite providing much of the energy that drove the opposition to the autocracy, were internally divided throughout this period. The hired employees were regarded with suspicion by many of the elected delegates as well as by the government; and in many areas the district-level zemstvos were on hostile terms with the provincial-level institutions, especially over the supervision of these hired employees, who administered educational programs, health care, veterinary services, road building and maintenance, vocational workshops, and the gathering of statistics (above all, for property tax appraisals).[40] During the thirteen years he was employed by the Viatka zemstvo, Charushin would both benefit and suffer from this connection.

The Viatka provincial zemstvo was, along with the Moscow zemstvo, one of the most energetic and progressive in Russia, in a period during which zemstvo activities as a whole were, after a rather somnolent two decades, being revitalized. Charushin's decision to leave friends and a comfortable life in Kiakhta had to a large measure been based on the perception that he could better pursue his societal goals through such institutions, which were sorely lacking in Siberia, and that he could throw himself purposefully into this emerging stream of public life.

Among his first contacts, and the person who employed him, was Avksentii Batuev. In 1890, at the age of twenty-nine, Batuev had been elected chair of the provincial executive board (*uprava*) and soon after gained national prominence for his initiatives, especially in popular education.[41] For Charushin it was a fortunate coincidence that zemstvos everywhere at the time were energetically adding staff for rapidly expanding programs in agronomy, health care, and education, many of whom, given their political records, had few alternatives for employment. Even more fortunate was the fact that the briefly serving governor of Viatka at the time, Fedor Trepov (1894–1896),[42] happened to look benevolently on the zemstvo, and formally approved of his appointment.[43] Elsewhere, and later in Viatka, a large number of the zemstvo employees were forced to work under the ruse of being "temporary hires," since the zemstvo was unable to gain approval of their appointments from more vigilant governors.

It was through the zemstvo that Charushin now channeled his efforts and continued to pursue goals he had developed in his youth, subsequently in exile in Kiakhta, and now in a radically changed environment. Zemstvo employees (the so-called Third Element) took up residence along with the

Charushins at the residence of V. Kliucharev—himself a district delegate to the zemstvo, who would later join the provincial executive board at a crucial time and fall afoul of the provincial administration. Among these figures were A. A. Gur'ev and G. Kugushev, P. A. Golubev (all later to join the SR Party), A. N. Baranov (writer, journalist, and zemstvo fire-insurance agent), D. P. Biriukov and M. P. Borodin (both employed at the zemstvo *kustarnyi sklad*)—an operation, including a warehouse, established to support small-scale cottage industries—and living in the Kliucharev residence, and N. P. Lozhkin (who worked at the zemstvo book warehouse and cooperative). Over the next few years this group became for the Charushins yet another circle of friends and collaborators, somewhat younger than those with whom he had shared the years of imprisonment and exile. Biriukov later wrote Charushin from St. Petersburg that their friendship had been especially meaningful, "I always turned to you in need."[44] All of these men shared in his trials and tribulations.

Looming above all these figures in prominence was Leonid Yumashev (see Figure 6.4). Of noble origin, he was a landowner in Sarapul district; in the 1880s he had been expelled from the Technological Institute in St. Petersburg. Returning home, he had taken up management of his mother's estate until, in 1891, he was selected by local peasants to become the chair of his district zemstvo board, without having first served in the assembly, the ordinary path to such a position. There he was forced to deal with the massive crop failures sweeping across European Russia at the time. He soon became a member of Batuev's close circle, energetically pursuing economic and cultural programs at the provincial level, until in 1900 he was elected chair of the provincial zemstvo *uprava* (executive board) by a wide margin.[45] In that powerful position, Yumashev was tasked with supervising the zemstvo's rapidly expanding affairs, including education, medicine, agronomy, veterinarian services, as well as the implementation of cadastral surveys. Thus, at a time when zemstvos all across European Russia were mobilizing politically, Yumashev was also responsible for building the socioeconomic infrastructure of this backward province roughly twice the size of Ireland.

By the early twentieth century Charushin's fate was entangled with that of Yumashev; initially as his employer (all zemstvo employees were hired by and accountable to the executive board rather than the assembly), then as an oppositionist figure in the 1905 revolution; as a co-member

FIGURE 6.4.

Leonid Yumashev, early 1900s. Kirov State Archive.

of numerous committees and boards under the provisional government. Together, they formed a "Supreme Soviet" and worked to prevent a Bolshevik triumph in 1917, and together they were arrested in December of that year. We have no written record of their correspondence, but in the letters between Charushin and other acquaintances, he frequently mentions turning to Yumashev as a reliable friend and backer.[46]

Yumashev also happened to be the nephew of the same Nikolai Chaikovskii whom we have met in earlier chapters. By now, having observed Chaikovskii's erratic trajectory in life,[47] Charushin treated this old colleague with a strong measure of skepticism, but Yumashev was cut from entirely different cloth—an effective leader and administrator, later a member of the Kadet Party and State Council (1906–1909 and 1915–1917).

BOOK MATTERS

When Charushin first took up work with the Viatka provincial zemstvo, it was with its statistical bureau. Virtually everywhere in Russia such bureaus had become nodes of political contention as the nobility took umbrage at the efforts of these bureaus to carry out accurate tax assessments of land holdings, and thereby to more fairly distribute the burden of taxation in the country.[48] Statisticians were accused of radical tendencies, and indeed the chief of the statistical bureau in Viatka, Gur'ev, was under police supervision. He later joined the SR Party, and in 1906, was exiled from the province. Gur'ev made sure the door to employment in his bureau remained wide open for others of Populist or Marxist inclinations. In fact, in 1903 a member of the provincial zemstvo *uprava* complained to the Minister of Interior that reports from that bureau were never completed in a timely fashion because its chair was so busy with politics he had no time for statistical work.[49] But as for Charushin himself the records are silent about any contribution to the work of the statistical bureau.

Employment with the zemstvo led also to an ill-defined connection with the official zemstvo newspaper, *Viatskaia Gazeta* (1894–1907), and then, through his acquaintance with Petr Golubev, with the independent, peasant-oriented newspaper *Viatskii Krai* (1895–1898), until it was closed down by the authorities.[50] He also became involved with the newly formed (1894) zemstvo book depository.[51] In joining these endeavors Charushin was renewing his life-long commitment to advancing social and cultural change through the printed word. His first published essay in 1895 was a sharp commentary on the deplorable state of the Viatka public library, which he had frequented thirty years earlier.[52] Now, joined by several others in his rapidly expanding circle of acquaintances, he plunged into zemstvo and public efforts to establish independent newspapers, a book distribution warehouse, and a cooperatively owned printing press.

The Viatka zemstvo had sporadically been tinkering with the question of how best to enhance peasant access to useful and uplifting books. The names Pavlenkov (1839–1900) and Blinov are well known to historians of education and the book trade for their efforts to create mobile schools, publish textbooks, and encourage readers. Both had been exiled to Viatka, both worked with local zemstvos in the 1870s, and both had extensive ties with the network of exiles as well as zemstvo figures in the entire Volga region.[53] But it was only when the youthful Batuev took the helm of the provincial executive board that a major effort was launched to establish "5-ruble" libraries in virtually every village of this vast province. Rapid progress was made in this area, but this brought up the question of finding a suitable printing press willing and able to keep costs down, and required the establishment of a distribution network. Charushin was soon drawn into both of these projects. Over the next ten years the operations of the book depository expanded rapidly, as did the number of staff employed by the zemstvo to promote and manage its activities.[54]

Batuev and his supporters[55] made rapid progress and soon gained renown for the Viatka zemstvo. To achieve this success however, questions of cost and distribution had to be quickly resolved. Initially, the zemstvo negotiated with presses in Moscow and St. Petersburg, first to obtain books on a commission basis (relieving the zemstvo of having to pay for them in cash in advance of sales), and then by negotiating significant discounts for the purchase of large quantities of the same title. Soon however the idea was floated of publishing one's own books; after all, Viatka's abundance of forests and of cheap labor created ideal conditions for printing presses, of which there were already six in this small city.[56] This notion gained urgency when, after the murder of Batuev in 1896 by a demented nobleman, elections produced a conservative-leaning provincial zemstvo assembly, which for the next three years was at odds with a more progressive *uprava*, and stymied the latter's efforts to expand programs.[57] In turn, Governor Trepov's replacement, Nikolai Klingenberg,[58] repeatedly enjoined the zemstvo to "spare the population excessive taxes" by reducing its expenditures,[59] and praised it for its "restraint"—a code word for limiting zemstvo activities.

The proposal to print one's own books promised significant cost reductions for the zemstvo but also hypothetically gave it greater control over which books could be placed on its distribution lists. Initially this selection was restricted to the notoriously restrictive and out of date list periodically provided by the censors at the Ministry of Education. The zemstvo had petitioned with mixed success to expand this list. Then the idea was floated of branching out into commercial publication. This could kill two birds with one stone; bringing in substantial revenues to help offset the cost of widespread distribution books to the Viatka peasantry,[60] but also significantly widening the audience among the educated public.

Zemstvo publishing activities continued to expand rapidly and by the turn of the century the warehouse was selling its books well beyond the boundaries of Viatka province; in the decade 1894–1904 it sold some twenty million books.⁶¹ Its sales of stationary, notebooks, and other writing paraphernalia were also hefty and brought in much of the operation's profits. But stubborn problems persisted in the enterprise. One was that of distribution: initially, the book warehouse used the existing network of traveling peddlers (*ofeni*) to distribute its wares, but it soon recognized the failure of that approach. Another was coordinating its efforts, providing information, and delivering books to a rapidly expanding school network in this huge province. The roads were so bad and the distances so great that individual schools were fortunate to have even one visit by an inspector in a given year, and teachers often felt completely out of touch with the "cultured" world. The solution was to set up separate warehouses in each of province's eleven districts, and by 1904 there were fifteen such branches.

But administering the branch warehouses was to cause its own set of problems after the turn of the century, contributing to accusations of poor accountability (see Chapter 7). In general, not only did the warehouse have to deal with skepticism from some members of the assembly and mixed support from its *uprava*; it also had to play a game of cat and mouse with the censors in order to publish the desired books. An unpopular law, promulgated by the autocracy on June 12, 1900, limited the growth of zemstvo tax rates to 3 percent a year at a time when the needs of the economy and population were rapidly expanding along with zemstvo activities. To make matters worse, on June 20, 1901, the minister of the interior, Sipiagin, issued a circular forbidding the zemstvo from engaging in publishing activities.⁶²

That decree prompted Charushin's friends to discuss establishing a private cooperative publishing firm. Shares were offered at 150 rubles each. Among those who signed up were Mikhail Borodin, Alexander Baranov, Petr Golubev, and Nikolai Lozhkin. Another was Alexander Charushnikov, long-time friend and schoolmate of Golubev and now a prospering publisher in St. Petersburg, who in the 1870s had been implicated in the Trial of the 193. Later he would be closely associated with Social Democrats. Charushnikov had signed a contract with the book warehouse to distribute his wares in Viatka; now he became a shareholder in the new publishing firm.⁶³ From this point on a bond of trust was formed with Charushin himself, who by now was also involved in the project. Such subsidies were crucial, since the contributions of more than 40 percent of the publishing cooperative's shareholders were in arrears.⁶⁴

In 1902, the Viatka Book Publishing Firm came into being as "the direct continuation of zemstvo publishing activities."⁶⁵ In the next two years it published twenty books in print runs totaling in all almost two hundred thousand copies. However, in 1905, the firm relocated to St Petersburg, where it continued to operate until 1918. Reasons given for the move were various: these included the relatively greater freedom from administrative controls in St. Petersburg, the closing of the N. A. Ogorodnikov printing press in Viatka, Viatka's distance from Russian cultural centers, and the "shortage of local literary talent."⁶⁶

When the Viatka Publishing House was established, Nikolai Charushin was selected as its nominal director, apparently with the agreement that Nikolai Lozhkin would be in charge of the daily operations. Accordingly, in 1905 Lozhkin moved to St. Petersburg to continue to direct the affairs of the press. What role Charushin played remains unclear,⁶⁷ but it seems from the fragmentary surviving correspondence from Lozhkin's daughter to Anna Kuvshinskaia that *she* was actively involved in the selection of books to be published and the overall direction of the press, even after the move to St. Petersburg. In one letter, for example, Lozhkina, writing to Kuvshinskaia about mail that had been lost by the postal service, provides indirect testimony of the latter's importance, "We always kept you closely informed of every move we made and believed you had a clear picture of everything that was going on ... we fully agree with your opinion about exactly what the countryside needs."⁶⁸ And in 1907, she is asked, "Would you be able to agree to a small expenditure on our part in order to obtain reviews of our publications in a number of journals and specialized publications?"⁶⁹

NIKOLAI CHARUSHIN: FIRE-INSURANCE AGENT

In 1896 Charushin also took up employment as a fire-insurance agent with the Viatka district zemstvo. As a member of the Chaikovskii circle, Charushin had been in the group that had argued for reaching out beyond students to the common people.⁷⁰ Now, it was Charushin's employment as fire-insurance agent and famine relief agent that provided him with a steady income, brought him closer to the actual policy makers in the zemstvo, and above all, complicated his views of the peasantry during his thirteen years traveling through Viatka district, adjacent to the city itself. The fact that his assignment was the district closest to the province's capital and the smallest in size in a huge province may have reflected his family connections, his fragile health, or both.

In her cultural history of fire and arson Cathy A. Frierson[71] has made a convincing case for the centrality of village conflagrations in the economy and politics of peasant life in late-Imperial Russia. Fires were not only frequent and often devastating; in the form of arson fire had deep roots in the countryside's material culture, internal family and village dynamics, and interactions with the outside world. In turn the state response, beginning in the era of the Great Reforms, of instituting mandatory fire insurance and re-ordering villages through rational planning, led to a series of fraught interactions with the peasantry.

It was precisely at the time Charushin began his employment during the 1890s that a massive effort was launched by provincial zemstvos across European Russia to introduce a series of measures designed to significantly reduce the incidence of fire as well as its devastating consequences for the Russian countryside.[72] Up to that point, "mandatory fire insurance" had been a laughable matter, since there were no agents to appraise the value of property, collect fees, or dispense compensation. In Viatka, the situation had even led to an epidemic of fires in two of its southern districts (Malmyzh and Urzhum), as peasants correctly appraised the situation by submitting inflated appraisals of the value of their structures and promptly burning them down, entire villages at a time. As a result, the provincial zemstvo had encountered debts mounting at an alarming rate.

A series of programs were launched. and for the first time. zemstvos began to employ permanent insurance agents, land surveyors, and other technical personnel qualified to address the situation. In all these spheres, Viatka province became one of a handful of leaders at the very time that Charushin found himself employed in an enterprise entirely new to him. The annual report by the Viatka zemstvo executive board to the provincial assembly in 1899 described the tasks of the fire-insurance agent, including verifying applications for loans and subsidies for the purchase of horses;

traveling to areas suffering from crop failures and dispensing aid; verifying the proper maintenance of existing equipment (especially, water-carrying carriages, or *obozy*) and of newly constructed buildings. But the most burdensome responsibility involved the mandatory loan operations designed to help peasants upgrade their buildings (primarily roofs) and make them fire resistant. The agent had to travel to a given village, inspect all the buildings, and investigate the creditworthiness of the applicant or village as a whole. The paperwork required for this and other responsibilities was considerable, and the agent then had the additional responsibility of supervising how the loan was used and making sure loan payments were made in a timely manner. A new program of optional insurance on moveable property rapidly gained favor in the 1890s and was added to these.[73]

In addition to the chores of recruiting and processing applications for loans, implementing these loans, and mobilizing fire patrol brigades, there was the larger program goal of *rasplanirovanie* (loosely, resettlement). This involved convincing both individual families and entire villages to relocate structures positioned at a suitable distance from each other to reduce the risk that a fire in one home would turn into a village conflagration, as often happened. Charushin, the Populist revolutionary, long-term exile, and denizen of the world of the intelligentsia had his work cut out for him; for the first time, he was tasked with a mission the completion of which required an intimate understanding of the daily life of the peasantry and the ability to reach across a daunting cultural divide. All the tasks performed by the agents involved interacting with peasants, largely through elders and other informal "brokers" mediating between the village commune and the outside world.

These interactions presaged the more famous, if no less problematic, and much-studied Stolypin land reforms initiated in 1906, which sought to end the dominance of communal life in the Russian countryside and create individual farmsteads. In both instances, grand schemes intended to address massive dysfunctions encountered the intricacies of a stubbornly resistant way of life that had its own rationale for doing things. As with the later Stolypin reforms, the relocation project represented a frontal challenge to an entire way of life, with overlapping political, economic, social and cultural dimensions. First of all, it required a nuanced understanding of peasant life and an ability to communicate with a subaltern community that quite justifiably tended to view all outsiders with suspicion and distrust.[74]

Up to this point, as we have seen, Charushin's actual contact with the peasantry had been minimal. How well did he now carry out this job? As the fire-insurance agent for Viatka district he mostly served villages that were situated close to the city, and his travel was not nearly as arduous as it was for the agents deployed to the far reaches of the region. Each year, the district zemstvos were asked to evaluate the performance of its agents in a report to the provincial-level executive board (which paid the agents' salaries). Many agents, Charushin included, regularly received ratings of "satisfactory" for their efforts. Only in 1899 was he, along with two others, "commended" for his contribution. But even the "satisfactory" ratings were of significance, for after 1900 tensions rose in the district zemstvos over the role of employees serving in the districts but employed by the provincial zemstvo; whenever possible, zemstvo employees whose performance was lackluster and political leanings suspect were singled out for criticism. Yet until the governor forced him out of him out of his position in 1907, there was never word criticizing his performance.

We actually hear his voice only once, in 1897, when, in a report on the topic of the mounted fire patrols, Charushin pointed out that such patrols were resented by the peasants, functioned only in a third of the time, and then only when direct supervision by the agent himself was possible. Charushin argued that such patrols were ineffective and his proposal that they be eliminated in villages with fewer than thirty homes was accepted.[75] That brief report suggests that Charushin took his responsibilities seriously enough to grasp the nuances of village ways.

His correspondence with Kuvshinskaia during her period of exile (1906–1907) is further testimony that he took his work seriously. Despite the chaos of the time, his political activism, newspaper concerns, and difficult family circumstances, he frequently mentions leaving the city on trips connected with work lasting two to three days. For example, on September 10, 1906, only days after Kuvshinskaia had been exiled, he writes to her, "Tomorrow I am departing and will most likely be on the road for five to six days, so don't expect my letters to arrive soon. Once my travel is over I'll be free, and after a bit, I should be able to drop everything and come to Perm' for a day or two. Today I am sitting at home dealing with paperwork."[76] A week later, he inadvertently reveals the everyday hazards of his travels, even in a district adjacent to the city, "The weather was almost always awful, the roads a mess, but I managed to get everywhere, do what needed to be done and return home whole. All this time my carriage flipped over only once[!] but did so considerately of my wellbeing, and my health held up while traveling ... once I file my reports I'll be done."[77] Furthermore, his correspondence with Kuvshinskaia, in general, was full of uncensored political commentary, but not when it came to work. Nowhere in these letters do we find evidence that he viewed his efforts to promote fire prevention methods primarily as an opportunity to propagandize a political agenda. Instead, the evaluations he received of "satisfactory" service testified to a concerted effort to improve peasant life according to the terms of his contract.

In terms of the amount of funds allocated, the zemstvo fire-insurance program in Russia outstripped all other measures undertaken by that institution after 1890, a period of revitalization and recommitment to public service in general, and Viatka was at the forefront of the project to insure and protect against fire damage and physically rearrange villages.[78] As the 1904 audit of Viatka province made clear, the results did not always live up to expectations. A few years later a special zemstvo commission found all manner of irregularities in the Viatka program: funds unaccounted for; the records of sales of firefighting equipment a mess, and optional insurance measures neglected. Yet all of this took place in a highly politicized environment; the record seems to indicate that despite the problems encountered in Viatka, some visible progress was certainly achieved with the fire-insurance measures and that Charushin played a role in this.

FAMINE RELIEF: THE ALL-ZEMSTVO ORGANIZATION

In late 1905 Charushin became engaged in another project that brought him further exposure to peasant affairs. In the fall of that year he was selected by the provincial zemstvo *uprava* to serve in the newly established position of authorized representative of the All-Zemstvo Famine Relief Organization.⁷⁹ This organization, which combined the efforts of twenty-nine of the country's thirty-four provincial zemstvos and was centered in Moscow, had originated in efforts to provide services to the wounded and facilitate the mustering of provisions during the Russo-Japanese War. Acting on instructions from St. Petersburg, the governors of the provinces had initially created obstacles to the formation of local committees of the organization, but a direct appeal to the tsar had changed the situation, making the appointment of personnel to these committees subject to verification only by the Red Cross, with whom the All-Zemstvo Organization was coordinating its activities.⁸⁰ With the end of the war, the organization began to disband its local units, but on August 30, a country-wide conference of representatives decided instead to redirect their activities to famine relief. The conference called on provincial zemstvo executive boards to select authorized representatives to attend a conference in Moscow, which convened on October 14, 1905, on the eve of the release of the October 17 Manifesto.

When, in March 1905, the All-Zemstvo Organization had come into being, the Viatka zemstvo had joined it, but instead of creating its own supply unit, it had sent along a sizeable sum to the Moscow organization for its efforts in relieving the conditions of soldiers in the Far East. But now it sent along two delegates, including Charushin.⁸¹ He was given instructions obliging him to form a committee out of zemstvo executive board members and one representative from each district zemstvo. Likewise, the district representatives he had selected were to create their own "boards of trustees" (*popechiteli*), which were to directly administer aid to the population.⁸² Funds were allocated by the general assembly in November, but the Viatka provincial committee swung into action only at the very end of the year, because, as Charushin explained, "only a small part of Viatka province had been affected by crop failures." The local committees had from two to fourteen members, and hired employees made up roughly two-thirds of all of the district committees. During this period, the Imperial Free Economic Society simultaneously recruited Charushin to help with its parallel efforts to provide famine relief as its authorized representative.

Despite administrative harassment of local branches of the All-Zemstvo Famine Relief Organization beginning in early 1906, Charushin continued to serve as its provincial representative until mid-June 1908, and the organization managed intermittently to provide food relief during a series of years of crop failures. On November 17, 1906, as an internal crisis was mounting in the zemstvo and Charushin's own position there becoming untenable (see Chapter 7), he wrote Kuvshinskaia of his ongoing work, "Soon I will leave for the district and after that most likely for a short time to the nearby towns in connection with famine relief matters."[83] Between January and June 1907, reconstructed committees in virtually all districts allocated funds to famine relief. The activities included organizing and funding hot school lunches and soup kitchens for adults and the targeted distribution of flour or even money directly to the neediest families in the more remote villages. Teachers and priests played a prominent role in running such programs, and doctors were also recruited to set up medical points to address health needs and diseases (especially scurvy) stemming from malnutrition.[84]. In April and May of 1907 the heavily agricultural southern districts of the province, where famine relief efforts had ceased entirely due to government delays in delivering promised funds to the famine relief organization, but also to mass firings and exile of zemstvo employees (who made up two thirds of all participants on local committees), now saw a revival of the committees, and Charushin himself directly administered their efforts.

As the person in charge of a vast province stricken by crop failures three years in a row, Charushin confronted enormous challenges. One report, provided by the chair of the Iaransk district zemstvo *uprava* in March 1907, provides a picture of the dire conditions prevailing in some areas as one crop failure succeeded another, and a lack of funding (partially for politicized reasons) limited the ability of local organizations to respond adequately. In this report, the author describes thirty-seven meetings of the local famine-relief committee in May and June 1906 to cope with crop failures and spreading infectious diseases. Despite the extremely limited funding, the organization had managed to set up seventy-one school canteens, feeding 2,032 pupils, as well as twenty-two soup kitchens for the general public (serving 1,889 people). Fifty food-distribution points had also been established for distributing flour and money to over ten thousand people. Yet the need was so great and resources so limited that "it's distressing to see the beautiful spring weather at a time when the starving peasants are desperate for a morsel of food." The aid given out (six pounds of flour for each person) was often consumed in just a few days; one widow with eight children received only eight pounds for her entire family. Teachers and priests reported that in schools with thirty pupils only two to three children could be given aid. As a result, "the children are listless and apathetic, constantly complaining of headaches and other ailments." As for begging, "despite dire need, the peasants are ashamed and remain at home hungry rather than to extend their hand."[85]

A report made by the Glazov district *uprava* to its assembly offers further detail—and bears mentioning because it later became a thorn in Charushin's side. On December 17, 1905, the provincial committee under Charushin appointed three "plenipotentiaries" and allocated one thousand rubles to get matters started in Glazov. A month later, the district zemstvo *uprava* appointed a committee, chaired by one of the plenipotentiaries and including eight other members, to implement a program that included a soup kitchen and the purchase of clothes and shoes for the needy, as well as to collect information on the scale of need in the district. The committee met thirteen times; by October 1906, it had spent 860 rubles on various relief measures; after that it itemized the 2,073 rubles it allocated: 1,600 rubles for hot lunches at schools, 53 rubles for clothing and shoes for schoolchildren, 120 rubles to individual families, 122 rubles for a food canteen for adults, 178 rubles for direct deliveries of grain to needy villages, and 851 rubles for peasant children attending municipal secondary schools. According to the report, the "committee moved to aid the population in diverse situations: for example, after fires, when children were orphaned or families experienced the prolonged illness of able-bodied members." It noted that available funds did not allow for the launching of ambitious undertakings, even though ongoing failures of flax and spring grain crops did not bode well for the district. The Glazov committee then asked that members of the zemstvo assembly inform them of dire cases of need, since only they were familiar with their individual areas; only then could the famine relief committee adequately address its limited funds properly.[86] Indeed, it was difficult to obtain reliable information on just which families or villages were most in need—and this was what became contentious (see Chapter 7).

ENCOUNTERS WITH THE PEASANT WORLD COMPARED

Sustained work to reduce the frequency and impact of fires on the village and to administer famine relief surely deepened Charushin's understanding of the daily lives of the peasantry, and of the complexity of undertaking measures to ameliorate their condition. But they involved two fundamentally different ways of interacting with the village. Once the zemstvo had managed to establish its own database of independent appraisals of peasant structures, the tasks of the insurance agent involved making contractual arrangements with individuals, families, and settlements based on verifiable information; discrete and enforceable commitments, as well as penalties; and explicit notions of the cost benefits between juridical entities.

The task of providing famine relief was of a different sort, providing more opportunity for the fraught traditional interactions between a dominant and a subaltern culture.[87] Here, the "weapons of the weak"—tactics of information concealment and downright deceit—were more evident; and here "meddling" by outside authorities, both "plenipotentiary" and "stranger" were likely to provoke either collective evasive behavior or stir up internal discord within the village.[88]

At roughly the same time, Vera Figner had a parallel experience trying to provide famine relief to the local peasantry in Kazan.[89] She had returned home to her family estate in Tetiushi district still searching for a place in the world after two decades of incarceration. The local population also suffered from crop failure, and in the spring of 1906 the Populist journal *Russkoe Bogatstvo* had forwarded her 800 rubles to disburse to the needy: "And my misfortune, my sour relations and unhappiness with the village began at that time, when I had money in my pocket and the surrounding population was suffering desperately. That was a time of distressing impressions and unpleasant relations with the peasants, the cause of disillusionment and the frustration, realizing that I was actually making mistakes irreparably depriving me of the respect of the villagers and sapping the love that up until then I had held in my heart for them."[90]

What went wrong? Virtually everything. First and foremost, Figner had taken up residence at the manorial estate of her brother and therefore "was from the start in the untenable position of a lady of the gentlefolk."

In so doing, she felt she had forgotten all the lessons she had learned in the 1870s of how to become, if not a genuine member of the village community, then at least a medic who could help its people, win their trust, and at the same time learn the ins and outs of the community. Instead she "came to occupy the position of a benefactor," causing the peasants to believe (here she uses biblical phrasing), "Ask, and it will be given you."[91] Because of this, and because there seemed to be no limits to her largesse, she was immediately mobbed from all sides by beseeching peasants of all colors and stripes. Young, strapping peasants would tell sob stories, bring along bedraggled urchins to make the point (and then it would turn out they had no children of their own). They would concoct elaborate plans to bring prosperity to the village and ask for an "investment" in the future. They would boast, cajole, and sometimes threaten her. Old women would come by, clearly in the last days of their lives, asking for help to keep their grandchildren from starving. She would give or not give without any idea of whether or not she had decided wisely. Finally, she found herself hiding out to avoid contact with the ever-growing number of peasants arriving from villages, nearby and distant, all displaying the combination of deference and wily self-presentation familiar to us now as the "weapons of the weak." Figner's experience, while not identical, resembled what seemed to have happened with the understaffed and improvised committees of Charushin's All-Zemstvo Famine Relief organization.

Aside from his own lived experience (and occasional correspondence with Figner and others of his circle) Charushin also had direct access to another trusted perspective, that of his brother Arkadii, whose two decades of efforts to analyze and shape resettlement policies had exposed him to conditions throughout the country. When Arkadii met with his brother, he unquestionably shared his own experience and knowledge. Thus, if in his early years as a member of the Chaikovtsy circle, Charushin's views of the people had been based on scanty information and contact, by the first decade of the twentieth century his picture of them was richer and more complex, reflecting multiple types of interaction and observation, including the perspectives of the state. To use the terms of James Scott, he could not only "see like the state" but had been part of making the countryside *legible*.

THE ZEMSTVO ON THE EVE OF 1905

Most historians place the beginning of the 1905 Revolution with the massacre of peaceful demonstrators in St. Petersburg on January 9 of that year; indeed, that catastrophe let loose the furies across the empire. But the tensions had been building some time among all classes and, for zemstvo circles, ever since the 1890 revised statute governing the zemstvo had reduced its autonomy. Across European Russia the heavy hand of the autocracy sometimes aggravated, but at other times occluded, the long-standing internal conflicts within the zemstvos, between employees, executive boards and assemblies, as well as between provincial- and district-level organizations. For different reasons the nobility who dominated the zemstvo assemblies and executive boards, as well as the professional employees providing services to the population, were by the turn of the century up in arms about harassment and autocratic restrictions of their activities. Decrees issued after 1900 only exacerbated the situation. The outbreak of the Russo-Japanese War in January 1904, and the accompanying outburst of patriotism in educated circles gave the autocracy a brief respite, but as the battlefield defeats mounted up, the truce between the zemstvo and government eroded.[92]

The fierce struggles that ensued between the provincial authorities and the zemstvo *uprava*, as well as the internal conflicts within the provincial zemstvo assembly, between it and the *uprava*, between the provincial- and district-level zemstvos, within those district zemstvos themselves, and finally, between the elected delegates and the hired employees of the zemstvo led to complicated and shifting alliances that sometimes were driven by ideology and other times not. This was the universe Charushin and friends had to navigate, one in which intervention by the heavy-handed provincial authorities only further roiled the waters—leading to unfortunate outcomes for many of them, but eventually, as we see later, for the governor as well. (See Figure 6.5.)

Why should events taking place in the zemstvo at this fraught time occupy so much space in a biographical work devoted to the lives of revolutionary Populists? The answer is simple: in Viatka, as elsewhere, the provincial zemstvos and municipal dumas, as well as the burgeoning local press, became a platform for oppositionist—both liberal and Populist—

FIGURE 6.5.

Viatka Zemstvo board, early 1900s. Yumashev is seated, third from the right; Gur'ev is standing on the far left; Prince Kugushev is standing in the back row, third from the left.
Kirov State Archive.

activities in the early twentieth century, the means by which they now hoped to effect the changes they had long dreamed of. The leading prerevolutionary historian of the zemstvo, Veselovskii, aptly writes, "Not notably active politically, the Viatka zemstvo of that time was nevertheless among the most progressive."[93] But now the provincial assembly moved from a focus upon progressive measures alone to join the mounting chorus of those demanding political change from "zemstvo Russia." In December 1904, having just returned from the landmark November 7–9 Zemstvo Congress of *uprava* chairs in St. Petersburg,[94] Yumashev read out its eleven resolutions, calling for representative government and civil, religious, and political rights. The Viatka assembly overwhelmingly voted its approval; yet the session of December 3, 1904, which heard and ended up endorsing Yumashev's report was nevertheless a tumultuous gathering.

We have three different accounts of the proceedings, which continued for several days. One is the official zemstvo journal drawn up by the *uprava* office; the second is by the provincial gendarme chief, and the third is by Charushin, from his biographical sketch of Yumashev, written in 1914 on the occasion of the fiftieth anniversary of the zemstvo. All three accounts agree on a basic narrative. Yumashev read out the resolutions and then asked for the assembly's endorsement, at which point the assembly chair, V. A. Shubin (himself a progressive but not a radical), called Yumashev out of order, arguing that discussion of the eleven points in Yumashev's report was not on the agenda; furthermore, a discussion of political questions was not within the purview of the zemstvo. Next, a commission was appointed to frame an address to the throne; among its members were A. A. Lopatin (Charushin's brother-in law) and Iakov Poskrebyshev (already familiar to us as municipal mayor). The commission then asked if it was within their writ to include the eleven points in their address, and therefore called for discussion of those points. When Shubin again protested the crowd noisily objected. At this point, Shubin demanded that the public leave the hall, which it refused to do. Shubin then adjourned the meeting and went to seek the governor's advice. Governor Khomutov summoned Yumashev to his office. (Shubin's actions add weight to the historian Veselovskii's assertion that the Viatka provincial zemstvo had a record that was progressive but not oppositionist. He had been in Batuev's inner circle in the previous decade and had eagerly supported advances in education and public welfare. Later, after 1909, he re-emerges to be the chair of the zemstvo assembly promoting this same agenda.[95] But in 1904, his actions make clear his view that the zemstvo's function was to concern itself solely with local affairs, that it should limit itself to societal improvement, not political change.)

Almost two hours later Shubin returned to the assembly hall to announce to the still assembled delegates that the governor indeed forbade any further discussion of the eleven points, and once again, he was met by loud jeers and protests.[96] According to the gendarme report, Shubin had to call in the police to help disperse the assembly. The police instead advised him to appeal to Yumashev for help, and indeed Yumashev, who had returned from the governor's office undaunted, complied, a few words sufficing to dispel the tension. The public left, cheering and clapping for Yumashev as it did so. On December 4, the assembly reconvened, and twenty-seven delegates insisted on clarification: did the assembly approve of the eleven points—without clarification, there could be no address to the Tsar. A vote was taken, and the motion approved. On December 7, a tedious debate followed; the official journal of the assembly (drawn up by the *uprava*) had for some reason indicated that the vote had been unanimous but apparently four delegates had actually voted against and wanted their negative votes recorded. Ultimately, after a lengthy splitting of hairs, the assembly voted "by a large majority" (so recorded) that the vote had been unanimous.[97] Several delegates insisted on adding their minority opinions to the report.

This episode as a whole offers a glimpse into the political dynamics at the time we have been discussing, the relations between state and society, and how the participants in the event read themselves into the moment of history. The zemstvo journal, the rough draft of which was written up by the *uprava* staff under the direction of Yumashev, describes an assembly that was fully aware of the significance of the moment, believing that it spoke for society[98] and anxious to record their individual voices in the transcript of history (hence the seemingly absurd splitting of hairs about unanimity—or perhaps out of worry about reprisals). Yumashev himself seems to emerge as one who took his obligations before the zemstvo extremely seriously. He saw himself and the zemstvo as agents of political transformation, but true to the convictions he subsequently manifested by joining the Kadet Party, he was concerned about acting legally, worried about the potential of large-scale violence, and ready to work with an amenable autocracy to avoid it.

Writing of these events in 1914 Charushin himself seeks to place Yumashev in the pleiad of three towering figures who had made the Viatka zemstvo among the most outstanding in Russia, and he fully ascribes to Yumashev's belief in the possibility of evolutionary political change through the instrument of the zemstvo. Charushin melodramatically compares Yumashev with Danton, and the mood of the zemstvo with that of the French National Assembly in revolutionary France. In his brief comments on the December 1904 session, as in his later newspaper account of Yumashev's removal from the zemstvo, the *public* appears fully united with the zemstvo, as it does in the transcript cited above, composed by the executive board itself—loyal to Yumashev.[99]

But who was this public? The *uprava* report and Charushin's account seem to elide the difference among the delegates, ex officio members in attendance, and the public at large. Here the gendarme's report, submitted on December 14, is revealing. In his account the crowd numbered as many as six hundred, but the number of delegates was under fifty. The gendarme notes that the audience was composed of zemstvo employees in large numbers, students at the zemstvo paramedical school, technical staff, and those under police supervision. In his view, the whole situation was dangerous because it was taking place in a province whose population was "backwards, coarse, rude and unbridled." The gendarme portrays Shubin as hapless, unable to control the zemstvo, and concerned mostly with demonstrating his own loyalty to authority. And the governor, soon to be removed from office, is criticized for vacillation. Yumashev, as well as (the Social Revolutionary) Gur'ev, emerge in this account as the only strong, if insidious figures, in full control of the situation, scripting events.[100] Thus, we have two conflicting discourses. In one, that of Yumashev and of Charushin, society is mobilizing, and change is underway; in the other, order is breaking down, and harmful elements are taking advantage of the situation. In one, the crowd is an agent of history; in the other, mob rule is just over the horizon.

But coming together in opposition to government restrictions meant papering over differences within the zemstvo. The margin of support the *uprava* enjoyed in the assembly was often paper thin, and at times its initiatives were thwarted. The number of new employees hired by the *uprava* but then rejected by the governor increased sharply at the time, from five in 1898 to sixty in 1902 and thirty-four in 1903.[101] Yumashev himself had seen his support from the assembly erode; when he was first elected chair of the *uprava* in 1900, the vote had been nearly unanimous, but when he came up for re-election in 1903, the margin of victory was narrow (twenty-nine to twenty-five), and the election of other board members was contentious. In 1903, the assembly voted by secret ballot to decline a request for 25,000 rubles to build more schools, as well as another request to increase the salaries of *uprava* members.[102] The activities of the book warehouse (which Yumashev had actively sponsored), the handicrafts workshop, and the statistical board came under withering criticism.

By this time, too, the district zemstvos were in open revolt against the provincial boards, encouraged by the autocracy here and elsewhere as part of a strategy to rein in, or even eliminate, the more liberal provincial zemstvos, and notably their *upravas*.[103] The Elabuga district zemstvo, dominated by prosperous merchants, was especially adamant in its protests against the activities of the provincial zemstvo. All were frustrated by the practice by which they were "given" agronomists, veterinarians, statisticians, and insurance agents who were nominally employees of the district executive boards, but were hired, paid, and relieved of their duties at the discretion of the provincial executive board.[104]

As we see in Chapter 7, the discontent carried over into the provincial *assembly*. District chairs of executive boards were also ex officio voting members of the provincial-level assembly, and by the turn of the century eight of the eleven serving chairs had been appointed by the Ministry of Interior rather than elected internally by their own assemblies The provincial assembly included a substantial number of other local notables who held their seats ex officio, and together these numbers made up a sizeable minority of voters who ordinarily were at the beck and call of the local governor.

Thus, while opposition to the autocracy was gathering force in zemstvo circles after the turn of the century, internal divisions were also growing apace in Viatka.[105] In January 1904, Governor Khomutov wrote to the chief of the gendarmes, Lopukhin, defending Yumashev against written complaints about Yumashev's left leanings filed by N. P. Saltykov, a fellow member of the provincial *uprava* and one of the longest-serving zemstvo figures in all of European Russia. Saltykov had for the previous fifteen years also been the member of the provincial *uprava* responsible for looking after the same fire-insurance program that employed Charushin. Now Saltykov claimed that Yumashev was both incompetent and had surrounded himself with radical elements in the zemstvo lacking the technical expertise required by their positions.[106] Apparently, since the departure of Charushin's brother in law as provincial zemstvo insurance agent, Yumashev had nominated several figures under police surveillance to that post; the governor had rejected each of these candidates, and the post had been vacant since at least 1902.

It is all the more remarkable, then, that until the end of 1906, Yumashev was able to muster majority support for himself if not all of his programs, and (as we see in Chapter 7) it took an order from the Ministry of Interior to remove him and his closest associate, Kliucharev, from their posts. And in his response to Saltykov's complaint, Governor Khomutov, who had been in that post since 1901, and had therefore been deciding which of Yumashev's candidates for employment to approve, argued that because of the shortage of educated cadres in Viatka, Yumashev had only limited choices when filling key positions, and that he himself represented "certainly the best to be found."[107]

FOUNDING OF A PROVINCIAL NEWSPAPER

The tide of revolution was sweeping over the country, having a drastic impact on Charushin, his family, and his friends, as well as on the zemstvo. But one move by the government, the Temporary Press Regulations issued on November 24, 1905, led Charushin to a decision that radically reshaped his life: the founding of a newspaper. The newspaper was *Viatskaia Zhizn'*, renamed subsequently *Viatskii Krai*, and then, from late December 1905 until December 2, 1917, *Viatskaia Rech'*.[108]

Viatskaia Rech' was an independently owned newspaper, funded by donations, with an annual subscription rate of six rubles. It soon gained a prominent place in local and regional affairs, often came to the attention of the capital city newspapers, and remained, at least until the outbreak of world war, a major thorn in the side of the provincial authorities—in 1908, Prime Minister Stolypin would label it "the most revolutionary of the provincial newspapers." *Viatskaia Rech'* was from this time on the focus of Charushin's public life, the main draw on his energies, and, after 1910 or so, his primary source of income.[109]

Charushin was no stranger to the newspaper business: during his years of exile he had maintained an active correspondence with S. Chudnovskii and Volkhovskii, both known to historians of Siberia as pioneering newspaper men.[110] Soon after arriving in Viatka, Charushin had taken an active role in the short-lived *Viatskii Krai* (edited by Gur'ev and Golubev), until it was closed down by government fiat. Now he brought into the operations of his newspaper most of his circle of friends employed in the zemstvo as well as sponsors from the larger educated and business communities, and even his connections in St. Petersburg and Moscow. The list of people associated with Charushin's new newspaper included two, Yumashev and Vera Tanaevskaia, who were simultaneously key figures on the staff of the official zemstvo weekly newspaper, *Viatskaia Gazeta*, but also Borodin, Baranov, Biriukov, and Golubev, all of whom appeared in our narration of the history of the book warehouse or served on the zemstvo statistical board.

SOCIAL NETWORKS IN VIATKA

Exiles in Nerchinsk and Chita had experienced cultural isolation. In Kiakhta, a handful of them had linked up with prosperous merchants to promote cultural institutions; others had played a major role in important Siberian newspapers. Now these aging revolutionaries were able to join efforts with a younger generation in a common project, one involving both zemstvo and newspapers, and in so doing they enacted the two key tasks of that earlier organization: book matters and reaching the people.

At the same time, we have seen the close connections between Nikolai Charushin and his brothers Ivan and Arkadii, both of whom were employees of the state, his brothers-in-law in the provincial administration, and still others serving as zemstvo delegates and officials. The crossing of political boundaries within families was widespread in Viatka. An official audit (*reviziia*) of the Viatka provincial zemstvo conducted by the MVD in 1904 noted just how often different members of the same family served either the zemstvo or the provincial governor's office:

> Another noteworthy feature of the hired employees of the Viatka zemstvo is the absence of the corporate insularity one encounters frequently in the zemstvos in the central provinces. For example, at the same time that in the Moscow zemstvo the notion prevails that service in the zemstvo is fundamentally different from employment anywhere else, in Viatka zemstvo personnel merge with the local intelligentsia, whose small numbers are made up largely of civil servants. To add to that we very often find

members of the same family—linked by the ties of blood—serving both in the zemstvo and the local administration.[111]

This purported lack of "corporate insularity" separating civil servants from zemstvo employees was reinforced by individuals switching employment in either direction, something the *revizor* (inspector or auditor) Zinov'ev described as widespread. But family ties were augmented by another dense web of connections linking a steamship magnate and philanthropist with powerful elected officials; Ivan Charushin, the provincial architect with the governor's office, and the same steamship magnate; exiles who were both zemstvo employees and newspaper editors (themselves also connected with the city's mayor, or *golova*); and Nikolai Charushin with his brother Arkadii in the central government.

In Viatka, state and society were tightly interlinked entities connected by a revolving door. All the more remarkable, then, was the polarization brought about by the turbulence that followed and was generated largely by events and forces outside the province. It also helps us understand why the headstrong governor Sergei Gorchakov, arriving in Viatka to restore order in the summer of 1906, was confounded by a seemingly united front of civil servants and public activists.

NOTES

1. On the railroad, see Viktor Berdinskii, *Istoriia goroda Viatka* (Kirov: Viatskoe knizhnoe iszdatel'stvo, 2002), 331–332.

2. On the eve of World War I, the population of the city was 48,630: *Viatskaia Rech'*, September 5, 1913; January 11, 1914, 3.

3. Nikolai Charushin, *O dalekom proshlom* (Moskva: Vsesouznoe Obshchestvo politkatorzhan i ssyl'noposelentsev, 1931), 218.

4. Months before his arrival in Viatka, the local gendarmes had been instructed to keep him under surveillance. Charushin arrived in mid-August of 1895. At first, it was open surveillance, requiring him to report to the police every week. Beginning on April 23, 1897, this was changed to secret surveillance, and in 1899, the police recommended that he be removed from surveillance. See GAKO, f. 714, op. 1, d. 50, l. 288 ob.; d. 11, ll. 183–193, 198, 205 ob.

5. *Deiateli SSSR i revoliutsionnogo dvizheniia v Rossii*, 294.

6. V. D. Sergeev, *Nikolai Charushin—narodnik, obshchestvennyi deiatel', izdatel', kraeved-bibliograf* (Kirov: n/p, 2004), 111.

7. This was Ivan L'vovich Iuferev, whose generosity had kept Charushin's family afloat in Orlov after the early death of his father. Viacheslav Iuferev was a graduate of the Riga Polytechnic Institute in agronomy, and worked initially in Viatka at the Viatka Agricultural Experimental Station. Sergeev, *Nikolai Charushin—narodnik, obshchestvennyi deiatel', izdatel', kraeved-bibliograf*, 112.

8. Charushin, *O dalekom proshlom* (1973), 25; the information about Lopatin is gleaned from *Pamiatnaia knizhka Viatskoi gubernii na 1896* II (Viatka, 1895), 8, 123, 126, 171, 180.

9. "Viatka i viatchane v vospominaniiakh uchenogo-agronoma Viacheslava Iufereva," *Gertsenka: Viatskie zapiski* 3 (2002): 155.

10. Ibid.

11. *Pamiatnaia knizhka Viatskoi gubernii na 1896 god* (Viatka, 1895), 29, *Pamiatnaia knizhka Viatskoi gubernii na 1901* (Viatka, 1900), 2.

12. RGIA, f. 391, op. 7, d. 3858, l. 7.

13. All in all, according to local historian Sergeev, he published a half dozen books on the peasantry. V. D. Sergeev, "Lishnyi shtrikh dostopamiatnoi epokhi: A. A. Charushin," *VIII Petriaevskie chteniia* (Kirov: n/p, 2005), 234–238.

14. "Viatka i viatchane," 157.

15. RGIA, f. 391, op. 7, d. 3858; f. 391, op. 2, d. 303, 322, 468, 488, 1077, 1284, 1571, 1592.

16. Peter Holquist, "In Accord with State Interests and the People's Wishes: The Technocratic Ideology of Imperial Russia's Resettlement Administration," *Slavic Review* 69, no. 1 (Spring 2010): 151–179.

17. "Viatka i viatchane," 158.

18. RGIA, f. 796, op. 438, d. 4733.

19. E. A. Andreeva, *Arkhitektor Ivan Charushin* (Izhevsk: n/p, 2007), 43.

20. In 1898 both Ivan and Arkadii were granted the status of hereditary nobility (RGIA, f. 796, op. 438, d. 4733, l. 3).

21. "Viatka i viatchane," 158.

22. On Bulychev (1847–1929), see the entry in "Entsiklopediia rossiiskogo kupechestva," n.d., http://www.okipr.ru/encyk/view/207, accessed 9/23/2012. Bulychev held the rank of *statskii sovetnik*, was town magistrate in Orlov, a member of the Viatka city Duma, served on numerous boards in the city, and was designated a "hereditary honorary citizen"; he had been awarded several official badges, including the Stanislav-2 and Anna-3. His property and enterprises were confiscated on February 3, 1918, and he died in abject poverty. See E. V. Berezin, "S 'Grazhdanina' nachalos': (k 150-letiiu viatskogo parokhodstva Bulycheva)," *Gertsenka* 23 (2013): 118–124.

23. Andreeva, *Arkhitektor Ivan Charushin*, 87–93.

24. See Erving Goffman, *The Presentation of Self in Everyday Life* (New York: Anchor, 1990).

25. M. S. Sudovikov, "Iakov Poskrebyshev: Portret gorodskogo golovy," *Gertsenka* 6 (2009): 99–104.

26. As mayor, Poskrebyshev, the former bureaucrat and now elected official, also convinced the city duma in 1904 to send a petition to the monarch calling for fundamental civil rights and representative government. This move almost cost him his life, when on October 22, 1905, a right-wing mob rampaging through the city came after him personally and he was forced to leave the city under cover.

27. R. I. Rabinowitch, *Opal'nyi millioner* (Perm': Knizhnoe izdatel;stvo, 1990), 61.

28. *Pamiatnaia knizhka Viatskoi gubernii. na 1906 god* (Viatka, 1905), 13.

29. Kugushev to Charushin, December 29, 1906–February 18, 1907 (RGALI, f. 1642, op. 1, d. 36, ll. 1–6 ob.)

30. Makushin to Charushin, January 17, 1909–May 29, 1909 (RGALI, f. 1642, op. 1, ed. 45, ll. 5–6.)

31. RGALI, f. 1642, op. 1, ed. 36, ll. 1–60b.

32. Alexander Charushnikov, the prominent Viatka-born St. Petersburg publisher, one-time exile, and lifelong friend of Charushin, also served as an insurance representative for another prominent firm, the Northern Insurance Society (Severnoe Strakhovoe Obshchestvo). Peshekhonov, a leading neo-Populist and editor of its influential journal *Russoe bogatstvo*, was also employed by an insurance company.

33. Those lifelong correspondents included Vera Figner, Ivan Popov, Dmitrii Klements, Anna Iakimova, Felix Volkhovskii, Leonid Shishko, Sergei Sinegub and Larisa Chemodanova, and Alexandra Kornilova-Moroz. Charushin mentions the later contacts with various Chaikovtsy in his memoir. See Charushin, *O dalekom proshlom* (1973), 118–119. Some of this correspondence has been preserved in the archives: Charushin to Chemodanova, February 28, 1910 (RGALI, f. 1291, op. 1, d. 39); Kuvshinskaia to Chemodanova, July 17, 1908 (RGALI, f. 1291, op .1, d. 38); Chemodanova to Kuvshinskaia, November 24, 1906; January 16, 1907; and November 15, 1907 (RGALI, f. 1642, op. 1, d. 105); Lazarev to Charushin, September 30, 1909 (RGALI, f. 1642, op. 1, d. 39; Kuvshinskaia to Figner (RGALI, f. 1185, op. 1, d. 818).

34. *Deiateli SSSR i revoliutsionnogo dvizheniia v Rossii*, 293.

35. Sokolov to Charushin, February 14, 1926 (RGALI, f. 1642, op. 1, d. 70, l.3).

36. Cited in Sergeev, *Nikolai Charushin*, 112.

37. Kuvshinskaia to Charushin, February 22, 1907 (RGALI, f. 1642, op. 1, d. 79, l. 48).

38. Tanaevskaia to Charushin, August 16, 1909 (RGALI, f. 1642, op. 1, d. 73, l. 26 ob.)

39. *Viatskaia Rech'*, January 13, 1909, 1.

40. Boris Veselovskii, *Istoriia zemstva za sorok let*, 4 vols. (S.-Peterburg, Izd-vo O.N. Popovoi, 1911), 3:349–515.

41. Batuev was a charismatic figure who in his brief time as chairman of the provincial zemstvo executive board immensely revitalized the zemstvo's activities (1891–1896). In November 1896, he was returning home from a zemstvo meeting when he was fatally shot by a deranged nobleman upset about his failure to find employment with the zemstvo. On Batuev, see *Entsiklopedia zemli Viatskoi. Znatnye liudi: biograficheskii slovar'*, vol. 6 (Kirov: n/p, 1996), 37; Veselovskii, *Istoriia zemstva*, 4:644–670, esp. 651–654.

42. *Biograficheskie spravki na Viatskikh namestikov i gubernatorov (1780–1917)* (Kirov: GAKO, 1996), 27–28.

43. The governor's approval of Charushin's appointment to the statistical bureau was dated April 24, 1895 (before he had returned to Viatka). In that letter of approval, he is simply referred to as "the son of a civil servant." He was appointed to his position as an insurance agent on April 10, 1896 (GAKO, f. 616, op. 10, d. 3375, ll. 1–2).

44. Biriukov to Charushin, September 9, 1906 (RGALI, f. 1642, op. 1, d. 12, l. 1).

45. For his work in the zemstvo, see GAKO, f. 587, op. 5, d. 355, ll. 1–38; op. 19a, d. 166, ll. 1–11.

46 For example, Tanaevskaia to Charushin, March 3, 1907, March 26, 1907, January 29, 1909, July 3, 1909, August 16, 1909 (RGALI, f. 1642, op. 1, d. 73, ll. 2, 5, 10, 15, 24, 26); Lipiagov to Charushin, February 11, 14, 1909 (RGALI, f. 1642, op. 1, d. 42, ll. 4, 6); Charushin to Kuvshinskaia, September 10, 1906, October 8, 1906, February 18, 1907, March 27, 1907, March 31, 1907 (RGALI, f. 1642, op. 1, d. 108, ll. 1 ob., 9, 43, 52, 53).

47. Chaikovskii had since then joined the Shakers in Kansas; he then became a blue-collar worker in Philadelphia and subsequently spent three decades working in a trading firm before returning to Russia in 1907 to provoke a rebellion among the Cossacks in the Urals. On Chaikovskii, see I. A. Solov'eva, "Nikolai Vasil'evich Chaikovskii," *Voprosy Istorii* 5 (1997): 38–48.

48. N. G. Koroleva, *Zemstvo na perelome (1905–1907 gg.)* (Moscow, 1995), 73–74. Arable, held primarily by the peasantry, was taxed at a rate twenty-five times higher than forest or meadow, held predominately by the nobility. Arable held by the peasantry was taxed at twenty-three kopeks per *desiatina*; that held by the nobility at twenty kopeks. Both the Ministry of Interior and many zemstvo assemblies hindered the land appraisal work done by the zemstvo statistical boards. For a recent work putting the endeavors of the statistical boards in an entirely new light, see Catherine Evtuhov, *Portrait of a Russian Province: Economy, Society, and Civilization in Nineteenth-Century Nizhnii Novgorod* (Pittsburgh, PA: University of Pittsburgh Press, 2011).

49. "The statistical bureau's land appraisals are extremely shoddy to the extent that they are worthless despite expenditures of more than 160,000 rubles in that area." Note submitted by N. P. Saltykov, member of the zemstvo executive board, November 20, 1903 (GARF, f. 102, D-3, 1903, op. 101, d. 2500, l.7).

50. Ten years later, introducing his new newspaper, *Viatskaia zhizn'* (soon to be renamed *Viatskii krai*, Charushin wrote in the lead editorial concerning his predecessor, "Its death, as was the case with most independent newspapers, was not a natural one." *Viatskaia zhizn'*, December 24, 1905.

51. Veselovskii mistakenly lists its opening date as 1893. See Veselovskii, *Istoriia zemstva*, 4:652. The material on the following pages on the book depository and publishing house is drawn primarily from V. G. Shumikhin, *Dlia zhizni nastoiashchei i budushchei: knizhoe delo Viatskogo zemstvo* (Kirov: Kirov Regional Library, 1996), 44–62. See also the account by N. P. Lozhkin, first published in the journal *Obrazovanie* 4 (1905), *Obrazovanie* 8 (1907) and reprinted in *Viatka: kraevedchiskii sbornik* (Kirov: n/p, 1972), 71–79. See also in Evgenii Petriaev, *Literaturnye nakhodki: Ocherki kul'urnogo proshlogo Viatskoi zemli* (Kirov: Volgo-Viatskoe knizhnoe izdatel'stvo, 1981), 121–130.

52. *Viatskii krai*, November 21, 1895, 2.

53. Florentii Fedorovich Pavlenkov, for example, was close to the Farmakovskii family as well as with such zemstvo luminaries as Gatsitskii and Portugalov, who figure prominently in Evtuhov, *Portrait of a Russian Province* (2011), chaps. 6, 8, and 10. For Pavlenkov's activities in Viatka, see Iu. A. Gorbunov, "Tret'ii put' izdatelia Pavlenkova," *Pamiatnaia knizhka Kirovskoi oblasti i kalendar' na 2009* (Kirov, 2009), 324–339.

54. Shumikhin, *Dlia zhizni nastoiashchei i budushchei*, 44–54.

55. On Batuev's circle, see Veselovskii, *Istoriia zemstva*, 4:654.

56. Shumikhin, *Dlia zhizni nastoiashchei i budushchei*, 55–56. The author compares the Kazan' and Viatka printing presses, noting that Viatka serviced all of Siberia. For a fuller, and less admiring, picture of the activities of the printing press in Viatka, see N. A Zinov'ev, *Otchet po revizii zemskikh uchrezhdenii Viatskoi gubernii* (Petersburg, 1905), 2:368. The revizor calculated that between 1899 and 1903 the cost of a printed page had unjustifiably risen by seventy five percent-something not replicated elsewhere.

57. Veselovskii, *Istoriia zemstva*, 4:654.

58. *Biograficheskie spravki na Viatskikh namestikov i gubernatorov*, 2.

59. Veselovskii, *Istoriia zemstva*, 4:655.

60. On the problematic use of the word "quality" in reference to book collections at the time, see Ben Eklof, "The Archaeology of 'Backwardness' in Russia: Assessing the Adequacy of Libraries for Rural Russian Audiences in Late Imperial Russia," in *The Space of the Book in Imperial Russia: Print Culture in the Russian Social Imagination*, ed. Miranda Remnek (Toronto: Toronto University Press, 2011), 108–136.

61. Shumikhin, *Dlia zhizni nastoiashchei i budushchei*, 47.

62. Veselovskii, *Istoria zemstva*, 3:523–537. The law on taxation was roundly criticized, and largely observed in the breach.

63. "Pis'ma A. P. Charushnikova v Viatku N. A. Charushinu (1900-e gody)," *Gertsenka* 24 (2013): 99–201.

64. E. D. Petriaev, *Literaturnye nakhodki: Ocherki kul'turnogo proshlogo Viatskoi zemli* (Kirov, Volgo-Viatskoe knizhnoe izdatel'stvo, 1981), 122.

65. Shumikhin, *Dlia zhizni nastoiashchei i budushchei*, 61.

66. Ibid.

67. That he remained engaged is indirectly clear from the draft of a document Charushin drew up on September 16, 1907, according to which the shareholders of the publishing house were to consent to an unsecured loan to *Viatskii krai*. In other words, Charushin felt comfortable proposing the shift of funds from one enterprise to the other, with, incidentally, a clause that no action would be taken should the loan not be repaid (RGALI, f. 1642, op. 1, ed. 2, l. 1). We don't know if this transaction ever actually took place.

68. Lozhkina to Kuvshinskaia, October 10, 1906 (RGALI, f. 1642, op. 1, d. 101, l. 1).

69. Ibid, l. 10 ob, 16 ob.

70. Daniel Brower, *Training the Nihilists: Education and Radicalism in Tsarist Russia* (Ithaca, NY: Cornell University Press, 1975), 201–207.

71. Cathy A. Frierson, *All Russia Is Burning! A Cultural History of Fire and Arson in Late Imperial Russia* (Seattle: University of Washington Press, 2002).

72. Veselovskii, *Istoria zemstva* (1909), 2:533–651; Zinov'ev, *Otchet po revizii*, vol. no 3 (1905), 35–58. See also *Sbornik postanovlenii Viatskogo gubernskogo zemstva za 21 god (1892—1913)* 4 (Viatka, 1914).

73. *Zhurnal VGZU v VGZS* (Viatka, 1899), 56.

74. Corinne Gaudin, *Ruling Peasants: Village and State in Late Imperial Russia* (DeKalb: Northern Illinois University Press, 2007); Carol Scott Leonard, *Agrarian Reform in Russia the Road from Serfdom* (New York: Cambridge University Press, 2011); Judith Pallot, *Land Reform in Russia, 1906–1917: Peasant Responses to Stolypin's Project of Rural Transformation* (Oxford: Clarendon Press, 1998); James C. Scott, *Seeing Like a State: How Certain Schemes to Improve the Human Condition Have Failed*. Yale Agrarian Studies (New Haven, CT: Yale University Press, 1998).

75. *Zhurnal VGZU v VGZS*, 10.

76. Charushin to Kuvshinskaia, September 10 (RGALI, f. 1642, op. 1, d. 108, l. 1).

77. Charushin to Kuvshinskaia, September 18, 1906 (RGALI, f. 1642, op. 1, d. 108, l. 2).

78. Veselovskii, *Istoria zemstva* 2 (1909), 2:607, 612, 625, 637.

79. The following information is from: RGIA, f. 1482, op. 1, d. 151 (1906) and f. 1482, op. 1, 7a; f. 1482, op. 1, d. 200 (1907); f. 1482, op. 1, d. 6 (1906); f. 1482, op. 1, d. 278; L.V. Zhenina, "Uchastie Viatskogo zemstvo v Obshchezemskoi organizatsii (1904–1907)," *Zemskoe samoupravlenie: organizatsiia, deiatel'nost', opyt. Materialy nauchnoi konferentsii* (Kirov, 2002), 124–129. See also, Veselovskii, *Istoriia zemstva* 3:590–605.

80. This coordination, actually subordination to the Red Cross, was a measure taken in order to gain relief from what its organizers described as stifling bureaucratic regulations. See Thomas E. Porter, *The Zemstvo and the Emergence of Civil Society in Late Imperial Russia 1864—1917* (San Francisco: Mellen Research University Press, 1991), 72—234; Mary S. Conroy, *Emerging Democracy in Late Imperial Russia: Case Studies on Local Self-Government (the Zemstvos), State Duma Elections, the Tsarist Government, and the State Council Before and During World War I* (Niwot: University Press of Colorado, 1998), 70–79.

81. From 1906, the selection of an authorized representative (*upolnomochennyi*) to administer the provincial-level program was made in Moscow rather than by the Viatka zemstvo, and Charushin remained Moscow's choice (that procedure, however, ultimately made him vulnerable during the righting of the zemstvo—see chapter 7).

82. In reality, a gathering in October of provincial zemstvo representatives and employees collectively decided on the membership of the provincial committee and itself selected district representatives and committees, with the proviso that these committees would also include ex officio the chair and members of the local zemstvo executive boards.

83. Charushin to Kuvshinskaia, November 17, 1906 (RGALI, f. 1642, op. 1, d. 108, l. 17).

84. Cite RGIA, f. 1482, op. 1, d. 151, ll. 4–111 for a listing of each such entity in Viatka province, its location, who opened and operated it and for how long, how much was spent, how many served, and what the per capita expenditures were.

85. RGIA, f. 1482, op. 1, d. 278, ll. 3–4.

86. GAKO, f. 587, op. 11, d. 228, ll.1–3.

87. For descriptions of the difficulties in Viatka, see *Viatskii Vestnik*, June 8, 1908, 1; and *Viatskaia Rech'*, June 19, 1908, 4.

88. Gaudin, *Ruling Peasants: Village and State in Late Imperial Russia*, 208.

89. Vera Figner, *Zapechatlennyi trud. Izbrannye Proizvideniia* (Moskva: Vsesouznoe Obshchestvo politkatorzhan i ssyl'noposelentsev, 1933), 3:97–128.

90. Ibid., 103. Lynn Hartnett, in her recent biography of Vera Figner, discusses this episode, but argues that Figner was primarily upset because there was not enough money to go around. We believe instead that it was the hierarchical nature of the interaction that she blamed herself for. She explicitly notes that she should have known better, that in the 1870s she and her friends had elaborately planned how to avoid such an asymmetrical relationship. See Lynn Ann Hartnett, *The Defiant Life of Vera Figner: Surviving the Revolution* (Bloomington: Indiana University Press, 2014), 188–189.

91. Figner is combining two passages from Matthew: Matt. 7:7; 11:28–30. She continued, "But how much? Nobody except I knew. But everyone believed that the supply of gold was inexhaustible and every petitioner was sure that there was plenty left when he came for assistance." Vera Figner, *Zapechatlennyi trud*, 104.

92. Korelova, *Zemstvo na perelome*, 78–101.

93. Veselovskii, *Istoria zemstva* (1911) 4:655–656.

94. Veselovskii, *Istoriia zemstva* (1911), 3:603; 4:38, 658.

95. Veselovskii, *Istoriia zemstva* (1911), 4:658.

96. The gendarme report differs on the sequence of events, placing the appointment of a commission to draw up an address after rather than before Shubin's departure to meet with the governor. The official zemstvo transcript of the meeting omits any mention of Yumashev returning to persuade the crowd to leave, as described in the gendarme report.

97. *Sbornik postanovlenii Viatskogo gubernskogo zemstvo za 21 god 1892–1913* (Viatka, 1914), 199–209.

98. Soon after, in a different discussion concerning the zemstvo's reaction to the Bulygin rescript, one delegate who had been an active participant in zemstvo matters, Ovchinnikov noted that nobody had actually ever checked to find out what "the people wanted" (Ibid., 217).

99. "Tri momenta," *Viatskaia Rech'*, May 20, 1914, 4–6. (This is a lengthy article by Charushin on the occasion of the fiftieth anniversary of the zemstvo, commemorating the "three most important" figures in the history of the zemstvo: Syntsov, Batuev, and Yumashev).

100. GARF, f. 102, D-3, op. 102, d. 2900, ll. 47–48ob.

101. Zinov'ev, *Otchet po revizii*, 1:252 (for a table). At the time, the provincial zemstvo employed roughly twelve hundred professionals, excluding teachers.

102. Ibid., 141, 153.

103. Veselovskii, *Istoriia zemstva* (1911), 4:54–78.

104. Zinov'ev, *Otchet po revizii*, 1:228–230, 241, 245, 259–262.

105. See Koroleva, *Zemstvo na perelome*, 72–82; Veselovskii, *Istoriia zemstva* (1911), 3:412–429, 473–478, 551–553; Zinov'ev, *Otchet po revizii*, 1:152–161.

106. GARF f. 102, D-3, op. 101, d. 2500, l. 6 ob.

107. Ibid., l. 22 (January 21, 1904). The accusations by Nikolai Petrovich Saltykov, himself a member of the uprava, are in the same folder, l. 6-ob, November 20, 1903. On Saltykov's length of service (1876–1879 and 1889–1905), see Veselovskii, *Istoriia zemstva*, 3:438. On P. Khomutov, who served from 1901 until December of 1904, see *Biograficheskie spravki na Viatskikh namestikov i gubernatorov*, 29–30.

108. To avoid confusion in a narrative already replete with names, we have everywhere called the newspaper by its final and longest serving name, but in the footnotes we refer correctly to the name that was current whenever an entry from its pages is cited. *Viatskaia Zhizn'*, December 24, 1905–August 22, 1906 (the paper was stopped in May, but several issues were published under the name *Viatskii Krai*). *Viatskii krai* was published again from 1906 to December 14, 1907 (114 issues in 1906 and 254 in 1907; *Viatskaia Rech'* from December 25, 1907 to December 2, 1917.

109. When Charushin's newspaper came onto the scene, it joined *Viatskii Vestnik*, the semi-official daily newspaper that had originally been published two to three times weekly as the unofficial section of *Viatskie Gubernskie Vedomosti*, and *Viatskaia Gazeta*, a publication of the zemstvo addressed to the peasantry of the province. P. A. Golubev and then A. A Gur'ev had published an independent newpaper, *Viatskii Krai*, from 1895 until 1898, when it was closed down by the censors, and in 1905 D. P. Biriukov had edited *Krestianskaia Gazeta*, until it too was closed down and he was exiled from the province.

110. Charushin, *O dalekom proshlom na poselenii* (Moskva, Vsesouznoe Obshchestvo politkatorzhan i ssyl'noposelentsev, 1931), 165, 170, 176, 199.

111. Zinov'ev, *Otchet po revizii*, 1:246.

After October

The Downward Spiral of Revolution

Yes, we are entering a difficult period, but I don't believe it can last long.

—Charushin to Kuvshinskaia, November 17, 1906

... the most revolutionary provincial newspaper in Russia, in which all kinds of filth is regularly collected and dished out to the public.

—Petr Stolypin commenting on *Viatskaia Rech'*, 1909

Both zemstvo activism and the oppositionist political journalism operating under the new press regulations provoked a strong reaction from the authorities and had serious consequences for Charushin, Kuvshinskaia, and their associates. In 1906 and beyond, fines, jail sentences, and exiles became the order of the day for those involved in Charushin's newspaper, and the zemstvo was subjected to extreme pressure. These misfortunes were so severe they even threatened the bonds of friendship that had held this tightly knit group together.

It is not possible to gain a detailed picture of Charushin's political activities in the years leading up to Bloody Sunday, or even between then and the October 17 Manifesto. By then, he was again under police surveillance (this time, however, secret). He had joined the influential Union of Liberation founded in 1904, and we next hear of him at a crucial gathering of its members in Moscow in October 1905, where he also learned of the October Manifesto and witnessed the subsequent jubilation in the streets of the city. We know that in the summer of 1905 he was also one of the organizers and members of the Peasant Union in Viatka. There too, roughly at that time he was also one of the initiators of the ephemeral Democratic Union coalition, which merged with the People's Socialist (NS) Party upon its establishment in late 1906. From then until his departure from politics in the midst of civil war in 1919, he was to adhere closely to the views and programs of that party.

Otherwise, what his actions and thoughts were at the time are lost to us. What were his responses to the unfolding violence in the country in the spring and summer of 1905? What were his feelings about the war with Japan, especially before it turned into a shocking series of military defeats? Once again, we are confronted with the reticence or silence of many Populist memoirs about the period in their lives between release from incarceration and exile and the 1917 Revolution. The silence is especially frustrating because of the fullness of Charushin's life at this time, the multiplicity of activities and commitments in the "outside" world in contrast to the era of confinement and isolation. However, the records of the zemstvo, the pages of his newspaper, personal correspondence, and governmental archives, both provincial and central, allow us to adequately reconstruct his activities and even gain glimpses of his and Kuvshinskaia's feelings in the crucial years of 1906 to 1909.

ENTER GORCHAKOV: "LIQUIDATION AND RENEWAL" POLICIES

Following upon the December 1904 events in the Viatka zemstvo and the complaints by the local gendarme chief about Governor Khomutov's excessive leniency, Khomutov was replaced in February by Alexander Levchenko, who set about restoring order in the city and the countryside, where peasant disorders were mounting. By then the tide of revolution was sweeping across Russia in the wake of Bloody Sunday, relentlessly bad news from the battlefront in the East, and continued autocratic intransigence. Levchenko's time as governor was brief. Despite his concerted efforts to purge the municipal duma, itself in turmoil, he was accused of indecisiveness and soon replaced.[1]

His successor, Sergei Gorchakov (1861–1926),[2] arrived in the city on July 25, 1906, with a writ to restore order and crush all opposition to autocracy. Gorchakov was a larger-than-life figure who seemed to welcome every opportunity to dramatize his presence. A rather hapless attempt by a student to assassinate him on the streets of Viatka, in 1908, gave him the opportunity to bask in comparisons to his distant relative and the most charismatic figure of the time Petr Stolypin, who, in 1906, had experienced a much more tragic and consequential attempt on his own life. The narration is even more colorful because Gorchakov used as his attack dog on the zemstvo a flamboyant and scandal-ridden figure with the improbable name "Count N. N. de Rochefort."[3] De Rochefort published incendiary articles in the semiofficial *Viatskii Vestnik*, and directed his antipathy at zemstvo programs and at Charushin and his associates personally. He became immersed in a scandal in the district of Sarapul when he physically assaulted a cashier in a store. He was eventually transferred to the Warsaw region, where he was appointed a land captain.[4]

Gorchakov's behavior as governor exemplified that "arbitrariness" (the word *proizvol* is resonant in Russian political discourse) for which the autocracy was so resented by liberal circles whose goal was to establish a law-governed state. Thus, a study of autocratic policies during the period of the "righting of the zemstvo" following the October Manifesto suggests that his actions closely followed a script written in St. Petersburg. What ensued in Viatka reflected policies enacted to one degree or another in all thirty-four zemstvo provinces and long ago described in Boris Veselovskii's monumental *Istoriia zemstva za sorok let* (1909–1911). Yet, if the script was provided from above, its enactment was shaped by the constellation of local societies.

In September 1908, under pressure for having employed what many saw as excessive measures, Gorchakov wrote in confidence to Stolypin, "I won't hide that when I first set out I believed Viatka province to be one of the most tranquil and amenable to guidance, and for that reason I was confident it would not be difficult to fully restore order there. But my expectations were cruelly dashed: I soon encountered a population but also a bureaucratic apparatus that was severely demoralized."

In Gorchakov's scheme, it was clear who was responsible for the demoralization, "The population has been corrupted in two ways: by the revolutionary propaganda of local zemstvo employees, and by equally revolutionary newspapers. He pointed out that in the absence of a landholding nobility its place had been occupied by a third element "completely saturated with social democratic tendencies." But that was not all: the ranks of the local civil service were filled primarily by people from the democratic intelligentsia. In Gorchakov's telling, the previous governors had been fooled by activists employed by the zemstvo boards:

> While conditions were seemingly tranquil and the third element assured the governor of its loyalty and willingness to completely submit to authority, zemstvo activists were perfidiously weaving a web, confusing and hypnotizing... the population.... A dominant role in these matters was played by the provincial and district zemstvo boards.[5]

Soon after arriving in Viatka in 1906, Gorchakov swung into action. On September 2 his office launched an investigation of the weekly newspaper *Viatskaia Gazeta* (published by the zemstvo board) for expanding its content to include political affairs, promoting an oppositionist agenda, and introducing the peasantry to a revolutionary vocabulary by publishing a glossary of political terms.[6] Also in that month Gorchakov, after visiting the Nolinsk district zemstvo and labeling its conditions "exemplary," then somewhat inexplicably engineered the removal of the chair of its executive board. Others were soon to follow, along with numbers of elected delegates, so that by the end of the year the composition of elected assemblies throughout the system had radically changed. In the meantime, the dismissal, arrest, and exile of zemstvo employees, which had begun well before he had arrived, soon accelerated.

Then, in his first address to the provincial assembly, on December 11, 1906, Gorchakov told the delegates in no uncertain terms what had to change. After noting that the "renewal" (i.e., purge) of the assembly[7] was complete, he next targeted the *uprava*, which, he argued, had repeatedly exceeded its writ. Gorchakov described the situation at its book depository as emblematic of all that was wrong in zemstvo affairs.

Indeed, as we saw in Chapter 6, the troubles with the book depository had been mounting since the turn of the century, when zemstvo delegates, and then the *revizor* from the Ministry of Interior had discovered financial irregularities, and several of its employees had been labeled politically unreliable. In 1902, the zemstvo assembly demanded to see the accounting records, along with the *kustarnyi sklad* (cottage industries warehouse), and then began to reject the book warehouse's annual reports as inadequate. At the 1903 meeting of the assembly, the executive board presented a report asking for additional financial support for the book warehouse; it was rebuffed, and the majority called for an audit of its financial records along with that of the *kustarnyi sklad*.[8] An internal auditing board was set up under the *uprava*, and then, in 1904, the assembly welcomed the arrival of the *revizor* Zinov'ev, who carried out a detailed review of all of the zemstvo's activities, including taxes and budgets, the assembly and *uprava*, its hired employees and its many "desks" dealing with public welfare and education; the *kustarnyi* museum; even the zemstvo's own internal review board (which he accused of incompetence); and finally the book warehouse.[9] Zinov'ev, who, despite the fact that he had clearly been sent to find dirt on the zemstvos,[10] was generally judicious in his evaluations, was scathing about business practices in the book warehouse: chaotic bookkeeping; erratic delivery of purchased goods; cost overruns and indebtedness; failure to collect monies due from purchasers; and infatuation with publishing on its own, without the authorization of the assembly, which had resulted in print runs far exceeding demand and a large stockpile of unsold wares.

During the 1905 Revolution, the book warehouse, among whose employees were several Social Democrats as well as Socialist Revolutionaries, had become an oppositionist meeting place, and the police launched several raids on it. One search, carried out between October 15 and 20, 1906, produced more than five thousand copies of censored books, and all the warehouse operations were suspended.[11] The warehouse was allowed to re-open in December 1906, but its commercial operations were permanently shut down, and only textbooks and school supplies could be marketed.

Finally, in 1908, following the report of a special commission reviewing the book warehouse (which since 1906 had been without a director), the zemstvo voted to liquidate all its holdings.[12] Yet the actual process of liquidation took over five years (until 1913) and filled many pages of the provincial zemstvo assembly's journal of that time with records of acrimonious debate about how to dispose of its inventory. As we shall see, Charushin also suffered personal humiliation and financial setback related to this matter.

A similar narrative could be provided for other programs, four of which were entirely dismantled in this period (Viatka ranked fourth among the thirty-four zemstvos in number of programs closed).[13] Among the zemstvo operations to suffer disproportionately was the statistical board; by mid-1906, its operations had already been virtually shut down by the dismissal, arrest, and exile of many of its employees, and in 1908, it was officially closed by vote of the assembly. This would have a drastic impact on Charushin's own work, for his labors in the area of famine relief depended on access to reliable statistical information about individual villages.[14]

As programs were closed down, the governor's office began to force the dismissal, arrest and exile of hundreds of teachers, veterinarians, doctors, insurance agents, and office staff in the *uprava*.

On September 14, 1906, Stolypin had issued a circular prohibiting all state and zemstvo employees from belonging to "anti-government" political parties. Most of the country's zemstvos neither resisted nor hastened to take action, leaving it up to local governors to follow up on this measure.[15] On November 20, Gorchakov "suggested" to the *uprava* that all zemstvo employees sign loyalty oaths,[16] and two months later he demanded an explanation, to be produced within three days, about why they were not forthcoming.[17] Indeed, if a report by the local city police chief to the governor (December 26, 1906) is to be believed, the provincial zemstvo board under Yumashev had been the command center of a vast plot to undermine the status quo, with its statistical bureau, extramural education, insurance, road-building and other programs all led by Populists, Marxists and liberals working closely together, the local teachers' and peasants' congresses (held in the summer of 1906) coordinated by the uprava, and the schools in the province run by teachers answering only to Yumashev's hirelings.[18]

By October of 1906, as the anniversary of the October Manifesto approached, the perception that a witch-hunt was underway was accompanied by fears of a repeat of the pogrom that had occurred in Viatka the previous year. Writing from exile in Perm', where she had been sent a month earlier, Kuvshinskaia described her premonitions in a letter to her husband, "I am very pessimistic; there is little stomach for revolution at the moment, and I am beginning to see things through the lenses of the 'reptile press.' I fear what might happen to you in October.... For some reason, I feel there will be pogroms and an outburst of patriotism just now."[19] Two months later, her mood was no better, "For some reason I can't rid myself of the thought that there will be throats slit, namely those of the intelligentsia. The clouds are darkening, people's brazenness getting worse... there is little to be happy about.... I fear for Viatka and tremble when I pick up the newspaper."[20]

Charushin was more optimistic, or so it seemed. On October 8, he hastened to alleviate her fear of right-wing violence with a rare nod to the governor, pointing out that the latter had given the police chief strict orders to prevent any pogroms in Viatka and let him know that he would be held directly responsible in the event there were.[21] Responding a month later to Kuvshinskaia's dismal prognosis of events, he conceded, "Yes, we are entering a difficult period," then he added, "but I don't believe it can last long."[22] After only a week, his optimism was more measured but still intact. He acknowledged the damage that had been done to the zemstvo, the mounting casualties in terms of careers, and the authorities' attempts to impose a new and durable order, but he still doubted that the damage to the country would be long-lasting: "Things are a mess here, people are being exiled one after another and without any obvious end to it... people are anxious, work is going poorly or not at all. Evidently a new purge of the zemstvo is looming and not only at the provincial level, for the elected district *uprava* are not being confirmed in office.... It looks like they are laying the foundation for a new and long lasting regime. But I still find this hard to believe."[23] And finally, in early in December: "They are exiling each and everybody, for what God only knows. Despite all that, my mood is not so bad."[24]

But by this time it must have been very difficult for him to remain upbeat. The expulsion of employees was already in full swing and continued well into the middle of the next year. The results were soon evident in the number of dismissals. In 1904, the number of specialists employed by the zemstvo (excluding teachers) numbered roughly 1,500, of whom 370 worked at the provincial level. *Viatskaia Rech'* calculated that by the middle of 1907 close to 200 employees had been expelled.[25] At the level of the provincial *uprava*, close to half of all those employed had lost their jobs. Indeed, of all the zemstvos in Russia, Viatka and Ufa would purge the most employees.[26] Soon Charushin himself would fall victim to the forces shaking the foundations of the zemstvo.

YUMASHEV, THE ZEMSTVO EXECUTIVE BOARD AND ITS NEWSPAPER *VIATSKAIA GAZETA*

Perhaps the most dramatic single episode in the campaign to "renew" the zemstvo was the effort to remove Yumashev from his powerful position as chairman of the executive board, change the composition of the board itself, and reduce both its powers and its budget. As in other provinces, the campaign was launched during the December 1906 session of the assembly; in Viatka, it lasted for two months until Yumashev and others on the board were forced to step down.[27] As was often the case elsewhere, it combined bitter personal attacks with accusations of malfeasance and incompetence, but it also accompanied an ideological struggle interwoven with a long-standing effort on the part of district zemstvos to incapacitate the provincial-level organ. The cards seemed to be stacked against Yumashev, since by now so many voting assembly delegates were serving ex officio (because of their positions in the church or the in local administrative apparatus or because they had been appointed in place of candidates whose elections had been vetoed by the governor).[28] One of Yumashev's fervent supporters and aides, Vera Tanaevskaia, complained bitterly that even many of the so-called peasant delegates had been handpicked by the governor In a letter that was purloined by the police, she wrote:

> The list of delegates makes me sick, especially the so-called "peasants." Who are these peasants anyway? One is a former constable, two are village scribes, then there are a policeman and seven or eight downright kulaks. You get the picture (even those who) more or less look like peasants... are sullen and suspicious, ignorant, barbaric to such a degree it is hard to describe. In their opinion they only thing zemstvo employees are good for is robbing them of their last crumbs of bread. I could even understand this hostility if it were directed against all privileged outsiders without

exception, but no you should see how these beasts kowtow to the generals. Their only enemies are the zemstvo workers.[29]

Yumashev, who earlier in the year had also been elected by the assembly to represent the Viatka zemstvo in the prestigious State Council,[30] was not about to yield to pressure.[31] Five days into the proceedings, a bloc of delegates asked the newly appointed (rather than elected) chair of the assembly, Kniazev, to hold an election for a new executive board, and crowds gathered in anticipation of a vote. But those opposed to a vote held sway for several days—many sensed a prolonged conflict; some wanted to buy time, and others simply to get home for the holidays—and a motion to postpone all further meetings of the assembly until February went forward.[32] Then Kniazev announced that the delay violated zemstvo rules, and that the governor ordered elections to proceed.[33] On December 20, when nominations were solicited for the position of *uprava* chair, Yumashev received the most votes (27), but with 28 voting against.[34] All candidates to the *uprava* except one received more negative than positive votes at the nomination stage, and so no one agreed to be put forward for an actual vote. The governor then insisted that the full board be elected on the following day.

Then, on December 21, after two more rounds of voting,[35] Yumashev was again re-elected, along with other standing members of the board, including V. P. Kliucharev as deputy chair and A. A. Lopatin (Charushin's brother-in-law) as well as the peasant I. I. Igoshin as members.[36] Charushin's newspaper reported that the results were greeted by wild applause from the spectators who had packed the meeting hall—even if in fact that "public" comprised mainly zemstvo employees and students. The vote was close; 29 voted for Yumashev, 21 against.[37] Nevertheless, it represented a reversal in his favor, mostly likely brought about by a reaction against the governor's heavy-handed tactics.

In any event, the governor again intervened, rejecting both Lopatin and Igoshin. As for Yumashev and Kliucharev, their positions as chair and deputy chair required that the Minister of Interior order their removal, and on December 30, Gorchakov filed such a request. A month later, on January 22, Stolypin signed the necessary papers, and the next day, the governor's office, citing the zemstvo executive board's refusal to follow limits imposed upon its newspaper, ordered Yumashev to step down.[38] Yumashev refused, but on January 31 the governor presented the executive board with a telegram from the Ministry of Interior dismissing Yumashev and Kliucharev from all official functions in the zemstvo—they remained in the assembly as elected delegates.

They were replaced by A. Sukhov and two other officials, both serving in the provincial administration.[39] For the first time in the history of the Viatka zemstvo, the entire provincial executive board had been appointed by the state. This created curious bedfellows in the assembly; vociferous objections were raised to what had happened, and a bitter struggled ensued over the salaries to be paid these appointed members of the *uprava*, the majority voting to significantly reduce their compensation from that paid to the previous elected members[40] (the governor insisted instead on *raising* the salaries under dispute.)[41] In March 1907, members of the assembly proposed a boycott of the new zemstvo executive board.[42] And in May, after an acrimonious discussion, the assembly voted "by an overwhelming majority" (including several figures who had otherwise participated in dismantling zemstvo programs), to file an appeal to the Senate over the issue of board-member salaries. As late as January 1908, the assembly was still at odds with the gubernatorial *prisutstvie*—the office entrusted with reviewing zemstvo practices—on this topic.

Likewise, the assembly response to the purge of zemstvo employees was mixed, even after it itself had been purged and directed "rightward." As was the case with the forcible removal of the executive board, the mass firing of employees was a divisive issue and provoked contradictory actions. A gathering of district chairs of executive boards in August of 1906 endorsed a recommendation by the Urzhum zemstvo to leave the positions of those who had been forcibly dismissed open for nine months and to pay two months' compensation to those who has lost their job.[43] As chair of the provincial executive board, Yumashev had endorsed this practice; the *uprava* had put aside 5000 rubles to that end. As late as 1909, delegate Yumashev was still defending that decision before a largely hostile assembly. He argued that it had been a humane gesture of appreciation for those who had been dismissed and forced into exile within a space of three days, leaving their families without any means of support. The matter was brought to a vote on January 21 that year, and the assembly decided (28–16) that the expenditure had been improper. But by a closer margin (23–19), it voted against seeking restitution from the previous *uprava*, which would have been a punitive measure directed at Yumashev.[44]

Finally, the same contradictory dynamic was evident in the closing of *Viatskaia Gazeta*, the weekly newspaper the zemstvo *uprava* had published since 1894.[45] Technically speaking, Yumashev had been forcibly evicted from his position as chair of the executive board because of a conflict over the newspaper's expanded content. In truth, *Viatskaia Gazeta* had become quite thoroughly politicized. Articles on taxation pointed out its inequities; ones on the Decembrists argued for their relevance to the present. A special appendix to one issue provided a booklet over a hundred pages long that introduced its readership to key political terms in less than neutral terms; others lambasted the government's handling of the food supply crisis. Under fire in early 1907, the paper defiantly continued this trend; but after the turnover in the executive board, in charge of the newspaper and the intervention by the Ministry of Interior, its status became untenable.

A few months later, on May 4, 1907, a heated argument erupted in the zemstvo assembly and, given the heightened restrictions that had been imposed, Yumashev recommended closing the newspaper down. By a vote of 46 to 5, his recommendation was adopted; but at the same time, the assembly voted 26 to 23 to express its support for the earlier expansion of the newspaper, and 28 to 22 to file a complaint against the actions of the provincial offices.[46] The votes were close, for as with the book and cottage industry warehouses, conservatives in the zemstvo had been nipping at the heels of Yumashev over the newspaper well before the governor's office intervened, objecting to excessive costs as early as 1901.

Yet support for zemstvo autonomy crossed political boundaries; delegates seemed divided—at times, resentful of the *uprava's* progressive activism; at other times, offended by the arbitrary and heavy-handed intervention in zemstvo affairs by the governor's office. No other explanation for the voting patterns makes sense. Discovering and explaining this erratic pattern of behavior at the time of the 1905 Revolution was one of the real challenges and findings of our research and casts new light on the history of the zemstvo.

CHARUSHIN'S NEWSPAPER UNDER FIRE: KUVSHINSKAIA'S EXILE

In his own words, Gorchakov had identified two villains in leading the population astray, one being the zemstvo, the other being "revolutionary newspapers." One such newspaper was now shut down; the other, Charushin's, *Viatskaia Rech'* devoted much space to unfolding dramas in the zemstvo and the municipal duma, where much the same was underway, and the impact of events on many of his friends.[47] The aggressive, relentlessly oppositionist, investigative journalism of the *Viatskaia Rech'* soon brought down upon itself a slew of repressive measures.

Persecution of the newspaper began soon after its first issue appeared on December 25, 1905. Its first editor, A. A. Gur'ev, was arrested in February, to be replaced by P. A. Golubev (both SRs had been connected with the earlier *Viatskii Krai*, which the authorities had closed down in 1898). Golub'ev lasted until June 1906. The fact that both were prominent SRs was certainly a red flag for the governor's office, but one incident in March brought *Viatskaia Rech'* to the attention of the authorities in St. Petersburg and set the pattern for relations between the press and the gubernatorial authorities for the next decade. A land captain in the Malmyzh district had filed a complaint, both with the governor and the Main Administration of the Press, that two of the paper's articles about him were libelous, and that as editor Golubev had rejected his demands for a retraction, insisting that the land captain provide exculpatory evidence.[48]

From that time on the newspaper and the gubernatorial authorities were engaged in a tug of war involving the reporting of current events at the local level and revolving around accusations of corruption or abuse of power by local constables, police agents, or land captains. This kind of investigative reporting often led to refutations written by the governor or vice-governor that would be printed in the newspaper (the law required that the newspaper provide space), and sometimes resulted in intervention by the MVD in St. Petersburg.

The newspaper was a thorn in the side of the authorities; accordingly, it experienced sustained harassment and pressure. Several issues were confiscated; local schools and offices were forbidden to subscribe to the paper; at one point the printing press with which it was contracted was closed down, and twice the courts seemingly shut *Viatskaia Rech'* down for good, only for it to soon re-emerge under a new name. Looking back in 1926, Charushin wrote, "Provided with enhanced powers, the authorities spared no effort in persecuting the newspaper: it took it to court, closed down the printing presses, the exile of staff and endless fines and jailings of editors, singularly and in batches."[49] Those penalized included figures closely affiliated with the newspaper[50] but also others who were unconnected with its activities and had volunteered to have their names put forward as "dummy" editors, despite the virtually certainty of that they would receive three-month prison terms. Looking back, Charushin marveled at the degree of support there had been for the paper in local society and confessed that without it the paper could not have survived (see Figures 7.1 and 7.2).

Survive it did, however, in March 1906, the governor delivered Charushin an ultimatum: either give up your position as publisher of the newspaper or end your employment with the zemstvo. Charushin elected to step down from the paper, and from that point on, until mid-1910, his name was removed from its masthead, but by all accounts, he continued to run it, traveling frequently to Moscow and St. Petersburg to raise funds for its operations and closely directing its content. He could not, however, collect a salary for his labors.

It was Kuvshinsaia rather than Charushin who was more severely affected by the governor's moves. In March 1906, she had stepped in to replace her husband as publisher, but in early September she was informed that she had been exiled from the province and given three days to leave.[51] Hastily arranged testimony from three doctors that she was seriously ill did not alter the decision,[52] and on September 8, the police arrived at their home and ordered her to depart within the hour. After some negotiation, she was given until the next day to make preparations. She left Viatka to live in exile with her recently widowed brother in Perm', where she remained until the order was rescinded on May 5, 1907.

In March 1907, seven months into her exile, Charushin gained an audience with a new *revizor*, Zviagintsev, sent to Viatka to address the multiple complaints that had been mounting against Gorchakov's actions. Describing his visit to Kuvshinskaia, he expressed optimism that he had persuaded the *revizor* of the merits of their case:

FIGURE 7.1.

Newspaper Viatskaia Rech' personnel, 1908. Charushin is seated on the front step; Vera Tanaevskaia is listed among those in attendance.
Herzen Regional Library, Kirov.

Dear Anya, just a few words for the moment.... I wanted to talk about you, about myself and about famine relief matters, but almost immediately suppressed all desire to talk and limited myself to your case. I was there for about an hour and more or less got my points across.... When we said good-bye he promised to bring the matter up with the governor in the next hour and to convince him to act on it. If that didn't work he said he would take your case to the minister, but he was sure he could resolve the

FIGURE 7.2.

Newspaper Viatskaia Rech' personnel, 1909.
Herzen Regional Library, Kirov.

situation here. Tonight I heard from an official source that your case has already been settled in your favor.[53]

Charushin clearly believed that he had "breached" the bureaucratic wall and persuaded the *revizor* of the merits of his case. But the report filed by Zviagintsev showed that Charushin had misread the situation:

> She [Kuvshinskaia] was exiled from the province as a result of a whole series of anti-government articles published in her newspaper.... Besides this, according to administrative sources, Charushin frequently holds gatherings of a revolutionary nature at his home. After she received the official order of exile, she [*sic*] presented Gorchakov medical testimony signed by four private doctors that she was too ill to travel. According to evidence gathered by an official assigned to the case by the governor, they had come to their conclusions without ever having seen or examined her. Subsequently, by order of the governor, the provincial medical inspector interviewed witnesses ... and it became clear that [Kuvshinskaia] was well enough to leave Viatka without suffering any harm.[54]

In this episode, as important as Charushin's misread were the dynamics of this situation: the Ministry of Interior had felt compelled to send out a delegation in response to an outcry against its own plenipotentiary; Zviagintsev had felt it necessary to meet with opponents of the regime and to hear their cases; and Charushin had entertained hopes that he could find redress by laying out the circumstances of the case and the situation. In fact, despite Zviagintsev's caustic report on the meeting, Kuvshinskaia was soon released. This may have been one in a long string of events that ultimately led to Gorchakov's transfer to a smaller province.

For some reason, Charushin himself remained personally outside the governor's reach. While events were unfolding, both he and Kuvshinskaia had been privately apprehensive he might be sent away, leaving their son Vladimir (Volodya) without a parent to look after him.[55] In his autobiographical essay, he noted that of course his continuing role in the newspaper was a "fact not unknown to the local administration." But "the latter for some reason did not take repressive measures against me, limiting itself to threats of exile, which it never carried out."[56] In a letter to Stolypin, written in 1907, Gorchakov complained that Charushin's ruse of employing surrogate editors had made him invulnerable, lamenting that "deprived of any opportunity to level fines against the main figure of that newspaper, I have to resort to punishing his subordinates."[57]

The practice of resorting to such editors was frequently used by the oppositionist press in Russia. Yet is it plausible that the autocracy found Charushin completely untouchable? After all, at the time hundreds of members of the Viatka intelligentsia were experiencing administrative exile, which required no due process, no legal proof of guilt, and not even any specific accusations. Why not use the same device to get rid of him? It remains a puzzle why the government here and elsewhere felt legal qualms about pursuing him.

FORCED RESIGNATION FROM THE ZEMSTVO

Whatever the explanation for Charushin's personal invulnerability as ghost publisher, it did not protect his employment with the zemstvo, which was his sole remaining source of income. In December 1906, when the meltdown of the zemstvo *uprava* was underway, Kuvshinskaia wrote her husband, "Well now Kolya, I've long been afflicted with worry about your future. I cannot figure out why Gorchakov might spare you and I fear he has something nasty in store. ... Judge for yourself: everybody's been sent away but why not you? Yikes, I can't think about what is going on there anyway."[58]

But in January 1907, Charushin lost his position as a zemstvo insurance agent.[59] Several other insurance agents were removed, some sent into exile, and the insurance offices of district executive boards were subjected to police raids. A year later, the zemstvo launched an investigation of the alleged misappropriation of funds by zemstvo insurance agents in other districts.[60] Accusations of corruption leveled against insurance agents in the troubled Glazov district appeared in the newspapers. The unfolding scandal was discussed in the zemstvo assembly in January 1908, and criminal court charges were brought against at least one agent.[61] Yet even though the Viatka district zemstvo, which was technically his employer, had earlier been dominated by a conservative majority, the quality of Charushin's own work and his integrity as an insurance agent were never impugned. Instead, it was his refusal to sign a loyalty oath that caused his dismissal.[62] In December 1906 he had written his wife, "Whether one actually belongs to political parties or not, the paper to be signed is so insulting ... that I don't have the strength to voluntarily commit this type of suicide and am inclined to refuse to sign. At the moment, it's hard to say what will come of it, but I can accept the consequences."[63]

Then, on January 13, 1907,[64] he wrote to inform her, "Dear Anya, my turn has come but not in full measure. According to the governor's resolution I have been dismissed, not according to martial law but rather for not complying with an order of the chairman of the zemstvo board, that is, for refusing to sign that damned paper."[65] He was hopeful that at some point, when matters, settled down he would get his position back. As always trying to cheer Kuvshinskaia up, he tried to look at the bright side, "In a few days I will clean out my desk and be a free citizen. I can even smile at the prospect of a bit of freedom, however short-lived."[66]

THE "URZHUM BROTHERS" AND FAMILY MATTERS

Other family members often appear in the correspondence between Charushin and Kuvshinskaia during this time of their troubles. On October 1, 1906, a month into her exile, she wrote her husband urging him to ask Arkadii to intervene, "You should write [him], maybe he can come up with something to better our situation."[67] During his frequent trips to St. Petersburg, Charushin usually stayed with Arkadii, and she forwarded important letters addressed to her husband to that address.[68] In October 1906 she also advised her husband to consult with his sister Yulia, "Get in touch with Yulia . . . ; she knows how to deal with such situations."[69] On December 12 she worried about his other sister's silence, "No news from Lydia? What's up with her; I'm puzzled that she hasn't answered. I fear that [without her assistance] you will be going about in rags, and that would make me unhappy."[70] She told her husband to turn to Ivan for help storing their possessions, including a piano, should they be forced to leave Viatka following his loss of employment. She adds, "Ivan Apollonovich must find room for our furniture." Then, rather preposterously, she concludes, "or else he's just another Gorchakov!"[71] For his part, Charushin wrote to her, on October 10, that Volodia was spending time at Ivan Apollonovich's house; later that month he described a visit by that brother, who had recently returned from family in Orlov, "where of course people are really upset with the state of affairs."[72]

Even though she was in her last years and living in nearby Orlov, Charushin's mother was still an active presence in their lives. On March 27, 1907, Charushin writes Kuvshinskaia, "I am forwarding you a very touching letter which mama sent me in response to mine. Do write to comfort her to the degree possible; I'm planning to do the same."[73] In 1908, writing to Larisa Sinegub about family affairs, Kuvshinskaia tells her, "So I've been thinking of traveling to Orlov to visit [Charushin's] mother; she's elderly but alive, walks with a cane, but embarrasses me—in the kitchen, at church, and at the mill, she does it all by herself. I haven't been there in several years and after all it is only fifty kilometers away."[74] Clearly, their ties with their extended family remained strong in this unstable time for Charushin and Kuvshinskaia.

Brother Arkadii was at the time also experiencing difficulties. Two years earlier, he had also reached a crucial juncture in his life that put an end to his career. That well-respected civil servant had, in 1905, made known his dissatisfaction with the views on peasant resettlement policies of A. A. Kaufman, a well-known scholar and specialist in the Ministry of Agriculture who, Arkadii believed, tended to put his own career ahead of the needs of both peasantry and state. In October 1906, he was offered a transfer to Tiflis to serve on the board of the Peasant Bank, most likely a demotion. Two days later he declined the position, citing his poor health and the fact that he was within two years of being eligible for a pension, "giving [him] reason to hope that [he] could complete [his] term without being uprooted from life in Petersburg." A week later, his superior responded that because of Arkadii's "categorical refusal" and "careless fulfillment of obligations it would be appropriate to ask for his resignation," adding that if he agreed, he would be recommended for an enhanced pension. If he refused, he would be transferred without pay to the Ministry of Agriculture, Kaufman's bailiwick. A medical examination showed that Arkadii, like his brother, had serious chronic medical problems, but we are left wondering what were the real reasons for this episode, given the high regard in which he had been held by colleagues in the Resettlement Bureau. On January 5, 1907, he retired with an ample pension of 2,700 rubles.[75] Some official in the Ministry of Finance wrote in the margins of the document confirming his pension, "He lucked out!" (*schastlivets!*)

The parallels in the two brothers' situations are striking: both were engaged in peasant affairs at a time of upheaval in the countryside, and both had been forced out of their work. But they emerged from their situations with drastically different financial prospects, and if the correspondence between Charushin and Kuvshinskaia is indicative, neither had a settled life after these events. Arkadii, rather than settle into a comfortable retirement, sought other means of applying his skills, with unknown results.[76] Nikolai continued to hope that once the political situation changed for the better he would be allowed to return long enough to be able to receive at least a partial pension. But his dismissal had put the family financial situation under serious stress. Kuvshinskaia wrote him on January 15, 1907, "I can't say, my dear Kolya, that your news delighted me . . . we have been tossed out on the streets and must find employment. You ask for advice, ay-ay, what can I say.... Kolya, drop your optimism and admit that things won't soon take a turn for the better and we need to save every penny that we have ... and it's awful that [their surviving son] Volodia might be put under someone's else's care.... What's worse is to be separated at a time when we need to discuss and weigh everything, and take measures."[77]

THE "SALTYKOV AFFAIR" AND DEPARTURE FROM THE FAMINE RELIEF ORGANIZATION

Even now, he still had one modest source of income. Since 1905 he had also been receiving a salary directly set and provided by the Moscow assembly of the All-Zemstvo Famine Relief Organization for his work in Viatka.[78] Aside from supervising local efforts, he continued to play a role in the affairs of the central organs of the famine relief organization in Moscow, attending several of its conferences. Charushin's position was seemingly inviolable in that he was the authorized representative (employee) of the famine relief organization in Moscow rather than of the provincial zemstvo itself.[79]

Now, however, the provincial zemstvo assembly was divided over Charushin's participation in, and Viatka's affiliation, with that organization. Its local branches had been under sustained attack since Gorchakov's arrival in 1906.[80] In that year, six of its local committees in Viatka were closed down entirely, and thirty-one of its participants suffered administrative measures (including twenty-nine of its fifty-three district representatives; most were fined, some were arrested, and others were exiled). After the purging of the zemstvo executive board at the end of the year, the activities of the provincial famine relief committee also temporarily ceased. But worsening conditions in the province in 1907 had forced the government's hand, and Charushin had taken direct charge of the efforts to provide relief to the hardest hit districts.[81] However, early in 1908, matters once again came to a head. The semiofficial newspaper *Viatskii Vestnik* published a series of articles and lead editorials accusing both the provincial and a district organization of incompetence, mishandling funds, self-aggrandizement, and even corruption, and this time Charushin's integrity was directly impugned.

The issue began as a squabble within the Glazov district zemstvo (see Chapter 6). In a close vote, 14 to 13, a group of delegates had recommended that the famine relief commission be commended for its worthy efforts to relieve distress at the local level. But then an angry letter was written to *Viatskii Vestnik* claiming that the zemstvo vote had been secretly organized by members of the commission, which had actually been shoddy and neglectful in its work, and four of its members had actually been among the zemstvo delegates voting in favor of the commendation. A caustic debate ensued in the pages of *Viatskii Vestnik* and *Viatskaia Rech'*, centering on one village of forty households and highlighting one of them: that of the Saltykov family. This family was allegedly one of the more prosperous in a village, but it had walked off with the lion's share of relief funds.[82] Charushin responded to the charges in the pages of *Viatskaia Rech'*, acknowledging that in such an extreme crisis, the need to dispense resources to the needy quickly, staff shortages, and the remoteness of villages could indeed have led to mistakes being made, but also challenging the specific accusations concerning the Saltykov family. The case was picked up by the provincial *prisutstvie*, which had also received the original letter of commendation, and which, on December 27, 1906, had moved to retract it.[83]

It is impossible to determine which side was right here; the problem of poor record-keeping had often come up in relation to the All-Zemstvo Famine Relief Organization. In June 1906, its assembly had taken note of the issue, especially in light of the government's insistence that if funds were to be forthcoming, the organization had to implement strict "accountability" at the local level. But the administration of the organization had recognized the difficulty of doing so: keeping track of how funds were used was extremely hard to do. Many provinces insisted on the right to look after their own affairs; operations were being carried out in a time of multiple major crises, of which famine was only one; most of the staff were volunteers occupied elsewhere at the same time; and relief committees often worked in parallel with the Red Cross, as well as with state food supply organizations.[84]

Charushin added to that mix the impact the disbanding of local famine relief committees and the dismissal and exile of its members, as well as the halting of the work of the zemstvo statistical committee, had had upon efforts to identify the needy and to keep records.⁸⁵ Because he had only scant reports from the districts, he had been unable to make a strong case for need before the All-Zemstvo Organization, and Viatka had initially not been identified as one of the areas most hard hit by crop failures. Because of this too, not all the funds allotted to Viatka had actually been distributed in the first year. In the second year, large sums promised by the central government in November 1906 had been held up, arriving in most places only in May of 1907, because of which in many provinces soup kitchens had been shut down and famine relief efforts in general had halted.⁸⁶ Delays on the part of the government in dispensing funds were caused in part because of its insistence that the All-Zemstvo Organization keep better records, but also, it was claimed, by officials in the MVD (namely, Gurko) wanting proof that individual villages petitioning for aid were not among the "politically unreliable."⁸⁷

In 1907, by sending out teams to individual districts to collect information from school and grain distribution points, Charushin had managed to put together a detailed itemization of who had organized these entities, when they had operated, how much they had spent, and how many people they had served. But as late as 1908, the All-Zemstvo Organization, listening to Charushin's appeal for more funds, asked him where he was going to find the personnel to allocate them properly. All in all, Charushin had been dealing with an excruciatingly difficult situation, and effort to impugn his integrity and competence seems misplaced, if not deliberately concocted.

Charushin may have seen the writing on the wall when, on January 31, 1908, the meeting of the provincial assembly selected not him but a delegate, N. P. Starodumov, to attend the upcoming congress of the All-Zemstvo Organization.⁸⁸ Then, on June 19, at the evening session of the assembly, the other shoe dropped. N. O. Branovskii, who had been prominent in the campaign against Yumashev and the zemstvo newspaper, criticized Charushin's annual report on famine relief for its messiness. On June 21, Branovskii argued that since the local branch of famine relief organization was not accountable to the zemstvo, the latter's role in famine relief had been reduced to that of cash cow. He added that Charushin, having lost his position as an insurance agent, was technically no longer a hired employee of that zemstvo. Moreover, he served Moscow as a famine relief officer only at the discretion of the assembly and should resign immediately.[89] Recognizing that his position was no longer tenable, Charushin submitted his resignation the very next day.[90] In October 1908, the operations of the provincial famine relief committee were completely shut down.[91]

All his ties with the institution he had served since 1895 were now cut. Charushin surely found the criticism—voiced at the recent sessions of the provincial assembly—of him and his work in both the fire-insurance and famine relief programs extremely demoralizing, for some of it had been scathingly personal.[92] But more was coming. On January 1, 1908, he had submitted a request to the uprava: in it he wrote that when he had first taken up work with the zemstvo, Batuev had approached him to copy edit a new edition of Nikolai Blinov's[93] Russian translation of Daniel Defoe's *Robinson Crusoe*, offering him an honorarium for his efforts. The book had been published in a print run of ten thousand copies, but at the turn of the century, as we have seen, the book warehouse was experiencing liquidity issues, and so Charushin, in his telling, had willingly deferred his own compensation. Now, he wrote, he was in straitened financial circumstances and was requesting the money due him. The *uprava* turned the request over to the liquidation commission that had been appointed to dispose of the inventory of the book warehouse; several months later the commission "found it impossible to honor his request" for 200 rubles. The commission hinted that the lack of paperwork documenting the contract made the request problematic.[94] Rubbing salt into the wound, it then reminded Charushin that he had an outstanding debt to the book depository of some sixty-eight rubles, and threatened that if he didn't pay, he would soon be facing a court case. In a repeat appeal, submitted in January 1909, Charushin lamented that his honor had been impugned, all over the "paltry sum I have patiently waited for" but which apparently never arrived.[95]

THE "VIATKA WARLORD" EXITS: ACCOUNTABILITY AND THE PRESS

Governor Gorchakov had triumphed, but in so doing had set in motion the processes that would lead to his undoing. Brusque and self-confident, he had flouted all semblance of legality, sometimes offending even conservatives within the zemstvo but also provoking opposition within the gubernatorial apparatus itself. Trouble was brewing as early as 1907 for the brash governor, even as he was running rampant with dismissals, arrests, and exiles. From Charushin's correspondence, we are already familiar with the arrival of Zviagintsev, in March of that year, to investigate "complaints... of administrative abuse... by certain public figures." Around that time, Charushin had received a letter from E. Alasheev, a deputy to Russia's parliament (the Second Duma), informing him that a delegation had met with Stolypin, who had promised to investigate Gorchakov's actions. Alasheev could not predict the outcome, since in his view Zviagintsev was of the same sort as Gorchakov himself, and "after all, 'wolves don't eat their own kind.'" But, he added, maybe Stolypin was looking for a way to get rid of Gorchakov; Alasheev urged Charushin to organize a campaign to depict Gorchakov as "a fool, drunk and petty tyrant who is undermining society by his behavior as is that of his clique."[96]

In his letter to Kuvshinskaia about meeting with the official from the Ministry of Interior to try to gain her release, Charushin had described his group's attempt to launch just such a campaign against Gorchakov, "Zviagintsev is a decrepit old man and typical bureaucrat.... (yet) our conversations from another realm... casting a different light on matters, seem to have considerably upended the misperceptions of this high ranking codger."[97] On that occasion his efforts seem to have fallen on deaf ears. But Alasheev's prompting of Charushin to compile and send to St. Petersburg a chronology of administrative abuse so that Gorchakov's behavior would become public knowledge ultimately had its effect. On September 15, 1907, the capital city newspaper *Rus'* published an anonymous letter describing how Gorchakov had left on a hunting expedition without properly delegating authority to anyone. During his absence, the Committee of Ministers had placed Sarapul district under martial law. Upon returning to Viatka, Gorchakov apparently decided that martial law was unnecessary, and instead sent his unofficial right-hand man, de Rochefort, to assume control over Sarapul. De Rochefort, at the time all of twenty-eight years old, had apparently been living at the governor's mansion ever since the latter had arrived in Viatka. There, he "had been leading a dissolute life and was well known in the city for his unseemly doings." A follow-up visit, in October 1907, by St. Petersburg officials uncovered a festering conflict between Gorchakov and his vice-governor, A. F. Shidlovskii, which had prompted this washing of dirty linen in public. Shidlovskii accused Gorchakov of charging the governor's office the large sum of 1,000 rubles for a hunting trip taken on the pretense of traveling to examine conditions in the countryside.

In this case, Shidlovskii was sent elsewhere in retribution for breaking ranks. However, Gorchakov was simultaneously having to defend himself publicly on other fronts. The war of words, fines, and arrests had continued, even after Gorchakov had welcomed the annual session of the provincial zemstvo, in 1908, by noting that it was time to "stop dismantling and begin rebuilding." Listings of the names of fired and exiled zemstvo employees and descriptions of the roughshod treatment of teachers by school inspectors, arbitrary behavior and the corruption of petty officials, and physical abuse of the peasantry filled the pages of *Viatskaia Rech'*. One of Charushin's close associates, Biriukov (who had also felt the heavy hand of Gorchakov), wrote Charushin from Petersburg chiding him for letting the struggle become so personal: "Nowhere else do the local governors take up so much space in the newspaper. Of course, it is all interesting, but really so much? As it is, space is limited."[98]

To be sure, the coverage went beyond personal invective. One example of the especially aggressive investigative reporting concerned the truly shocking treatment of peasants in Kotel'nich district.[99] By 1908, a series of crop failures had left the peasantry in dire straits, and mounting arrears led to Gorchakov to send police and army units into the villages to forcibly extract the overdue sums. Reports (many compiled by local correspondents for *Viatskaia Rech'*) came out of Kotelnich of floggings and other harsh measures used on individuals, families, and even entire villages. The governor himself toured the area on a "fact-finding" mission and concluded that the accusations were concocted, but Viatka delegates to the Duma picked up the story. An investigation was launched, the capital city newspapers reported on the "*Viatka interpellation*," and in February 1909, a delegation was sent to meet with Stolypin on the matter.[100]

Once again, Stolypin was publically steadfast in his support of Gorchakov. In the words of a Kadet deputy and former school inspector from Viatka, S. Lipiagov, "When I began to lay out the circumstances to Stolypin, he interrupted me by saying . . . that he was fully aware of just what kind of source this was: 'the most revolutionary provincial newspaper in Russia, in which all kinds of filth is regularly collected and dished out to the public.'"[101]

Yet, even as Stolypin was loudly defending Gorchakov and removing the vice-governor, his ministry was conducting an internal investigation of the harsh measures the governor had used against the newspaper. In August 1908, Gorchakov was forced to respond to an article in *Viatskaia Rech* describing the incarceration of a female editor who had been thrown into jail with common criminals for refusing to pay the fine leveled against her for her work. It is unlikely that Gorchakov's bizarre response—namely, that her infractions had not been political in nature, satisfied his superiors.[102] That Stolypin's patience with Gorchakov was by then exhausted is clear from a letter he sent Gorchakov on August 26. In it he wrote, "I can't ignore the fact that all these administrative exactions ... rather than facilitating the task of overall pacification have instead have prompted justified complaints against arbitrary behavior by the authorities."[103] Stolypin then provided Gorchakov with a list of the administrative measures he had resorted to and heartily recommended retracting them.

Defending his actions, Gorchakov described *Viatskaia Rech'* as "the last gasp of what was revolutionary Viatka." He averred that the measures he had taken had come at a great cost to his reputation, "My name has reverberated across the entire country, becoming almost an epithet—you can hardly find a single left-leaning newspaper which doesn't feel obliged to mock the 'Viatka warlord,' and the humor journals are peppered with caricatures of me." Yet the results had been worth it, "I am profoundly gratified that I can now say that my efforts have not been in vain.... My trip around the province the past summer turned into a triumphal tour."[104] He argued that by retracting the fines, arrests, and other measures he had taken would severely damage the respect for strong authority that had been restored.

Stolypin was not convinced; in exasperation, he wrote in the margins of Gorchakov's letter, "Will someone tell that man that his recent actions have nothing in common with the struggle against revolution? Instead, he has handed weapons to the enemies of order in their efforts to discredit authority." He agreed that forcing Gorchakov to repeal measures already taken would only undercut his position but "recommended" that henceforth Gorchakov proceed much more carefully.[105]

Gorchakov left the scene soon after this. In the spring of 1909, after yet another *reviziia* by the Ministry of Interior,[106] he was transferred to Kaluga.[107] Charushin and his circle regarded the dispatch of Gorchakov as vindication of the importance of the newspaper, an assertion which finds confirmation in the archives.[108] As A. N. Baranov, writing from exile in Orenburg, gloated, "For sure even that one last exposure of police brutality leading to Gorchakov's transfer speaks volumes about the significance of the newspaper."[109] And one recent historian examining the documents in the Shidlovskii case concludes that "[Gorchakov's] stubborn character and lack of diplomatic tact had to undergo incessant public criticism. He was able to remove those in his administration who didn't suit him, but he couldn't find a way to silence the community of journalists, even those working in his own territory."[110] It is tempting to conclude from the denouement of these overlapping scandals that there were limits to governmental arbitrariness. Gorchakov knew he could get away with all kinds of administrative measures flouting legality, but at some point, a combination of journalistic exposure, societal opinion, and internal administrative conflicts forced Stolypin to remove his acolyte. Viatka was no longer the "City of Dunderheads" so famously described by Russia's greatest satirist, Saltykov-Shchedrin.

Still, Gorchakov's departure did not stop Charushin from continuing to publish a stream of articles exposing the peccadillos of the former governor and his ongoing self-indulgences, both on the way to and while serving in Kaluga. Never one to avoid fanfare or scandal, Gorchakov had left rather noisily and, it seems, "without turning out the lights,"[111] for it soon emerged that he had left unpaid a large bill, accumulated over several months, for electrical services provided to the governor's mansion. The city Duma voted overwhelmingly to forgive the debt in gratitude for his services, but Gorchakov's successor instead made a point of picking up the tab himself. In addition, according to *Viatskaia Rech'*, on leaving Viatka, Gorchakov made a side trip to pick up a luxurious yacht he had ordered and appropriately named *Viatka Warlord*, on which he continued his journey to his new home. Later, settled in Kaluga, he created yet more waves by allegedly encroaching upon the property of a neighboring landowner.

Gorchakov's successor, Petr Kamyshanskii,[112] who was most likely selected because of his reputation as a respected St. Petersburg legal expert, announced he would no longer impose fines upon the newspaper, but he did threaten Charushin with exile if *Viatskaia Rech'* continued to "discredit the work of the police."[113] Charushin later wrote that it was precisely because of his reputation for legal probity that Kamyshanskii was "more dangerous, more insidious" than his predecessor. On December 8, 1909, Kamyshanskii simultaneously arrested eight editors (the one actual serving and seven who were listed as standing in reserve) for the article "Political Revenge" published in No. 262 that year.[114] Each of the editors was fined 500 rubles; three were arrested, and four were forced to hastily depart the province to avoid being arrested themselves. As Biriukov noted sarcastically, "Dear Nikolai Apollonovich! How are things going? Matters going no better under the province's new boss? I see that he is your constant companion."[115] The situation remained difficult enough that Baranov, living peripatetically in exile, wrote Charushin, "From my distant perch I continue to closely follow the affairs of *Viatskaia Rech'* and was profoundly depressed to learn that the situation is critical. Apparently, things have improved, for the newspaper continues to appear? You must somehow persevere!"[116]

In fact, events unfolded in a familiar pattern. On December 10, Padarin sent a telegram to the MVD reporting the situation; the next day a deputation from the Duma, again led by Lipiagov, requested an audience with Stolypin, after which Stolypin responded that he had to seek further information before acting. On December 12, he demanded an explanation from the governor, who responded the next day that he "considered all the editors responsible and his actions correct." On December 15, Stolypin told Kamyshanskii that his measures were against the law and should be withdrawn, something that took place the following day.[117] From that point until his sudden death in late 1910, Kamyshanskii caused no further waves. Between then and the outbreak of war in 1914, the arrests, fines, and exiles of editors continued under a new governor, and individual figures were sometimes treated quite harshly, but gradually this abated,[118] and the pattern of gubernatorial accountability to the press had been firmly established.[119]

Charushin and friends had reason to be proud of their hard-won achievements; through their adept use of the periodical press they had been instrumental in bringing about a fundamental change in the dynamics of state and societal relations by bringing local affairs to the attention of the central government in a way that forced a response to abuse.

IN THE AFTERMATH: LOOKING TO THE FUTURE

But achieving some stability with the newspaper was hardly the end of Charushin's woes. Financial difficulties, domestic concerns, and then Kuvshinskaia's death in 1909 left him with their only surviving child to look after. With her passing he also lost his partner in running the newspaper. On the occasion of her death, staff members wrote to *Viatskaia Rech'* that she had been a constant presence at the newspaper, "[S]he gave advice, provided moral support, but at the same time the slightest slips, inevitable in work observing strict deadlines, had made her miserable."[120]

By the middle of 1910, Charushin (see Figure 7.3) had reasserted his formal status as publisher, and from that point on, he was in direct charge of nearly all the daily operation of *Viatskaia Rech'*, as well as its general stewardship and orientation. He wrote to Chemodanova not long after

FIGURE 7.3.

Nikolai Charushin, c. 1910.
Herzen Regional Library, Kirov.

Kuvshinskaia's death, "Not much to say about myself. I am alone at the moment, Volodia being in Moscow. As usual I am struggling with the newspaper and it takes up all my time. We are being seriously squeezed but we are still alive and have no plans otherwise. We've been under pressure for five years now, but don't want to retreat."[121]

The newspaper remained his only source of income, and fortunately by this time its financial situation had stabilized. Nevertheless, the events of recent years, and especially the violence, repression, and failure of the 1905 Revolution had inevitably put a strain on the personal relationships among Charushin's peers. We find abundant evidence confirming this in their correspondence, which is replete with accusations of scheming, dishonesty, arrogance, indifference to the well-being of others, and lack of fortitude or commitment to the cause.[122] The frequent changes of editors, arrests, fines, and the constant threat of the newspaper's closure ended up putting all of them at odds with each other. At several points, Charushin had to hastily find a replacement for an editor who had been forcibly removed, and not everyone welcomed his approaches. When Gur'ev's wife was asked to step up, Gur'ev himself angrily forced her to withdraw and send an indignant letter to Charushin accusing him of indifference to her well-being.[123] Charushin wrote Kuvshinskaia, "Everyone is just looking after themselves with no regard for the common good."[124] Golubev had resigned from his position as editor because of the newspaper's refusal to adopt SR positions, and he had demanded the right to make his complaints public in its pages. Given the perilous state of the newspaper, Charushin found his actions inexcusable and at the same time was terribly upset about the break with Golubev, as was Borodin, who vainly called for a court of honor in this case as well (Golubev later apologized to Charushin). The list of such demoralizing incidents was a long one.[125]

Disillusionment with each other extended to the level of the revolutionary parties as a whole. On December 23, 1907, Gur'eva wrote to Kuvshinskaia, from Ozerki in Finland:

> Revolutionaries today are a bad lot. The cultural level of these people seeking to "change history" is abysmal.... The NS Party in St. Petersburg is melting away. There are no organizers and no work among the masses. The most capable people there are preoccupied with party affairs, which would make some sense if something came out of it all, but nothing ever does.

I've come to the conclusion that in the NS Party nobody is willing to risk anything for their convictions. About the leaders I have nothing more to say; they are writers rather than activists.[126]

At first glance, all this bickering and displeasure would seem to contradict the picture we have elsewhere drawn of the group's sturdy relationships. In this chapter, we are reading about these lives through contemporaneous letters, whereas our descriptions of the Chaikovskii circle and of life in exile are filtered through the memoirs, as part of a carefully constructed "traveling narrative" (see chapter 9). Could we be wrong in emphasizing the solidarity of this group? Indeed, in the 1920s, as the aging Populists sought to inscribe their legacy by writing memoirs, Kornilova-Moroz would vent her anger at Sazhin for wanting to include their disagreements during this earlier period in his own.[127] But, in fact, these complications and outbursts did not in the long run alter their fundamental ties. They settled down and continued to work together in their public endeavors, and after 1917 renewed or maintained close contact with each other, sought and gave help when the need arose, wrote recommendations for each other, and reached out for verification of their recollections when writing their memoirs.[128] Nevertheless, the striking contrast in tone between letters written at the time and memoirs written two decades later is a noteworthy one.

The ties between former exiles may have been renewable, but there is no denying that the stress of events had cut deeply into their optimism about the future. The violence of the 1905 Revolution, the waves of summary executions and exiles, and disillusionment with the revolutionary potential of the people brought about a soul-searching and profound disillusionment with the political process among the intelligentsia as a whole that has been amply studied by historians. It was no different for our group of tightly knit provincials. In the letter to Kuvshinskaia, cited earlier, Gur'eva assessed the chances for positive change in somber terms, "How are you enduring this bloody reaction and what path forward do you see, Anna Dmitrievna? Must we make a new and huge expenditure of energy in the serendipitous hope of casting off this heavy burden, or decades of exhausting gradualist efforts, the outcome of which is hidden in the murky future? It's hard to be reconciled with that last one."[129] And on March

15, 1908, Dmitrii Biriukov wrote to Charushin, "I realize that everything now rests upon efforts to spread culture much more deeply in society, but how can that be achieved nowadays given such debasing conditions, just how? How does one suppress one's hopes for something bigger to happen, and return instead to living life in small doses as we did six or seven years ago? I don't know how, and there are lots of people wandering about in a fog, adrift on a huge, melting iceberg floating who knows where to. It's a miserable situation."[130]

In contrast to the mood of many in his circle, Charushin had retained a measure of optimism about the country's future, "My view of the future is not bleak and I think that with time matters will improve and we'll all be able to breathe a bit more freely."[131] Yet within a decade his convictions would be tested again. A new seismic wave of events, including war, revolution, civil war, and incarceration awaited him, and Charushin was forced to find a new personal path in the fundamentally transformed landscape of Soviet Russia.

NOTES

1. *Viatskaia zhizn'*, April 12, 1906; April 21, 1906, 5; April 22, 1906, 1, 3; April 26, 1906, 2; June 28, 1906, 3; June 29, 1906; July 1, 1906, 2; *Viatskii krai*, December 14, 1906.

2. On Gorchakov, see V. E. Musikhin, "Viatskii gubernator Sergei Dmitrievich Gorchakov," *Iz istorii Viatskogo kraia* (Kirov: Viatskii gosudarstvennyi pedagogicheskii universitet,1997), 37–53.

3. As preposterous as it seems, and despite the parallels with the agent of Cardinal Richelieu in Dumas's *The Three Musketeers*, as far as the authors can determine this was the actual name of Gorchakov's shady agent.

4. *Viatskaia Rech'*, June 18, 1908, 3.

5. Sergei Gorchakov to Petr Stolypin, September 5, 1908 (RGIA, f. 776, op. 21. 2, d. 277. 1, 1907, ll. 49 ob.–51 ob.).

6. *Tolkovatel' slov. Spravochnik pri chtenii gazet* (Viatka: n/p, 1906). RGIA, f. 1288, op. 2, d. 19, 1906, ll. 30–94. See more V. V. Tanaevskaia, "Vnimaniiu viatskikh iuristov," *Viatskii krai*, February 28, 1907, 2–4.

7. In Viatka, the number of delegates who had been forcibly removed or not confirmed equaled 16% of the total for all thirty-four zemstvos in European Russian. See Boris Veselovskii, *Istoriia zemstva za sorok let* (St. Petersburg: Izdatel'stvo O. Popovoi, 1911), 4:48.

8. *Viatskii Vestnik*, May 5, 1907, 3.

9. GAKO, f. 616, op. 1, d. 1357.

10. An initially promising search for the file on the Zinov'ev-led audits of several other provinces, which was registered in the archival holdings of RGIA, led to the discovery that it had been discarded in the 1950s.

11. See *Viatskii krai*, November 8, 1906, 2–4, for a lengthy article on the closing of the book warehouse on that date. Charusin, in a letter to Kuvshinskaia at the time, expresses puzzlement

at the raid, and claims that no compromising materials were actually found (RGALI, f. 1642, op. 1, d. 108. l. 11, November 3, 1906). As he put it, "[W]hy it was shut down only Allah knows."

12. *Viatskii Vestnik*, June 25, 1908, 2.

13. It is rather puzzling why some programs were targeted, and others not. It is understandable, for example, why the statistical boards, which were responsible for land tax appraisals, and in most provinces worked to make the land taxes more equitably distributed between peasants and nobles, came under fire. But why veterinarian and fire insurance programs? If Viatka is studied in isolation from other zemstvos, the likely conclusion would be that oppositionist figures, including former exiles, had been employed rather randomly, as openings occurred and because of the shortage of educated personnel. But as Veselovskii shows, these very same programs were crippled or dismantled in other provinces, with few variations. Veselovskii, *Istoriia zemstva* (1911), 3:606–645 and 4:74.

14. See *Viatskaia Rech'*, August 15, 1909, for a discussion of the impact of dismantling the statistical bureau. The statistical bureau was reinstated in 1911. *Sbornik postanovlenii Viatskogo gubernskogo zemstva za 21 god (1892–1913)* 1 (Viatka, 1914), 630–645, 567–675).

15. Veselovskii, *Istoriia zemstva* (1911) 4:42, 61–62.

16. RGIA f. 1288, op. 2, d. 19, l. 248.

17. *Viatskii Vestnik*, December 10, 1906, 1; RGIA, f. 1288, op. 2, d. 19, l. 248.

18. GAKO, f. 582, op. 168, d. 482. l. 101-ob. Virtually all of the board employees listed in this report were exiled in January 1907.

19. Anna Kuvshinskaia to Nikolai Charushin, October 6, 1906 (RGALI, f. 1642, op. 1, d. 79, l. 18).

20. Kuvshinskaia to Charushin, December 19, 1906 (ibid., l. 30).

21. Charushin to Kuvshinskaia, October 8, 1906 (RGALI, f. 1642, op.1, d. 108, l. 8 ob.)

22. Charushin to Kuvshinskaia, November 17, 1906 (ibid., l. 16).

23. Charushin to Kuvshinskaia, November 26, 1906 (ibid., l. 18).

24. Ibid., l. 26.

25. *Ukazatel' soderzhaniia gazety Viatskaia Rech'. 1908–1917 gg.* Vyp. 1. Ch. 1 / Sost. G. F. Chudova (Kirov, typescript, 1974), 78–105. The local archives contain a more or less complete listing of district and provincial zemstvo employees who lost their jobs between February 1906 and December 1908. GAKO, f. 616, op. 9, d. 46, ll. 1–26 ob.

26. Veselovskii, *Istoriia zemstva* (1911), 4:59–64, 74.

27. See A. P. Korelin, *Zemskoe samoupravlenie v Rossii. 1864–1918*, 1 (Moskva: Nauka, 2005), 40–44.

28. *Viatskii krai*, December 13, 1906, 1.

29. GARF, f. 102, op. 265, d. 256 (n.p.)

30. *Viatskaia zhizn'*, April 19, 1906, 2–3.

31. Yumashev's narration of Gorchakov's "rampage" in his first nine months as governor can be found in a complaint filed with the Ministry of Interior on March 25 1907 (GARF, f. 102, D-5, 1907, d. 378, ll.52–58 ob).

32. *Viatskii vestnik*, December 17, 1906, 3.

33. *Viatskii vestnik*, December 23, 1906, 3.

34. RGIA, f.1288, op. 2, d.19 (1906), ll. 255–257.

35. Initially, of fifty-five voting members, Yumashev received twenty-seven votes, just short of a majority; according to *Viatskii Vestnik* of those nominated to the board declined, some "decisively" or "categorically," and ultimately only four accepted their nominations. See *Sbornik postanovlenii*, 352–354.

36. *Viatskii krai*, December 22, 1906, 1.

37. RGIA, f. 1288, op. 2, d. 19 (1906), l. 255. As for the other members, Kliucharev received twenty-six affirmative and twenty-four negative votes; Lopatin, a notary public in Orlov, received thirty affirmative versus twenty-one negative votes, and Igoshin received the most in favor: forty-one as opposed to nine against.

38. At one o'clock in the afternoon of the same day, it carried out an unannounced audit of the finances of the *uprava*, of deposits to the Viatka branch of the State Bank, and of sums held at the uprava office and stored at the provincial *treasury*. *Viatskii Vestnik*, January 24, 1907.

39. RGIA, f. 1288 op. 2, d. 19 (1906), l. 254, 258. Initially, Gorchakov sought to nominate to the as chair a young circuit judge from Yalta, D. V. Novitskii, but at the last moment he declined "for health reasons," perhaps finding the climate, both political and weatherwise, unfavorable (GAKO f. 587, op. 7, d. 257, l. 109). Sukhov, widely seen as an opportunist from the Viatskii district, had failed on several occasions to win elections both to the zemstvo board and the municipal assembly (*duma*). *Viatskii krai*, March 6, 1907, 3.

40. See Vera Tanaevskaia's long essay in *Viatskii krai*, February 28, 1907, on the legal implications of this affair. For a radically different, and rather colorful, perspective, see *Viatskii vestnik*, January 21, 1907.

41. *Sbornik postanovlenii*, 349.

42. *Viatskii vestnik*, March 9, 1907, 2.

43. *Viatskii vestnik*, January 8, 1907, 2.

44. RGIA, f. 1288, op. 1, d. 19, ll. 249–269. *Sbornik postanovlenii*, 360–365.

45. RGIA, f. 1288, op. 2, d. 19; ll. 248–258. The file contains a letter from the governor to the Ministry of Internal Affairs discussing possible justifications for removing Yumashev, including the argument that Yumashev had been elected to the State Council in April, and the distance from St. Petersburg to Viatka would prevent him from carrying out his duties as a zemstvo official. Materials are also included on the famine relief and food supply efforts of the government. Ultimately, it was decided to both remove and indict him and Kliucharev over the handling of *Viatskaia Gazeta*, but the diverse content of the file suggests how interwoven many of the issues were in the minds of those involved. Several official meetings took place at the governor's office, in 1907, to deal with the fate of *Viatskaia Gazeta*. *Viatskii Vestnik*, January 24, 1907, 2–3; February 23, 2–3; February 24, 2–3.

46. *Viatskii vestnik*, May 6, 1907, 3–4. For the continuation of the conflict within the zemstvo, see *Viatskaia zhizn'*, May 8, 1907; 3; May 3, 1907, 2; October 4, 1907, 1–2; *Viatskii krai*, August 23, 1907, 2–3.

47. Gur'ev, Tanaevskaya, Kugushev, and Lozhkin were among those who suffered.

48. These articles were published in *Viatskaia zhizn'*, January 22, 1906, 4; February16, 1906, 4 (RGIA, f. 776, op. 21. 2, 1906, d. 11, ll. 7. 13–13 ob).

49. *Deiateli SSSR i revoliutsionnogo dvizheniia v Rossii* (Moskva: Sovetskaia entsiklopedia, 1989), 294.

50. He calculated the scale of administrative measures taken against *Viatskaia Rech'* (from 1908); the total was thirty-two fines amounting to 15,000 rubles and seven years and seven months of time spent in prison or exile by its editors. In those seven years, beginning in 1908, the paper had twelve editors, with an average length of service of seven months (RGALI, f. 1642, op. 1, d. 1, ll. 1–7 ob).

51. GAKO, f. 714, op. 1, d. 256, l. 10.

52. *Viatskii krai*, September 28, 1906, 2–3; October 19, 1906, 2–3; March 24, 1907, 3–4.

53. Charushin to Kuvshinskaia, 1907 (RGALI, f. 1642, op. 1, d. 108, l. 74).
54. GARF, f.102, D-5, 1907, d. 378, l. 117 ob.
55. Kuvshinskaia to Charushin, January 19, 1907 (RGALI, f. 1642, op. 1, d. 79, l. 40).
56. *Deiateli SSSR i revoliutsionnogo dvizheniia v Rossii*, 295.
57. E. D. Petriaev, *Liudi, rukopisi, knigi* (Kirov: Volgo-Viatskoe knizhnoe izdatel'stvo, 1970), 200.
58. Kuvshinskaia to Charushin, December 1906 (RGALI, f. 1642, op. 1, d. 79, l. 33).
59. See GAKO, f. 616, op. 10, d. 3375, ll. 9–14 ob., 69–75.
60. GAKO, f. 616, op. 9, d. 41, ll. 2–13; d. 45, ll. 1–23, 44–76 (Sarapul, Urzhum, and Elabuga).
61. *Sbornik postanovlenii*, 367–368.
62. Among those also dismissed was A. N. Baranov, a close associate of Charushin, who had previously worked in Malmyzh as an insurance agent (while simultaneously engaged in literary matters and politically involved in the notorious Multan affair). In 1902 Baranov was transferred to this huge district of Slobodskoi to become an insurance agent; he became energetically immersed in peasant affairs and in 1905 organized a group of zemstvo employees to help distribute oppositionist literature among the peasantry there. But like Charushin, he refused to sign a loyalty oath and on Gorchakov's order was dismissed. In February 1907, he moved to Viatka and took up employment on the editorial board of *Viatskaia Rech'*. However, he was soon forced to leave for Ufa, where he again received a position as an insurance agent and wrote frequently about insurance and fire prevention measures in following years.
63. Charushin to Kuvshinskaia, December 1906 (RGALI, f. 1642, op. 1, d. 108, l. 26). On the campaign to collect signatures in other provinces, see Veselovskii, *Istoriia zemstva* (1911) 4:61–62.
64. The decision to dismiss him had been taken by the district zemstvo earlier, on December 23, 1906 (we recall that, in April 1906, the right to hire and fire zemstvo employees was transferred from the provincial to the district uprava, something that profoundly troubled those employees, a fact highlighted in *Viatskaia zhizn'*, April 21, 1–2; April 26, 1906, 2; April 27, 1906, 3.
65. Charushin to Kuvshinskaia, January 13, 1907 (RGALI, f. 1642, op. 1, d. 108, l. 30).
66. Ibid., l. 30 ob.
67. Kuvshinskaia to Charushin, October 1, 1906 (RGALI, f. 1642, op. 1, d. 79, l. 14 ob.).
68. Ibid., l. 66 ob.
69. Kuvshinskaia to Charushin, October 7, 1906 (ibid., l. 19).
70. Kuvshinskaia to Charushin, December 19, 1906 (ibid., l. 31).
71. Kuvshinskaia to Charushin, January 15, 1907 (ibid., l. 37 ob.).
72. Charushin to Kuvshinskaia, September 21, 1906 (ibid., d. 108, l. 5).
73. Charushin to Kuvshinskaia, March 27, 1907 (ibid., l. 27).
74. Kuvshinskaia to Chemodanova, July 17, 1908 (RGALI, f. 1291, op. 1, d. 38, ll. 1–1 ob.)
75. RGIA, f. 391, op. 7, d. 3858, l. 94.
76. In fact, in October 1909, the Department of State Domains filed a request for Arkadii's service record (*formul'iarnyi spisok*), indicating that it had, or was considering offering him a position. However, his trail disappears there, and we only know of his membership in a literary society, after 1917, and of his death in 1922.
77. Kuvshinskaia to Charushin, January 15, 1907 (RGALI, f. 1642, op. 1, d. 79, l. 36).
78. RGIA, f. 1482, op. 1, d. 7a, l. 6.
79. Ironically, at a conference in Moscow, in June 1906, Charushin had spoken up in objection to a new charter for the famine relief organization, one in which its authorized

representatives would be selected by that organization's assembly (made up of the chairs of all provincial zemstvos, as well as some ex officio members from other organizations) instead of by the local zemstvos themselves. Charushin and others believed that this would lead to overcentralization and promote passivity on the part of individual zemstvos (a similar charge was made by members of the interministerial group formed in St. Petersburg to coordinate famine relief efforts between the government's food supply commission, the Red Cross, and the All-Zemstvo Organization). Nevertheless, the new charter passed (if only partially implemented), and Charushin was elected unanimously (49 to 0) to continue to serve as its representative. Serving as the All-Zemstvo Organization's elected and salaried authorized representative to the zemstvo, rather than as a representative to the central organization from the provincial zemstvo, gave Charushin some protection during the wave of dismissals of zemstvo employees in 1906–1907, but in June 1908, it served as a convenient argument within the zemstvo to force him out of this position.

80. In his report to the Moscow famine relief organization in 1908, Charushin described in detail how its district committees had suffered from the repressive measures of the state. The greatest number of dismissals of members had taken place in Slobodskoi, Iaransk, and Kotelnich. Among those dismissed were Charushin's friends A. N. Baranov and V. I. Lozhkin, as well as several colleagues as insurance agents. See RGIA, f. 1482, op. 1, d. 151, ll. 3–6. In a similar letter to the famine relief organization, the Iaransk district zemstvo board depicted a catastrophic situation of famine and disease in the area and confirmed that the local famine relief committee had been paralyzed by massive purges launched by Gorchakov, to the extent that people qualified to pitch in were nowhere to be found. Ibid., d. 278, ll. 1–6.

81. *Zhurnaly Viatskogo gubernskogo zemskogo sobraniia ekstrennoi sessii 17–21 iiunia 1908 goda s prilozheniiami* (Viatka, 1908), 481–497.

82. *Viatskii vestnik*, June 8, 1908, 1; July 2, 1908, 1; December 12, 1906, 3.

83. *Viatskaia rech'*, June 19, 1908, 4; GAKO, f. 587, op. 11, d. 28, ll. 1–2.

84. RGIA, f. 1482, op. 1, d. 78, 1906, ll. 44, 49.

85. On the impact of the closing of the statistical bureau, aside from Charushin's testimony to the All Zemstvo Org., see *Viatskaia Rech'*, October 5, 1910, 2.

86. This picture is drawn from Charushin's own reports to the All-Zemstvo Organization, that institution's journals of its meetings, a Duma investigation in the summer of 1906, and reports of the interministerial commission set up by the MVD in August 1906: RGIA, f. 1482, op. 1, d. 151; f. 1482, op. 1, d. 7a;

87. RGIA, f. 1482, op. 1, d. 7a, l. 20.

88. *Sbornik postanovlenii*, 227.

89. *Viatskii Vestnik*, June 24, 1908, 3.

90. Notification was posted in *Viatskaia Rech'* on June 22. This did not stop Charushin from subsequently criticizing the (deliberate?) inertia of his replacement, F. I. Platunov, who was reportedly close to government circles.

91. '*Viatskaia rech'*, April 19, 1909, 3. Following the new representative's appointment, on October 31, the committee had not met again; in the words of *Viatskaia Rech'*, "[S]o, if this organization has died, we should be informed of the fact." On the recent poor harvest and the failure of the provincial zemstvo to provide seeds or aid, see *Viatskaia Rech'*, June 25, 1909, 1.

92. Later, Charushin was once again appointed to be the authorized representative of the Imperial Free Economic Society in Viatka (headed by N. Chaikovskii) in its efforts to provide famine relief. *Viatskaia rech'*, December 13, 1911, 2. But he was immediately summoned to the governor's office with a warning. *Viatskaia Rech'*, December 15, 1911, 2.

93. The priest Nikolai Nikolaevich Blinov (1839–1917) was a notable figure at the time. Exiled to a remote village in Viatka, he had worked with the Udmurt (Votiak) population promoting literacy, published several primers for that population and was been active in zemstvo affairs; he then gained dubious prominence during the notorious Multan affair in the 1890s for breaking with the rest of the intelligentsia, including Korolenko, and asserting that the Udmurt population did in fact carry out human sacrifices. A. A. Rashkovskii, "Sviashchenik i kraeved," *Pamiatnaia knizhka Kirovskoi oblasti i kalendar' na 2009 god* (Kirov, 2009), 340–343; V. D. Sergeev, *Poborniki prosvetitel'skogo sluzheniia: Iz istorii Viatki* (Kirov, 2004), 31–36. The volume in question by Blinov was entitled *Zhizn' Robinzona (v chem schast'e)*. The work that gained him infamy in educated society was *Iazycheskii kul't Votiakov* (Viatka: n/p 1896).

94. In a repeat request, submitted in 1909, Charushin argued that under Batuev, "oral commitments" had been the norm, and cited Lozhkin, Borodin, and former uprava member Gromozov as witnesses. *Zhurnal Viatskogo gubernskogo zemskogo sobraniia* (Viatka, 1909), 1513–1515.

95. Ibid.

96. RGALI, f. 1642, op. 1, d. 6, l .2.

97. Charushin to Kuvshinskaia, 1907 (ibid., d. 108, l. 74).

98. Biryukov to Charushin, 1909 (RGALI, f. 1642, op. 1, d. 12, l. 11).

99. See Charushin's description of this event (RGALI, f. 1642, d. 1, ll. 3–4).

100. RGALI, 1642, op. 1, d. 42, ll. 1–10.

101. Lipiagov to Charushin, February 14, 1909 (ibid., l. 6).

102. Most likely anxious about the *zapros*, Gorchakov did, however, show concern about her well-being by moving her to a prison hospital (GARF, f. 102, D-4, d.15, ch. 8 (1908), l. 17).

103. RGIA, f. 776, op. 21, ch. 2, d. 277, ch. 1, 1907, l. 36.

104. Ibid., ll. 52 ob.–53.

105. The complete exchange can be found in RGIA, f. 776, op. 21, ch. 2, d. 277 ch. 1 (1907), ll. 35–49.

106. *Viatskaia rech'*, February 28, 1909, 2.

107. *Viatskaia rech'*, April 2, 1909, 1; April 26, 1909, 3.

108. GARF, f. 102, D-4, d. 15, ch. 8 (1908), ll. 1–13.

109. Baranov to Charushin, May 29, 1909 (RGALI, f. 1642, op. 1, d. 8, l. 4).

110. S.V. Liubichankovskii, "Smushchenie v tsentre gubernskoi tverdoi vlasti obostraietsia": dokumenty Kirovskoi oblasti o konflikte viatskogo gubernator S.D. Gorchakova s vitse-gubernatorom A. D. Shidlovskiim. 1907g. *Otechestvennyi arkhiv* 2 (2007). The article includes the full text of letters from both sides in the conflict held at GAKO, f. 582, op. 148, d. 371. The article in *Rus'* was published on September 15, 1907, 2–3. The report of the Spring and October, 1907 MVD visits to Viatka are located in RGIA, f. 1284, op. 47, 1906, d. 63, and RGIA, f. 1284, op. 47, 1906, d. 63, ll. 68–78.

111. Ibid., May 1, 1909, 2.

112. Before he arrived in Viatka to assume the responsibilities of governor, on April 20, 1909, P. K. Kamyshanksii was the procurator for the Petersburg judicial chamber (1904–1909; GAKO, f. 583, op. 603, d. 868). The Kadet Party leader Ariadna Tyrkova-Williams remembered him as a typical prosecutor calling for severe penalties in political cases for the accused and describing them as dangerous political criminals. Ariadna Tyrkova-Villiams, *Na putiakh k svobode* (New York: Izdatel'stvo imeni Chekhova,1952), 159.

113. *Viatskaia rech'*, August 19, 1909, 3.

114. *Deiateli SSSR i revoliutsionnogo dvizheniia v Rossii*, 295.

115. Biryukov to Charushin, 1909 (RGALI, f. 1642, op. 1, d. 12, l. 11).
116. Baranov to Charushin, May 29, 1909 (ibid., d. 8, l. 4 ob).
117. RGIA, f. 776, op. 21, ch. 2, d. 277, ch. 1, (1907), ll. 108–123.
118. Fines and arrests declined significantly between 1910 and 1912, rose slightly in 1913, and then spiked significantly in 1914, before stopping almost entirely in 1915 and 1916. Charushin later wrote, "[I]t was only in its very last years that the local administration began to regard us as a necessary evil and resorted less frequently to repressive measures." *Deiateli SSSR i revoliutsionnogo dvizheniia v Rossii*, 295. For a full list of exiled and fined editors, beginning in 1908, see RGALI, f. 1642, op. 1, d. 1, l. 7 ob.
119. The pattern was already in place at the time of Gorchakov's departure. For a small sample of such reported incidents in a three-month period alone, and attempts by the governor's office to refute charges against local officials, see the following items in *Viatskaia rech'*, April 12, 1909, 3; April 22, 1909, 2; April 26, 1909, 2; May 5, 1909, 3; May 20, 3; June 5, 3–4; June 7, 3; June 17, 1909, 3; June 18, 1–3; June 19, 3; June 30, 3; and June 24, 3, 4. For another incident illustrating this pattern, see the protracted case (1911) of one land captain from Sarapul, a certain Miliukov: *Viatskaia rech'*, January 25, 1911, 3; March 3, 1911, 3; April 7, 1911, 3; May 25, 1911, 2. The government response to the incident can be found at RGIA, f. 776, op. 21, ch.2, d. 277, ch.1, ll. 203, 217, 253–253 ob.
120. *Viatskaia rech'*, January 15, 1909, 1.
121. Charushin to Chemodanova, February 28, 1910 (RGALI, f. 1291, op. 1, d. 39, l. 1 ob.).
122. RGALI, f. 1642, op. 1, d. 107, l.
123 Ibid., d. 22, ll. 6–6 ob.
124. Ibid., d. 108, ll. 48–48 ob.
125. Ibid., d. 21, l. 1.
126. GARF, f. 102, op. 265, d. 256, l. 45.
127. Kornilova-Moroz to Figner, August 31, n.d. (RGALI, f. 1185, op. 1, d. 602, ll. 66–66 ob.
128. RGALI, f. 1642, op. 1, d. 87, l. 1.
129. GARF, f. 102, op. 265, d. 256, ll. 45–45 ob.
130. RGALI, f. 1642, op. 1, d. 12, ll. 2–3.
131. Charushin to Kuvshinskaia, March 11, 1907 (ibid., d. 108, l. 48).

8

The Revolution Followed Its Own Scenario (1917–1919)

How little I understood the course of the revolution, how myopic, unreflective and politically unprepared I was.

—Vera Figner, 1923

Yes, in my conversations with workers we touched upon social revolution as a way out of the present situation, but this was always an abstract conversation unrelated to the tasks at hand.

—Charushin, 1876

THE NEW ORDER

Rumors of massive strikes in Petrograd arrived in Viatka as early as February 25, 1917, and three days later, employees at the train station received a telegram relaying the news that a revolution had taken place.[1] More detailed telegrams followed, but before they could be published in the newspapers the police confiscated them pending a decision by the governor, N. A. Rudnev to do so. On March 2, after the abdication of Nicholas II, Rudnev, a popular figure in Viatka, publicly confirmed what had happened and proclaimed his willingness to submit to the authority of the Provisional Government, as did the municipal duma. By then, most district towns had already been informed about events. On March 4, *Viatskaia Rech'* published official greetings sent by Rudnev, as well as by the chair of the provincial zemstvo *uprava* (P. I. Pan'kov) and the municipal mayor (P. I. Shkliaev) to G. E. L'vov, the new head of the Provisional Government. The next day, instructions arrived from Petrograd telling all governors and vice-governors to turn over control of their provinces to the chairs of the *upravas* (again: provincial zemstvo executive boards), who were simultaneously to serve as the newly established local commissars of the Provisional Government. Indeed, on March 6, Rudnev handed over the reins of government to Pan'kov.

On March 3, even before the governor had stepped down, an expanded session of the municipal duma in active consultation with the governor had voted to establish the Committee of Public Safety to assume power in the locality and take control over the local police. Representatives from both zemstvo and duma were sent to regimental headquarters and quickly won the assent of both soldiers and officers to support the new authorities. As historian Yuri Timkin observed, the political situation in the Viatka garrison in early March differed sharply from that in Petrograd. The commanders maintained control over the situation and the circulation of information, provided their assessment of unfolding events, while the soldiers themselves did not arrange their own meetings or demonstrations. In his account the Committee of Public Safety played a decisive role in shaping the mood and behavior of the garrison, and a similar situation developed with other garrisons located in the province.[2] Thus, calm and order marked the transition.

Despite the prevailing calm, multiple nodes of authority emerged and initially who was in charge—that fledgling institution, the zemstvo or municipal duma was unclear. Viatka soon witnessed the proliferation of cooperatives, professional unions, soldiers' committees, officers' councils, and, finally, the establishment of a Soviet of Workers' and Soldiers' Deputies. By March 18, the Provincial Committee of Public Safety (now called the Executive Committee) included within its ranks representatives of all of these organizations as well as of all the major political parties. District and even *volost'* (county) branches of the committee were established, but its relationship with the Provisional Government in Petrograd remained ill-defined. As historian V. I. Startsev has ably shown, similar organizations made up with more or less the same list of institutional participants arose spontaneously at the same time across Russia, following the precedent of Moscow. In some areas their influence was short-lived, fading by sometime in April; in others, it persisted.[3] In Viatka, of the seventy-two times the committee met in 1917, more than half (thirty-seven) took place in the first month.[4]

As historian V. Bakulin wryly comments, shared power in Viatka evolved over time into no power at all.[5] Yet despite the multiplicity of organizations giving voice to long pent-up demands, enthusiasm and support for the Provisional Government held sway in Viatka city, the district towns, and the villages longer than in Petrograd and many other areas, and the polarization of society was slower to emerge.[6] Only in factory towns, such as Izhevsk, Sarapul, and Votkinsk, did a robust working-class movement make itself felt early. Elsewhere, Bakulin notes, "the working class at this time wasn't inclined toward a direct conflict with the holders of power and capital."[7] The Soviet of Workers and Soldiers' Deputies as well as the newly resurrected Peasant Union found common cause with the Provisional Government; the municipal dumas as well as provincial and district zemstvos remained prominent in politics. Although enthusiasm for the new order waned by late spring, disorders in the countryside surfaced only in late summer as famine began to stalk the central and northern districts, and food requisition policies generated tensions in the fertile southern areas of Viatka province.[8] Local garrisons (including the pivotal 106th regiment in Viatka city), as well as local soviets on the whole remained loyal to the Provisional Government and looked forward to the Constituent Assembly right up to and even after the October Revolution in Petrograd.

"THE JOY WAS SHORT LIVED ... ANXIETY OVERTOOK ME"

The historian M. M. Bogoslovskii wrote in his diary at the time: "Enjoying a burst of energy, our society is too infatuated with revolution and believes that we are seeing heaven on earth emerge. All cautionary talk aimed at sobering people up is fruitless."[9] We have no correspondence which might provide tell us about Charushin's own response to the February Revolution. Judging solely by the lead editorials in *Viatskaia Rech'*, it was. affirmative if not euphoric.¹⁰ True to his lifelong beliefs, in a signed editorial, on March 23, he noted that "no committee could carry out a revolution by itself," and expressed happiness that the "blinders had finally been removed from the peasants' eyes." At the same time, he counseled patience, restraint, and the preservation of order in the villages, and in the vocabulary of an earlier generation he urged the intelligentsia, to "go forth to the people" (an article in *Viatskaia Rech'* was even so named).¹¹ He himself was certainly no idle bystander of events. In his 1926 autobiographical sketch, written perhaps with an eye to the Soviet censor, he speaks sparingly and selectively about his own experience in the months following the February Revolution, "In Viatka as elsewhere revolutionary organizations emerged spontaneously and in the aftermath of the February Revolution I was obliged to play a very active role, especially in the Executive Committee."¹²

Despite his advanced age (he turned sixty-six in December 1917) Charushin seemed to be everywhere. On the eve of the revolution he was serving on several committees official and unofficial, including those providing aid to the wounded and to families of the enlisted, financial support for university students, the auditing commission of the Economic Society of Consumers as well as the board of trustees of the library. Now he joined the provincial executive committee of the Committee of Public Safety¹³; served on the local food-supply commission (*prodovol'stvennaia komissiia*), which was key to the survival of the new regime under its chair Leonid Yumashev;¹⁴ and was active once more in zemstvo affairs. Now, however, he was an elected delegate to the "renovated" assembly rather than a hired employee. Likewise, he was elected to serve as a delegate to the municipal duma, joining his brother Ivan there.¹⁵

On March 18, following the lead of the reconstituted People's Socialist (NS) Party in Moscow he took the initiative in resurrecting the Peasant Union in Viatka, serving as the chairman of its executive committee. When in June it merged with the Soviet of Peasant Deputies Charushin was unanimously elected (against his better judgment) to its provincial executive committee. Charushin was also instrumental in organizing a Political Red Cross to aid recently released political prisoners.¹⁶ Even if, at times, he may have been appointed primarily as an honorary chair, this was an impressive list for an "old freedom fighter" (as he was frequently labeled) whose opinions were still held in high esteem.

One wonders, however, whether this elderly revolutionary fully shared in the generally ecstatic mood of the country during the "Springtime of Freedom," marking the month or so after the abdication of Nicholas II. The work of O. N. Znamenskii modifies the conventional narrative by describing considerable anxiety and trepidation among the intelligentsia of Petrograd as events on the streets unfolded in late February and March. There was anxiety about outcomes and fear of the unfamiliar, as well as apprehension about the prospects of anarchy and what millions of armed veterans might bring to politics. Shock at the rapidity of change, a feeling that the bottom had dropped out, and general discomfit were widespread.[17]

Underlying Charushin's burst of energy and activism, did this reserved and self-contained veteran have his own moments of doubt? Did the lead editorials in *Viatskaia Rech'* leave out any misgivings or apprehensions he might have felt? It seems so. Later, speaking, on September 20, of that year to the assembled 192 delegates at the Third Provincial Peasant Congress, he recalled his emotions at that earlier date, "Naturally, like others I was happy, but that happiness was short-lived. Almost from the start of the revolution I experienced overwhelming anxiety."[18]

For Vera Figner as well, the February Revolution seemed to prompt mixed feelings from the start: optimism, yes, but caution as well, and a certain melancholy about the long road taken to this point. Turning to a friend in mid-March, she wrote, "[I]t's difficult to reconcile what could turn out to be magnificent with what seems ominous in what has happened around us. For the first few days I was even downhearted, for my thoughts kept returning to those who had fallen or been crushed during the past thirty-seven years of relentless struggling for freedom, not to mention those who came even before them."[19] A few years after the revolution her recollections of it were even more poignant, "We had waited so long for this moment but strange as it seems, I didn't experience unbridled joy; instead, I was made uneasy by a mix of happiness, sadness [for what had come before] and anxiety. Everything had come about too easily and too fast."[20]

VIATSKAIA RECH' AND THE PEOPLE'S SOCIALIST PARTY

Whatever his true feelings were and despite his multiple commitments, Charushin focused on the two activities which had characterized his political efforts since the turn of the century: *Viatskaia Rech'* and the Peasant Union. After the outbreak of World War I subscriptions to *Viatskaia Rech'* had soared, from four thousand to over ten thousand, and in this revolutionary year the newspaper remained the major source of news for the educated classes in the city and in the province as a whole.

Just as Charushin was unwavering in his support of the coalition Provisional Government, so he insisted that his paper remain free of party affiliation. Yet the general drift of the paper did consistently reflect the positions of the rejuvenated People's Socialist (NS) Party (which in June had merged with the like-minded Populist Trudoviks). In 1917 the party platform[21] called for the establishment of full civil rights for all men and women regardless of faith or nationality; for a single-chamber parliament with full legislative powers; a federal system of governance with regional autonomy and local self-government of the village commune and the zemstvo; an independent judiciary, exclusively public trials, abolition of all special courts, the election of judges, accountability of all officials and replacement of a standing army with popular militias. Calling for popular sovereignty in its fullest form, the NS-ers nevertheless recognized that it could only gradually be implemented given the weight of Russian tradition, Russia's level of development, and current circumstances. The party believed that at this time Russia "lacked the spiritual and material base" for immediately introducing socialism. Many party members, including its most prominent leader, Alexei Peshekhonov, had more than dabbled in revolutionary politics and had recognized the need ultimately to resort to force to topple the autocracy, and even tacitly supported terror as a last resort.[22] But by 1917 their perspective was clearly evolutionary, even if they sought what was essentially revolutionary redistributive justice and transformational political change.

Most important for the ultimate victory of democracy was elimination of all noble landholdings and the turning over of all land to the peasants, to be held on the basis of the labor principle (essentially, "he who works should have access to the land as a stewardship"). But this also could take place only gradually, with the nationalization of all state, crown, and monastic holdings. In their opinion expropriating all private land risked alienating the substantial proportion of the more enterprising peasantry who also held land in private ownership. Unlike the Socialist

Revolutionaries they also insisted that expropriation of private land take place with compensation from the state to its owners. The NS Party adamantly rejected both class warfare in the countryside (and a class-based politics in general), and making a wager solely on the "middle peasantry"; that is, ignoring the needs of the poorer stratum in the countryside, as it was accused of doing.

As it had in its previous iteration drawn up in the immediate aftermath of the 1905 Revolution, the NS program emphasized the need for a strong state *(gosudarstvennost')*, both in the current conditions and in general as a mediator between the needs of the country's diverse constituencies. The National Socialists differed from the far more popular and influential SRs in that they believed a strong state fit both the age-old psychology of the peasantry and the contemporary needs of the country. The program also put much weight upon the country's intelligentsia, to whom it ascribed pivotal sociological features giving them both much in common with, and the potential to be leaders of, the people as a whole. Finally, the party's program emphasized that the goal of any just society should be individual self-realization as much as it should be the common good.

The NS Party consistently called for a coalition government as the only means of effecting an orderly transition and, in the long run, of providing authentic democracy. In June 1917, it (with Charushin serving on its executive committee) called for full support of the Provisional Government insofar as it pursued truly democratic goals; the elimination of "dual power"; the vigorous promotion of a defensive war; and the equally vigorous pursuit of forming a unified Populist party. It expended considerable energy in its efforts to create a new umbrella party of like-minded thinkers, ultimately with little result.

Both earlier and now, in 1917, the NS Party existed in a fluid and triangulated relationship with both SRs and Kadets; it had members looking both right and left. As for the SRs, its right (or moderate) wing had many ties with the NS Party, both personally and politically; ties evident in Charushin's own life and in Viatka politics in general. But these ties with the left were dashed by the return of militant exiles and growing prominence of more radical SR party elements over the course of the summer.

The NS party had about 150 organizations, with a membership not exceeding eleven thousand, of whom roughly 80 percent were members of the intelligentsia. The absence of a popular base was reflected in elections to the Constituent Assembly, which produced only three (or, according to a recent account, five) delegates from the NS Party. On the other hand, it was well represented in public organizations; the zemstvo structure; and the administrative and executive branches of the Provisional Government, including two ministers, six deputy ministers, and a large number of high-ranking officials there. In the face of sagging morale later in the summer, *Viatskaia Rech'* continued to defend the war effort as well as the Provisional Government.[23] That, the rejection of "soviet power" and its determination to keep the empire together, albeit within a federal structure; its power base within the Provisional Government; and its faith in the ability of zemstvos to satisfy the needs and earn legitimacy in the eyes of the population did not bode well for its prospects.

In the summer of 1917 Charushin traveled to Moscow and Petrograd, meeting there with Petr Kropotkin, newly returned from years of exile, and with Nikolai Chaikovskii, both for the last time. At his meeting with Chaikovskii, at a time when the country was in ferment and being pulled in multiple directions, Charushin asked his comrade what he thought was in store for the country, and the latter responded firmly, "a bourgeois-democratic government."[24] Given the common belief in a predetermined path, progressing in stages to socialism, why he did not feel an urgent need to act more forcefully becomes more understandable. It is also understandable why, in 1927, the author of an article on the October Revolution in Viatka put the NS Party closer to the Mensheviks than to the SRs, with whom they had long-standing ties.[25] After all, it was the firm conviction of the Marxist Mensheviks that, historically, socialism would be preceded by an extended period of bourgeois dominance.

In fact, by May of 1917, with the appointment of the Socialist Revolutionary P. T. Salamatov as provincial commissar[26] most key institutions in the city (including the municipal duma) and the province came under the sway of moderate SRs and Mensheviks. Even the local branch of the liberal Kadet Party was dominated by intellectuals whose world views were strongly influenced by Populist ideas.[27] And conversely, one of the NS Party's most prominent leaders, V. A. Miakotin, revealingly wrote about its allegiances, "if forced to choose, better the Kadets than the Bolsheviks!"[28]

THE PEASANT UNION AND THE "OLD REVOLUTIONARY AND FREEDOM FIGHTER"

Such an arrangement was much in accord with Charushin's own views about an "umbrella" coalition of moderate socialist forces. He believed that oppositional organizations must remain scrupulously free of party affiliation in order to present a united front against monarchist and reactionary forces, as well as to work effectively with the peasantry. This conviction also governed his role organizing the newly reborn Peasant Union. The relationship between the Peasant Union and the Soviet of Peasant Deputies was a fraught one. The latter, established in May in Petrograd, was from the start largely the creation of the SR Party and initially drew much of its membership in that city from military units (soldier-peasants, it was argued) garrisoned there. After some complicated negotiations, the leadership of the Peasant Union, operating out of Moscow, decided to keep its distance from the other organization.

Perhaps because of lingering memories of its significant role in the Revolution of 1905–1907, the Peasant Union initially garnered significant support among the Viatka peasantry.[29] From the moment of its founding in March, local branches rapidly sprang up across the province.[30] Yet this early support was fading by May because of the leadership's endorsement of the war effort and insistence that land reform had to await the Constituent Assembly. Although historians have concluded that many peasants made no distinction between the two organizations, as the summer approached many local organizations drifted toward the burgeoning Soviet of Peasant Deputies. At the time of the first Provincial Congress of Peasants (June 6–10)[31] the momentum in Viatka was clearly on the side of the Soviet of Peasant Deputies, and at a meeting of the executive committee of the Peasant Union chaired by Charushin, it was decided over his objections[32] to merge the two organizations. Charushin was selected its honorary chair at that congress not because of his specific views but in recognition of his status as an "old revolutionary and fighter for freedom." He was also unanimously selected to serve on the executive committee of the newly enlarged Soviet of Peasant Deputies.[33]

None of these organizations had the wherewithal to continue in existence on their own. Discussions at subsequent congresses and at the last session of the provincial zemstvo, in December 1917, leave no doubt that the local soviet of peasant deputies functioned only because of ongoing subsidies from the zemstvo and local cooperatives. By the end of the summer, contributions from the village, never substantial, had entirely dried up. To continue operations, the local soviet needed five thousand rubles monthly and another seven thousand to meet its obligations in fees to the national organization, but in October had it collected only 1,500 rubles from the localities.[34.]

Despite that reality and disregarding Charushin's insistence that the Soviet of Peasant Deputies and the periodical peasant congresses remain independent of party affiliation, the SR Party was steadily tightening its grip on such organizations. At the Second Provincial Congress of Peasant Deputies, which opened on August 12,[35] its executive committee worked up a program and a list of delegates for the Constituent Assembly exclusively forged by the SRs. Distraught by this seeming takeover by a single party, even one that was notoriously lax in party discipline in 1917,[36] and hurriedly departing to attend the State Conference in Moscow, Charushin abruptly resigned from the executive committee of the Soviet of Peasant Deputies without having argued his case in public, something for which he was roundly criticized. A month later, on September 20, as the Third Provincial Peasant Congress convened,[37] he published a long letter responding to his critics and arguing against immediate expropriations without compensation from private landowners, which was a bone of contention between the SRs and NSs. Charushin accused the local SR leadership of deviousness and hypocrisy: deviousness, because the SR-dominated executive committee had taken advantage of the low turnout (fifty-two participants) at the August conference to ram through its own program; and hypocrisy because at the first Peasant Congress V. N. Makushin had even apologized to his "peasant comrades" for the possibility that the SR promises might mislead the peasantry. Charushin complained that the leadership of the party fully realized that the question of land redistribution was complex and that expropriation of land from the nobility without compensation was unrealizable, "[They] knew this but did not have the civic courage to admit openly and forcefully that this was deceit."[38]

By forwarding only SR names in its selection of candidates to the forthcoming Constituent Assembly which was to determine the future of the country, Charushin argued that the Viatka executive committee had gone even further than its national leadership, which, by contrast, had included NS leaders in its list, and which acknowledged the inevitability of compensation by the state to owners of private property for expropriation of that land. Nor, he continued, was it true, as SRs claimed, that that the Peasant Union had won over only a narrow sliver of the "more conscious" peasantry. As evidence of this he pointed to the unexpected victory in district and county peasant elections of unaffiliated candidates despite the concerted efforts of the SR Party to influence these elections. For all these reasons Charushin was offended by the selection at the poorly attended August Conference of a monolithic bloc of twenty-five SRs to its executive committee.

At the same time, strongly objecting to party politics within the Soviet of Peasant Deputies, Charushin described the peasantry as being "not only without party affiliation, but also not prepared [without tutelage] to make sense of party programs, or cope with the complex problems brought by the current situation."[39] It was this reality, he argued, that in June had convinced the Peasant Union of the need to join forces with others, "[A]t this critical moment, what was needed for the defense of peasant interests was a class-oriented, supra-party unifying all the laboring peasantry 'from top to bottom.'" Still, Charushin concluded his letter to the delegates convening on September 20 with a plea for unity: at a time "when terrible dangers are besetting the revolution and the country from all sides" he urged them to take their task seriously and resolve the issues before them, "keeping in mind that every false or incorrect step only brings our homeland that much closer to that abyss to which we are hurtling precipitously due to our own mistakes and internal quarrels."[40]

Soon, however, at this Third Peasant Congress, with 192 delegates present, Charushin became involved in a heated dispute with SR delegates, and gave one of his most plaintive speeches, which he prefaced by saying, "I didn't join the revolution yesterday, fellow citizens, I've been at it for a long time, dating back forty-six years." Referring back to his arrest, imprisonment, and prolonged exile he continued, "While in prison the dream of emancipating the country never left my thoughts, and I never betrayed the ideals of my youth." Describing his long-held conviction that preparing the peasantry for active participation in politics would take generations, he asserted that as long as the peasantry did not move to emancipate itself any revolution would be reduced to dust.[41]

Turning to current events, he bitterly described the evolution of the executive committee, his own reluctant election to it, and the exit of its NS members in protest against the local committee's decision not to publish a brochure by (NS theoretician) Peshekhonov, *The Nationalization of Land*. Responding to warnings that he was out of order and repeating that it was his "profound conviction" that the organization had to remain above party affiliations, he argued, "Don't lose track of the fact, my fellow citizens, that until only recently the village had been closed to any free exchanges of opinion. So now it is being educated and led in one direction alone by a single party line."[42]

Finally, on October 1, he returned to the topic once again in a signed article in *Viatskaia Rech'* entitled, "At the Viatka Peasant Congress: Some Personal Impressions."[43] He described a hall full of peasants, many wearing soldiers' jackets, and, in contrast to the first such congress six months earlier, actively participating and responding boisterously to every speech. At the same time, instead of relying on their own observations and common sense, those present were largely under the sway of "whoever plays most upon their emotions and grievances, whoever best stoops to demagogy and calculates the mood of the moment." Referring of course to the leftist SRs, Charushin again lamented their advocacy of expropriation without compensation, their cry that if the Constitutional Assembly vetoed that, the revolution would need to be defended by force of arms instead of through the Assembly itself. He argued that "the peasant party" was now at a crossroads: up to this point it had sought to agitate the peasantry using simple slogans that would be readily understood by the "benighted peasantry" among whom the "urge to destroy" prevailed. "But now, given the universally acknowledged societal collapse what was needed was 'sacrifice,' practicality, and impartial evaluation of existing conditions and strengths. Instead, what had been sown were unfounded illusions and promises, which only worsened (*ugliubliali*) the situation."[44] He was to use that word—which could also be translated as "deepened"—often from that time on.

"THE DEEP COUNTRYSIDE IS MIRED IN IGNORANCE"

While managing a newspaper and struggling with developments in peasant organizations Charushin was also attentive to developments at the national level. He and 2,500 others had attended the noisy State Conference in Moscow on August 12–15, and been exposed to the evident disarray and growing polarization there.[45] We have no correspondence with friends by which to determine his mood at the time, although his comments from the Third Provincial Peasant Conference certainly indicated his growing frustration with those with whom he had hoped to cooperate.

From Charushin's speeches in 1917 it is evident that his views on the mutual relationship of the intelligentsia and peasantry remained consonant with his earlier positions and "preparationist" views. Views similar to Charushin's have been expressed by the modern historian Orlando Figes, who has argued that peasants "had a limited view of citizenship... that did not go beyond the village borders... and could not understand complex political terms."[46] Indeed, a prominent article in *Viatskaia Rech'* in early October repeated a well-used phrase of the time, "The deep countryside is mired in ignorance."[47]

The views of both fit well with what Aaron Retish, has called the "constricting discourse" of the Viatka zemstvo intelligentsia. In recent decades historians have often underscored the hegemonic aspects of educated Russia's discourse on its peasantry, seeing it as controlling rather than emancipating—a conclusion drawn from the axiomatic linking of knowledge and power today on the pages of academic journals.[48] Retish argues instead that contrary to the intelligentsia's fears of backward villagers, "by autumn, peasants' political acumen had ripened and they no longer showed... patience with educated society's political tutelage."

Resentment of the privileged classes was certainly widespread among Russia's lower classes, and the distinction between education and privilege could be a fine one when outsiders came to the village.[49] However "political acumen" overstates the sophistication of most peasants mobilized into politics. For Retish, that term seems to imply that the peasantry were now full-blooded participants in civil society, able to distinguish between party programs, and resentful of attempts to educate them. Peasant grievances were indeed egregious, and their actions certainly displayed "agency," but intrusion into politics in 1917, outside of the demand for land and an end to the war, was by no means always disciplined or focused for more than a small minority. Peasants could and did act rationally, as one of the authors of this work demonstrated in a study of popular schooling at the turn of the twentieth century.[50] But "agency" could also be ill-informed, irrational, and self-defeating. Nor did the peasantry much care for doctrinal differences among the parties; rather it moved in favor of those they came to believe were generally "for the peasantry." They were understandably ready to vote for any party that offered peace and land.[51] There were significant exceptions—notably the one to two million peasants who had gone beyond a primary education to become a "peasant intelligentsia" of some import for Russian society and politics. Soldiers returning from the front also altered the situation, but for the most part, the long-standing perspective recently repeated by Rex Wade, namely that peasant politics were above all local, still holds.[52]

As for the argument that the regional zemstvo intelligentsia had established no lasting ties with the peasant village, it does not do justice to what was in fact a complex, shifting, and multidimensional relationship that had emerged, especially since the 1890s. After all, in many areas zemstvo budgets had increased fivefold in the previous twenty years, and the number of hired employees (doctors, teachers, insurance agents, etc.) active in thirty-four provinces and 441 districts had grown exponentially. Excluding teachers, some 75,000 were working in the villages of European Russia by 1914.[53] As Scott Seregny's thorough studies of rural teachers and Ilya Gerasimov's work on agronomists in the cooperative movement have shown, by World War I the rural intelligentsia, including teachers, zemstvo activists, and those in the cooperative movement had established a "crucial direct link into rural life."[54] It is understandable, then, why against all odds Charushin continued to believe both in the mission of the zemstvo and to hold out hope that a unified educated elite could rise above party loyalty to provide the peasantry with the tools it needed to understand events, and together lead the country out of the morass it was entering late in 1917.[55]

"EVERYONE IS FED UP WITH EMPTY PHRASES AND INACTION"

Charushin was no naïve outsider. He had carried out difficult and often frustrating ameliorative work with the peasantry through the operations of the zemstvo and as a famine-relief agent between 1896 and 1907. He was well aware that peasant frustration and wrath was at times directed at outsiders of all stripes.[56] He was surely alarmed at the angry outbursts of the soldiers and peasantry directed at his colleagues in the professional intelligentsia. Articles in *Viatskaia Rech'* expressed dismay at the downward spiral of events and growing disorder in the countryside. The newspaper published stories about attacks against individual households that had left the communes; resistance to the authorities' attempts by to take timber for military needs or by the military to find deserters; resistance to the activities of land surveyors and the beating up of grain assessors, pollsters for the ongoing All-Russia Agricultural Census, and the local chair of the food supply commission; arson in *volost'* offices; seizures of church land; and the chopping down of treasury forests.[57] At roughly this time, the historian Bogoslovskii commented in his diaries about the misplaced idealism of the zemstvo intelligentsia, "And that the very people for whom they had sacrificed their own well-being now call them 'bourgeois' and harbor the worst feelings toward them. The peasants don't want to hear about the zemstvo and just want to see it eliminated ... where is the border between idealism and myopic stupidity?"[58]

Indeed, the tone of *Viatskaia Rech'* grew increasing sober as the year unfolded. When celebrations of the May 1 holiday in Urzhum took an ugly turn and a crowd turned against progressive zemstvo figure A. S. Depreis and the chair of the district zemstvo board, forcing their arrest, Charushin, in an article titled "Urzhum Outrage," inveighed against "demagogues" who were leading the people astray. Charushin surely knew Depreis (he had been elected chair of the local zemstvo executive board in 1906 but was rejected by Governor Gorchakov, and was now the head of the local food-supply commission and the district commissar).[59]

But another incident of crowd violence early in July came even closer to home. V. A. Treiter,[60] a doctor well known to Charushin, was badly roughed up by a hostile crowd at the Viatka railway station (where he also served as doctor). According to *Viatskaia Rech'*, as an American delegation (which included the statesman Elihu Root) was traveling through Viatka on its way from General Staff Headquarters, a fire broke out in a number of warehouses at the train station. It had spread to several empty freight cars on the train and was threatening other cars that were filled with explosives. The American delegation was forced to abandon the train and was rerouted to continue its journey by steamship on the Viatka River; in the meantime, the deputy commissar Treiter tried to have the cars with explosives moved out of harm's way. However, the soldiers and the mixed crowd misunderstood his intentions, set upon him, and beat him senseless, as they did the stationmaster who sought to intervene; both received medical assistance before being sent to the hospital. Treiter languished there in critical condition before finally recovering to participate in events alongside Charushin.[61]

Reporting on the incident, *Viatskaia Rech'* underscored the mob violence and *samosud*, a term describing the "rough justice" of the peasants taking the law into their own hands. By contrast, in the Urzhum incident Charushin had blamed Bolshevik agitators for the assault on zemstvo and the Provincial Government officials. Like Vera Figner, Charushin made it clear that he thought that the activities of the Bolsheviks were beyond the pale. As early as April 27, *Viatskaia Rech'* warned against the preachings of Lenin, arguing he was trying to undermine the Provincial Government, establish a dictatorship of the proletariat, and sow the seeds of anarchy and civil war.[62] In June, *Viatskaia Rech'* expressed concerned about the growing Bolshevik influence among the soldiers of the local garrison.[63] And the newspaper was not the only forum in which Charushin made his views on the Bolsheviks abundantly clear. Speaking out at a session of the municipal duma in September, he argued against the Kadets present who were opposed to sending a representative to the upcoming "Democratic Conference" in Petrograd (September 14–22), convened to rally democratic forces in support of the Provisional Government. He pointed out that unless the "healthy wing" of democracy were present the field would be left to the Bolsheviks.[64] He consistently portrayed that party as stirring up the country's obscurantist elements, both benighted and criminal.

Once again, Vera Figner's letters to friends are suggestive. Writing in September about that conference she also rued the course of events and railed against the Bolsheviks, "Everyone is fed up with empty phrases and inaction as we tie ourselves up in knots, hopelessly obsessing about our differences. Only the Bolsheviks have managed to float like flotsam and jetsam in the sea of turmoil, and with their unbridled and unfulfillable promises to the benighted masses are shamelessly giving the country over to the Germans while at the same time unleashing the forces of reaction."[65]

By August and September of 1917, discontent was rife among soldiers garrisoned throughout Viatka province and in towns with sizeable working-class populations, adding to the turmoil in the countryside brought about by the requisitions of the food-supply committees seeking to feed the towns.[66] By September, food-supply organizations in a number of towns and districts were warning of approaching conditions of starvation and called for firm action.[67] Yet the NS Party's efforts to address the deteriorating situation were instead directed primarily at drawing up candidate lists and preparing for elections to the Constituent Assembly (which finally took place only in late November, early December.) It did not bode well.

In her letter of September 21 Figner had also shared the apprehension that the crush of events and the direction the country was taking had stripped people of any urge to take the high road or to make sacrifices for the common good. She lamented that resources, both spiritual and material, were simply not adequate to the tasks at hand, "Nobody shows any trace of the earlier surge of ennobling feelings and willingness to sacrifice. Some are simply incapable of such strengths, but others are just worn out both physically and spiritually, crushed by the enormity of what needs to be done and by the miserly resources—both human and material—at hand to make it all happen."[68] Indeed, by this time Figner's despair was profound:

> Because of all the difficult experiences making up my past life I had few illusions about the spiritual capacities of most people. For that reason, from the start I didn't have much hope that freedom would take root without us undergoing painful shocks, or that this painful war wouldn't crush Russia. There were other people who positively radiated with ecstasy, who believed that the old order had been cast aside and the new one would not be sullied in the process. Where have those people gone? Instead, now everyone is sullen, irritable, and quarrelsome. Of course, there is no reason to give up hope entirely—where there is life there is hope, but the

situation today has revealed terrible sores on the body politic it is impossible to breathe freely or sleep peacefully in light of them.[69]

Was the situation really so hopeless at the time? Concerning Viatka, three historians have presented different perspectives on the viability of the Provisional Government there. Retish emphasizes conflict, peasant activism, and hostility to the zemstvo and the intelligentsia, hence only tepid support for the Provisional Government. In his view, by midsummer this support had all but vanished.[70] Bakulin emphasizes that the February Revolution in Viatka had been bloodless because it was a revolution in name only. In his view, it had been little more than a changing of the guard, leaving the ruling classes in power, with new administrators drawn essentially from the same pool, and the needs of workers and peasants needs unmet.[71] For both historians popular support for the Provisional Government had been tepid from the start; hence its erosion was foreordained.

In contrast, Yuri Timkin points to the problems the Provisional Government had inherited, but argues that the *volost'* (county) zemstvos established in the late summer of 1917, had they reached deeper into the countryside, could have served as a viable foundation for a new political system if provincial officials had moved more quickly in the months after dual power was established. Elections to establish such county zemstvo organizations, scheduled for August 13 through 20 and intended to bring that organization closer to the peasantry, had, in fact, gone extremely poorly. Timkin points out that they had come just as several other elections were also taking place in quick succession, exceeding the capacity of local sponsors to organize and implement them. He implies that had such elections been better staged and less frequent, participation might well have been far more robust. As it was, weary and preoccupied constituents had little time to sort out what was happening, and teachers, agronomists and other zemstvo personnel were not available to pitch in.[72] Had they been on hand to work more closely with the peasantry, perhaps the links established over the previous fifty years could have helped move the peasantry in a different direction.

In her study of neighboring Kazan province Sarah Badcock, while emphasizing the rift between the peasantry and the local intelligentsia,[73] has observed that the events of 1917 exacerbated the situation by pulling the latter out of the village, mobilizing them into national electoral politics and recruiting them to carry out administrative tasks for a Provisional Government extremely short of administrative talent.[74] If so it was a bitterly ironic twist of fate—those who could have provided a link with the countryside had been removed from the scene just when they were most needed.

Whatever the case, it was not to be. As the Provisional Government's hold on the country, never firm, slipped away in the late summer and early autumn, the war effort imploded, the country's centrifugal forces accelerated, and polarization became the name of the game.

SURELY NOT ALL OF RUSSIA IS INFECTED WITH BOLSHEVISM!

When the Bolsheviks came to power in Petrograd on October 25, Charushin was attending the first session of the newly reformed zemstvo assembly on which the Provisional Government had pinned its hopes for creating a robust vertical linkage with the provinces and revitalizing local government. In his 1926 autobiographical sketch, Charushin's description of his own role is markedly laconic, perhaps reflecting the political climate at the time, "In October, 1917 ... the capital was in turmoil and soon the open struggle for soviet power was to begin. All normal contacts between the provinces and the capital were interrupted. Therefore, the provincial assembly was obliged to assume all the functions of governance until such time as authority was restored in the capital. It proclaimed Viatka province an independent republic and elected an executive organ, the Supreme Soviet consisting of eighteen members including myself."[75]

If, however, we turn to his responses to events at that time a much more vivid picture emerges. Just a day before the Bolshevik coup in Petrograd, on October 24, *Viatskaia Rech'* had greeted the opening of the fifty-ninth session of the Viatka provincial assembly in several articles, calling it the "first democratic assembly" and urging it to "save the motherland."[76] On that day the assembly convened with eighty of one hundred delegates and ex officio members present. The chair of the *uprava*, P. P. Pan'kov, greeted the members, proclaiming that this session was the first to reflect the country's "reformed structure" and that for the first time in history the assembly's composition genuinely reflected "the will of the people." Then there was a vote for a new (largely honorary) chair of the assembly, and the SR provincial commissar Salamatov was elected by a strong majority; Charushin, for the first time in his life an elected delegate from his home town Orlov (as well as to the Viatka municipal duma)[77] was made a member of the auditing commission by a vote of 69 to 11.[78]

In his speech, Salamatov argued that up to the present the zemstvo had largely "stood to the side in the rush of events," but now, under the new law that added county-level units to the existing district and provincial level zemstvos its structure could facilitate "integrated and sustained" action. Deputy chair of the assembly E. V. Serapikhskii noted that "everybody knows that up until now there is no trust in the zemstvo on the part of the people"; for that reason, winning that trust had to be the first task. The SR V. N. Makushin (whom Charushin had recently roundly excoriated at the Third Peasant Congress), and then Charushin following him, emphasized the huge problems facing the country and region. Both, however, expressed optimism that the situation was temporary, and that ultimately popular sovereignty would triumph. On October 26, the public face of the new regime was completed when by a vote of 72 to 11, Leonid Yumashev was returned to the post of *uprava* chair, after an interval of ten years. P. S. Basov[79] was selected deputy chair and A. A. Zonov[80] (of peasant origin and, like Basov, a member of the NS Party) was made a member of the new *uprava*. Clearly, Charushin's entourage was well-represented by this leadership.

In his introductory comments on October 24, Basov noted that whereas previously the zemstvo had largely been entrusted with administrative tasks and cultural development, its mission now was one of governance.[81] Yet to understand the ineffectiveness of Charushin's circle in the ensuing events it is crucial to keep in mind that in the growing turmoil, zemstvo men were confronted simultaneously with a political crisis of unprecedented dimensions, one requiring bold measures, and tasked with keeping the schools and hospitals open, collecting taxes, ensuring that factories received the raw materials they needed to keep operating, and myriad other functions, not to mention the record-keeping such matters involved. On October 24 and then again on the twenty-fifth, after the introductory speeches assessing the general condition of the country and the role of the zemstvo, the assembly turned immediately to these more humdrum matters.

For this reason, the pages recording the October 24 meeting seem to emit an audible sigh of relief from the assembled members that the Provisional Government had created a new food-supply council; now the zemstvo would no longer have to occupy itself with grain supply issues, which had provoked such hostility from the peasantry. The newly elected chair of the provincial *uprava* had himself only recently resigned from the food-supply commission.[82] Yet other issues loomed, such as establishing a centralized medical council to deal with infectious diseases; reorganizing the governance of primary and secondary schools; addressing the working conditions of zemstvo employees; dealing with the mounting crisis in tax collections and related looming school and hospital closures; the need to create a new "social welfare" bureau; collections of firewood in preparation for the advancing winter; and the conditions of Muslim schools in the province. Over the following days, as the assembly grappled with organizing resistance to the Bolsheviks, it continued to discuss the ongoing revenue and supply issues, delegating functions to the new county-level zemstvos; popular resistance to exactions; support for the local SR newspaper;[83] the reimbursement of delegates for travel expenses; and especially, implementation of a new and completely overhauled educational system.[84] Charushin weighed in often on these issues.

As it was deliberating these practical matters, the newly elected assembly chair reported, on October 26, the rumors that there had been "seizure of power by the Soviet of Soldiers and Workers Deputies" and recommended establishing a special council, a *sovet* (or soviet) to be made up of members of the zemstvo and municipal duma, with authorization to take prophylactic measures in response to unfolding events. Among those voting in favor of establishing this council were Yumashev and Basov; Charushin, however, did not.[85]

At the fateful evening session on October 27, Salamatov confirmed the rumors, noting that news had come via the telegraph, which was now available only in Siberia (since postal workers in St. Petersburg had shut down the city's telegraph).[86] Searching for something positive to report, the SR Salamatov pointed out that the St. Petersburg Soviet of Peasant Deputies had issued a call to the provinces to reject the Bolsheviks, and urged the country to unite around the slogan "All Power to the Constituent Assembly." Salamatov asked the assembly what stance it wished to take. Charushin was one of a long list of speakers who lined up to speak. Basov spoke first, addressing the call by the municipal committee of the Bolshevik Party for all organizations to support the new authorities, "We must proclaim loudly and clearly to the rest of the country . . . that we do not recognize the authority of the Bolsheviks and will not submit to them. . . . We will operate under the rule of law and that only."[87]

When Charushin came to the podium he minced no words about what had happened and who was to blame, "Citizen delegates! That which we fearfully anticipated has indeed happened. In Petrograd, a civil war has been declared. On top of the ongoing collapse at the front and in the rear, we now have more calamity. I believe we share the blame with the old regime for this terrible situation, for we devoted ourselves exclusively to intensifying the revolution, and we intensified it until we arrived at Bolshevism."[88]

As we have seen, Charushin had begun to use the phrase "intensify the revolution"[89] as a cautionary against exacerbating tensions in the country. Now accepting a share of the blame for the deteriorating situation in Russia, for the first and perhaps only time he seemed to suggest that the Bolsheviks were in some way an unholy extension of, rather than deviation from the revolutionary tradition he himself had espoused. Charushin's phrasing closely matched that of a diary entry Bogoslovskii had made in September to the effect that the imminent arrival in power of the Bolsheviks represented "the extreme boundaries of the free Russian revolution, its far left shore, after which movement back in the opposite direction would be inevitable."[90] Charushin, after conceding that the political movement to which he had devoted his life may have contributed to the anarchy and now dictatorship descending on Russia, urged his compatriots to regroup. "I think this is the end point—we can go no further and we will turn back in the opposite direction. I am sure that for the majority their urge for a functioning government (*gosudarstvennost'*) will resurface and bring the country together. After a few days or weeks this crisis will past. After all, not all of Russia is infected with Bolshevism."[91]

In the meantime, objecting to other delegates' suggestions that the zemstvo assembly be temporarily adjourned, he instead urged that it remain in session and for the delegates to stay in the city until the crisis had been resolved, that all democratic forces unite to devise a common response to the situation, that the district assemblies convene, and that appeals to be sent out to the population at large.[92]

MY POSITION ON THE CLAIMANTS TO POWER: A MATTER OF CONSCIENCE

Later, under arrest, Charushin was to say repeatedly that he believed that the October Revolution was illegitimate; he refused to acknowledge any guilt for his actions but also minimized the role he had played in events, "I do not acknowledge the accusations and accept no guilt.... I reject the authority of the soviet people's commissars as a catastrophe [lit. a "plague"]. The Supreme Soviet had no connections with the counterrevolutionary White Guard."[93] In fact, using the zemstvo to mobilize and coordinate resistance to the Bolsheviks in the hope of rebirthing (a healthy) state authority was very much what he had had in mind in his speech to the zemstvo assembly. It is also evident that contrary to later statements, he was at least initially optimistic about the balance of forces in the region and the country as a whole and the potential for restoring some version of the Provisional Government.

The provincial zemstvo assembly had voted to reject Bolshevik claims to legitimacy in the name of the workers and peasant soviets, instead calling for the establishment of their own "soviet" (in Russian the word simply means "council") under the provincial commissar and proclaiming Viatka an independent republic until order could be restored in the country as a whole. The council, which by now had twenty members, including Basov, Treiter (who had been roughed up by the crowd at the railway station earlier that year), Charushin's longtime associate Yumashev, and Charushin himself,[94] was soon reorganized as a Supreme Soviet (see Figure 8.1) claiming legitimate authority over the province, and serving under the provincial commissar and SR Salamatov.[95] A telegram was sent on October 27 to Alexander Kerensky, the head of the now defunct Provisional Government, announcing these developments;[96] similar telegrams were sent to the heads of district dumas and zemstvo *upravas*. On the

FIGURE 8.1.

Supreme Council of Viatka, 1917. Charushin is seated third, Yumashev fourth and Treiter fifth, from left to right; standing, from right to left, Basov is second and Serapikhskii third.
Kirov State Archive.

same day, the Viatka Soviet of Workers' and Soldiers' Deputies resolved that "the seizure of power by the Bolsheviks, in the current conditions of societal and economic disarray, marks the beginning of a fratricidal civil war among the forces of democracy ... all power to the Constituent Assembly."[97] A few days later the executive committee of that organization in a joint session with other public organizations decided, by a vote of 88 to 46, to recognize the authority of the newly formed Supreme Soviet.[98]

Yet the Supreme Soviet soon proved ineffectual in halting the tide of events. Perhaps the word "tide" is inappropriate here, for as in several other provinces in European Russia, the balance of forces in Viatka was not at first weighted in favor of the Bolsheviks. Across the country, after a brief initial period lasting until early August, when the new claimants to power won over several major cities, there was then a month-long pause and regrouping of forces.[99] In Viatka (both the city and province), most factory workers supported the Provisional Government until at least the end of November; nor was the local garrison ready to support the Bolsheviks.[100] It is hard to avoid the conclusion that what followed was an externally imposed regime, rather than a revolution from below.

At the same time, Bakulin is also probably right in arguing that the willingness of the Supreme Soviet to put their hopes in elections to the Constituent Assembly gave the new authorities in Petrograd time to assess the situation, send Red Guard units to the province, and change the balance of power in the region.[101] And some inept handling of dangerous situations, including a notorious "drunken *pogrom*,"[102] when the contents of the local distillery were emptied into the frozen river, by whom it is unclear, did nothing to establish the legitimacy of the Supreme Soviet and forced Salamatov to resign and leave the province (Treiter replaced him). On November 23, a meeting of the regimental committee produced a majority calling for turning over all power in the province to the provincial Soviet of Workers' and Soldiers' Deputies.[103] After intense discussion, the Soviet of Workers' and Soldiers' Deputies resolved to take power, in a vote of 83 to 37.[104] When Bolshevik power was proclaimed in Viatka on December 1, the Supreme Soviet committee cut off the city's electricity, water, and telegraph; organized a strike of public organizations and employees; and sought to disband the 106th regiment.

The sixtieth and final session of the Viatka provincial zemstvo convened on December 16, 1917, with only thirty-one delegates and seven representatives from the municipal duma (which was meeting at roughly the same time) present, amid reports of seizures of estates in Urzhum and elsewhere, the burning down of mills, factory offices being broken into, the closing of the prosperous fur factory in Slobodskoi, and the arrests of municipal delegates in Kotelnich.[105] Even now, Charushin opposed taking radical measures to win the support of the peasantry. A candidate to the Constitutional Assembly, one N. I. Evseev, argued that "the plenitude of power" could be established only if the issues of peace, bread, and land were addressed immediately by issuing executive orders in the name of the upcoming Constitutional Assembly to be delivered by the authorities directly to the villages. Charushin strongly disagreed, noting that until its legitimacy had been fully established (it was to convene in two weeks), there could be no talk of mandates addressing peace, bread, and land.[106]

On December 19, Charushin was nominated to a new Supreme Soviet made up of only three individuals (the others being Basov and Treiter). In his 1926 autobiographical sketch he described his feeling, repeating a claim he had made in 1918 while under arrest by the Bolsheviks, namely that he had "seen the writing on the wall." "I was aware that the position of the new [Supreme] Soviet was untenable and long held out against participating but in the end gave in to the pleading of the delegates. My premonitions were soon fulfilled and the Soviet had virtually no opportunity to function."[107]

Charushin was arrested the next day, December 20, along with twenty-five others connected with the Supreme Soviet, including Treiter, Basov, and Yumashev. Two weeks earlier, on December 2, his beloved *Viatskaia Rech'*, to which he had devoted fully twelve years of his life, had also been permanently shut down.[108] His personal trials and tribulations now began, and his role in the short-lived and quixotic Supreme Soviet was to cost him dearly.

INCARCERATION REDUX: REPEATING THE TRIALS AND TRIBULATIONS OF YOUTH

Writing to a friend on January 11, 1918, and having recently arrived in Viatka from Petrograd, the accomplished librarian and acquaintance of notable liberal figures Elena Gogel', exclaimed, "I like it here. The town is very pleasing to the eye, like a big village set upon hills; every street seems to wander off into a field or forest; the vistas are beautiful. The days have been sunlit, the snow a dazzling white, the evenings are moonlit, it is all so magical."[109]

Charushin and Gogel' would cross paths again and their lives would become intertwined, but his observations at the moment could hardly have corresponded with hers, for he was then incarcerated. To be sure, fleeing the turmoil in the Petrograd, Gogel' wore no blinders, for she had ended her lyrical letter on a different note, "[A]nd it's so upsetting, to see resort to the axe [i.e., violence] and turmoil all around."[110] Gogel' also commented on the suppression of *Viatskaia Rech'*, which had occurred shortly before her arrival, and in blistering language she described the newspaper the Bolsheviks established to replace it, "We are now cut off from the world, since the last issue of the newspaper was January 5 and the local press has been wiped out ... instead we have the local [Bolshevik] *Pravda*, and like all the other *Pravdas* that have been established, it is illiterate, hypocritical, and what is worst, stupid, a parody of a newspaper."[111]

The "axe" was now hovering over Charushin's head: over the course of the next year and a half, Charushin was arrested four times, brought up before a revolutionary tribunal thrice, and, finally, held hostage in imminent danger of facing a firing squad before he was ultimately released. At his first appearance before the Revolutionary Tribunal (January 20, 1918), he and others were charged with organizing resistance to the new authorities and trying to forcibly disband the 106th regiment billeted in the city.[112] However, all except one[113] were exonerated and released in light of "their irreproachable political past, their service to the people, the shackles they had worn and persecution endured under the tsarist regime."[114] Dissatisfied with the verdict, the bulletin carrying this story was even more irked that when it was announced spectators in the hall had loudly applauded, "whereas the Revolutionary Tribunal itself received no such acknowledgement."

Displeased with the outcome, the Viatka city soviet met the following day and, under pressure from a leading Bolshevik, M. M. Popov,[115] replaced the members of the Revolutionary Tribunal with new faces, rearrested Charushin, Yumashev, and others, and convened another trial on March 2.[116] In his testimony, Charushin made the assertion, repeated later in his memoirs, that we have cast doubt on, "While agreeing to serve on the Supreme Soviet I couldn't imagine how it could actually function and knew its situation was hopeless, but signed on only at the urging of the assembly.[117] As for his present position being under arrest he testified, "All authority in the country should rest in the hands of the Constituent Assembly elected by popular vote.... I see Soviet power as something temporary to be replaced by a government established by that Assembly. I repeat what I said after my arrest on December 20, namely, that power in the province should reside with the provincial zemstvo assembly. My stance toward Soviet power is thereby critical, but I submit to it."[118]

This time all of the accused were convicted and deprived of their political rights for a year.[119] Once more released on the condition he disengage from politics, and with his health shattered, he retreated to a site in the countryside near his native Orlov district. But on October 22, 1918, he was arrested for the third time, procedures against him began on October 29, and hearings were held from November 14 to 16. On November 14, he wrote a long letter to the provincial-level secret police (*Cheka*). In it, he laid out in detail his role in events and his subsequent treatment by the authorities.[120] He expressed his frustration and professed bewilderment at being been prosecuted again, "Since then I have completely withdrawn from politics, something my poor health also called for. . . . For the first time in a long and fraught life, buffeted about by fate, I finally had time to rest, but that was rudely interrupted. . . . Why I am here and how long my incarceration will last I have no idea . . . and if, given the political situation in Viatka at the time, it is understandable why I was first arrested, this last arrest is totally incomprehensible."

Then, as he had done on several occasions in 1917 when challenged, he brought up his credentials as a lifelong revolutionary:

> I am already elderly, sixty-seven years old [*sic*: he was still sixty six], and have given up politics; my health is shattered, which should not come as a surprise given what the revolutionary tribunal itself called my "irreproachable past," purchased by means of four years of preliminary detention in the Peter-Paul Fortress, eight years of hard labor and a long period of forced colonization in distant Siberia, as well as the relentless persecution and deprivation of rights in recent times, ending only with the February Revolution. What crimes have I now committed which justify my present treatment?[121]

His brother Ivan had rushed to his aid, sending a letter to the Viatka Cheka on November 8, pleading for Nikolai's release. Ivan described his older brother as returning from a lengthy exile a gray-haired elder who had nevertheless spent the following years working for the betterment of the people. Ivan wrote that the best testimony to his brother's revolutionary credentials could be found in the gendarmes' and governors' reports to the Ministry of Interior. He described Nikolai's health as broken by his exile and endless tribulations.[122] As it turned out, on December 14, the provincial Cheka again decided that in light of the "absence of the body of a crime" and once again in view of his "irreproachable past" to release Charushin from confinement.

Yet in April 1919, he was arrested along with two veteran SRs: Sergei Krest'ianinov and a certain Zhuikov. It turned out that earlier, when Charushin had languished under arrest and concerned about possibly incriminating evidence lying about, Krest'ianinov had taken Charushin's papers from his apartment and entrusted them to Zhuikov's safekeeping. Zhuikov, who had been on the NS Party's list of candidates to the Constituent Assembly) had unfortunately parted on less than amicable terms with his lady friend, with whom he shared an apartment. She had turned these papers over to the authorities, hoping, one presumes, to make life less pleasurable for her former partner.

Once again, Charushin's case was examined, but the legal department of the provincial secret police decided that these papers contained nothing describing counterrevolutionary actions in the recent past (later, Stalinist prosecutors wouldn't make such fine distinctions). The charges were essentially dismissed, but the Cheka decided nevertheless to retain all three as hostages, given their "their popularity and status as long-standing and committed members of the Socialist Revolutionary Party [sic]."[123] If a year earlier his revolutionary credentials had been a ticket out of jail, now they made him an invaluable commodity on the hostage "market" of the bloody civil war.

On April 12, 1919, he was finally released for the last time. According to his own later account, his release came through the personal intervention of the legendary Marshall Bliukher, then commander of the Urals front for the Red Army organizing resistance to the approaching White armies.[124]

THE REVOLUTION FOLLOWED ITS OWN SCENARIO

Throughout this fraught period Charushin steadfastly continued to take pride in his status as an "old revolutionary." Yet by now he was also rethinking the role of the revolutionary movement in Russia's political culture. We recall his admonition to the delegates of the Third Viatka Provincial Congress on September 19, of 1917: "due to our own mistakes and internal quarrels the country was heading toward an abyss."[125] In other words, the inability of the left intelligentsia to resolve its issues had contributed to the disarray and turmoil. Then in his statement to the zemstvo assembly on

October 27, 1917, on hearing news of the Bolshevik coup in St. Petersburg, "I believe we share the blame with the old regime for this terrible situation, for we devoted ourselves exclusively to intensifying the revolution, and we intensified it until we arrived at Bolshevism." By this, he surely had in mind the activities of the left wing of the SR Party since the 1905 Revolution; by "we" he must also have meant the notion of "no enemies to the left," so widespread throughout Europe and Russia in the nineteenth and early twentieth centuries. Charushin's use of the term "intensify" by way of self-criticism both reflected the debate (following the 1905 Revolution) about the harmful impact of the revolutionary inclinations of the Russian intelligentsia and foreshadowed the heated arguments among the émigré community in the decades after 1917.

To be sure, in the crush of events it was not an easy task to orient oneself or to act with any reasonable hope of predictable outcomes. Looking back in 1923, Vera Figner wrote of reading the Menshevik Nikolai Sukhanov's classic chronicle of the revolution, after which "I came to the uncomfortable realization just how little I had understood about the course of the revolution at the time, just how myopic, unreflective and politically unprepared I was."[126] Still, it can fairly be argued that Charushin's unstinting support for continuation of the war effort, even on these terms, was short-sighted and untenable by the summer of 1917 if not before—even if the other options were equally unfeasible. Moreover, the argument of the NS Party that "influencing public opinion" while awaiting the convening of the Constituent Assembly could be effective was commendable but led to political passivity in the face of growing challenges to pursuing democratic path, from both right and left. Simply put, by November that was a fatal strategy, if one at all.

The reluctance of Charushin and his friends to address the question of force left them virtually powerless in confronting the Bolsheviks. We recall that by the early summer *Viatskaia Rech'* was warning of impending anarchy and civil war and apprehensive of the dangers of mounting polarization. Polarization was what Lenin welcomed; in his view, it created stark black and white choices for the country favoring the Bolsheviks, who offered, as William Rosenberg has pointed out, "a capacity for organization, an ideological clarity, and a social positioning that facilitated affiliation with the radical relocation of power and authority."[127]

But were Charushin and his kind really so wrong-minded in their hesitancy and reluctance to violate their ethical principles in domestic politics? A case can be made that for Russia as a whole the outcome of the revolution was not foreordained. Even Rosenberg, while listing the strengths of the Bolsheviks, cautions against such a perspective.[128] If in the minority, other reputable historians today still believe that had a government been formed "which was able to proceed with land reform and democratization," and other choices made at critical moments, events might just have turned out otherwise. Unless we consider the consequences of the October Revolution (civil war, famine, and later, the mass exterminations and incalculable hardships imposed upon the Soviet people by its leadership) to have been inevitable we might consider in another light the perspicacity of the views of Populists and other activists like Charushin.

Was it wholly unrealistic for Charushin to place his hopes upon the Constituent Assembly? He viewed matters from the perspective of Viatka and could hope only to help shape events in that enormous province. By the autumn of 1917 the situation was certainly unsettled but it was not unreasonable to hope that the gathering scheduled for January 5 could produce a mandate legitimizing the agenda most parties on the left supported, and halt the drift toward anarchy and civil war. In Viatka, as in several other provinces, the Bolsheviks did not command the support they had in Petrograd and came to power only with the help of armed forces sent from the center.[129] Instead, an informal coalition of moderate socialists held sway. As Timkin has argued, had events in the country as a whole moved in a different direction, or had Viatka been left on its own to sort out its affairs, no such outcome would have been likely.[130] Both Timkin and Bakulin describe considerable resistance to Bolshevik rule in Viatka's rural districts lasting well into 1918.

As one historian recently put it, "[T]hat the revolution took a different turn was the misfortune, not the fault of the NS party."[131] Misfortune was indeed the bitter pill Charushin had to swallow; to be arrested by revolutionaries, many of whom had themselves suffered from arrest and exile under the tsarist regime and who had seemed to be comrades at arms, even if from an early date he had been repulsed by the doctrinarism and unethical tactics of the Bolsheviks. In a letter to his interrogators, dated November 14, 1918, he wrote, "At the same time that the Soviet authorities are acknowledging the debt they owe to those who gave their lives in the cause of freedom, offering up every manner of commemoration to my comrades in the revolutionary struggle, even planning to build monuments to [Sofia] Perovskaia, [Andrei] Zheliabov and others—at the same time, I repeat, those with an 'irreproachable political past' who remain among the living and merit the same treatment, can in fact find no place in the Soviet socialist republic except the prison!"[132]

No less crushing was the seeming popular indifference to or even collusion in the round-up, arrest and incarceration of him and his closest colleagues. He vented his bitterness to the Cheka, "I'm not afraid of prison, for I have spent the better years of my life there. Neither am I afraid of a violent death if it were for a good cause. But I am oppressed by the thought of the utter ingratitude of that very "emancipated people" in whom I believed, for whom I without regret or hesitation relinquished my freedom and devoted my entire life, and who are paying back those who were their unfailing friends by putting them prison."[133]

Disillusionment with a revolutionary movement to which one has devoted one's lifetime; rejection by the very people whose lives one sought to better, how does one recover from such misfortunes? In the aftermath of October, bowing to a situation outside of his control, Charushin refused to acknowledge the legitimacy of the Bolshevik regime, but he also chose not to leave the country. Others did leave, including Nikolai Chaikovskii, who resided in Paris until his death in 1926. Still others, such as the leader of the NS Party, Peshekhonov, were forced out of the country—and spent the rest of their lives seeking to return. Like Charushin, the librarian Gogel' wrote in 1925, when asked why she remained in Russia, "I simply can't imagine making a clean break with my native land."[134] It remained for Charushin to come to terms with this new reality and find a way to live out the rest of his life in accordance with the goals he had set long before, only now stripped of the teleology of transformation he had envisioned. Now sixty-eight years old, like many other veteran revolutionaries he also had to find a way to provide for himself as well as to defend the legacy of his lifetime endeavors.

NOTES

1. Iu. N. Timkin, *Smutnoe vremia na Viatke: Obshchestvenno-politicheskoe razvitie Viatskoi gubernii vesnoi 1917-osen'iu 1918 gg.* (Kirov, 1998), 6. For a slightly different account, see Aaron

B. Retish, *Russia's Peasants in Revolution and Civil War: Citizenship, Identity, and the Creation of the Soviet State, 1914–1922* (Cambridge: Cambridge University Press, 2008), 68.

2. Timkin, *Smutnoe vremia na Viatke*, 7.

3. V. I. Startsev, *Vnutrenniaia politika vremennogo pravitel'stva* (Leningrad: Nauka, 1980), 193–198, 204–205. A detailed description of events in Kursk can be found at: GARF, f. 5881, op. 1, d. 115, ll. 1–6. Автограф. http://www.alexanderyakovlev.org/almanah/inside/almanah-doc/71775 (accessed October 12, 2014).

4. A rare firsthand account of the activities of the Committee of Public Safety, later serving as the Provincial Executive Board under the Provincial Government Commissar for Viatka province, by its chair V. V. Ammosov, read to the assembly on October 31,1917, can be found in GAKO, f. 616, op. 1, d. 26, ll. 102–105.

5. V. I. Bakulin, *Drama v dvukh aktakh: Viatskaia guberniia v 1917–1918 gg* (Kirov: Viatskii gosudarstvennyi gumanitarnyi universitet, 2008), 12.

6. For a narrative of events in the early days after the February Revolution, see the chronicle in *Viatskaia rech'*, March 8, 1917, 3; March 9, 1917, 3; March 21, 1917, 3; March 24, 1917, 3.

7. Bakulin, *Drama v dvukh aktakh*, 21–22.

8. Retish, *Russia's Peasants*, 101–105.

9. M. M. Bogoslovskii, *Dnevniki (1913–1919)*: Iz sobraniia GIM (Moskva: Vremia, 2011), 343.

10. See the items in *Viatskaia Rech'* for March 1, 1917, 1; March 14, 1917, 3; March 15, 1917, 2.

11. *Viatskaia Rech'*, March 23, 1917, 2.

12. *Deiateli SSSR and revoliutsionnogo dvizheniia v Rossii.* Entsiklopedicheskii slovar' Granat (Moscow: Sovetskaia Entsiklopediia, 1989), 295.

13. *Viatskaia rech'*, March 5, 1917, 1–2; March 7, 1917, 3.

14. *Viatskaia rech'*, April 16, 1917, 3.

15. G. F. Chudova, "Nikolai Apollonich Charushin (1861–1937)," *Gertsenka: Viatskie Zapiski* 24 (2013): 88.

16. *Viatskaia Rech'*, March 23, 1917, 3; March 24, 1917, 3.

17. O. N. Znamenskii, *Intelligentsiia nakanune velikogo Oktiabria* (Leningrad: Nauka, 1988), 32–42, 51–58, 73.

18. *Viatskaia rech'*, September 22, 1917, 3.

19. Figner to Natalia Kupriianova, March 14, 1917 (RGALI, f. 1185, op. 1, d. 231, l. 89).

20. *Deiateli SSSR i revoliutsionnogo dvizheniia v Rossii*, 243–255.

21. For more detail on the activities and platform of the People's Socialist Party, both after 1906 and during the 1917 Revolution, from which most of this information is drawn, see the excellent essay by G. Anonpieva and N. Erofeev, in *Politicheskie partii Rossii, konets XIX-pervaia tret' XX veka: entsiklopediia*, ed. V. V. Shelokhaev (Moskva: ROSSPEN, 1996), 619–626. See also *Modeli obshchestvennogo pereustroistva Rossii. XX vek*, ed. V. V. Shelokhaev (Moskva: ROSSPEN, 2004), 438–461; O. L. Protasova, *A.V. Peshekhonov: chelovek i epokha* (Moskva: ROSSPEN, 2004), 46–52.

22. On the views of its chief theoretician, A. V. Peshekhonov, on terror, and violence in general in politics, see O. L. Protasova, *A.V. Peshekhonov*, 24, 40.

23. *Viatskaia rech'*, March 8, 1917, 2.

24. Charushin, *O dalekom proshlom* (1973), 120.

25. See M. Favorov, "Oktiabr' v Viatke," *Oktiabr' i grazhdanskaia voina v Viatskoi gubernii*. Ed. by A. Novoselov (Kirov, 1927), 1–19.

26. *Viatskaia rech'*, May 7, 1917, 2. The executive committee unanimously selected Salamatov and, as a second choice, A. A. Gur'ev (former chief of zemstvo statistical bureau and editor of *Viatskaia Zhizn'* in 1906. V.A. Treiter was selected a member of the provincial executive committee at this time as well. For a listing of the activities of the Executive Committee in Viatka, see *Viatskaia Rech'*, July 28, 1917, 3

27. Timkin, *Smutnoe vremia na Viatke*, 14–15.

28. *Modeli obshchestvennogo pereustroistva Rossii*, 457.

29. In his volume on the peasantry in the Volga region during the revolution and civil war, Orlando Figes omits any mention of the Peasant Union and offers a very different perspective than the one presented here: *Peasant Russia, Civil War. The Volga Countryside in Revolution (1917–1921)* (London: Phoenix, 1989), 30–69.

30. On the activities of the peasant union see *Viatskaia Rech'*, March 19, 1917, 3; June 6, 1917, 3; June 17, 1917, 2–3 and 3–4; June 13, 1917, 2–3; June 15, 1917, 3; August 13, 1917, 3; August 15, 1917, 3–4; August 17, 1917, 3–4; September 6, 1917, 3; September 22, 1917, 3; September 23, 1917, 3–4; September 24, 1917, 2; September 26, 1917, 3–4; October 1, 1917, 3.

31. On the First Viatka Provincial Peasant Congress, see *Viatskaia Rech'* from June 6 to June 17, 1917, 2–3 and 3–4, in the chronicle section of the newspaper.

32. According to his retrospective account in *Viatskaia Rech'*, September 20, 1917, 4.

33. *Viatskaia rech'*, June 13, 1917, 2–3; and June 15, 1917, 3.

34. GAKO, f. 616, op. 1, d. 266, ll. 45–54; *Viatskaia Rech'*, October 1, 1917, 4.

35. For the August congress, see *Viatskaia rech'*, August 13, 1917, 3; August 15, 1917, 3–4; and August 17, 1917, 3–4.

36. In the opinion of Sarah Badcock, dissent within the party was so widespread it was the norm rather than the exception. Sarah Badcock, *Politics and the People in Revolutionary Russia: A Provincial History*, New Studies in European History (Cambridge: Cambridge University Press, 2007), 67–68.

37. On the Third Peasant Congress, see *Viatskaia Rech'*, September 23, 1917, 3.

38. *Viatskaia Rech'*, September 20, 1917, 3, for Charushin's announcement of his resignation.

39. Ibid., 4.

40. Ibid.

41. *Viatskaia rech'*, September 22, 1917, 3–4.

42. Charushin could have added, as another delegate did, that the Congress itself, and the Soviet of Peasant Deputies, was kept afloat only by large subsidies from the zemstvo and local subsidies, was unable to pay its dues to the national organization, and had received only paltry financial support from local branches, many of which were still functioning as units of the Peasant Union. *Viatskaia Rech'*, September 22, 1917, 4.

43. *Viatskaia rech'*, October 1, 1917, 3.

44. Ibid. "Essentially, we are being urged to continue to 'intensify' the revolution, but now it is time to build, to construct."

45. In John L. Keep's opinion, the State Conference was convened as a substitute for the promised Constituent Assembly originally scheduled for that time. See *The Russian Revolution: A Study in Mass Mobilization, Revolutions in Modern World* (London: Weidenfeld & Nicolson, 1976), 247.

46. Orlando Figes and B. I. Kolonitskiĭ, *Interpreting the Russian Revolution: The Language and Symbols of 1917* (New Haven, CT: Yale University Press, 1999), 141–144.

47. *Viatskaia rech'*, October 12, 1917, 2. The article treats the peasantry with great sympathy, but much like Anton Chekhov's famous short story "Peasants," it depicts squalid conditions

of life, from which no informed participation in political life could emerge. Chekhov, like the author of this article, was a doctor.

48. Kotsonis, Yanni, *Making Peasants Backward: Agricultural Cooperatives and the Agrarian Question in Russia, 1861–1914* (New York: St. Martin's Press), 1999.

49. Retish, *Russia's Peasants in Revolution and Civil War: Citizenship, Identity, and the Creation of the Soviet State, 1914–1922*, 6, 9, 99, 112–113, 128–129.

50. Ben Eklof, *Russian Peasant Schools: Officialdom, Village Culture, and Popular Pedagogy, 1864–1914* (Berkeley: University of California Press, 1986).

51. Retish, *Russia's Peasants*, 89, 92, 126–127.

52. Rex A. Wade, *The Russian Revolution, 1917*, 2nd ed., New Approaches to European History (Cambridge: Cambridge University Press, 2005), 144–145.

53. Peter Waldron, *Governing Tsarist Russia*, European History in Perspective (New York: Palgrave Macmillan, 2007), 110.

54. Scott J. Seregny, "Zemstvos, Peasants, and Citizenship: The Russian Adult Education Movement and World War I," *Slavic Review* 59, no. 2. (2000): 290–315; and "A Wager on the Peasantry: Anti-Zemstvo Riots, Adult Education and the Russian Village during World War One: Stavropol' Province," *Slavonic and East European Review* 79, no. 1. (2001): 90–126; I. V. Gerasimov, "On the Limitations of a Analysis of 'Experts and Peasants' (an Attempt at the Internationalization of a Discussion in *Kritika*)," *Jarhrbucher fur Geschichte Osteuropas*, Neue Folge 52, no. 2 (2004): 261–273.

55. For a similar appraisal see Jane Burbank, *Intelligentsia and Revolution: Views of Bolshevism, 1917–1922* (New York: Oxford University Press, 1989).

56. Articles in *Viatskaia Rech'* at the time reflected Charushin's conviction that the transformation of the countryside should be gradual and his fear of anarchy and the appeal of demagogues.

57. See, for example, the article in *Viatskaia rech'*, August 25, 1917, 2–3, on the spread of peasant resistance to the grain monopoly; *Viatskaia rech'*, September 20, 1917; September 2, 1917, 4; August 29, 1917. A complete list of such items can be found in the unpublished index of *Viatskaia rech'* held at the Herzen State Library: Gali Chudova, Ukazatel' soderzhaniia gazety "*Viatskaia rech'*" 1908–1917, 10 vols. (Kirov: typescript, 1975), vol. 9, items 1029–1068, 1083–1094.

58. Bogoslovskii, *Dnevniki (1913–1919)*, 359.

59. *Viatskaia rech'*, May 19, 1917, 3; May 3, 1917, 3; May 5, 1917, 3.

60. Treiter's services were regularly advertised in *Viatskaia Rech'* (quite possibly an indirect subsidy of the newspaper), was the provincial health inspector, a member of the provincial executive committee (formerly Committee of Public Safety) in the Provincial Government, and later, along with Charushin, of the ill-fated Supreme Soviet, as well as Provincial Commissar.

61. *Viatskaia rech'*, July 1, 1917, 3. See also July 4, 1917, 3–4.

62. Ibid., April 25, 1917, 2.

63. Ibid., June 25, 1917, 3.

64. Ibid., September 12, 1917, 3.

65. Figner to Kupriianova, September 21, 1917 (RGALI, f. 1185, op. 1, d. 231, l. 115).

66. *Viatskaia rech'*, August 25, 1917, 2–3.

67. Timkin, *Smutnoe vremia na Viatke*, 18–20.

68. Figner to Kupriianova, September 21, 1917 (RGALI, f. 1185, op. 1, d. 231, l. 115 ob).

69. Ibid., ll. 115–116 ob.

70. Retish, *Russia's Peasants*, 9, 32, 66–67, 84, 93–94, 99, 104, 8–19, 27–29.
71. Bakulin, *Drama v dvukh aktakh*, 8, 13, 24.
72. Timkin, "Demokraticheskaia vlast' i viatskoe obshchestvo v 1917 g.," *Vlast' i obshchestvo: istoriia i sovremennost'* (Kirov, 1998), 75–76.
73. Badcock, *Politics and the People in Revolutionary Russia*, 123–144.
74. Ibid., 121, 62, 93–94.
75. *Deiateli SSSR i revoliutsionnogo dvizheniia v Rossii*, 295.
76. "Save our Homeland: The Old and New Zemstvo," *Viatskaia Rech'*, October 24, 1917, 1–3. The 59th zemstvo session convened under new rules set by decree of the Provisional Government on May 21 and had to institute new procedures and functions in a very complex and unstable environment (GAKO, f. 616, op. 1, d. 268, ll. 3–17).
77. In the archival record of the 59th session, Charushin is listed as a "member" (ex officio) rather than as a delegate; however, in the record of the extraordinary 60th December session, he is registered as a "delegate" from Orlov (GAKO f. 616, op. 1, d. 274, l. 9). The difference may reflect changing status or simply the fluid situation in the zemstvo caused by the new law passed in the summer, together with the mounting chaos.
78. GAKO, f. 616, op. 1, d. 268, l. 39 ob.
79. P. S. Basov, member of the NS Party, was a teacher of peasant origins, arrested in 1905 but then allowed to return to his position. Between 1911 and 1915 he was in charge of the education bureau of the Urzhum district zemstvo, then secretary of the provincial zemstvo executive board. He was first elected a delegate to the zemstvo assembly in 1917, was chair of the Viatka district executive committee of public safety, then district commissar and a member of the organizing committee of the Viatka Peasant Union. Bakulin, *Drama v dvukh aktakh*, 205; *Viatskaia rech'*, October 20, 1917, 2–3; GAKO, f. 616, op. 1, d. 266, ll. 54–54 ob.
80. A. A. Zonov was an agronomist of peasant origin serving in the Slobodskoi district zemstvo, active in the cooperative, and in 1917 served as chair of the local land committee (*Viatskaia rech'*, October 20, 1917, 3).
81. GAKO, f. 616, op. 1, d. 267, ll. 54–54 ob.
82. Ibid., ll. 7, 98–102, 106–108.
83. Funding this newspaper (*Krest'ianskaia Gazeta*) was an issue entwined with party politics; a review of its practices seemed to indicate that despite protestations, it was indeed an SR Party mouthpiece. Nevertheless, after a heated discussion, money was allocated by the zemstvo to keep the newspaper alive (GAKO, f. 616, op.1, d. 267, ll. 45–53, 70–71).
84. Ibid., ll. 113–139.
85. Ibid., l. 60; *Viatskaia rech'*, October 29, 1917, 2.
86. GAKO, f. 616, op. 1, d. 267, ll. 54–57.
87. GAKO, f. P. 1322, op. 1, d. 49, ll. 38–39 ob., 41. *Viatskaia Rech'*, October 27, 1917, 3–4.
88. GAKO f. 616, op. 1, d. 267, l. 66.
89. *Viatskaia rech'*, October 1, 1917, 3.
90. Bogoslovskii, *Dnevniki*, 419.
91. GAKO, f. 616, op. 1, d. 267, l. 69; *Viatskaia Rech'*, October 29, 1917, 2.
92. GAKO, f. 616, op. 1, d. 266, l. 69.
93. GAKO, f. 1322, op. 1, d. 49; GASPIKO, f. R-6799, op. 4, d. 4577, l. 22.
94. The point at which Charushin joined what was to be known as the Supreme Soviet remains murky. Charushin seems deliberately vague on this score; Gali Chudova's account is not clear; not do the archival records help in establishing the date.
95. Valentin Sergeev, *Nikolai Apollonovich Charushin* (Kirov, n/p, 2004), 195.

96. *Viatskaia rech'*, October 29, 1917, 3.
97. Ibid., October 28, 1917, 3.
98. Ibid., November 4, 1917, 3; November 5, 1917, 1.
99. Wade, *Russian Revolution*, 205–207.
100. Bakulin, *Drama v dvukh aktakh*, 24–25.
101. Ibid., 96–97.
102. Ibid., 103–104; Timkin, *Smutnoe vremia na Viatke*, 26–27.
103. *Viatskaia rech'*, November 21, 1917, 3; November 26, 1917, 4.
104. Timkin, *Smutnoe Vremia na Viatke*, 32.
105. GAKO, f. 616, op. 1, d. 268, l. 41.
106. Ibid., l. 47.
107. *Deiateli SSSR i revoliutsionnogo dvizheniia v Rossii*, 273.
108. A month earlier, struggling to keep the newspaper alive, Charushin had appealed in the name of the *Viatskaia Rech'* to the Supreme Soviet to release and procure 1000 pud of paper for its use. See GAKO, f. 1345, op. 1, d. 9, l. 284; *Viatskaia Rech'*, October 29, 1917, 2.
109. Gogel' to Koni, January 11, 1918, *Gertsenka* 12 (2007): 14–15.
110. Ibid., 15.
111. Ibid., 14.
112. This regiment had strongly supported the Provisional Government and was initially resistant to Bolshevik overtures after the October coup, but now it was gravitating to the other side. In his testimony Charushin denied that the Supreme Soviet had tried to disband, instead "releasing" the unit, once it had swung in favor of the Bolsheviks.
113. The one not exonerated was Treiter, who was deprived of his political rights, but for only one month.
114. This was the rendition provided by the *Izvestiia Viatskogo gubernskogo Ispolnitel'nyi Komiteta*, cited in K. A. Palkin, *K istorii stroitel'stva sovetskoi sudebnoi systemy v Viatskoi gubernii god 1917–1918* (Kirov, 1966), 28–32 (typescript manuscript held at the Herzen State Library).
115. Timkin, *Smutnoe vremia na Viatke*, 50. This same Popov was to briefly become the director of the Herzen Library in the 1930s, shortly after Charushin resigned his position there in the heat of the Cultural Revolution. On Popov, see *Getsenka* 17 (2010): 4–5.
116. GAKO, f. 1322, op. 1, d. 49. The historian K. A. Palkin notes that even elementary rules of procedure were ignored, for nobody on the revamped tribunal had legal training of any sort. Many of the accused were absent, and the court could not even enter their first names or patronymics. In 1918, the Revolutionary Tribunal underwent several restructurings, and when Charushin faced it again in 1919, it was far more organized and militant. See also M. Favorov, "Oktiabr' v Viatke," 19.
117. GAKO, f. 1322, op. 1, d. 49, l. 55.
118. Ibid.
119. The testimony of the accused can be found at GASPIKO f. 6799, op. 4, d. 4577, l. 70–77).
120. The entire file on Charushin, originally held in the FSB archive, but then turned over to the State Archives of the Social and Political History of Kirov Oblast (GASPIKO) can be found in f. 6799, op. 4, d. 4649 (Ugolovnye-sledstvennye materialy na lits, podvergshikhsia politicheskim repressiam i reabilitirovannykh v ustanovlennom zakonom poriadke, Upravleniia Federal'noi sluzhby besopasnosti Rossiiskoi Federatsii po Kirovskoi oblasti. Ugolovno-sledstvennoe delo Charushin Nikolai Appolonovich, 1851 g.r. Vol. 1 (April 12, 1919 to September 19, 1930), 166 pages.)

121. GASPIKO, f. 6799, op. 4, d. 4577, ll. 8–19, 22–22 ob. For the complete file on the process, ibid., ll. 1–77.
122. Ibid., ll. 18–19.
123. Sergeev, *Nikolai Apollonovich Charushin*, 109–112.
124. *Deiateli SSSR i revoliutsionnogo dvizheniia v Rossii*, 295.
125. *Viatskaia rech'*, September 20, 1917, 4.
126. RGALI, f. 1185, op. 1, d. 231, l. 141.
127. Edward Acton, V. I. Cherniaev, and William G Rosenberg, *Critical Companion to the Russian Revolution 1914–1921* (Bloomington: Indiana University Press, 1997), 29–30.
128. See Donald J. Raleigh, "Echoes of the International across the Historiographies," in *Russia's Home Front in War and Revolution, 1914–1922. Book 1: Russia's Revolution in Regional Perspective*, ed. Sarah Badcock, Liudmila G. Novikova and Aaron B. Retish (Bloomington, IN: Slavic Publishers, 2015), 387.
129. Bolshevik support in the capital, on the other hand, has been convincingly argued in the work of Alexander Rabinowich, *The Bolsheviks Come to Power: The Revolution of 1917 in Petrograd* (New York: W. W. Norton, 1976).
130. Timkin, *Smutnoe vremia na Viatke*, 4, 29, 39, 45, 81–83.
131. *Modeli obshchestvennogo pereustroistva Rossii*, 459.
132. GASPIKO, f. 6799, op. 4, d. 4577, ll. 22–23 ob.
133. Ibid.
134. Gogel' to Koni, dated "Easter eve," 1925, *Gertsenka* 12 (2007): 20.

Remembrances of a Distant Past

We are bound together by a shared, irretrievable past.

—Egor Lazarev to Fanni Stepniak-Kravchinskaia

We must find a way to cope with this spiritual agony and despair.

—Elena Gogel' to Anatolii Koni

"THE THINNING RANKS OF THE LIVING AMONG US"

The period following the revolution and civil war in Russia was marked by what historians have labeled an "explosion" of memoir writing, motivated by both the policies of the new Soviet regime in the realm of history and the establishment of the Society of Former Political Prisoners and Exiles (OPK) in 1921.[1] Many of the memoirs of the surviving members of the revolutionary movement were published by the OPK, whether in separate volumes or as articles in its house journal, *Katorga i Ssylka* (*Hard Labor and Exile*).[2] The memoirs of Vera Figner and Charushin were prominent among these. In 1926, the first volume of Charushin's memoirs, *Remembrances of a Distant Past* was published (covering his childhood, participation in the Chaikovskii circle, incarceration, and Trial of the 193). A sequel covering the time he spent at the Kara gold mines was published in 1929, and in 1931 a final part concerning his time as a penal colonist was issued.

Yet another signature moment in the publication of Populist memoirs was the monumental but never completed "bio-bibliographical dictionary" titled, *Figures in the Revolutionary Movement in Russia: From the Predecessors of the Decembrists to the Fall of the Autocracy*. In the two decades following 1917, those who had participated in the revolutionary movement—including the 1870s generation—and present at the events and places marking the struggle against autocracy, gradually emerge as symbolic sites of memory (*lieux de memoire*). The notion of a "seventies generation" as a stage in the revolutionary narrative becomes a fixture in the popular imagination. In the preface to the bio-bibliographical dictionary, the editors wrote, "That which existed in embryonic form in the 'sixties' and was contemplated in the abstract, was actually embodied in practice in the following generation."[3]

By that time, however, Charushin and his friends felt little connection between their life's endeavors and the new political order. The writing of the memoirs was more an integral part of efforts by Charushin and his peers to reconnect with their "distant pasts" (a phrase appearing in the titles of several such works) and to defend their collective life stories from erasure in the increasingly hostile environment of Soviet Russia in the decade following the revolution and civil war. On the individual level, this and other activities by the aging Populists sought to address their deepening feelings of despair, isolation, and pointlessness in the new society and to help them cope with feelings of loss.

Several important figures in this story passed away in this decade; as Charushin wrote to a long-time acquaintance Maria Shebalina, "The grim reaper is busy culling the already thin ranks of surviving veterans."[4] Yumashev had died in 1920, earning but a paragraph-long obituary in the local newspaper, *Viatskaia Pravda*. Charushin's brother Arkadii had died in 1922. Vera Figner also wrote of her losses: her brother Nikolai had died in December 1918 (another brother, Petr, had passed away in April 1916); her sister Olga died in September 1919; her niece Vera, in March 1920.) To be sure, during this stretch Charushin was not entirely alone, nor were his colleagues in the library his only contacts. He continued to be close to his son Vladimir (who at some point took up employment with Gosplan) and with his brother Ivan and his family. Since at least 1918 he had been living with Olga Koshkareva, who, judging by his correspondence, provided domestic warmth and comfort in these years (they registered their marriage in 1931).[5] He received letters from Larisa Chemodanova and Anna Iakimova expressing relief that rumors of his execution were untrue and filling him in about their own lives, how they were adapting to the new realities.[6] Chemodanova wrote from Siberia, "We simply refuse to belief such a rumor: you, shot? You, the old revolutionary who did so much to promote the cause—it cannot be!"[7] Chemodanova also shared news of her own tribulations during and after the civil war, including the loss of several children.

Nor was Figner all alone: she still had her sister Evgeniia (Sazhina) and her cousins Natalia and Lidia Kuprianova, all of whom looked after her, as did her Populist friends and fellow veterans of Shlisselburg prison. The ravages of age and the disappointments of the past years led not to isolation but to a closing of ranks, an enhanced appreciation of those left standing, a common search to find a meaningful place in the new society, and a determination to defend their legacy.

"I WITHDREW COMPLETELY FROM THE ARENA OF POLITICS": THE LIBRARY AS REFUGE AND OUTLET

In the autobiographical sketch Charushin wrote in 1926 for the volume *Figures of the Revolutionary Movement* he described in an extremely parsed sentence—restraint being his wont when matters were delicate or painful—his turn away from politics, "After 1918 because of advanced aged and the damage inflicted upon my health by a lifetime of stressful experiences, I completely withdrew from the political arena." He added, "Forsaking politics I nevertheless remained committed to cultural affairs, and in recent years have devoted as much energy as I have to that sphere."[8] Indeed, Charushin spent the next decade busily at work. Initially, he reconnected with the burgeoning cooperative movement, a natural step for many of his peers, and one fitting the ideological framework of the Populist movement, especially of the NS Party, now of course dissolved in the single-party state. At some point in 1919 he rejoined the activities of the Viatka

Economic Consumer Society, and "for some time" served on its governing board. In the autumn of that year he was also elected to the presidium of the Soviet of Cooperative Congresses and soon was elected its chairman, serving until that organization was liquidated in the spring of 1920.

While employed by the cooperative movement, Charushin was delegated to serve on the governing board of the (newly renamed) Herzen Public Library—at that time, the cooperative shared space with the library. Toward the end of 1921 he became a full-time employee of the library, serving first as the social sciences librarian, and then in 1923 as director of its local history collection (*kraevedcheskii otdel*), a position he held until his resignation under duress in January 1930.[9] Charushin arrived at the library at a time when everything was topsy-turvy in Soviet Russia; institutions were being dissolved or destroyed; others were emerging haphazardly; opportunities were disappearing, others arising; uncertainty and instability were the name of the game; and few could glimpse the contours of the future. All this evoked both anxiety and hope. For Charushin, taking up work in the library was both a new endeavor and a return to his roots— the cause of the book, founding libraries, and acting as a "culture-bearer," albeit in an environment shorn of the illusions of the past.

The Herzen Regional Library, today a fine and vibrant institution serving as the cultural center of the city of Kirov (as Viatka was renamed in 1934), had itself undergone a rather turbulent history in recent years. Founded in 1837 it had struggled along without reliable funding ever since. In his memoirs Charushin nostalgically recalled the many blissful hours he spent in his youth exploring the world of books within its walls, only to find it in a dilapidated condition on his return from exile. As a child, the noted historian Pavel Luppov had passed the library on his daily walk to school, but had never seen a single soul entering or leaving the building. Especially after 1905, when the rapid expansion of secondary schooling increased the demand for books, prominent citizens (including Ivan Charushin and the mayor, Iakov Poskrebyshev) served on its board of trustees, and the regional collection was established under Alexei Luppov (a local civil servant). Despite efforts at revival the library remained in a parlous state. Funding sources were few and far between; staffing was woefully inadequate and lacked professional training; most "employees" were local bureaucrats assigned to work there without pay, in addition to their regular work—in compensation for their efforts they were provided housing in the library itself. The collection itself remained in disarray; no card catalogue existed; books were purchased irregularly or not at all, and those in circulation were not kept track of. Some books that had been received in 1912 had still not been registered as late as 1917.[10]

Efforts to put the library on firmer ground gained momentum immediately after the February Revolution. Under the leadership of Alexei Luppov and the remarkably energetic head of the zemstvo's extramural education bureau Alexander Lebedev, a plan was drawn up to place the library under the aegis of the provincial zemstvo in order to ensure reliable funding and turn it into a provincial-level research center. A new board comprising five directors was to administer its affairs and select from its members a chairman (initially Luppov, then Lebedev). The plan was approved by the board of trustees in July 1917 and endorsed by the provincial congress of public education the following month. By December all the documents were readied and ceremoniously handed over to the provincial zemstvo; unfortunately, only a month later that very institution was abolished.

Yet suddenly the library was deluged with volumes confiscated from the offices of the provincial governor, zemstvo, and the church. The remnants of private collections, both confiscated from and donated by local merchants and other notables, had to be sorted, catalogued, and shelved. But there were few people to do this, no catalogue to augment, and no available space in the dilapidated building.[11] Lebedev, like many other former zemstvo employees who had promoted the cause of the book, was now confronted with a serious moral dilemma. On the one hand, he and others were appalled by the Bolsheviks' confiscation of private homes and belongings, including in many cases substantial book collections from prominent local figures who had been benefactors of the schools and libraries. On the other hand, they fervidly wanted to preserve these collections intact at a time of large-scale looting and ransacking of homes and institutions. They thus felt compelled to take part in the morally objectionable confiscations in order to prevent the destruction of valuable holdings. Lebedev and his colleagues ended up in the uncomfortable position of taking part in the smashing of cultural sites in Viatka, laboring at the same time to preserve their valuable artifacts.[12]

It was at this time that Elena Gogel' and her close friend and colleague Adol'fina Pallizen[13] arrived on the scene from Petrograd. Gogel,' whom we briefly met in chapter 8, had fled the dire conditions in that city, but had also come to look after her elderly mother (her brother had served as the director of the local art museum but had recently left Viatka). Gogel' had studied at the famous Bestuzhev Courses for women, as well as at the Sorbonne and spoke several languages; at the time of the revolution she was the librarian at the Petrograd Pedagogical Institute, directed by the renowned historian Sergei Platonov. She maintained contact with him and with the noted liberal jurist Anatolii Koni until the end of their lives.

At loose ends in Viatka and in the midst of the case subsequent to the Bolshevik takeover there, the two women volunteered to help maintain the library's collection. As Gogel' told Koni on January 11, 1918, "How can a librarian live without books? Moreover, it seems I'll be offered a small salary, which will surely help."[14] On January 23 she continued, "I really enjoy this work, and for me Viatka strikes a deep chord."[15] Her organizational abilities and professional expertise were soon recognized, and she was offered the post of academic librarian. She and Pallizen set about reorganizing the collection; they divided the library into seven sections, and in general established the standards that prevailed in St. Petersburg and that had been set by international library congresses, in which she had played an active role.

Despite the tumultuous times, they made rapid progress. Gogel' was inspired by the goal of turning the library into a regional cultural and scholarly center. As she wrote to Koni on February 28, 1918, "These folks have grandiose plan to transform the region, but they lack the personnel, and for that reason they are holding fast to me. I don't know how it will all turn out, but the idea of creating a cultural center for an entire region is certainly appealing." Yet the letter also has a wary note, "There are ample funds available; now if only we can overcome the prevailing climate of downgrading and nullification of culture left and right.... Yesterday, for example, the local 'comrades' occupied the building that had been designated for expanding our library." But despite the disturbing intrusion of the "comrades," she still considered "the possibilities to be endless here."[16]

Both her hopes and her fears would be realized over the next few years. In 1919, a new statute was drawn up. The board of directors was eliminated (several of its members had been arrested in 1918); a new elected board was established; and Gogel' was named the director of the library. The library itself was granted autonomy and officially designated a research institution, a status that meant it would be more reliably funded by Moscow rather than locally. Staff were added (an increase from three to twenty-nine employees). Courses in librarianship were offered, and the library's collection began to grow rapidly. In 1920 it was placed on the select list of twenty libraries receiving mandatory free copies of all publications forthcoming in the Russian Federation.[17] The architect Ivan Charushin stepped in to design a capital renovation of the building (both floors had by now been given over fully to the library); working with Lebedev, the librarians drew up a budget for the project and supervised its completion.[18] In 1924 a reference section was opened, book circulation renewed,[19] and finally in 1929 a magnificent new reading hall, with space for 450 visitors, was opened.

Yet it was far from smooth sailing for the library. Despite the support from Moscow, "some local commissars" (as Gogel' put it) had little use for the "rubbish" (as they put it) housed in the library and persistently schemed to appropriate its limited space for other uses.[20] Then, in 1919, at a time when the civil war was raging and Charushin was being held as a hostage, disaster struck the library. As Kolchak's White Army approached Viatka from the south, the order went out to evacuate the library's holdings to Moscow; the entire collection was hastily boxed up, loaded onto ten freight cars and hauled away.[21] Frantic efforts were made to prevent its departure, but by the time Trotsky (who was coordinating the defense of Viatka) and the Moscow authorities intervened, the train carrying the library holdings had already arrived in the capital. In 1929 K. V. Driagin, who later succeeded Gogel', noted that if the boxes been unloaded and distributed throughout the city there would have been no way back.[22] As it was the collection was returned but a substantial portion of it had been damaged or disappeared; what remained had to be catalogued and arranged once again. In short, all that had been achieved since 1918 was lost. Gogel' recalled, "How very much, both bad and good, we had lived through together! At first, building (a collection); stressful, urgent, consuming all our physical and spiritual energies; the reading hall, new building, and then, in the course of two days, collapse, evacuation... devastation."[23]

Moreover, the library had by this time been "repurposed" to house an orphanage and other agencies. When on the orders of General Bliukher the building was given back to its owners, it had been stripped of furniture, its fixtures torn out, and left in partial ruin. This was incidentally the very same famed Bliukher who was intervening at the time to obtain the release of Charushin (and himself later fell a victim of Stalin's purges). In 1920, what remained of the collection was further threatened by instructions and lists now being issued by Moscow to get rid of "outdated and harmful" literature. It was recommended to purge libraries of all monarchist, religious literature and pre-revolutionary histories of Russia, but Gogel' had spoken up forcefully against such measures. Fortunately, when the decree was promulgated the governing statute of the Herzen Library had granted it absolute autonomy over its affairs, so implementation of the 1920 instructions was left up to local (that is, her) discretion. She chose to leave the collection intact.[24] Another threat was posed however by the introduction of New Economic Policy (NEP), whereby funding and administration of cultural institutions was turned over to local bodies that were essentially bankrupt. Libraries and schools were largely left on their own to find resources.[25] Other developments were also ominous. In 1921, provincial authorities stepped up the pressure to politicize the activities of the library, and on April 11, 1922, a new statute eliminated the board of trustees and provided that the library's director thenceforth would be appointed from above rather than elected from within.

Despondent over the loss of autonomy as well as the looming cutoff of funding, and missing the pace of life and comforts of a big city, Gogel' solicited and received an offer of work from the prestigious Rumiantsev Museum in Moscow. Despite obstacles put in her path by the Provincial Department of Education, which was reluctant to part with highly trained staff (even while undercutting their autonomy) Gogel' departed, taking Pallizen with her. On June 12, 1922, she wrote, "To my surprise, over the past four years I have made some good friends, and the Herzen Library I have helped found has become the 'pride of Viatka.'"[26] The two women were not the only figures to depart the scene; Lebedev, who had vigorously fought the provincial authorities against the new statute, was forced to leave Viatka for Perm', depriving the city of one its most energetic cultural figures in the area of museology, archival preservation, library affairs, and extra-mural education.[27]

One of the good friends Gogel' referred to was Nikolai Charushin. It is difficult to determine when they first met or the nature of their interactions during the period when they were both involved in library affairs, but mostly likely it extended from the time of his release in mid-1919 until her departure for Moscow in 1922. What is certain is that by then they had established a strong bond based on mutual respect and even friendship. After she left Viatka she wrote him a warm letter of regard, and they continued to correspond for years. Soon after leaving she turned to him for help retrieving some important documents she needed in Moscow. Later, she describes her own work, asks for detail about the Herzen Library, and urges him to draw up plans for expanding the activities of *kraevedcheskii otdel*, over which he had been placed in charge in 1922, and which was to be the focus of his efforts over the next eight years.[28] Gogel' wrote him from Moscow, "It's so gratifying to know that now there is somebody as dedicated and engaged as you are in the local history branch of the library."[29]

As we know, such work was already familiar to Charushin from his time in Siberia. Ivan Popov later recalled that "toward the turn of the century cultural promotion activities unfolded all across Siberia in a far more vibrant manner than in European Russia. Culture building went hand in hand with the study of Siberia, which led to the founding of museums. As early as 1888, Dmitry Klements, on returning from an expedition to Mongolia, gave a lecture entitled "'Museums and a Passion for One's Native Region,' and in this lecture one heard the term . . . *kraevedenie* (local history)."[30] Indeed, the term became a mainstay of the vocabulary, and *kraevedenie* flourished in the early Soviet era—a practice to which disenchanted intellectuals from the pre-revolutionary era flocked.[31]

For Charushin as well as Popov (see Figure 9.1) such endeavors represented a return to their pasts. While Charushin labored at the Viatka library, Popov was engaged in Moscow at the Central Bureau of *Kraevedenie*. It is likely that in the picture of Popov and Charushin mulling over some papers in Figure 9.1, they are engaged not only in matters concerning the OPK but also with local history topics. The same can be said of Alexei

FIGURE 9.1.

Nikolai Charushin, Ivan Popov, 1920s.
© Russian State Archive of Literature and Art, Moscow.

Kuznetsov (who taught Charushin photography), founder of museums in Chita and Nerchinsk and continuing his efforts in that sphere after the revolution. Popov wrote about the old Siberian exiles meeting up at local history conferences throughout the 1920s. We know too, that Charushin presented a paper about his work with the Herzen library at just such a gathering in Viatka in June 1923, in which he outlined plans for the expansion of that branch of the library and expressed that hope that it would become an authentic center for such studies.[32]

In fact, Charushin was to achieve remarkable results for the fledgling local history section of the library, carrying out with only limited assistance the Herculean tasks of cataloguing materials and compiling extraordinary bibliographies. These works (some were published, but most are available only in typescript at the Herzen Library itself) included a listing of more than seven hundred titles of articles and books about national minorities in Viatka province; a detailed index of every document produced by the Viatka zemstvo (both provincial and district units) from its inception in

1867 until 1916, as well as of the city duma (1870–1916), a prodigious effort organized both by date and by theme; indices to *Viatskii Krai* (1894–1898); to his own newspaper (*Viatskii Krai* and *Viatskaia Zhizn'*, 1905–1907, and *Viatskaia Rech'*, 1908–1917—the latter completed only long after his death. He also pored over sixty capital-city journals, more than 7,400 periodical volumes to produce, in 1928, a booklet listing in all 548 articles about Viatka. He created unique album-format catalogs listing all the holdings of the local history section of the Herzen Library (all in all, forty-nine such albums). One needs to work with this rich body of bibliographic source— as the authors of this book did—to fully appreciate his contribution to the history of Viatka and the extraordinary energy and diligence of this fragile, elderly man, now in his seventies. It is no wonder that his memory is venerated even today by the staff of that library.[33]

"YOUR EFFORTS WERE ALL IN VAIN": THE TURN TO WRITING MEMOIRS

Such productivity also helped to combat the relentless onslaught of feelings of emptiness and despair. As Gogel' confessed, "My spirits are low; the future looks dim, all light has gone out, our fellow travelers wander wearily about, stumbling through the surrounding muck and ashes, lacking the energy to deal with reality. But we can't let things go, we must find a way to cope with this heartache and hopelessness."[34] Charushin's letters to Gogel' are lost to us, yet is not a far stretch to infer that he shared her emotional mix of commitment and despair. Both found renewed meaning in their efforts to restore the library. Both also sought security in working within the discrete boundaries of an institution that needed to be shielded from the increasingly shrill propaganda campaigns and harsh repressive measures of the Bolshevik regime. By committing their entire workday to the cause of scholarly and cultural development, both could partially shut out those aspects of the outside world they found repulsive. But repulsive they nevertheless were, and the process of withdrawal could go only so far.

Others of this generation recorded feelings of outrage and despair similar to those vented by Gogel'. In the summer of 1920 Mikhail Frolenko wrote Figner, "Old age, inadequate diet, but most important, the dreariness and oppressive state of anticipation, always hoping for something better but at the same time anguishing about the present; you feel dejected being surrounded everywhere by ruin and at the same time feel completely helpless about alleviating the situation—all of this is deadly for body and soul."³⁵ Most of the Populists rejected the October Revolution, viewing it as a political coup d'état rather than a social revolution. Echoing Charushin's own response to events, Egor Lazarev lamented:

> Fifty-five years of struggle for political freedom! I sat in solitary confinement for five to six years, and on three occasions was subjected to administrative [rather than judicial—authors] exile in Siberia. Oh, how many years spent abroad in emigration and in flight. Finally—an end to autocracy! Russia undergoes the greatest of revolutions and in March 1917 the ossified tsarist order is overthrown! And what kind of absurdity do we now see, when thousands of socialists, having paid for their free-thinking with years of confinement and hard labor, are once again scattered over the endless tundra of Siberia and exile only to experience conditions immeasurably harsher than under tsarism.³⁶

Disillusionment and isolation compelled the Populists to look to the past for consolation, a past they increasingly thought of as "distant." Testimony to this can be found in the title of the memoirs Charushin produced at this time—*Remembrances of a Distant Past*—but also in the abundant surviving correspondence between Populists, and the very fact that they made sure to preserve these letters. Remembrances kept the 1870s generation together in these difficult times; writing to the widow of Kravchinskii soon after the death of Ekaterina Breshko-Breshkovskaia, Lazarev affirmed, "We are bound together by a shared, irretrievable past."³⁷ Of course, for the older generation of revolutionaries recounting their past was a way of fleeing from the unkind present into a realm in which their youthful energy and optimism had run rampant.

Psychologically, memoir writing was also an individual tool to overcome the traumatic experience of prison and hard labor as well as to facilitate the adaptation to life under the difficult new conditions. Even in the late Tsarist era former revolutionaries had had trouble orienting themselves to life outside prison. Perhaps the only way to do so was to put down one's experiences on paper? Newly in search of meaning in their lives and given the impossibility of simply picking up where they had left off, a commitment to such endeavors provided an exit from political and societal isolation. Figner described her own path in this way, "In 1913, I confronted the emptiness of my situation: there were no revolutionary tasks I could apply myself to, indeed nothing that could serve the common cause. So instead I turned to a task my friends had long urged upon me and about which I had myself been thinking for some time. I began to write."[38]

If this was the case in the aftermath of the 1905 Revolution, it was even more so after the far more cataclysmic events of 1917–1921. Elderly Populists regarded memoir writing as fulfilling a debt to their fallen comrades, those who had died in prison or in exile or during revolution or civil war. The need to reinforce the heroic image of Populist revolutionaries as figures with high moral standards may also have been urged on by the opening of the archives of the Tsarist secret policy and the discovery that some among their midst had actually betrayed the cause to become agents of the police.

The urge to write became stronger as the decade passed. Populists sought to ward off "erasure" brought on by the passage of time but also by an increasingly hostile environment. In 1921, Figner encountered what was for her an entirely unexpected and shocking challenge to her sense of her place in history and her very identity. In a letter to a colleague she described what had happened:

> Yesterday I was at the [now renamed] Petrovsky Academy of Agronomy at the invitation of students who sent along fifteen or twenty queries in advance. But it was late and I didn't get around to reading them; I also knew there would be some unwelcome questions which I had no wish to address. I had already had the occasion to respond to the likes of 'what is your stance toward the current political order?' or 'why don't you belong to the party in power today?' But I certainly didn't anticipate what I read in one of the notes I perused after returning home from my presentation; concerning the historical significance of the People's Will: it read: 'your efforts were all in vain, your energies were expended heedlessly and produced no results.'[39]

The political trials of the 1920s profoundly disturbed exiles and prisoners of the Tsarist era who them as a repeat of the past. They sought to use their moral authority as opponents of the old regime to speak out against the restoration of the death penalty and ease the conditions of those incarcerated by the Bolsheviks. Such efforts even led the Central Committee of the Communist Party in 1922 to consider shutting down the only recently formed OPK, whose strivings to promote revolutionary morality were potentially quite disruptive.[40] It persistently sought to preserve in the public memory the repressive tactics employed by the Tsarist prison authorities; it served as a link between the community of former exiles and the outside world, and it actively agitated against the persecution of Socialist Revolutionaries in the notorious 1922 trials, refusing to expel from its own ranks anarchists and SRs who were under investigation. Moreover, it even continued to publish their memoirs.[41]

Many of the veterans familiar to us took part in this movement by signing an address to the party Central Committee protesting the execution of the SRs. They called the death penalty antithetical to the spirit of socialism and humanitarian values. They referred to their own tragic experiences in tsarist prisons and the horror of anticipating one's own execution, and in so doing sought to deploy their "symbolic capital" as martyrs to the socialist cause. Their letters at the time frequently cite the moral obligation they felt to speak truth to authority. In 1925 and 1927, the Populists repeated the demand that the death penalty be expunged from the judicial process.[42]

"I URGE YOU TO WRITE DOWN YOUR RECOLLECTIONS"

If one of the postulates of memory studies is that collective memory is not so much the result of recollections as it is a societal process, then we can stipulate that as a whole the Populists' memoirs represented both a struggle to preserve the legacy of Populism and to assimilate the present as much as they reflected an individual apprehension of events or a coming to grips with one's own demons. It was in this context that in 1922 Vera Figner convinced Charushin to register with the OPK—admittedly for different reasons: she wanted to help him arrange a pension and to make his life more comfortable as well as less isolated. He was drawn into the activities of that society, defending the legacy of Populism against increasingly militant attacks mounted by young Bolsheviks and historians. But the process was gradual and his reluctance to write evident. Early in

January 1924, Figner wrote in a note to Charushin, "I urge you to write down your recollections about the origins, activities and organizations of the Chaikovtsy in several cities. Such a history of the circle, remarkable in all ways, is lacking, and you must put on paper all that you know about it directly and what you have heard from others."[43]

In reply, Charushin pointed out:

> I've been waiting all along for one of the better informed members of my circle to fulfill this task, but up to now have been disappointed in that expectation. Yours is not the first time I have heard such a request, but I confess that with all the unremitting cares of daily life, when matters of the present can swallow up one's attention, there has simply been no time to think about the past. Now however, with almost none of the Chaikovtsy still alive, I feel even more acutely the obligation to fill the gaps in that area to the best of my abilities.[44]

Two weeks later, on January 29, 1924, Figner again urged Charushin to write his memoirs, describing the act as a moral debt to those who were no longer among the living; otherwise much would be forgotten and then irretrievably lost. She wrote, "So for all these reasons you must get down to business and please, no more delays. Otherwise what if you are taken ill and won't be able to recall the details? After all this is a debt owed to the public by those of us who have outlived our comrades. I am so happy I have already made my own contribution—if I had to start today and write the way I did then—I just couldn't do it."[45]

Figner was not the only one pestering Charushin; fellow member of the Chaikovskii circle and his lifelong friend Alexandra Kornilova-Moroz added her voice to the choir, in what was certainly a heartfelt request, though most likely made at the behest of her dear friend Figner, "All of us who remain have the obligation to finally clarify in a truthful and comprehensive way the many activities of that circle which ... put it at the forefront of the movement."[46]

In their letters to Charushin we again see the emphasis on a debt to one's departed comrades of the Chaikovskii circle as well as the striving to fix in the memory of generations to come the prominent role that that circle had played in the history of the revolutionary movement as a whole. This idea had arisen much earlier, during their collective imprisonment awaiting trial in the middle of the 1870s and after release at the turn of the century, but now it had even more urgency.⁴⁷ In the correspondence of the old revolutionaries we note the oft-repeated stress on the need to give as full and reliable a version of the activities of the circle as was possible ("what you know, in what you participated, what is known about others"), for the claim to authenticity would be legitimized both by the fact of direct participation in the affairs of the circle itself as well as by the testimony of others.

In December of 1924, Kornilova-Moroz prepared to send Charushin the memoirs of Leonid Shishko⁴⁸ for use in his own account of events and inquired of Charushin—had he actually begun writing yet? Once more, in February 1925, she urged him to begin, and let him know that Vera Figner had confirmed the veracity of his replies to Kornilova-Moroz's queries about the early activities of the Chaikovskii circle (for her own book), as well as his commentary on Shishko's memoirs. She was writing a biography of Sofia Perovskaia (who had been executed for her role in the assassination of Alexander II). In March 1925, Kornilova-Moroz wrote Charushin that she had "fulfilled her own obligation" by completing her recollections of Perovskaia and was sending him part of this text.⁴⁹

It seems that by this time Charushin was genuinely turning to the task of writing, for he sent Kornilova-Moroz a letter with a list of queries about the political stances of members of the circle, the details of the program of the Chaikovtsy, and their understanding of the practical tasks confronting them. But she was taking no chances. He received a detailed response from her in which she once again invoked the importance of contributing his recollections, "Your recollections are extremely valuable... please get down to this soon."⁵⁰

In short, Charushin set about the task of putting in words his recollections only after prolonged procrastination and despite deep reservations, at the urging of his friends. Perhaps Charushin's lengthy hesitation had stemmed from his awareness of the perils of relying upon individual recollections alone. He wrote in 1926 about the doubts that had beset him when he first took up the project, "Over the years the memories had faded, much had been entirely lost. Most importantly, I was apprehensive that in my efforts to reproduce and evaluate the events of the past would be involuntarily colored by the atmosphere of subsequent times and that the result would convey a distorted picture of what I was describing."[51]

That the "atmosphere of subsequent times" was also beginning to impinge on this conversation is clear from the correspondence. Vera Figner was writing an introduction to the collected works of Lev Tikhomirov, the member of their circle who had turned against the revolutionary movement and written the brochure "Why I Am No Longer a Revolutionary" that had profoundly shaken the group (see chapters 1 and 5). Figner was still reflecting on his actions when she set about recruiting survivors of the movement to contribute their autobiographies to the *Granat* collection. Bewildered by Tikhomirov's account of his early years, which she found "muddy and slapdash, as if he himself hadn't written it," she asked Charushin to send her his recollections of Tikhomirov's participation in the Chaikovskii circle and an explanation for why Tikhomirov had acted as he did. But she ended that letter with the words "I really need this, *but not for print.*"[52] Even at this time she wanted to keep their conversation confidential.

When he finally set about the task of writing his memoirs it was not only because of the persistent entreaties of Vera Figner, who enjoyed enormous authority among the older revolutionaries, or Kornilova-Moroz, or even his own sense of moral obligation to his generation. Also weighing in were the core of old revolutionaries in the OPK, whose circle he had joined. Evidence of this can be found in brief comment in a letter Charushin sent in 1927 to one of its members, Maria Shebalina: "Please give my warmest greetings... to the circle, *whose assignment I received last summer and now have carried out,* for better or worse."[53]

COLLECTIVE AUTOBIOGRAPHY AND
TRAVELING NARRATIVES

In his review of the first volume of Charushin's memoirs, the young historian Shmuel Levin noted that the author had "put pen to paper after all of his comrades and contemporaries themselves had done so and [he] had access to all of these texts as well as to a number of recently published important documents pertaining to his circle. Because of this his own work should be treated as a summing up of all that had been written before him."54

Charushin's memoirs were indeed written with a keen eye to the accounts of other members of the Chaikovskii circle, citing these accounts, and utilizing a voluminous correspondence with others in the movement. Earlier, as his correspondence shows, he had paid close attention to the memoirs written by his peers: in 1906 he had written to Kuvshinskaia living in exile in Perm' to describe his excitement on reading the memoirs of Sinegub and Shishko for the first time, "The mail has arrived, bringing new issues of *Byloe* and *Russkoe Bogatstvo* and I was absorbed reading ... about those 'old' times."55 Those two journals with a Populist orientation had begun publishing memoirs of the seventies generation, many of whom had only recently been released from exile. Charushin had discussed these memoirs with Kuvshinskaia, encouraging her to write down her remembrances since he felt that those of Sinegub were incomplete and excessively subjective. Even more, they were "simplistic and imprecise, to the degree that he even makes me out to be a died-in-the wool anarchist."56 It should be added that despite this criticism Charushin had tried to convince his acquaintance, the noted Moscow bookman and sponsor of Charushin's newspaper Alexander Charushnikov, to publish Sinegub's memoirs as a book, in order to help out his friend "Silych'" (as he affectionately called him) financially.57

In the second volume of his memoirs describing his life at the Kara gold mines and penal settlement, Charushin made use of both Shishko's and Sinegub's memoirs, writing in the foreword, "Life at Kara at that time has already been described in part by Sinegub and, less so, Shishko; for that reason, there is some inevitable repetition in my own narration, something unavoidable if I wanted to give a full picture of what life was like there."58

In 1924, when he was still only contemplating writing his own memoirs, Charushin had also read carefully those of Ivan Popov, and confessed to the latter that in doing so, "I was pleased and even surprised at how luminous were your recollections of that relatively distant past—so much so that I am now intimidated at the thought of launching such a project."59 Years later, writing his recollections of his time spent as a penal colonist, instead of describing Kiakhta at length himself he directed the reader to Popov's "much richer" account. In 1929, he described rereading the five volumes of Figner's recollections with "enormous pleasure."[60] After he had started writing, he also discussed his recollections regularly with Kornilova-Moroz. In April 1926 she wrote him, "If you find it more opportune to meet with me in Moscow to go over your memoirs, I will be able to travel there in May."[61]

Moreover, in the introduction to the first volume of his memoirs Charushin underscores the fact that Kornilova-Moroz had given her seal of approval to the manuscript.[62] This in his view was testimony to the veracity and authenticity of his account. After the memoirs were published, Charushin welcomed the proposal made by members of the OPK that Kornilova-Moroz and nobody else should write a review, most likely for *Katorga i Ssylka*, the OPK journal. He agreed that she was the best person to do it because she was a veteran of the Chaikovskii circle and her testimony that "what I had written did not doctor up the facts ... will carry a lot of weight. When she does write the review she can also compensate for any omissions on my part."[63]

In 1926, a circle of "elders" was established in the OPK. As Kornilova-Moroz wrote, "[T]hey met weekly, ... one of them would relate his own life story, which was then taken down by a stenographer, and later turned into an article for the journal."[64] Charushin continued working on his own memoirs, now focusing on the period of exile, turning to his peers in this group to verify dates and to clarify the historical context. For example, Charushin noted that Mikhail Chernavskii's memoirs had helped him substantially in his description of the ignominious Uspenskii episode as he grappled with it in his own volume.[65]

Turning to the accounts of other revolutionaries was characteristic of this generation and led to something resembling a "unified" or "collective" remembrance. On occasion, a former Chaikovtsy might even directly borrow a passage from the works of someone else without acknowledging its origins, simply merging the words into his or her own text—something only a close word-by-word analysis of these memoirs has revealed. For instance, Kornilova-Moroz borrowed freely from the memoirs of Chaikovskii, Kropotkin, and Figner. She made it clear that doing so was part of the normal creative process of writing. She wrote:

Thanks to books I obtained, in my status as a bona fide writer from the [local] library.... I was able to insert (into my own account) some really interesting passages, such as the one of the colorful scene from the Trial of the 193 when [Hyppolite] Myshkin finished his speech and the gendarmes dragged him by force out of the courtroom. [Vasilii] Bogucharskii himself borrowed this from the newspaper published in Geneva in 1877–8. I also took the obituaries of [Anatolii] Serdiukov and [Mikhail] Kupreianov from Lavrov, which I found there. As for the depiction of the Chaikovskii circle, I borrowed that from Kropotkin, and pulled a couple of passages from (Figner's) *The Imprint of Life's Endeavors*.[66]

Other Populists also acknowledged the overlapping of texts; after reading Mikhail Novorusskii's remembrances of their time at Shlisselburg, Vera Figner wrote him, "Despite all the differences in tone and construction... I found so much agreement on so many occasions... *that you might even think we copied from one another*—which given the time of writing could not have been the case. I got a good laugh reading the first part of your foreword: the draft of my own foreword... is virtually the same, word-for-word!"[67] While concluding the third and final installment of his memoirs, about his period as a penal colonist in Nerchinsk and Kiakhta, Charushin once again sought confirmation and clarification of his recollections.[68]

Thus we find considerable evidence of, to use the term loosely, "intertextuality"—if not what we today would call outright plagiarism—in the Populists' memoirs. It is important to emphasize, however, that the former Chaikovtsy did not see matters that way; rather they sought to speak in unison. The process of constructing memoirs involved relying upon individual memory, but also turning to the already formulated recollections of other participants in the revolutionary movement, as well as, when possible, discussion of key moments, all of which in the end led to the creation of a social memory. At the same time the commonality of views, the collective experience and even—one might say—of identity, led on its own to the construction of similar narratives written largely in isolation from others.

CHARUSHIN LAUDED AND REWARDED

When the first volume of Charushin's memoirs[69] appeared in 1926, the five-thousand-copy print run so exceeded his expectations that he wondered if it was not in fact excessive. Later he received an honorarium. Believing it to be immodest to inquire about payment in March, 1927, he instead had asked his friend Maria Shebalina, employed by the Kropotkin Museum in Moscow, to find out. Displaying his typical reticence, he had written, "The question is of course important to me, but I can't get myself to bring it up."[70] In May of that year he thanked Shebalina for talking with the publishers, after which he had received a portion of the sum owed him.[71] A month later he received another 150 rubles with a promise of more to come as well as notice that his volume had been approved for school libraries. That fact along with the publication in 1929 of the second volume in an inexpensive format led G. G. Sushkov of the OPK to assure Charushin that sales would be brisker because of its lower cost, "but also because [the second volume's] content is simpler and more accessible."[72]

Living in exile in Viatka, the anarchist philosopher Alexei Borovoi[73] wrote in his diary on October 15, 1929, "I read with great pleasure both volumes of Charushin's memoirs which he had given me.... The writing is clear and unpretentious, but also redolent. Nothing superfluous there. Most appealing is the portrait that emerges of the narrator himself: modest, serious, a luminous figure. He sees the best in people and never seeks to settle scores. Approaching his eightieth birthday, he writes simply and with a light touch without drawing attention to himself—the rarest of righteous people he is!"[74] Charushin's old friend Baranov was similarly impressed; he wrote the author on January 29, 1928, "I read your book with pleasure and interest. I found seductive the unembellished language and authenticity of tone."[75]

The published reviews were also positive. One prominent historian and editor, Boris Koz'min, commended the conscientiousness and exceptional meticulousness Charushin demonstrated as a memoirist as well as his striving to minimize the subjectivity inevitable in any memoir and to provide as impartial as possible a picture of events. He concluded that as a history of the Chaikovskii circle it would take its place along with Aptekman's description of *Land and Liberty* and Vera Figner's *People's Will*.[76] Charushin was surprised at the positive reviews of the first volume and embarrassed to find his work put on the same level as Figner's. Calling Koz'min's praise "overblown," he found many shortcomings in his portrait of the Chaikovskii circle, believing that "it should have been more vivid and substantial, but for a number of reasons I didn't have the strength to carry it off."[77]

MEMORY WARS

As we have seen Charushin was not the only one to write his memoirs during this period. The majority of such works met a positive reception. Especially valued were those written by authors who "had experienced the full weight of repression of the tsarist regime." Their didactic worth was pointed out by the popular author Dmitrii Furmanov, "The will to struggle is hardened by contact with such vibrant and convincing texts."[78] That writer cited Figner's memoirs as exemplary.[79] Indeed, the multitude of letters Figner received on the publication of her recollections testify to the appeal of those who had struggled heroically against the autocracy, who held themselves to high moral standards and who sacrificed their own well-being and even lives for the common good.[80]

But even at this date positive reviews sometimes contained what amounted to backhanded compliments. For example, Koz'min praised Charushin for confessing that factory workers of peasant origin poorly comprehended the concept of socialism, responding instead to discussions of land question, the nobility, taxes, and obligations. This observation was a timely one, for the Soviet authorities were at the time trying to develop appropriate policies for the countryside and to have a prominent Populist rue the peasants' lack of political savvy fit their current needs well without inconveniently embellishing the image of the Populists themselves.[81]

The topic of the political struggle also raised eyebrows among reviewers. In 1927 Levin chided (his much senior) Charushin thusly, "It seems a bit naïve for Charushin to argue that the Chaikovtsy were not unfamiliar with political questions, that such questions were sidetracked 'only' by the enormity of the task of mobilizing the population into the emancipation struggle. After all, the failure of the seventies generation was precisely in their failure to comprehend the link between mass movements and the political tasks facing the country."[82]

Compared with what was to come this language and criticism was measured. Soon, publishing the memoirs became far more problematic as Bolshevik Party's control over content tightened and historical memory became even more contested. Manuscripts had to be first closely vetted for approval internally by the OPK and were sometimes simply returned to the author without any explanation. Writing of their experience of incarceration, former exiles had often included along with tales of horror their ability to organize study groups and instances of benevolent treatment by those supervising them. Such depictions now brought on accusations from the Bolsheviks of whitewashing the truth and misleading the young. One fervid critic wrote, "The nightmarish conditions behind the walls of the prison, the inhumane humiliation, torture and mockery of human dignity and individuality of revolutionaries that characterized the police state that Russia was—all find their apologist (in these memoirs)."[83] Charushin wrote to Shebalina in March 1927, that he was finding writing about his time at Kara difficult: "Continuing my memoirs has gone slowly; the mood is not there and I'm not at all sure that what I have to say merits publication."[84] It is more than likely that this reluctance stemmed from the disparity between the current political climate and his nuanced recollections. After all, Kara had been a mixed experience of oppression combined with bonds of friendship, mutual support, and even optimism about the future.

Despite these difficulties, by 1928 Charushin had managed to complete the manuscript and send it off to his publisher at the OPK. In July of that year he wrote to Shebalina, "I still haven't heard a word about the fate of my manuscript . . . and have no clue why."[85] In September, he repeated the same lament.[86] Then in October he wrote, "My manuscript is stuck somewhere, and nobody has told me why. To be sure, Ivan Popov wrote me on October 1 that the editorial board had decided to publish only the section dealing with Kara, but to reject what I wrote on the period of penal colonization, and that Koz'min himself was going to write me about this. For some reason he hasn't done, who knows why? I'm not upset that the second part was turned down, for even I was not happy with it; it doesn't have much of general interest and could have been done differently, certainly more concisely."[87] Finally in November he learned that the book was being readied for publication and set about writing an introduction. The second was published in 1929, but without the section on penal colonization and with a decidedly mixed foreword written by Felix Kon, who had been a participant in the events described (see below).

Shortly thereafter there was talk of publishing a new and combined edition of the volumes of *Remembrances of a Distant Past*, at which point the topic of finally publishing his recollections of life as a penal colonist in Siberia was broached, apparently by Popov. On January 16, 1930, Charushin wrote a letter to Popov conveying his ambivalence:

> I fully agree with you it would be much better to publish the memoirs in the form in which I originally wrote them. But my section on penal settlement was tossed aside without any explanation and for that reason I didn't even venture to suggest including it in the new edition. Several people read the sections on Kara and penal settlement ... but I never saw their reviews. It could be they found nothing new in the latter, especially since the bulk of it is devoted to Kiakhta, about which you had already written much more adequately. I myself had my doubts about the value of that section and saw no point in insisting on publishing it. It's likely that the censors' rejection of it was categorical, so who am I to bring it up again? Of course you see it differently, but that theme is dear to you [so] just how objective can you be? Had we the completely candid opinion of someone impartial ... then we might know better, but how can I myself judge? Maybe it would be better to try a different publisher. What are your thoughts on the matter?[88]

After all was said in done, however, *Life as a Penal Colonist* (the third volume of *Remembrances of a Distant Past*) was published separately in 1931, perhaps as a result of Popov's intervention.

"WE NEED MORE BOLSHEVIK VIGILANCE!"

In the opinion of Sandra Pujals, the years 1931 to 1934 were ones in which the tonality of class warfare was turned against the older generation. A struggle erupted within the OPK reflecting the strivings of a younger generation of Bolsheviks to assert party control over its functions, to direct not only its present activities but its past as well—that is, the process of memoir writing—and in so doing, to crowd out the society's Populists. The struggle to define a "genuinely Leninist" path to building socialism provided a way to eliminate revolutionaries of another time. Challenges to the objectivity of the memoirists' attempts to describe historical events were combined with innuendos about the ability of senile old figures to accurate recall earlier times.[89]

By the close of the 1920s, the place the Bolsheviks had allocated to their predecessors in the new and triumphal historical narrative of the revolution had become clear. As the fiftieth anniversary of the Trial of the 193 and the formation of the People's Will approached the press gave much coverage to the place of Populism in the "prehistory" of the Bolshevik Party, with emphasis on the former's utopian views and the principal ideological and class differences between Populism and Marxism. Now histories of Populism were supposed to highlight its mistaken ways and the task was to demonstrate the political impotence of an older generation who had no idea how to make a revolution. The older Populists had entertained unrealizable dreams about "socialism about which they had a faulty understanding even if they had written a brilliant page in the history of the struggle against autocracy."[90] In contrast, the Bolshevik Party had chosen the right path and had no need of prominent historical antecedents. In this new iteration history really began with the formation of that party, its struggle against the autocracy—but also against the Mensheviks, Socialist Revolutionaries, and other "deviationists." The culture and propaganda sector of the party's central committee issued a pronouncement in which it continued to pay homage to the "huge contribution" made by the People's Will in the "heroic" struggle against autocracy.[91] But that resolution also repeatedly pointed out that Populism was but a past stage in the revolutionary struggle, now superseded by the proletarian stage, and that workers had intensified that struggle *despite* the influence of Populism.[92]

Felix Kon's foreword—mentioned above—to the second volume of Charushin's memoirs was indicative. Kon, a fellow former exile, was now chief editor of *Katorga i Ssylka*. In the foreword, he directed several criticisms at Charushin's cohorts who, in Kon's view, had not paid enough attention to the fundamental differences that had existed within the ranks of the opposition to autocracy. Kon was also perturbed by the author's description of camp commandant Kononovich as a "humane civil servant." He wrote condescendingly of the inability of members of the Chaikovskii circle to "properly understand" their situation, and of the absence of a "class-based" approach to matters.

Charushin wrote a measured response to Kon, but held out little hope that it would be published. Privately, he wrote caustically to Popov, "[Kon] couldn't resist slamming the old activists for not drawing a clear line between revolutionaries and [the liberal opposition] and for their [non-plebeian] social origins. And the soul of that bard couldn't bear my relationship with [the camp commandant] Konovovich."[93]

Ominously, in 1931, an official communist faction was formed within the Society of Former Political Prisoners and Exiles. The plan was to carry out a reorganization of the OPK that would place a party leadership in full control of its apparatus.[94] In 1932 the OPK was accused of ignoring the history of the Bolsheviks who had endured hard labor or exile. In 1932, at a meeting between that faction and representatives of the Communist Party Central Committee in attendance resolved to direct the scholarly endeavors of the OPK to the "proletarian" period of the emancipation movement, to increase the number of communists on the OPK journal editorial board, to reduce the number of non-communists in the society itself and to make the editors of its journal personally responsible for the content of published manuscripts. An article published in the journal *Class Struggle* in 1933, appropriately titled "We Need More Bolshevik Vigilance," sharply criticized the editorial board of the OPK journal despite the fact that it had already confessed to the "errors of its ways" and to manifesting "rotten liberalism."[95] Its sins included publishing memoirs that "ignored" the role of Bolsheviks in the revolutionary movement and evincing political "myopia" or even failing to confront "falsifiers of history" (meaning the Mensheviks and anarchists), but also describing revolutionary Populism as a forerunner of Leninism.[96]

Matters just got worse. In 1934, responding to a query by Anna Iakimova, the prominent ideologue Emel'ian Iaroslavskii explained that since all articles by former SRs were prohibited, and since Populists tended to repeat the same formulations as the SRs, they too should be forbidden access to the press. "We cannot be indifferent to attempts to propagandize SR views, the harmfulness of which should be amply evident from the history of recent decades, and especially the time of the proletarian revolution."[97] He expressed his consternation that the Populists were not grateful to a regime that—despite their principled differences, and out of profound respect for their revolutionary past—had previously abundantly published their recollections.[98]

In reality, by that time the editorial board of *Katorga i Ssylka* was under intense pressure over its attempts to defend the legacy of Populism. In 1935, a resolution of the Central Committee of the CPSU stated, "We need to emphasize that Marxism evolved here in a struggle against a Populism *which was its mortal enemy* by obliterating its basic tenets and rejecting its means of struggle."[99] Speaking before the newly formed Union of Writers in 1934, party ideologue Andrei Zhdanov called for the creation of new heroes to replace Zheliabov and Perovskaia, the assassins of Alexander II.

As a form of protest against Soviet-era repression Vera Figner had long held out against joining the OPK. In 1932 (on the occasion of her eightieth birthday) she had written a letter to that institution pointing to its endorsement of capital punishment as the reason she could not join. She was also offended by attempts to turn the OPK into a communist organization, by refusing to admit those belonging to other political parties and by carrying out a campaign verifying the political loyalty of existing members. She had written, "Following the example of what is taking place in the government itself the Society has immersed itself in politics, is carrying out a 'purge,' violating the very sanctity of the individual and demeaning human dignity in a way offensive to any thoughtful person. Instead it should be raising its voice in protest against the methods of control being used which go against everything essential to the revolutionary ethics of earlier times."[100] Her name does appear on a 1934 registry of OPK members, but recent research in the archives strongly suggests that she was more or less coerced into joining.[101]

The esteem in which Figner was held as the very symbol of the revolution, made clear by the outpouring of eightieth birthday congratulations as well as the prolific correspondence she received from incarcerated SRs and anarchists, could not but perturb the authorities, who nevertheless dared not touch her because of her unmatched popularity. In 1935, she joined with Maxim Gorky in an effort to save the OPK, but in vain; it was forced to close its doors in late 1935. The publication of *Katorga i Ssylka* ceased, and holdings removed from libraries and the roundup of its members began.[102] The memory politics of the time now entered a new epoch.

Many former Populists were arrested, often along with their families, in 1937 and 1938.[103]

As Shebalina had written Charushin in 1926, soon after the publication of his memoirs, what she found most appealing about that work was it "simplicity and truthfulness in describing the prodigious efforts carried out by the Chaikovtsy, something completely lacking in works published today."[104] Those words seem all the more poignant in light of subsequent events, for the task the Populists had set for themselves in the early 1920s of providing a comprehensive rendition of the activities of the "remarkable" Chaikovskii circle and to preserve a "collective representation" of their own generation was never realized. Despite their best efforts, their "memory" was never consolidated in commemorative practices; instead it was suppressed by the official Bolshevik narrative. Nor was it prolonged through family or group memory or demanded by a new generation; rather it gradually fell out of the society's historical consciousness.

"STILL, I AM NOT YET READY TO GIVE UP . . . "

Charushin was hardly immune from these developments. To be sure, he continued to live peacefully for most part. As late as March 1927 he could still write to Shebalina in Moscow, "Here in Viatka all is quiet and peaceful. Incidentally, just recently I was pleased to attend a lively conference of *kraevedy*; we were impressed too by the European atmosphere prevailing at that conference."[105] As the decade came to a close, he did not seem at all concerned about his own fate or to be personally affected by the mounting ideological pressure all around, but he did try to help those who were in trouble. For example, he put in a word for another former prisoner of the Shlisselburg Fortress whose manuscript the OPK group had rejected for publication. He asked the Shebalins to write an appeal in support of a Viatka agronomist who Charushin believed had been wrongly arrested.[106]

Other Populists also maintained ties with their peers of an earlier time. For example, Egor Lazarev, living in Prague, kept up a correspondence with Sazhin, Shebalin, Figner, and others. In each other's eyes, they remained comrades. They were united by their past struggle for emancipation, court trials, and periods of imprisonment, and not even deciding to leave the country—and in so doing rejecting the Soviet system—could separate them emotionally or politically. It is revealing that in their self-identification and descriptions of their peers, the "remote" and "distant" past is prominent, as are their references to a "bygone era" and their self-labeling as "relics." In the same letter Lazarev refers to his colleagues as "archeological digs," suggesting not only the remoteness of their era but its disconnect from the present.

In reality Charushin's own situation was worsening as well. At one point, he had found himself caricatured and mocked on the pages of *Viatskaia Pravda* for his "false" ideological credentials, and he was described as a tool of the ruling classes in a 1927 history of the October Revolution in Viatka. Roughly at that same time even his bibliographic work was being scrutinized for its ideological defects. In a secret letter to the library, the deputy director of the Viatka Communist Party historical commission, one S. V. Tokarev, had written that Charushin's introduction to his bibliography of *Viatskii Krai* (1905–1907) made false claims for the "independent" and "oppositionist" nature of that newspaper and needed to be rewritten from a Marxist perspective.[107] In January 1930, unable to work with the new administration brought in by the ongoing Cultural Revolution he resigned from his position in the library.[108] And in 1933 the successive waves of searches and arrests of political exiles in Viatka finally reached him. In letter to Borovoi from February 18, Charushin wrote of ongoing searches and deportations and then of a thorough ransacking of his residence by the secret police, "I can't make any sense of this; among those currently living in exile here, few of whom I know, there hasn't been any kind of activity calling for repercussions of this nature."[109]

Charushin now confessed to being shaken by these events, "This entire mess has had an impact on my already fragile nervous system and has put me badly out of sorts."[110] It could scarcely have been any comfort to him to know that three years earlier as "untouchable" a figure as Vera Figner had also had her premises searched, a story reported abroad but denied by the Soviet authorities—proof that it had actually happened was in the correspondence between her and Charushin that was confiscated when his residence was searched.

After his departure from the library Charushin lived a life of penury; he was often in poor health and seldom left his home. That home, before the revolution always open to zemstvo activists, journalists, and members of all oppositionist political parties, was now rarely graced by the presence of others. As he wrote to Borovoi in 1933, "We ... often remember you. Viatka has lost many of those close to us personally and your visits, rare as they are, always livened up a rather monotonous life devoid of vivid impressions. This is especially the case for me, for I have rarely stepped outside the house during the past two years."[111] When Viatka was renamed Kirov in 1934, Charushin was confronted with yet another indication that the history with which he was so intimately familiar was being erased in front of his eyes, leaving him even more alone in a world alien to his sensibilities.

His health continued to deteriorate; in the fall of 1934 he wrote, "The past year was not a good one. . . . [m]y legs are refusing to serve me any longer and I must make my peace with that. In a word, my health is not the best."[112] A document found in the local archives, dated 1936, provides further testimony to his declining health and impoverished state. According to that note, Charushin, was a category-1 invalid (the most severe) and was to be granted a subsidy of 150 rubles.[113]

Yet Charushin retained his strength of character and emotional resilience, despite his failing health. On January 13, 1935, he wrote to Borovoi, "Yes, I am now 83, and I'm still not as yet ready to give up even if the time has come for me to face the facts, stop worthlessly taking up space and burdening the lives of those close to me. You are quite right; it is my intrinsic nature that is to be blamed, for I am incapable of pessimism and can easily overcome assaults such as pneumonia . . . and when all is said and done, you can't change who you are."[114]

Strength of character characterized his friends as well, and it is what helped them deal with new trials in life. But some faltered. Many surviving Populists were overcome with disillusionment and misery brought on by both the political situation in the country and their own tribulations. After the death of a close friend, Kornilova-Moroz wrote Figner, "My sweet, dear Verochka . . . your extraordinary willpower and capacity for mental concentration allows you to retain your vitality and interest in life around you, that same life which has some of your contemporaries so unhappy."[115] In 1928, Kornilova-Moroz found herself homeless and forced to impose upon the Sazhins (Evgenia Figner was married to Mikhail Sazhin) for a place to eat and sleep, was then given a room at a house for pensioners, but she then left for the village to help out her son's family. She wrote Charushin in 1933, "Please be magnanimous and forgive my extended silence. I have been overcome by lassitude and pursued by personal misfortune, so much so that since I returned from the village I have been unable to continue writing about the Chaikovskii circle."[116]

Charushin constantly fretted about Kornilova-Moroz's situation and often asked about her in letters to Shebalina. Figner also tried to support her, for they were the closest of friends. As she wrote her, "The narrower the circle remaining the more my friends mean to me, and I think of you as a sister, or in some ways as even closer than that."[117] For it was "Sashechka" (as Figner called Alexandra Kornilova) who, just to be sure Figner would not be left on her own at that precarious time, had shared her humble quarters in Arkhangelsk province in Russia's far north after Figner's release from Shlisselburg. It was she who later accompanied Figner to Italy and Switzerland and was by her side in the 1930s past the death of her sister Evgeniia.

In his twilight years, Charushin had his son Vladimir nearby (see Figure 9.2), as well as his grandson Leonid (see Figure 9.3), named after Charushin's older son who had died in the Caucasus at the turn of the century. Nearby also was Ivan, who had managed to continue his career as an architect after 1917. Ivan designed a large hotel in the center of the city; many of its rooms, however, were given out to members of the secret police. According to his biographer, Ivan was able to see to fruition many projects of some architectural value, but nevertheless felt himself constricted by the dictates of the Stalinist era. He was also terribly distressed to see many of the churches he had designed torn down during the antireligious campaigns of the time.

Nikolai Charushin died on March 6, 1937, at the age of eighty-five. Ten years younger than his brother, Ivan had retired in 1937 and moved to Leningrad to be near his son, soon to be a well-known illustrator and author of children's books. During World War II and the siege of Leningrad, Ivan was evacuated to Kirov, where he died in 1945. Charushin's grandson Leonid also died of malnutrition as a result of that siege.

FIGURE 9.2.

Nikolai Charushin and his son Vladimir, 1930s.
Herzen Regional Library, Kirov

FIGURE 9.3.

Nikolai Charushin and his grandson Leonid, 1930s.
Herzen Regional Library, Kirov

NOTES

1. For a magisterial recent history of the OPK, see Mark Junge, *Revoliutsionery na pensii: vsesoiuznoe obshchestvo politkatorzhani ssyl'noposelentsev, 1921–1935* (Moscow: AIRO, 2015).
2. Based on a meticulous study of the journal *Katorga i Ssylka*, L. A. Kolesnikova identified 1149 works, written by 572 memoirists, ranging from fragmentary notes and reviews, introductions to publications of documents, obituaries, and full-blown memoirs and autobiographies. L.A. Kolesnikova, *Istoricheskie i istoriograficheskie problemy na stranitsakh zhurnala "Katorga i Ssylka"* (Nizhnii Novgorod: Gosudarstvennyi arkhitekturno-stroitel'nyi universitet, 2001), 4.
3. *Deiateli revoliutsionnogo dvizheniia v Rossii. Biobibliograficheskii slovar'. Ot predshestvennikov dekabristov do padeniia tsarizma*, ed. F. Kon, A. Shilov, B. Koz'min, V. Nevskii, (Moskva: Vsesouznoe obshchestvo politkatorzhan i ssyl'noposeletsev, 1929), 2:X.
4. TsIAM, f. 2241, op. 1, d. 138, l. 4.
5. Their marriage was formally registered in Viatka on March 1, 1932 (*Viatskii nabliudatel'*; December 14, 1991). Koshkareva, born in 1889 in the Viatka district, completed the Bestiuzhev Higher Education Women's Courses in St. Petersburg and taught literature in a secondary school. It is clear from the correspondence between Gogel' and Charushin that the former was also acquainted with Koshkareva (GAKO, f. P-1970, op.2, d.66, l.36). The Russian National Library in St. Petersburg holds an extensive correspondence she maintained with Charushin during a prolonged hospitalization in 1934—a correspondence that reveals a close emotional relationship (f. 1139, d.428 and d. 422: E.D. Petriaev).
6. Anna Yakimova to Nikolai Charushin, December 13, 1922 (RGALI, f. 1642, op. 1, d. 24, l. 1).
7. Larisa Chemodanova to Nikolai Charushin, January 10, 1920 (ibid., d. 66, l. 2).
8. *Deiateli revoliutsionnogo dvizheniia v Rossii. Biobibliograficheskii slovar'*, 295.
9. Ibid., 296.
10. A. N. Luppov, "O Viatskoi publichnoi biblioteke," *Gertsenka: Viatskie zapiski* 10 (2006): 3–13; Gogel' to Koni, January 11, 1918, *Gertsenka: Viatskie zapiski* 12 (2007): 14.
11. Despite this large influx of volumes, the future director Driagin bitingly describes a catastrophic lost opportunity during this period, when entire large school libraries and private collections were ransacked, plundered, damaged, and lost, partly because of the chaos and disorganization, but also because of thuggery, theft, and indifference on the part of ignorant local officials. K. V. Driagin, "Biblioteka za 10 let revoliutsii," *Gertsenka: Viatskie zapiski* 12 (2007): 28–29.
12. See the recent biography by V. Zharavin, *Aleksandr Lebedev–prosvetitel' i kraeved* (Kirov: GASPIKO, 2011). Lebedev also played a substantial role in establishing a local archive, preserving priceless government and private collections of documents, and sought to turn a much-coveted church refectory into a cultural center, and in so doing incurred the wrath of more powerful figures looking to appropriate that building for themselves.
13. N. D. Popyvanova, "A.V. Pallizen (1883–1943)–zaveduiushchaia mestnym (kraevedcheskim) otdelom Viatskoi biblioteki im. Gertsena," *Gertsenka: Viatskie zapiski* 16 (2009): 127–133.
14. Gogel' to Koni, January 11, 1918, *Gertsenka: Viatskie zapiski* 12 (2007): 14.
15. Ibid., 15.
16. Ibid., 16.
17. V. N. Kolupaeva, "K istorii Gertsenki (1917–1922)," *Gertsenka: Viatskie zapiski* 3 (2002): 13.
18. Driagin, "Biblioteka za 10 let revoliutsii," 34.

19. The practice of allowing books to be circulated had earlier been suspended, since no mechanisms for tracking or policies of enforcement were in place, which only aggravated the disorder caused by the lack of a systematic catalogue of holdings. Librarians blamed the "low culture" of the region's readership.

20. Kolupaeva, "K istorii Gertsenki," 12.

21. V. S. Zharavin, "A. S. Lebedev i Viatskaia publichnaia biblioteka," *Gertsenka: Viatskie zapiski* 2 (2001): 27. Lebedev followed the boxes of books to Moscow and apparently succeeded in preventing them from being opened and the books scattered to different sites until he could arrange for help from the higher-ups.

22. Driagin, "Biblioteka za 10 let revoliutsii," 27–40. About Driagin, see E. V. Lobanova, "K. V. Driagin: uchenyi, pedagog, lichnost'," *Gertsenka: Viatskie zapiski* 3 (2002): 175–181.

23. V. N. Kolupaeva, "'Vse s knigami i o knigakh'. E. V. Gogel' (1864–1955) i Viatskaia gubernskaia publichnaia biblioteka im. A. I. Gertsena," *Gertsenka: Viatskie zapiski* 11 (2007): 34.

24. A future director of the library, Stepan Shikhov, was, in 1936 and 1937, to suffer humiliation and dismissal, for failing to remove "harmful" literature from the library's collection, as well as for keeping on the library's staff "remnants of the old order" and even Trotskyites. See V. S. Zharavin, "Stepan Kuz'mich Shikhov–direktor Gertsenki," *Gertsenka: Viatskie zapiski* 18 (2010): 3–14.

25. Even before this, in 1920, the replacement of the extramural bureau of the Commissariat of Enlightenment (Narkompros) by the Glavpolitprosvet, the Herzen Library had been subordinated to that largely propagandist organization and, in 1922, turned over to the Gubono, soon losing its status as an academic institution

26. Elena Gogel' to Anatolii Koni, June 12, 1922, *Gertsenka: Viatskie zapiski* 12 (2007): 18.

27. V. S. Zharavin, "A. S. Lebedev i Viatskaia publichnaia biblioteka," *Gertsenka: Viatskie zapiski* 2 (2001): 29–30. Lebedev later left for Ekaterinburg, where, in 1937, he was arrested and executed.

28. GAKO, f. 2483, op. 1, d. 384, l. 19. See: Gali Chudova, "N.A. Charushin–bibliograph," *Sovetskaia bibliographiia* 4 (1984): 41–45; Valentin Sergeev, "N.A. Charushin i biblioteka imeni A.I. Gertsena," *Gertsenka: Viatskie zapiski* 1 (2000): 25–31.

29. Elena Gogel' to Nikolai Charushin, February 22, 1923, *Gertsenka: Viatskie zapiski* 12 (2007): 23.

30. Ivan Popov, *Zabytye stranitsy: Zapiski redaktora* (Irkutsk: Vostochno-sibirskoe knizhnoe izdatel'stvo, 1989), 13.

31. On *kraevedenie*, see Francine Hirsch, *Empire of Nations: Ethnographic Knowledge and the Making of the Soviet Union* (Ithaca, NY: Cornell University Press, 2005).

32. See Nikolai Charushin, "Organizatsiia kraevedcheskogo Otdela pri Viatskoi gubernskoi publichnoi biblioteke imeni Gertsena i zhelatel'naia postanovka sootvetstvuiushchikh otdelov v bibliotekakh na mestakh," *Gertsenka: Viatskie zapiski* 16 (2009): 21–28.

33. For a complete list, see *Nikolai Apollonovich Charushin (1851–1937). Bibliograficheskii ukazatel' ego rabot i literatury o ego zhizni i deiatel'nosti*, sostavitel' G. F. Chudova, (Kirov, typescript, 1989).

34. Gogel' to Koni, April 19, 1918, *Gertsenka: Viatskie zapiski* 12 (2007): 16–17.

35. Frolenko to Figner, July 3, 1920 (RGALI, f. 1185, op. 1, d. 805, l. 57).

36. Sergei Mikhailovich Kravchinskii Papers, box 1, Bakhmeteff Archive, Columbia University Rare Book and Manuscript Library, New York.

37. Ibid.
38. Vera Figner, *Zapechatlennyi Trud* (Moskva: Mysl', 1964), 1:42. To be sure, Figner's correspondence suggests that she had actually started writing earlier and had given lectures on the conditions of political prisoners, and written articles, with such frequency that she finally had to make a conscious choice about whether to concentrate solely on her memoirs or continue to give lectures.
39. Vera Figner to Mikhail Novorusskii, October 23, 1921 (RGALI, f. 1185, op. 1, d. 239, l. 185).
40. On the early struggles of the OPK with the Bolshevik authorities, see Iunge, *Revoliutsionery na pensii*, 96–152.
41. Mark Iunge, "Ugroza likvidatsii OPK v 1922 godu," *Vsesoiuznoe Obshchestvo politkatorzhan i ssyl'noposelentsev. Obrazovanie, razvitie, likvidatsiia. 1921–1935*. Materialy mezhdunarodnoi nauchnoi konferentsii (Moskva: Memorial–Zven'ia, 2004), 23–66.
42. By veterans of the revolutionary movement, including Vera Figner, Mikhail Shebalin, Anna Iakimova, Mikhail Sazhin, Mikhail Frolenko, Evgeniia Figner-Sazhina, Mikhail Ashenbrenner, Mikhail Chernavskii, Osip Aptekman, Anna Korba-Pribyleva, and others. Ibid., 72–74.
43. RGALI, f. 1642, op. 1, d. 77, l. 1.
44. RGALI, f. 1185, op. 1, d. 817, l. 5.
45. RGALI, f. 1642, op. 1, d. 77, l. 3 ob.
46. Ibid., d. 51, l. 1.
47. GARF. f. 112, op. 2, d. 2468.
48. RGALI, f. 1642, op.1, d. 51, l. 2 ob.
49. Ibid., l. 9.
50. Ibid., l. 12 ob.
51. Nikolai Charushin, *O dalekom proshlom* (Moskva: Mysl', 1973), 17.
52. Figner to Charushin, February 22, 1925 (RGALI, f. 1642, op.1, d. 77, l. 5.)
53. Charushin to Shebalina, March 3, 1927 (TsIAM, f. 2241, op. 1, d. 138, l. 1a). On the collective endeavors of the OPK to preserve the past, see Junge, *Revoliutsionery na pensii*, 206–226.
54. Shmuel Levin, "N.A. Charushin. O dalekom proshlom," *Istorik-Marksist* 4 (1927): 242.
55. Charushin to Kuvshinskaia, November 3, 1906 (RGALI, f.1642, d. 108. l. 11 ob.–12).
56. Charushin to Kuvshinskaia, November 17, 1906 (ibid., l. 16 ob.).
57. Charushin to Kuvshinskaia, February 10, 1906 (ibid., l. 41 ob.).
58. Nikolai Charushin, *O dalekom proshlom na Kare* (Moskva: Vsesouznoe Obshchestvo politkatorzhan i ssyl'noposeletsev, 1929), 8.
59. Charushin to Popov, April 24, 1924 (RGALI, f. 408, op. 1, d. 114, l. 1).
60. Charushin to Popov, December 26, 1929 (ibid., l. 15).
61. RGALI, f. 1642, op. 1, d. 51, l. 18 ob.
62. Charushin, *O dalekom proshlom* (1973), 18.
63. TsIAM, f. 2241, op. 1, d. 138, l. 2 ob.
64. RGALI, f. 1642, op. 1, d. 51, l. 15 ob.
65. Petr Uspenskii, a member of Nechaev's organization, had been sent to the Kara mines in 1875, where he intermingled with the Chaikovtsy until 1881, when he was transferred to the prison in the Lower Kara region, along with others who had been consigned to hard labor. There, because he was wrongly suspected of betraying his comrades who had been digging an escape tunnel, he was murdered. In his memoirs Charushin depicts Uspenskii's psychological state and his conflicts with the other prisoners, and searches for an explanation of what led

his comrades to falsely suspect Uspenskii of treason, leading to that tragic outcome. Writing about this episode was particularly painful to Charushin, for a number of reasons, and caused him great distress.

66. RGALI, f. 1642, op. 1, d. 51, l. 14–14 ob.
67. Vera Figner to Mikhail Novorusskii, May 17, 1920 (RGALI, f. 1185, op. 1, d. 239, l. 145).
68. RGALI, f. 1185, op. 4, d. 29, l. 1–2. For example, in considering the visit of the Stakhevich family (of which Vera Figner's sister Lydia was a member) to Troitskosavsk in 1894–1895, Charushin turned to a daughter in that family to resolve his own doubts about the exact times of their stay, since Mikhail Sazhin's recollections were different, and Charushin received a trove of information from her based on things she found in the Stakhevich family archive.
69. Strictly speaking, the three volumes of Charushin's memoirs were not published as a set (or listed as vols. 1–3); however, each was labeled *O dalekom proshlom* (and then given a separate subtitle: *Kruzhok Chaikovtsev*, *Na Kare*, and *Na poselenii*), and the narrative in each subsequent volume proceeded chronologically. We have taken the liberty of treating his memoirs as a multivolume unit, as Charushin himself did in his correspondence.
70. TsIAM, f. 2241, op. 1, d. 138, l. 1a.
71. Ibid., l. 2.
72. RGALI, f. 1642, op. 1, d. 72, l. 1, 4.
73. Shebalina to Charushin, n.d. (RGALI, f. 1642, op. 1, d. 82, l. 3).
74. RGALI, f. 1023, op. 1, d. 173, l. 85.
75. RGALI, f. 1642, op. 1, d. 8, l. 6.
76. Boris Koz'min, "N.A. Charushin. O dalekom proshlom," *Pechat' i revolutsiia* 13 (1927): 157. Koz'min was on the editorial board of OPK press and *Katorga i Ssylka*
77. TsIAM, f. 2241, op. 1, d. 138, l. 1a.
78. *Pechat' i revolutsiia* 1 (1926): 189.
79. Ibid., 1 (1923): 184.
80. 1 Figner, *Zapechatlennyi Trud* (Moskva: Mysl', 1964), 1:34–35.
81. RGALI, f. 1642, op. 1, d. 51, l. 4 ob, 23 ob.-24.
82. Shmuel Levin, "N. A. Charushin. O dalekom proshlom," *Istorik-Marksist* 4 (1927): 243.
83. G. Arkad'ev, "Za bol'shevistskuiu perestroiku. K voprosu o rabote izdatel'stva byvshikh politkatorzhan," *Bor'ba klassov* 6 (1933): 130.
84. TsIAM, f. 2241, op. 1, d. 138, l. 1a.
85. Ibid., l. 3.
86. Ibid., l. 5 ob.
87. Ibid., l. 6.
88. RGALI, f. 408, op. 1, d. 114, l. 17.
89. Sandra Pujals, *When Giants Walked the Earth: The Society of Former Political Prisoners and Exiles of the Soviet Union, 1921–1935* (PhD diss., Georgetown University, 1999).
90. G. Arkad'ev, "Za bol'shevistskuiu perestroiku. K voprosu o rabote izdatel'stva byvshikh politkatorzhan." *Bor'ba klassov* 6 (1933): 129.
91. Tezisy k 50-letiiu 'Narodnoi voli,'" *Pravda*, April 9, 1930, 4.
92. See George M. Enteen, *The Soviet Scholar-Bureaucrat: M. N. Pokrovskii and the Society of Marxist Historians* (University Park: Pennsylvania State University Press, 1978), 122–128; John Barber, *Soviet Historians in Crisis, 1928–1932* (New York: Holmes and Meier, 1981), 80–99; J. Frankel, "Party Genealogy and the Soviet Historians (1920–1938)," *Slavic Review* 4, no. 25 (1966): 563–603. Our thanks to Dr. Larry Holmes for suggesting these sources.

93. Charushin to Popov, February 15, 1929 (RGALI, f. 408, op. 1, d. 114, l. 10).
94. On this, see Junge, *Revoliutsionery na pensii*, 364–427.
95. P. Kazanskii, "Bol'she bol'shevistskoi bditel'nosti," *Bor'ba klassov* 5 (1933): 122–128.
96. The criticism of the journal began appearing as early as September 1930 in the journal *Proletarskaia revolutsiia*. See Sandra Dahlke, *Individuum und Herrschaft im Stalinismus: Emel'jan Jaroslavskij (1878–1943)* (Munich: R. Oldenbourg Verlag, 2010), 194–206.
97. GARF, f. 533, op. 2, d. 2387, l. 88.
98. Ibid., l. 90.
99. *Tolkovyi slovar' russkogo iazyka*, red. D.N. Ushakov (Moskva: Sovetskaia entsiklopediia, 1938), 2:414.
100. RGALI, f. 1185, op. 1, d. 85, l. 2 ob.
101. See Junge, *Revoliutsionery na pensii*, 442, 494. Lynne Hartnett wrongly claims that Figner never joined the OPK. See *The Defiant Life of Vera Figner: Surviving the Russian Revolution* (Bloomington: Indiana University Press, 2014), 254.
102. Junge, *Revoliutsionery na pensii*, 468–516.
103. *Vsesoiuznoe Obshchestvo politkatorzhan i ssyl'noposelentsev. Obrazovanie, razvitie, likvidatsiia. 1921–1935*, 222–316.
104. Shebalina to Charushin, April 28 (RGALI, f. 1642, op. 1, d. 82, l. 7).
105. TsIAM, f. 2241, op. 1, d. 138, l. 1a.
106. Ibid., ll. 3, 4, 5 ob.
107. GASPIKO, f. 45, op. 1, d. 232, ll. 154, 290.
108. He submitted his resignation on January 15, 1930. A copy of the original letter is in *Gertsenka: Viatskie zapiski* 17 (2010): 6–8.
109. RGALI, f. 1023, op. 1, d. 761, l. 1.
110. Ibid., l. 2.
111. RGALI, f. 1023, op. 1, d. 761, l. 2.
112. Ibid., l. 14.
113. GAKO, f. 1965, op. 1, d. 2, ll. 16, 22–23.
114. RGALI, f. 1023, op. 1, d. 761, l. 16.
115. Kornilova-Moroz to Figner, August 17, 1934 (RGALI, f. 1185, op. 1, d. 602, l. 16).
116. Kornilova-Moroz to Charushin, April 18, 1933 (RGALI, f. 1642, op. 1, d. 51, ll. 29, 30 ob.).
117. Figner to Kornilova-Moroz, undated (RGALI, f. 1185, op. 1, d. 237, l. 9).

In Search of the Real Charushin in the Perestroika Era

If we look at the big picture, how one remembers Charushin comes down to two different views of our history as a whole.

—Valentin Sergeev to Gali Chudova, February 17, 1991

Personally I think very highly of Charushin despite his Populist worldview.

—Gali Chudova, letter, May 26, 1988

EMERGING FROM THE DUSTBIN OF HISTORY

With the passing of Charushin and the last survivors of his revolutionary cohort in the 1930s the generation of the 1870s departed this life to become a part of history. Or so they hoped; they had made every effort in their last years to ensure that the memory of their deeds was preserved. It reality, however, their movement was threatened with oblivion. As Leon Trotskii had thundered in a speech aimed at the Mensheviks at the Second Congress of Soviets—when they fatefully left the hall in protest against the Bolshevik seizure of power in Petrograd—"Your role in history has been played out, so be on your way into the dustbin of history where you now belong."[1] By the 1930s, the striving to send the Populists in the same direction was evident in the accusations directed at them of the errors of their ways, their petty-bourgeois and then even counter-revolutionary views. Now it was no longer necessary to struggle against the old Populists—better to forget them entirely! The political regime needed its own heroes, which they wished to craft themselves. At its worst the Populists became "enemies of the people" in Stalin's Russia.

The "Thaw" in Soviet life under Khrushchev and move away from Stalin's notorious Short Course of History of the Communist Party (first published in 1938) after the Twentieth Communist Party Congress led also to a re-examination of the Populist legacy. In a lead article in the prominent journal *Voprosy Istorii* (*Issues in History*) it was admitted that many Marxists had begun their political lives as Populists, that it was lamentable that historians had neglected the contribution made by the revolutionaries of the 1870s and 1880s and ignored the continuity in the evolution of the revolutionary movement. In so doing—the article continued—they had forgotten the very words of Lenin to that effect.[2] Soon afterward followed an article by P. S. Tkachenko[3] calling on historians to return to the study of Populism, taking off from the work done in the first decade of Soviet power before the onset of Stalinism.

In the next few years a stream of works on the history of Populism emerged, with contributions made by historians such as Boris Itenberg, Boris Koz'min, Shmuel Levin (two elderly historians who had been involved in evaluating Charushin's memoir in the 1920s), Vasilii Antonov, and Mikhail Sedov. Nikolai Troitskii, who himself made a significant contribution to the history of the topic, wrote, "Needless to say, not all scholars immediately rejected the basic postulates put forth in the *Short Course*.... It took long, frequent and heated discussions to make progress after 1957; such conversations took place at the Institute of History of the USSR Academy of Sciences on several occasions between 1957 and 1966 and simultaneously in the journals *Voprosy Literatury* (*Issues in Literature*; 1960) and *Istoriia SSSR* (*History of the USSR*) (1961–1963)."[4] A major outpouring of research followed on topics such as the place Populists should occupy in the Soviet pantheon of revolutionary heroes and whether or not the two decades after the Emancipation of 1861 could be treated as one generation. If the latter were the case, the revolutionary Populists would be linked with Chernyshevskii and Herzen—two towering figures in the Soviet hagiography of opposition to autocracy who had survived the depredations of Stalinism ideology. Discussion also continued about the purported shortcomings of the Populist movement.[5]

In the 1970s a political "freeze" set in once again concerning research on Populism. Troitskii, who himself continued to write prolifically on the topic,[6] later noted, "Publishing houses were reluctant to accept manuscripts on this theme, and when they did they demanded that the word "Populism" be removed from the title. Instead, in order to avoid the censor, revolutionaries of that generation were to be called *"raznochintsy,"* a term denoting commoners who didn't fit into Imperial Russia's societal categories and therefore left their specific political leanings undefined."[7] At the same time, perhaps by the force of inertia, a string of biographies and anthologies of the works of Populists continued to appear in print. In 1973, a new and richly annotated edition of the first volume of Charushin's memoirs was published with an introduction by Itenberg. In it Itenberg called the Populists ideologists of peasant democracy and noted the admirable moral standards of that generation of oppositionists, their readiness to sacrifice themselves, and their fortitude in the struggle against the autocracy. An appendix was added containing an essay by Levin and his correspondence with Charushin from the 1920s. In those letters, Levin inquired about the political views of the Chaikovskii circle and, especially, the influence of the anarchist Bakunin. Itenberg noted that the topics had not lost their timeliness in the 1970s and that polemics around publishing a new edition of Charushin's memoirs were themselves interesting both from a historiographic perspective but also as a commentary on the present.[8]

Soon after the republication of Charushin's memoirs, local historians in Kirov considered ways to call attention to his life and work. At the center of this effort was the Herzen Library—the very same place where Charushin had spent his last years as a librarian. There, on March 28, 1975, a session of the local book club dedicated to Charushin was organized. The historian Valentin Sergeev told the well-attended gathering about Charushin's activities in Viatka, and the venerable local chronicler Evgenii Petraiev, who had almost single-handedly reconstructed the cultural life of Viatka in the nineteenth and twentieth centuries, discussed Charushin's length stay in Siberia, where Petraiev himself had spent an extended interval. Indicative of the continuing shadow looming over the study of Populism were the emphases on holding this meeting innocuously as a "library session" and the wording of the announcement for the event that identified Charushin only as a "book-lover and bibliographer."

However, in December 1976, when the library organized a meeting within the rubric of its traditional "Thursday local history evenings" in order to commemorate the 125th anniversary of Charushin's birth, it ventured to call Charushin a "prominent representative of revolutionary Populism and a progressive societal and cultural figure of the Viatka region." The invitation to this gathering included a brief summary of Charushin's life, which mentioned his revolutionary activities in St. Petersburg, exile to Siberia and cultural endeavors there, work as a photographer, participation in the work of the zemstvo, the founding of the newspaper *Viatskaia Rech'*, and work in the library after 1917, as well as his membership in the Society of Former Political Prisoners and Exiles. No mention was made, however, of his whereabouts during the events of 1917. Noteworthy, too, was the fact that two figures highly respected in Kirov—Petriaev and the librarian Gali Chudova—were identified as the authors of this short "blurb." This was likely done to add weight to the assertion that Charushin was a "prominent representative" of the city and in anticipation of objections to this characterization of a figure whose legacy was still contested.

And indeed far from everybody was happy with the text or the event itself. A local historian from the Kirov Pedagogical Institute, by the name of Sukhodoev, protested against attempts to restore the good name of a figure he personally found disreputable. However, one of his colleagues and a revered historian of the Viatka region, Anatolii Emmausskii,[9] stood up at the meeting and challenged Sukhodoev to provide documentation of the charges he had made against Charushin, something the complainant was unable to do. Sukhodoev continued his campaign, however, by writing to the editors of the *Soviet Historical Encyclopedia* urging that in its forthcoming new edition the brief entry on Charushin present him more critically or be deleted entirely. Chudova later recalled that in the late 1970s Sukhodoev and another figure, Komarov,[10] had filed a protest with the local party authorities against the Herzen Library for "spreading propaganda about Charushin," who was "an enemy of the people, provocateur and dissimulator." The then secretary of the regional Communist

Party had called together local historians to consider those charges, and the commission declared them unfounded.

A few words about Gali Fedorovna Chudova (see Figure 10.1) are called for, for she plays a major role in the struggle over defining the Charushin's legacy in the late Soviet era. She was born in Tula, just south of Moscow in 1904, studied at a gymnasium in St. Petersburg, and left the city with her family for Samara on the Volga in 1919. There in 1925 she began working as a librarian and continued her studies as the Moscow Library Institute, but completed her degree only after World War II. The war found her in Kaluga on the direct path of the German invasion. She was evacuated along with hundreds of thousands of others to the Viatka/Kirov region, where she worked on a collective farm in the countryside until

FIGURE 10.1.

Gali Chudova (1970s). Herzen Regional Library, Kirov

being offered a position in Kirov at the Herzen Library, there rapidly rising to a position of prominence. Retiring on a pension in 1960, she continued to spend virtually every day in the library for the next thirty years, as Charushin had done before her, focusing her efforts on bibliographic compilations. At the same time, she gave hundreds of public lectures and endeavored to promote "the cause of the book" in Kirov. Among her many bibliographic works were the completion of Charushin's monumental but unfinished index to the newspapers *Viatskaia Rech'* (a titanic ten-volume effort rendering visible the daily life of an entire province over more than a decade); a bibliography of all publications by and on Charushin himself; an article in the journal *Sovetskaia Bibliografiia* (*Soviet Bibliography*) describing in detail Charushin's contribution to knowledge of the region. Chudova also published a volume on the history of local studies in Viatka and left behind two unpublished volumes of her memoirs. Regardless of political persuasion, Chudova was drawn to her predecessor in the library because of their kindred efforts in the areas of cultural promotion, local studies, and bibliography. But soon she would be forced to articulate her views on his opposition to Bolshevism.

PERESTROIKA MEMORY WARS

Soon after Mikhail Gorbachev assumed the post of General Secretary of the Communist Party in the Soviet Union and introduced the policies of Glasnost and Perestroika, interpretations of the past became hotly contested. The "blank spots" or silences in the official rendition of the twentieth century were soon filled in as archives were opened and collections of previously unseen documents were published. New perspectives on events, a new emphasis on the roles of individuals in history—good and bad—and the question of alternative outcomes to the past were forthcoming.

Many believed that a fresh examination of the past was vital to the advancement of democracy, bitter medicine needed to cure the country of the effects of totalitarianism, and the only way to renew the country's vitality. Others however found such endeavors disturbing, traumatic, if not traitorous. One side sought to defend the heroic narrative of the

Soviet experience that was firmly entrenched in officialdom and with deep roots in the popular consciousness as well. As evidence of this we need only recall the stormy public reaction at a crucial moment in 1988 to the letter published in a prominent newspaper (and probably initiated by high-ranking conservative Party politicians) by an irate Leningrad chemistry teacher, Nina Andreeva, "I Cannot Forsake My Principles."[11] Andreeva expressed consternation and apprehension that Soviet youth might be captivated by the new "nihilistic" interpretations of the past stressing Stalin's purges as well as the pervasive fear coursing through Soviet society. She fretted about the damage done to the "founders of socialism." She criticized the widespread deviation from a "class-based Party position" in the treatment of history, lamented the corrosive influence on the young of the popular plays of Mikhail Shatrov and works on Stalinism by Viktor Suvorov, and saw the perfidious hand of the West working together with Soviet emigrés to undermine the Soviet system.

Others vehemently disagreed and sought to restore to their rightful place figures whom Soviet history textbooks had consigned to oblivion, to do away with ideological dogma, to point to the alternative paths not taken at crucial moments, and above all to defend pluralistic interpretations of history. The publication in 1989 of a volume entitled "Historians Argue Their Case" was indicative of the efforts being made by scholars to rethink crucial periods and events in their own history. Yet at the same time, this rethinking was still—much as in the aftermath of the Twentieth Party Congress two decades earlier—to take place within a "Leninist" framework, meaning by that the relative freedom of interpretation enjoyed during the 1920s without challenging the very foundations of Communist Party rule. The positions taken in the ongoing debates over history became a litmus test of one's views on political events underway in the Soviet Union in the Gorbachev era.

These debates unfolded in the capital cities—drawing the most attention of foreign observers—but were equally heated in the country's regions, including Kirov. There on May 26, 1988, an article signed by L. I. Zhdanov, deputy chair of the local board of the Society for the Preservation of Historical and Cultural Monuments appeared in *Kirovskaya Pravda*[12] noting that the Kirov planning commission had scheduled demolition of Charushin's dilapidated residence in the middle of the city to make way for developers. However an amateur local historian by the name of Alexander Reva had gone to the municipal soviet asking instead that the home be preserved as an historical monument with a plaque honoring Charushin. Because, as Zhdanov put it, Charushin was a "remarkable personality, if one both complicated and contradictory," a follow-up meeting of the Society for the Preservation of Monuments was called to discuss the topic. This meeting revealed sharply polarized views and its members issued an open invitation to submit opinions to the newspaper about what to do with the house and about the name of Charushin himself.[13]

On June 16, *Kirovskaia Pravda* published a passionate letter from Reva stressing Charushin's authenticity, service to the people through the zemstvo, and founding of "what was virtually the most democratic newspaper in Russia."[14] For Reva it was of utmost importance that Charushin's home had been "an unofficial center for the forces of democracy," open to all comers in Viatka. In the same note and with the same overtones he argued that whatever others might think Charushin "never wavered, never repented of his convictions" after 1917. Although one could understand why some might have been angry at him in 1917, today (Reva concluded) given the subsequent history of the country, any such attacks on him could only be labeled obscurantism. In this portrait, the currents of the Perestroika era are evident in the striving to democratize the country and to connect the past and the present by identifying alternatives to the Bolshevik pleiad of heroes. Reva's characterization of Charushin as a "knightly figure" portrayed him as a standard bearer of the intelligentsia, a heroic figure, and a democrat in both actions and beliefs.

On July 28, Chudova weighed in with her own letter, drawing on her familiarity with Charushin's life and works to make her case. She pointed to his memoir as a classic highly regarded by scholars; to his "contribution to the cultural life of the province" through his work in the zemstvo, as well as in the famine relief efforts; to his "progressive newspaper" and "struggle for freedom of the press"; to the distinguished work he had done in Siberia as a photographer and an organizer of museums and libraries; and to his monumental contribution to the Herzen Library as a bibliographer. Acknowledging that Charushin had dropped his straightforward opposition to the autocracy during World War I, Chudova sought to justify that choice by implicitly appealing to a deeply patriotic Soviet audience for whom the memory of a more recent German invasion was still fresh—resistance to invaders of the homeland transcended party loyalties. She argued that it was his belief in the inevitability of a peasant revolution that, though misguided, explained his inability to see the "inevitability" of the Bolshevik Revolution. On balance then, she urged that a memorial plaque be placed on the home of his birthplace in Orlov, where such a plaque already existed for his brother Ivan, and that "the people of Kirov should never forget Charushin." However, she concluded that unlike others from Viatka who had risen to national stature, his cultural contributions had been only regional, and as a Populist he had been among the "modest and self-sacrificing" rank-and-file; therefore, she believed there was no reason to save the home on MOPR[15] Street in Viatka from the wrecking ball.[16]

We see that while Reva and Chudova differed on the virtues of preserving Charushin's residence, their views coincided in their high estimation of him and on the need to memorialize his name. But they came to that conclusion from different angles: Reva valued Charushin's contribution in political terms, as an advocate of democracy and freedom—like, he surely had in mind, the intelligentsia in the Perestroika era—while Chudova lauded his contribution to the region's progress in the area of culture.

Such views did not go unchallenged. The fireworks began on August 25 with a letter submitted to the newspaper by Komarov and Sukhodoev—the same two who had a decade earlier objected to commemorating Charushin's legacy. Titling it "In Violation of the Truth" (*Vopreki pravde*), they criticized Reva and Chudova for failing to read documents through a "party and class" lens and accused Charushin of concealing the truth about his life in his memoirs. In particular, they asserted his family had not struggled after the death of his father for their mill had continued to bring in profits and in 1874, after Charushin's incarceration, his mother had written him that she "had no material needs." Charushin, they wrote, had been a revolutionary for all of two years and had then repented before the Tsar. During his exile, he and Kuvshinskaia had tutored the jail commandant's children; in 1884, his civil status had been restored—at a time of intense police repression; he was issued a passport that contained no mention of his arrests, and was then granted the right to travel as a photographer to China. In general, they claimed, his photography business had brought him big financial dividends. Returning to Viatka, he had "vacillated between the [liberal] Kadets and SRs," and "taken advantage of the 1905 Revolution to enhance the power of the bourgeoisie." Furthermore, he "had exploited the people's trust" to get them to contribute to his newspaper. And why was it that several contributors to and editors of *Viatskaia Rech'* had been persecuted, but not Charushin himself? Could this have been a coincidence? What is worse, they opined, he had tried to undermine the appeal of Bolshevism, personally spreading dirt about Lenin in his newspaper throughout 1917. At the October 27 session of the zemstvo assembly immediately following the Bolshevik Revolution, he "had proposed the formation" of a "Supreme Soviet" to become the "general staff of the counterrevolution," which sought to forcibly disband the local military unit; was instrumental in organizing a "drunken pogrom" in Viatka to confuse the public, and set out to organize a "[counterrevolutionary] White Guard." When Bolshevik power was proclaimed in Viatka on December 1, this committee cut off electricity, water, and the telegraph to the city, and organized a strike of public organizations and employees. Citing local Communist Party verification commissions from the 1920s, the authors challenged Charushin's claim that (after his fourth arrest by the Bolsheviks) he had been released by General Bliukher. In his later life, he had "taken advantage" of young historians such as Levin (who had corresponded extensively with Charushin and then written a favorable review of his memoirs) distorting his past in his correspondence with them. We also learn that Charushin had "exploited" his acquaintance with 'members' of the Society of Former Political Prisoners and Exiles ("he was never a member")[17] to receive a personal pension, which the Central Pension Commission of the Soviet state withdrew in 1935 after reviewing a letter from the Kirov City Welfare Board. Komarov and Sukhodoev concluded their testimony by noting that "we have only scratched the surface of the truth about Charushin here."[18]

The letter was sprinkled with terms that were familiar to those who had lived through the 1930s: Charushin was a "renegade," a "provocateur." That it drew from secret police (NKVD) files is likely, because the language closely replicates denunciations of that period combining accusations of political misdeeds with those of deceit, moral degeneration, profiteering at the expense of the people, and false self-representation of one's personal and political history. For the Russian reader in particular, the vocabulary they deployed to make their point is reminiscent of denunciations that can be found in the archives of the NKVD. Chudova made the same point when she stated that Komarov and Sukhodoev's letter reminded her of 1937, when her father along with hundreds of thousands of others had been arrested. The entire thrust of the attack was to prove that Charushin was from early in his life wily, devious, self-promoting, and an opportunistic counterrevolutionary. That this was a smear campaign of half-truths, distortions and outright fabrications should be clear to the reader of this book.[19]

For the next eight months, the newspaper was silent on the issue of saving or tearing down Charushin's home. Chudova however was not silent. Despite her advanced age and fragile health and outraged by developments, she went to the archives to find evidence contradicting the charges made in "In Violation of the Truth" and then wrote a long second letter to the *Kirovskaia Pravda* refuting her opponents' arguments line by line. When her letter was not published, she wrote increasingly angry follow-up notes to the editors wanting to know why the newspaper had fallen silent on the issue. She emphasized her lifelong membership in the Communist Party and sought to influence a party newspaper by citations from the articles and speeches of Mikhail Gorbachev at the time calling for "taking clear positions on issues."[20] In all likelihood Chudova regarded Perestroika to be an extension of the Khrushchev Thaw, referring to it as a "revolutionary *renewal*," a term Gorbachev had himself used to describe the program in his first year as general secretary.

Then on September 7 she wrote a letter to distinguished historian of the Populist movement Troitskii asking him to defend Charushin.[21] In response he and three other historians (Itenberg, Antonov, and Sedov) sent a letter, dated December 27, 1988, to the Kirov regional party committee in which they claimed that Sukhodoev and Komarov poorly understood the history of the revolutionary movement and "had no qualms about fabricating the facts." They, too spoke of Charushin's "errors and meanderings" in the aftermath of the October Revolution, "which, by the way, the Soviet authorities had forgiven." These distinguished historians asserted that "such errors and deviations should not be allowed to cloud Charushin's contribution to the revolutionary movement." In their view, Populism was indeed a predecessor of Social Democracy, rather than a wrongful departure from the true path. This was "irrefutable and universally recognized in competent circles," as was Charushin's loyalty to the Soviet system after the revolution. Without a doubt, they insisted, the name of Charushin deserved to be memorialized.²²

Another figure speaking up in defense of Charushin at the time was Valentin Dmitrievich Sergeev (1940–2006) (see Figure 10.2). He had grown up in Charushin's own hometown Orlov in a family of teachers, doctors, zemstvo employees, and priests (one of his relatives had apparently crossed paths with Charushin). As a youth, he had suffered through the times of dire scarcity following World War II and had first learned of Stalin's crimes at the age of thirteen, when family relatives returned from the Gulag. Completing his undergraduate degree at the Kirov Pedagogical Institute in 1964 he served in the army and then worked at the museum of local history before writing a graduate-level dissertation in the 1970s on the subject of

FIGURE 10.2.

Valentin Sergeev, 1970s.
Herzen Regional Library, Kirov

the *raznochintsy* (again, the code word at the time for Populists).[23] He was then invited to teach at his alma mater, the Kirov Pedagogical Institute. But his stay there was a rocky one: according to archivist Vladimir Zharavin,[24] Sergeev never fully realized his potential as a scholar because he was hounded out of his position at the Pedagogical Institute by the older Stalinists there, who made life difficult for him at every turn. This led to his departure in 1980 for Petropavlovsk in distant Kamchatka. Later, Sergeev wrote Chudova that when he had received a letter from the Pedagogical Institute he couldn't bring himself to open it, "I had such painful memories, especially about my department, even though there were many fine people at the institute as a whole."[25] Once he became eligible for a pension in 1995, he returned to Kirov. In order to augment his meager pension in those difficult times he continued to teach at a number of institutions rather than devote himself full time to archival research and scholarship.

Zharavin describes Sergeev as a warm human being who, however, was never inclined to conceal his beliefs. He was close to some scholars in Kazan', especially the charismatic and quite unorthodox Grigorii Wol'fson, who is much venerated today by a younger generation of Kazan' academics who studied under him. Speaking to one of the authors of this book, Sergeev's son Alexander rejected the notion that his father had considered himself a representative of the "sixties generation" (the Thaw era) in the Soviet Union. The son generously provided the authors autobiographical sketches his father had written about his childhood, family, and acquaintanceship with nearby relatives of Charushin. These notes vividly testify to Sergeev's free and independent spirit but indeed do not suggest that he was a dissident. Still, all accounts describe him as a free-thinker, a nonconformist, and someone who though soft-spoken and generous to others, refused to spout Party dogma. And others do remember him as a man of the sixties who could never reconcile himself to the bureaucracy or the Communist regime as a whole, and who read to his close friends, out loud and with gusto, passages from the works of Alexander Solzhenitsyn and Vasilii Aksenov.[26] His political convictions are also suggested by a photograph taken in July 2006, a month before he died of a heart attack, in which he is standing in Kirov's central square holding high a placard calling for restoring the city's earlier appellation, Viatka (recall Charushin's distress in 1934 when the city was renamed after a communist noteworthy).

Chudova had been keeping Sergeev posted on events in 1988, and at some point he took to writing his own refutation of the charges against Charushin. In an early draft of a letter he sent to Chudova he made no apologies for Charushin. Instead of discussing whether Charushin's "sins" were balanced out by his "contributions" Sergeev lauded his resistance to the October Revolution and (like Reva) called him prescient for anticipating what was to come. Sergeev approvingly quoted Charushin's description of the Bolsheviks as "a plague, a bacchanalia [of violence] launched against the peasantry, an assault on the gene pool of the Russian nation [a notion current in the Gorbachev era], a mockery of the historical past, a sullying of democracy leaving no guarantees of a person's dignity or even life."[27] Yet Charushin was never a counterrevolutionary, for he had never sided with the White movement, never sought to emigrate and was, Sergeev insisted, an "old revolutionary," a "revolutionary democrat," a "revolutionary propagandist."[28] Neither did Sergeev mince his words when it came to the essay by Sukhodoev and Komarov, which also reminded him of the era of the purges, "So what is the period we are living through—is it 1988 or 1938?"[29]

Despite their shared repugnance at the accusations leveled against Charushin, the different perspectives of Sergeev and Chudova are evident in their treatment of his behavior in 1917 and his stance toward the Bolsheviks. For Chudova, his rejection of the Bolshevik seizure of power was a cardinal error, a serious misstep stemming from his Populist affiliations and non-Marxist convictions. As she put it, "Personally I hold Charushin in high regard *despite* his Populist worldview, which caused him to go astray in 1917."[30] In her opinion he could be *forgiven* for his sins because his opposition was only in word rather than in deed. She argued that Charushin should not be blamed just because people around him "took advantage of his good name" as a public activist, newspaper publisher, and venerated Populist.

Was Chudova's perspective on Charushin merely a tactical move governed by the somewhat controlled discourse of the time of Perestroika? Was she parsing her words when she spoke of "missteps" rather than guilt? After all, the phrase she used, *zabluzhdenie* ("straying off track"), was part and parcel of official Communist Party rhetoric, sprinkled throughout the texts of party congresses and resolutions to signify shortcomings but not "crimes," such as were perpetuated by "enemies of the people." However, by all accounts of people who knew her well, she was part of a generation of highly intelligent and ethically honest true believers in the mission of the Communist Party. In her letter to the regional party committee she pointed out, "I have been a member of the Communist Party of the USSR for forty years now, and never in that time have I dishonored that name." Like others she believed that a "bright future" for the country could be ensured if only the doctrine of Marxism-Leninism were truly followed in the spirit of the Twentieth Party Congress and "unsullied by the excesses of Stalinism."[31] Both the tone of her letter and the nature of her evaluation of Charushin, whether it concerned his youthful participation in the revolutionary movement or his later "errors," seek to validate him from an "authentically" communist perspective—this was no tactical positioning. Of course, being a bibliographer and *kraeved* herself, she could not but admire his contributions in that area in the 1920s. All of this compelled her to make peace with his unfortunate straying from the true path in 1917 and to speak up in his defense when the time came.

Sergeev also highly valued Charushin's cultural endeavors. But his unpublished letters in 1988 make it clear that his views on Populism and Charushin's role in history differed from those of Chudova. If for Chudova the Populists were the genuine *predecessors* of the Social Democrats, for Sergeev, they represented a path not taken, an unfulfilled *alternative* to the trials and tribulations brought on by Soviet power. "Alternatives" in history were also an integral part of the discourse during Perestroika, as revisionists sought to tear down the rigid historical determinism of the official ideology. In Sergeev's own scholarship he drew vivid portraits of the provincial revolutionary intelligentsia in the 1860s and 1870s, emphasizing their high moral standards, the fervor of their convictions, and their devotion to the cause. Here we see just how embedded Sergeev also was in his own times; like others, he was seeking what was "authentic" and "genuine" in a Soviet society in which words and deeds had become so disconnected in public discourse, and falsity seemed ubiquitous.

On March, 19, 1989, still waiting for a resolution to the conflict over commemorating Charushin's name, Chudova wrote a dejected letter to Sergeev, in which she at the same time tried to boost his spirits while in "exile" by comparing him to one of his mentors, the *kraeved* Petriaev, "Ruefully, the situation faced by Viatka local historians is not an enviable one. Earlier E. D. Petraiev had to battle against fraudulent local historians... but to no avail, for mediocrity always prevails. I really empathize with your position as a 'refugee,' but will you be able to return home?"[32]

Finally, in the spring of 1989, after more letters from Chudova urging the local party committee to resolve the issue (letter writing was a venerable practice in Soviet society, replacing more open modes of communication) the newspaper published the conclusions of a commission established to review Charushin's legacy.[33] Noting both Chudova's and Sergeev's unpublished letters ("which were in the briefcase of the editor"), the commission concluded that Charushin's revolutionary credentials were genuine as were his contributions to the public life of Viatka. Yet, as they put it, "Life is what it is, never black and white," and Charushin had "made serious mistakes" and also "truly" taken part in counterrevolutionary activity. The commission concluded that the idea of memorializing this local figure "was valid, but only if proper account were taken of both his real contributions and those errors and missteps which he took."[34]

This was clearly a measured compromise, probably satisfying nobody, but understandable coming from a party commission and given the times. Why, they thought, make a bad situation worse? To us today the language that Charushin made "serious mistakes" is dated or entirely alien. But it was a strategic term used by all sides at the time as Perestroika lurched forward and backward, and the fate of the country's future—as well as its past—hung in the balance. As we have seen, all the participants in this debate resorted to the term ("mistakes"), although for Reva it was a case of "well, he might have made mistakes, or maybe not, it is beside the point."[35] Sergeev also employed the word "mistakes" in the letter he sent to the authorities, but it had clearly been added to make his strong statements more palatable to the authorities, for it is missing in the draft of that letter held in the Herzen library.

The commission's conclusions were not the end of the story, for Chudova was clearly not satisfied with the outcome. As late as September 1989 she suspected that efforts to write about Charushin were still being hampered by underhanded means.[36] Frustrated at her inability to find a local publisher willing to produce biographies of outstanding Viatka culture bearers and determined to bring the Charushin episode to the national stage, she wrote to the editors of the prominent historical journal *Voprosy*

FIGURE 10.3.

"Lenin Street, 1990." (Former Offices of Viatskaia Rech').
Painting by Viktor Kharlov (1949–). Used with permission.

Istorii, in Moscow, hoping that it would commission an article about the debate over his legacy. The editors acknowledged the significance of the topic but replied that since the issue had already been resolved by commission's report such an article would be superfluous. Instead, they suggested that she turn to local publishers. She apparently replied that this would be difficult (her letter is not in the file, so her explanation is not clear); *Voprosy Istorii* once again expressed its regrets and also cautioned her against seeking other interested publishers in Moscow, most of which were controlled by reactionaries, for "any contact with such organizations could only besmirch a person's good name."[37]

Disappointed at the failure to convince the editors of *Voprosy Istorii*, she must have felt uplifted in 1990 upon receiving a letter from Sergeev in

Kamchatka saying that he had finally sat down to write a biography of Charushin.[38] For her Charushin was a man "who had dedicated his entire life to the goals of freedom and democracy, enlightenment and cultural uplift."[39] She had to have been delighted that Sergeev would have the final word. After returning to Kirov in 1995, he completed a short volume (published locally in 2001) and participated in numerous events at the library honoring both Nikolai and Ivan Charushin. In 1998, he wrote the script for a film directed by M. Dokhmatskaya[40] entitled (in Russian) *Nikolai Charushin: History Seen Through an Individual Life*. The film portrays Charushin as already being disillusioned with socialism by the time he returned from exile in Siberia at the turn of the century. The script homes in on the events of 1917, highlighting Charushin's resistance to the Bolsheviks and his negative views on the newly established post-revolutionary order. It argues that the Bolsheviks had little support in Viatka and had managed to seize power only with the help of outside forces. Charushin is presented as a chivalrous human being who had devoted his entire life to the welfare of the people but who became a victim first of the autocratic, and then the soviet systems. He emerges from the film not so much a revolutionary but rather as a freedom fighter, above party or ideology, isolated but never broken morally.

IN SEARCH OF THE REAL CHARUSHIN

Was Charushin a genuine revolutionary, and does anyone care? Like the language used in the debate about Charushin's legacy during Perestroika the question sounds odd to the ear today. But to the early Populists it was everything and at the end of the nineteenth century it remained—along with the newly emergent professional identities available to the educated class—important to them. After the revolution, being labeled a revolutionary of the tsarist era was central to one's social status, not to mention employment opportunities or access to a pension.[41] At the same time, it was a plastic identity the meaning of which changed with the times. As for Charushin, once formulated in his youth, it remained a constant. For our purposes, it can be argued that his goals remained revolutionary in the sense of transformational: the search for a just society based on the redistribution of wealth and elimination of private property. At the same time,

FIGURE 10.4.

Nikolai Charushin, 1937.
© Russian State Archive of Literature and Art, Moscow.

his views (like those of the NS Party) on the right way forward became evolutionary. On the surface this represents a major shift from the time when the young men and women of the 1870s talked freely of a popular uprising. Yet again, Charushin's (and Kornilova-Moroz's) recollections of revolution as something "detached from time and space" suggest otherwise. Charushin continued to see himself as, take pride in, and when challenged, insist on his status as an "old revolutionary," even if by the 1920s, all that was left to him of his Populist identity was that of a culture bearer (without an end goal), and even the memory of his earlier life as a revolutionary was challenged and then officially erased.

Yet in the second half of the twentieth century, authenticity and the search for genuine moral attributes were a long-brewing reaction to the double-speak of Soviet life—the pervasive phenomenon in politics of saying one thing and meaning quite another.[42] However illusory it may have been, the intelligentsia in Russia at the time of the Thaw, and again during Perestroika, were drawn to the belief that a "critically thinking person" could remake the world. For many living in the post-Stalin era, more important than the failed strategies of the Populists or even their identities as revolutionaries were their ideals and their insistence that word and deed be inseparable in life.

NOTES

1. Nikolai Sukhanov, *Zapiski o revoliutsii*, 3 vols. (Moskva: Politizdat, 1992) 3:337.
2. XX s"ezd KPSS i zadachi issledovaniia istorii partii," *Voprosy istorii* 3 (1956): 5–6.
3. P. Tkachenko, "O nekotorykh voprosakh istorii narodnichestva," *Voprosy istorii* 5 (1956): 34–45.
4. Nikolai Troitskii, *Russkoe revoliutsionnoe narodnichestvo 1870-kh gg. (Istoriia temy)* (Saratov: Izdatel'stvo Saratovskogo universiteta, 2003), 21–22.
5. See S. Volk, *"Narodnaia Volia" (1879–1882)* (Moskva, Leningrad: Nauka, 1966).
6. Troitskii, *"Narodnaia Volia" pered tsarskim sudom (1880–1891)* (Saratov: Izdatel'stvo Saratovskogo universiteta, 1971); *Bezumstvo khrabrykh. Russkie revoliutsionery i karatel'naia politika tsarizma 1866–1882 gg.* (Moskva: Mysl', 1978).
7. Troitskii, *Russkoe revoliutsionnoe narodnichestvo 1870-kh gg.*, 30.
8. Nikolai Charushin, *O dalekom proshlom* (Moskva: Mysl', 1973), 15.
9. On Anatoly Emmausskii, a distinguished historian who himself had a complicated path to follow in the Stalinist era, see the many references in Larry E. Holmes, *War, Evacuation and the Exercise of Power: The Center, Periphery and Kirov's Pedagogical Institute, 1941–1952* (New York, NY: Lexington, 2012).
10. V. Sukhodoev taught at the Kirov Pedagogical Institute; N. Komarov was a former associate of the Kirov local history museum and archive.
11. Nina Andreeva, "Ne mogu postupit'sia printsipami," *Sovetskaia Rossiia*, March 13, 1988, 2.
12. *Kirovskaya pravda*, May 26, 1988, 3.
13. L. Zhdanov, "Kto on, N.A. Charushin?" *Kirovskaia pravda*, May 26, 1988, 3.
14. A. Reva, "Sluzhil narodu," *Kirovskaia pravda*, June 16, 1988, 2.
15. MOPR is an acronym in Russian for a Comintern organization established to aid veterans of the movement. The authors can testify that virtually nobody on the streets of Kirov today can decipher its meaning.
16. Chudova, "Kto on, Charushin?" *Kirovskaia pravda*, July 28, 1988, 3.
17. For his membership, see *Politicheskaia katorga i ssylka. Biograficheskii spravochnik chlenov Obshchestva politkatorzhan i ssyl'noposelentsev* (Moskva: Vsesouznoe Obshchestvo politkatorzhan i ssyl;noposelentsev, 1934), 700.
18. N. Komarov and V. Sukhodoev, "Vopreki pravde," *Kirovskaia pravda*, August 25, 1988, 2.
19. On Charushin's family situation, see chapter 1; on the request for a pardon and on Charushin's photography and "teaching," see chapter 5; on *Viatskaia Rech'* see chapter 7; on the Supreme Soviet and on Charushin's arrests, see chapter 8; on Charushin's pension and membership in the Society of Former Political Prisoners and Exiles, see chapter 9.

20. Chudova to Tatarenkov, October 2, 1988, KOUNB, f. D, p. 21.
21. Chudova to Troitskii, September 7, 1988, KOUNB, f. D, p. 15.
22. Antonov, Itemberg, Sedov, Troitskii to Chudova, December 27, 1988, KOUNB, f. D, p. 2.
23. Even using this euphemism, the VAK (the official bureau that certified all dissertations in the USSR) had received an anonymous denunciation that Sergeev was too sympathetic to the Populists and, specifically, Charushin, who figures prominently in his dissertation.
24. Interview with Vladimir Zharavin, Kirov, February 22, 2015.
25. Sergeev to Chudova, February 17, 1991, KOUNB, f. D.
26. *Gertsenka: Viatskie zapiski* 11 (2007): 3–24. Vasily Aksenov (1932–2009) was a writer who was especially popular among the young in the 1960s—it was a review of the work in which he had first coined the term *shestidesiatniki*, or "sixties generation." Aksenov was deprived of his citizenship in 1980. His novel *The Island of Crimea* circulated underground in the late Soviet era, and was a sensation when published in the Perestroika era.
27. Sergeev, "S kompetentnost'iu i bez neterpimosti (K sporam o N.A. Charushine)," *Kraevedenie v razvitii provintsial'noi kul'tury Rossii* (Kirov, n/p, 2009), 271.
28. Ibid.
29. Ibid., 274–275.
30. Chudova to Prezidium Oblsoveta VOOPIK, May 26, 1988, KOUNB, f. D, p. 2.
31. Chudova to Karacharov, November 18, 1988, KOUNB, f. D, p. 34.
32. Chudova to Sergeev, March 19, 1989, *Gertsenka: Viatskie Zapiski* 4 (2003): 16.
33. Iu. Karacharov, A. Lakhman, V. Ponomarev, "Esche Raz o N. A. Charushin," *Kirovskaya Pravda*, April 27, 1989, 3. The letters from Itenberg and Troitskii are preserved in the local section of the Herzen State Library. However, our search of the letters-to-the-editor archive of the newspaper, conducted at GASPIKO, did not produce these letters, or any others that may have been sent during the winter of 1988/9. Karacharov, who headed the commission, was at the time serving as director of the regional party archives, but he had been the power regional party secretary investigating the charges leveled against Charushin in the late 1970s.
34. Karacharov, Lakhman, Ponomarev, "Esche raz o N. A. Charushin," *Kirovskaya pravda*, April 27, 1989, 3.
35. Reva, "Sluzhil narodu," *Kirovskaia pravda*, June 16, 1988, 2.
36. Chudova to Sergeev, September 2, 1989, *Gertsenka: Viatskie zapiski* 4 (2003): 16.
37. V. Polikarpov to Chudova, November 23, 1989, KOUNB, f. D. The author specifically referred to the *series Zhizni zamechatel'nkh liudei*, the publishing house *Molodaia gvardiia*, the journal *Nash Sovremennik*, and the memorial society *Pamiat'*.
38. *Viatskaia zhizn'*, no. 4, 2003, 17.
39. Chudova to T. Ashikhmina, April 21, 1989, KOUNB, f. D, p. 38. By now, Chudova was in her late eighties; by 1991, physically infirm, losing her eyesight and mobility, unable to read or attend lectures, she moved to Perm' to be with her son's family. She died in 1997. In the end, in 1997, the house on MOPR Street where Charushin had spent a good part of his life after returning from exile, was torn down.
40. She was born in Kirov in 1948, graduated from the Leningrad Theater Institute, Music and Cinematography, and after 1967 worked in television.
41. See the recent, appropriately named, study of the OPK, *Revolutionaries on a Pension*. Mark Iunge, *Revoliutsionery na pensii* (Moskva: AIRO, 2015).
42. See Ludmilla A. Trigos, *The Decembrist Myth in Russian Culture* (New York: Palgrave Macmillan, 2009), x–xi, 147–150.

Conclusion

IN THE PAGES of this book the authors have navigated between telling Nikolai Charushin's life story and providing a collective biography of a generation of romantic revolutionaries, most of whom came of age early in the 1870s. Along the way we have journeyed through the turbulent history of modern Russia from the mid-century Great Reforms to the era of high Stalinism and beyond. We have offered a fresh picture of Populism as a movement, focusing less on organizational questions than on personal ties, collective strivings, generational identity, and social memory. In the process, we combined micro- and macrohistory and challenged some of the prevailing stereotypes about women's role and the balancing of the private and the public in the lives of this generation as a whole, as well as about the lived experience of incarceration and exile.

We have deployed the term "generation" as a subjective labeling and means of group identity rather than as a demographic term as such. Our focus has been upon the ethics and principles this group formulated early in their lives—at a time when their individual identities were also in the making—but especially on how their earlier experiences defined their subsequent lives. Their world views were formed in the late 1860s and early 1870s; even then, they differed on the question of whether or not they were followers of Lavrov or of Bakunin and on how they should focus their efforts to effect change. Later their paths in life and party affiliations sometimes diverged: some became Socialist Revolutionaries, others Social Democrats and some even liberal Kadets. Nevertheless, as a group they kept up strong ties and maintained a collective generational identity throughout their lives.

What was it that held together the Chaikovskii circle despite the members' different trajectories taken after imprisonment and exile? We argue that above all it was ethical rationalism which sustained these bonds. Concerning the *terrorist* movement in the Populist midst, Susan Morrissey has aptly used the term "moral economy" to describe the "complex of ethical orientations" this faction put forth in order to *justify* their violent actions. Yet for the Populist movement *as a whole* we see the focus on ethics differently. In our view it was more integral, functioning not as a means of self-justification but rather as the *core* of its members' identity and the wellspring of their actions.[1] Ethics defined their actions in advance rather than providing justification or rationales after the fact. At the same time, while acknowledging that recent research in psychology cautions against drawing sharp boundaries between thought and emotion,[2] we also emphasize the *rational* component of their ethical orientation in life. For that reason we are skeptical of interpretations that look for signs of widespread psychological imbalance among the ranks of Populists or label the movement a religious quest in all but name.

This is not to deny that terrorism and the issue of violence in general posed serious ethical and strategic problems for this generation—under what circumstances could it be justified? This question divided the movement in the 1870s, leading the organization Land and Liberty to split into two groups—the Black Partition and the People's Will—the latter orchestrated the assassination of Alexander II in 1881. In exile, the Chaikovtsy heatedly debated supporting the terrorist acts of the People's Will—their friends. They rejected such acts in principle but accepted them as a temporary exigency. The question of terrorism also plagued the Socialist Revolutionary Party in the first decade of the twentieth century. In reality, Charushin's friends never managed to reconcile political violence with their ethical codes, which left them at a terrible disadvantage in 1917. Yet as one historian whom we cited earlier put it, "[T]his was their misfortune, not their fault." In any event, as important as terrorism was at moments of crisis it did not define Populism as a whole; exclusive focus on it has the result of obscuring what was a much larger and impactful movement in modern Russia.

CONCLUSION

Moving beyond terrorism allows us to get a clearer picture of the balance between the public and the private in the lives of Populists. We have discovered different models of marital and familial relationships among revolutionaries of those times: we have seen fictive marriages and authentic ones, divorces and second marriages or even remarriages, large families and small. We have observed companionate relationships and partnerships but also hierarchical arrangements based on differences in education or social status; dominant and domineering males, resourceful and decisive women, long-standing and short-term ties. As for Charushin and Kuvshinskaia, theirs was a stable lifelong marriage with a strong emphasis on domesticity, but also a partnership and in which there was mutual support for their societal endeavors—even if in her later years, she lamented that she had always played the role of second fiddle.

Like terrorism, incarceration and exile are familiar tropes of the narrative about Populism. We, too, have devoted considerable attention to the lived experience of that long interval in the lives of the Chaikovtsy, acknowledging the considerable hardship and cruelty they endured. At the same time, we also avoid treating this period exclusively as one of martyrdom and suffering. The long years the Populists spent stripped of their civil status and branded as criminals served also to reinforce their generational ties, and they later recalled fondly the "democratic" community they had established in exile as the "Republic of Kara." Shared experience did not exclude personal conflict, especially in the demoralizing aftermath of the Revolution of 1905—something which their memoirs written in the 1920s tended to conceal but was evident in their correspondence at the time. Despite this, their generational ties endured, even as after exile they found themselves scattered about different regions and cities of this vast empire.

Moreover, during their time in Siberia many Populists became photographers, newspaper men, ethnographers "culture bearers" for the region. Recent research has for good reason looked askance at narratives that treat the Siberian exiles as bringing civilization and light to a barbaric and backward region, but there can be no doubt that human capital was in short supply there and that the exiles left a legacy of museums, libraries, and scholarly research. More importantly for our purposes, in the process they developed *professions* even if they were largely self-taught or learned their skills through apprenticeships rather than a specialized education.

Professional training was something they had missed out on at a crucial developmental stage in their lives after having been pulled out of universities into the revolutionary movement, and then out of civil society entirely.

Nor did their life stories end with arrest and exile, as one might think from reading their memoirs. Instead, after they were released, they continued to nurture these professional careers, in the process becoming an integral part of a society of which the newly emerging and self-aware professions were a boisterous component. It would be tempting to conclude that the Chaikovtsy grew out of their shells as "professional revolutionaries" (a term that was new at the time). Yet Charushin and most of his generation also continued to participate in oppositionist politics and to repeatedly affirm their identities as "old revolutionaries" in the new twentieth century and until the end of their lives. This was something more layered and nuanced than the age-old and universal story of emerging from the radical dreams of youth to stolid position of respectability in a stable society.

Charushin's decade-long career as a fire-insurance and famine relief agent while he was employed by the zemstvo introduced him to the pragmatic politics of provincial life. His experience running a newspaper from 1905 until 1917 only deepened that knowledge even if it left some scars. Even as they actively participated in public affairs and in the burgeoning cooperative movement, they cultivated their connections with the business world. They had good friends in local government, the professions, educational and cultural organizations, and voluntary societies. Thus, while many have pointed out that the Russian Populists of the 1870s were naïve, inexperienced in the give and take of politics, and ill-informed about the peasantry they yearned to serve, such a charge can scarcely be made of them by the early twentieth century, for these enterprises gave them both a close-up look at the complexities of agrarian society and hands-on experience in the arena of local politics. The majority of revolutionaries and political exiles in Charushin's world also made every effort to live a full-blooded existence. They took pleasure in travel, interacting with others, sharing holidays, getting out into nature, participating in scientific expeditions, even hunting.

It is another question how they partook of "modernity," a concept that scholars link closely with the notion of generation but that exploring would take us too far afield here, given the range of issues we have addressed.³ Yet a few words are in order. Obviously, in terms of human organization and experiences (family structure, material culture, urban life, and means of communication), Populists did participate in the modern world. Notions of individual rights and secularism were characteristic of this generation, as were their solidarities, political affiliations, and professional identities—the bourgeois individual subject dominated. But among the "multiple modernities" competing for scholarly attention today, the one prevalent among historians of fin-de-siècle Russia fits the Populist movement poorly. Historians such as Laura Engelstein, Daniel Beer, and others have argued that the early twentieth century brought criminology, social psychology, anthropology, the medical sciences—and the inevitable accompanying anxiety and trepidation about the human condition—into the mainstream of Russian culture, displacing an earlier and more optimistic liberalism.⁴ There can be no doubt that these disciplines and the massive street violence during the 1905 Revolution brought some to a more pessimistic view of the human condition. Yet we search in vain for evidence of these trends in the correspondence of the seventies generation—who were entering their fifties at the turn of the century. The Populists we have studied continued to adhere closely to the far more optimistic views of humanity and progress presented by the "neo-Enlightenment" (the term used by A. Walicki to describe the dominant views in the immediate aftermath of the Great Reforms of the 1860s), whose tenets they had imbibed in their youth and which were reproduced in the Neo-Populist movement of the subsequent generation. Given the widespread appeal of Populism as a worldview in both the provinces and the capital cities, we suspect that such an approach to reality was considerably more widespread in Russian society than was the modernist angst and skepticism about the human condition described by Beer, Engelstein, and others—and which better defines our own culture today.

Like millions of others, Charushin was faced with difficult and momentous choices in 1917. He cast his lot with the Provisional Government and the democratic revolution in general, but categorically rejected the importuning of the Bolsheviks. In his newspaper and in his many public speeches he warned of approaching anarchy and of the consequences of the collapse of the state. He urged his compatriots to await the convening of the Constituent Assembly before seeking a resolution of the land question, the war, and other burning issues. He remained true to the convictions he had formed early in life about the need to educate and enlighten the population before it could participate fully in politics. At the same time, he believed that no political revolution could be successful unless it was combined with a social transformation and brought on by the people themselves.

We have avoided discussing how realistic his views were. However, our portrayal of the events of 1917 through the eyes of Charushin and Vera Figner allowed us to frame these events in a highly personalized way and—without pretensions to be doing a complete rewrite of that revolutionary year—to suggest the viability of alternative outcomes, at least in some areas of the country. It also allowed us to provide, without whitewashing, a more empathetic explanation of the despair and distress with which many moderate revolutionaries responded to the tide of events.

Whatever the validity of his convictions, Charushin remained true to his beliefs in word and deed. He took the momentous decision to join the Supreme Council set up by the zemstvo leaders in order to coordinate resistance to the Bolshevik Revolution. He may have realized the hopelessness of the effort—we cannot be sure that his testimony to that effect is fully accurate—but the principles he had worked out as a member of the Chaikovskii circle would not allow him to stand on the sidelines as these events unfolded. Charushin's actions found parallels in the deeds of others of his circle, including Nikolai Chaikovskii. Also believing in a gradual democratic transformation, the latter took charge of the Supreme Soviet of the Russian North (in Archangel'sk). However, after unsuccessful attempts to obtain support and condemned in absentiia to death by a Bolshevik tribunal, Chaikovskii fled the country (he died in Paris in 1926). We don't know if Charushin actually had a choice to leave, but at least the striving to make a meaningful contribution to society while living under a hostile regime was a familiar—in fact, lifelong—ethical choice for him.

All that remained for the seventies-generation Populists in the 1920s and 1930s was their memory of a past that now seemed so distant—but at the same time urgently necessary to preserve. Working collaboratively with others in the Society of Former Political Prisoners and Exiles, Charushin wrote down his recollections at a time of "memory wars" in the Soviet Union. We have noted that these memoirs were part of a collective project which created a "traveling narrative;" one combining the efforts under duress of several surviving figures from that generation to "get history right" and provide an authentic rendition of their life experiences.

The revolutionary cohort of the 1870s was cast out of the new triumphal historical narrative of the Stalin era, but they resurfaced in the renewed memory wars of the Thaw and Perestroika. Now historians and the general public sought to recover the interwoven but by then occluded connections between revolution and freedom, along with notions of personal honor and ethical behavior that many felt had been erased in their own lifetimes—but which the Russian version of Populism stood for.

NOTES

1. Susan R. Morrissey, "The 'Apparel of Innocence': Toward a Moral Economy of Terrorism in Late Imperial Russia," *Journal of Modern History* 84, no. 3 (2012): 607–642; idem, "Terrorism, Modernity, and the Question of Origins," *Kritika: Explorations in Russian and Eurasian History* 12, no.1 (2011): 213–226; Claudia Verhoeven, *The Odd Man Karakozov: Imperial Russia, Modernity, and the Birth of Terrorism* (Ithaca, NY: Cornell University Press, 2009).

2. William M. Reddy, *The Navigation of Feeling: A Framework for the History of Emotions* (Cambridge: Cambridge University Press, 2001), 31–32.

3. For a thorough discussion of the evolution of the term *modern* and its variants, see the article in *Slovar' osnovnykh istoricheskikh poniatii* (Moskva: NLO, 2016), 241–296. See also the several essays devoted to the topic in the *American Historical Review*, 116 (3) (June, 2011).

4. See Laura Engelstein, *The Keys to Happiness: Sex and the Search for Modernity in fin-de-siècle Russia* (Ithaca, NY: Cornell University Press, 1992); Daniel Beer, *Renovating Russia: The Human Sciences and the Fate of Liberal Modernity, 1880–1930* (Ithaca, NY: Cornell University Press, 2008).

BIOGRAPHICAL SKETCHES

Included here are figures referred to often in the text or whose memoirs are frequently cited. The biographical descriptions of other personalities who play a significant role in this story are included in the text itself and can be found using the index. Still others who make only cameo appearances are described in endnotes directly attached to their names at first mention.

Bakunin, Mikhail. 1814 (Tver')–1876 (Bern). Scion of a legendary liberal aristocratic family, European anarchist theoretician and activist, participant in the First International and fervent opponent of Karl Marx, Bakunin was educated at Petersburg Artillery School; lived overseas from 1840 to 1851; participated in the 1848 revolutions; expatriated to Russia; was imprisoned until 1857, then exiled to Tomsk, then Irkutsk in Transbaikal; in 1861, escaped to England; duped by Sergei Nechaev to take part in the latter's fictitious international conspiracy; between 1871 and 1874 wrote *State and Revolution* and other foundational anarchist tracts while taking part in uprisings in Italy and Spain. In the eyes of many he was the archetype of the anarchist revolutionary.

Chaikovskii, Nikolai. 1850 (Viatka)–1926 (Paris). From the nobility. Student at Petersburg University, and member of Chaikovskii circle from 1869. Chaikovskii emigrated to United States in 1874, where he founded a commune in Kansas and lived with the Shakers; returned to Europe in 1879; was among the founders of the Free Russian Press in London; a member of the Central Committees of the United Trudovik-NS Party, in 1917, and of the Soviet of Peasant Deputies and the Petrograd Soviet of Workers and Soldiers' Deputies; delegate to the Constituent Assembly from Viatka; until February 1920 leader of the opposition to the Bolsheviks centered in Arkhangelsk; emigrated to Paris; uncle of Leonid Yumashev.

Chemodanova-Sinegub, Larisa. 1850 (Viatka)–1923 (Tomsk). Daughter of a priest, she studied at the Viatka Diocesan School; in 1872, she entered into a fictive marriage with Sergei Sinegub, and in 1973 joined the Chaikovskii circle in St. Petersburg. Along with Liubov Kornilova participated in the Political Red Cross; she followed her husband into exile in Siberia, where she remained for the rest of her life.

Chudnovskii, Solomon. 1849 (Kherson)–1912 (Odessa). Son of a merchant, Chudnovskii studied at Petersburg Medico-Surgical Academy, from which he was expelled for his role in student disorders in 1869 and exiled to Kherson. From 1871, he was a member of the Odessa branch of Chaikovskii circle; from 1872 to 1873 studied in Vienna; in 1878 was sentenced to five years of hard labor, commuted to exile in Tobol'sk province, where he produced studies of the peasant commune, took part in geographic expeditions, and contributed to the newspaper *Vostochnoe Obozrenie*. In 1893 he returned to Odessa, where he engaged with the legal periodical press; he joined liberal Kadet Party in 1905 and worked with prominent liberal journals.

Debogorii-Mokrievich, Vladimir. 1848 (Chernigov)–1926 (Bulgaria). From a family of the impoverished nobility, in 1871 Debogorii-Mokrievich graduated from Kiev University and joined revolutionary circles there. In 1873, he was introduced to Bakunin in Switzerland and became an adherent of his views; he returned to Kiev, where he was employed as a factory worker, and took part in the Kievan commune and then the Going to the People movement; sought to organize peasant uprisings, notably in the famous Chigirin episode; and helped several incarcerated revolutionaries escape. At the end of the decade he renounced anarchism and sought to find common ground with zemstvo liberals; was arrested numerous times after 1873 and in 1879 sentenced to fifteen years of hard labor, but en route exchanged documents with a common criminal and returned to European Russia. From 1881 to 1894 he lived incognito in France, moved to London, the United States, and finally to Bulgaria, where he became a citizen.

Deutch (Deich), Lev. 1855 (Podolsk)–1941 (Moscow). From a merchant family, Deutch studied at the gymnasium in Kiev and in the philosophy department at Basel University. He was a member of Land and Liberty and Black Partition (the Populist organization that rejected terrorism); emigrated in 1880; was one of founders of the Emancipation of Labor—the predecessor to the Marxist movement; arrested multiple times and sentenced to hard labor and exile in Siberia.

Figner, Vera. 1852 (Kazan province)–1942 (Moscow). Born into the nobility, Figner studied at a finishing school for noble girls in Kazan and at the medical faculty of Zurich University. She was a member of the executive committee of the People's Will organization involved in the assassination of Alexander II and sentenced to death in 1884; her sentence commuted to life in prison, she spent twenty years in solitary confinement in Shlisselburg prison; in 1906, following her release, she traveled abroad and worked to publicize the situation of political prisoners in Russia. After 1917, she wrote her memoirs and collaborated with the journal *Katorga i Ssylka*. Her sister Lydia was also exiled for Populist activities; her brother was a prominent opera singer.

Kornilova-Moroz, Aleksandra. 1853 (Petersburg)–after 1938. The daughter of wealthy merchant, she was the close friend of Sofia Perovskaia and Vera Figner. Sentenced in 1878 to exile in Perm' and Tobolsk provinces, after 1894 she lived in Moscow, participated in the work of the Political Red Cross; after 1917, she worked in the museum of the Society of Former Political Prisoners and Exiles; sisters Liubov and Vera were also members of the Chaikovskii circle.

Kropotkin, Petr. 1842 (Moscow)–1921 (Moscow). Legendary anarchist from a princely family, he served as a page at the imperial court; a member of the Chaikovskii circle, in 1874 he was arrested; in 1876, escaped abroad and lived in Switzerland, Great Britain, and France before returning to Russia in 1917. He was an international founder of the anarchist movement and Jura Federation of the First International; a prominent Russian geographer and geologist and author of oft-cited memoirs and works on Russian and French prisons.

Kuznetsov, Alexei. 1845 (Kherson)–1928 (Moscow). From a merchant family, he studied at the Petrovsky Agronomy Academy; was arrested in connection with the Nechaev affair, sentenced to hard labor at Kara, then sent to the penal settlement in Nerchinsk, where he engaged in photography and founded the region's first museum; in Chita, he organized a branch of the Geographic Society; in 1906, he received a death sentence, which was commuted to ten years' hard labor; thereafter he was exiled to the remote Yakutsk region, where he became the founder and director of the local museum; published works on ethnography, archeology, and the history of Transbaikal region.

Lavrov, Petr. 1823 (Pskov)–1900 (Paris). From the nobility, he was a Populist theoretician; graduate of Artillery School in Petersburg and from 1844 to 1866 taught math at military educational institutions there; in 1866 was arrested and exiled to Vologda province, where he wrote *Historical Letters*. He escaped abroad to Paris, joined the First International, took part in the Paris Commune in 1871; editor of the journal *Vpered* from Zurich and London.

Novorusskii, Mikhail. 1861 (Novgorod)–1925 (Leningrad). From the clergy, he studied at a church school and then the Petersburg Ecclesiastical Academy; in 1887 he was sentenced to death for his role in a conspiracy to assassinate Alexander III; the sentence was commuted to life in exile, then in turn to imprisonment at Schlisselburg. Released in 1905, he became a popular science writer, author of children's books, memoirs, and biographies. After 1917 he was the director of the Petrograd Agricultural Museum.

Popov, Ivan. 1862 (St. Petersburg)–1942 (Moscow). The son of a staff sergeant, Popov was a graduate of the St. Petersburg Teachers' Institute; a member of the People's Will in 1885, he was exiled to Kiakhta; from 1894, he lived in Irkutsk and served as editor of newspaper *Vostochnoe Obozrenie* and the journal *Sibirskii Sbornik*. After 1906 he lived in Moscow, was affiliated with the Kadet Party and parliamentary commissions; a member of the Political Red Cross; worked in a consumer cooperative network, in publishing, and in the Moscow regional museum. He was a member of the OPK.

Sazhin, Mikhail. 1845 (Izhevsk, Viatka province)–1934 (Moscow). The son of a petty clerk, Sazhin was a student at Technological Institute in Petersburg; he joined the revolutionary movement in mid-1860s; in 1868, exiled to Vologda, he escaped to the United States, where he was a factory worker; in 1871, he participated in the Paris Commune and joined the Jura Federation of the International; in 1872, connected with Bakunin he took part in the Italian revolutionary movement and an uprising in Herzegovina; sentenced in the Trial of 193 to five years of hard labor, after which he lived in Riga and Nizhnii Novgorod; from 1906 to 1916, he was on the staff of the Populist journal *Russkoe Bogatstvo*; a member of the OPK.

Shishko, Leonid. 1852 (Podolsk)–1910 (Paris). From the nobility, Shishko studied at the Petersburg Artillery School, was commissioned, then joined the Chaikovskii circle. Sentenced in the Trial of 193 to nine years of hard labor at Kara, then to a penal settelement in the Transbaikal region, in 1887 he relocated to Tomsk and, in 1889, fled from exile. He played an active role abroad in the Free Russian Press.

Sinegub, Sergei. 1851 (Ekaterinoslav)–1907 (Tomsk). From a family of noble landowners, in 1871 he graduated from the Minsk gymnasium and enrolled in the Technological Institute, before in the same year joining the Chaikovskii circle. In 1878, he was sentenced in the Trail of 193 to nine years of hard labor, then to penal settlement in Chita; in 1896, he relocated to Blagoveshchensk in the Far East, and then to Tomsk.

Stepniak-Kravchinskii, Sergei. 1851 (Kherson)–1895 (London). Son of a military doctor, he studied at the Mikhailov Artillery School in Petersburg; joined the Chaikovskii circle and in 1874 took part in the Going to the People movement before emigrating; in 1878, he returned to Russia and joined Land and Liberty, gravitated to terrorist activities and famously assassinated the head of the gendarmes, General Mezentsev, with a dagger. His book *Underground Russia* was translated into several European languages, circulated widely, and was admired by George Kennan. He was the prototype for the hero of Emile Zola's novel *Germinal*.

Tikhomirov, Lev. 1852 (Gelenzhik)–1923 (Sergiev Posad). From the nobility. Tikhomirov was a student at Moscow University, a member of the Chaikovskii circle and Land and Liberty (1876); he served on the executive committee of the People's Will, was the editor of Populist publications and represented the People's Will abroad. In 1888, he repented and asked for clemency, writing his infamous "Testament," and becoming a staunch monarchist.

SELECTED BIBLIOGRAPHY

ARCHIVAL SOURCES

Moscow

GARF, State Archive of the Russian Federation (Gosudarstvennyi Arkhiv Rossiiskoi Federatsii)
  f. 102—Department of Police, Ministry of Internal Affairs (MVD)
  f. 112—Special Office of the Senate for investigating crimes against the state and illegal organizations
  f. 533—The All-Union Society of Former Political Prisoners and Exiles
RGALI, Russian State Archive of Literature and Art (Rossiiskii Gosudarstvennyi Arkhiv Literatury i Iskusstva)
  f. 1642—N. A. Charushin
  f. 1185—V. N. Figner
  f. 408—I. I. Popov
  f. 1291—S. S. Sinegub, L. V. Sinegub
  f. 1023—A. A. Borovoi
  f. 1435—M. V. Muratov
TsIAM, Central Historical Archive of Moscow (Tsentral'nyi Istoricheskii Arkhiv Moskvy)
  f. 2241—M. P. Shebalin

St. Petersburg

RGIA, Russian State Historical Archive (Rossiiskii Gosudarstvennyi Istoricheskii Arkhiv)
  f. 391—Resettlement Administration
  f. 776—Main Office of Press Affairs of the MVD
  f. 796—Chancery of the Synod
  f. 1284—Department of General Affairs of the MVD
  f. 1288—Main Office of Local Economic Matters of the MVD
  f. 1482—The All-Zemstvo Organization for Famine Relief
TsGIA SpB, Central State Historical Archive of St. Petersburg (Tsentral'nyi Gosudarstvennyi Istoricheskii Arkhiv St. Peterburga)

f. 492—Technological Institute
IRLI RAN, Institute of Russian Literature, Russian Academy of Science (Institut Russkoi Literatury [Pushkinskii Dom])
    f. 675—S. S. Sinegub
Russian National Library, Manuscript Division
    f. 1139 E.D. Petriaev

Kirov

Kirov Regional (Herzen) Library (Kirovskaia Oblastnaia Nauchnaia Universal'naia Biblioteka imeni A. I. Gertsena)
    f. "D"—unpublished documents held by the local history (*kraevedcheskii*) section.
GAKO, Kirov Region State Archive (Gosudarstvennyi Arkhiv Kirovskoi Oblasti)
    f. 582—Chancery of the Viatka Governor
    f. 583—Viatka Gubernatorial Office (*upravlenie*)
    f. 587—Viatka Provincial Bureau (*prisutstvie*) for zemstvo and muncipal affairs
    f. 616—Viatka Provincial Zemstvo Executive Board (*uprava*)
    f. 714—Viatka Provincial Gendarmerie
    f. P-1322—Viatka Provincial Revolutionary Tribunal
    f. P-1965—Kirov regional branch of the All-Union Society of Former Political Prisoners and Exiles.
    f. P-2483—The Kirov Regional (Herzen) Library
    f. 205—The Chancery of the Director of Schools, in Viatka province
    f. 221—The Viatka diocesan women's school
GASPIKO, State Archive of the Socio-Political History of Kirov Region (Gosudarstvennyi Arkhiv Sotsial'no-Politicheskoi Istorii Kirovskoi Oblasti)
    f. 45—Material relating to the history of the Communist Party and October Revolution in Viatka province held by the Party History Commission (ISTPART)
    f. 69—Communist Party editorial board of *Kirovskaia Pravda*
    f. R-6799—Materials from criminal investigations of individuals subjected to political repression and legally rehabilitated. Offices of the Russian Federal Security Bureau (FSB), of the Kirov region

New York

Columbia University, Rare Book and Manuscript Library, Bakhmeteff Archive
The Sergei Mikhailovich Kravchinskii Papers
The Boris Sapir Papers

Newspapers

Viatskaia Zhizn' (December 24, 1905–May 4, 1906; June 1–August 22, 1906)
Viatskii Krai (May 1906; September 1, 1906–December 14, 1907)
Viatskaia Rech' (December 24, 1907–December 2, 1917)
Viatskii Vestnik (1904–1910)
Viatskaia Gazeta (1894–1907)
Kirovskaia Pravda (1988–1989)

Journals

Katorga i ssylka (1921–1935)
Byloe (1906–1907)

Golos minuvshego na chuzhoi storone (1926–1928)

PRIMARY SOURCES

Aksel'rod, Pavel. *Perezhitoe i peredumannoe*. Berlin, 1923.
Arkad'ev, G. "Za bol'shevistskuiu perestroiku. K voprosu o rabote izdatel'stva byvshikh politkatorzhan." *Bor'ba klassov* 6 (1933): 129–130.
Bogoslovskii, M. M. *Dnevniki (1913–1919)*: Iz sobraniia GIM. Moskva: Vremia, 2011.
Chaikovskii, Nikolai. "Detskie gody," *Golos minuvshego na chuzhoi storone* (1926).
Charushin, Arkadii. "Brat'ia Urzhumovy." *Katorga i ssylka* 1 (1926): 63–92.
Charushin, Nikolai. "Chto bylo na sobranii u professora Tagantseva." *Katorga i ssylka* 2 (1925): 99–102.
———. "Organizatsiia kraevedcheskogo Otdela pri Viatskoi gubernskoi publichnoi biblioteke imeni Gertsena i zhelatel'naia postanovka sootvetstvuiushchikh otdelov v bibliotekakh na mestakh." *Gertsenka: Viatskie zapiski* 16 (2009): 21–28.
———. *O dalekom proshlom na Kare*. Moskva: Vsesoiuznoe Obshchestvo politkatorzhan, 1929.
———. *O dalekom proshlom. Kruzhok Chaikovtsev. Iz vospominanii o revoliutsionnom dvizhenii 1870-kh gg*. Moskva: Vsesouznoe Obshchestv politkatorzhan, 1926.
———. *O dalekom proshlom*. Moskva: Mysl', 1973.
———. *O dalekom proshlom na poselenii*. Moskva: Vsesoiuznoe Obshchestvo politkatorzhan, 1931.
Charushnikov, A. P. Pis'ma A. P. Charushnikova v Viatku N. A. Charushinu (1900–e gody). *Gertsenka* 24 (2013): 99–201.
Chekhov, Anton. "Ostrov Sakhalin: (Iz putevykh zapisok)." *Polnoe sobranie sochinenii i pisem: v 30 t*, t. 14–15. Moskva: Nauka, 1978.
Chudnovskii, Solomon. *Iz davnikh let. Vospominaniia*. Moskva: Vsesoiuznoe Obshchestv Politkatorzhan i ssyl'noposelentsev, 1934.
Dan, Lidia. *Iz vstrech s V. N. Figner*. New York: Inter-University Project on the History of the Menshevik Movement, August 1961.
Debogorii-Mokrievich, Vladimir. *Vospominaniia*. Petersburg, 1906.
Deiateli revoliutsionnogo dvizheniia v Rossii. Biobibliograficheskii slovar'. Ot predshestvennikov dekabristov do padeniia tsarizma. Red. F. Kon, A. Shilov, B. Koz'min, and V. Nevskii. Moskva: Vsesouznoe Obshchestvo politkatorzhan, 1927–33.
Deiateli SSSR i revoliutsionnogo dvizheniia v Rossii. Entsiklopedicheskii slovar' Granat. Moskva: Sovetskaia Entsiklopedia, 1989.
Deich, Lev. *16 let v Sibiri*. Zheneva, 1905.
Driagin, K. V. "Biblioteka za 10 let revoliutsii." *Gertsenka: Viatskie zapiski* 12 (2007): 28–29.
Figner, Vera. "Zheny dekabristov." *100-letie vosstaniia dekabristov*. Sbornik statei i dokumentov zhurnala *Katorga i ssylka*. Moskva: Vsesoiuznoe Obshchestvo Politkatorzhan, 1927.
———. *Zapechatlennyi trud*. 2 vols. Moskva: Mysl', 1964.
———. *Polnoe sobranie sochinenii v 6 tomakh*. Vols. 1–6. Moskva: Vsesouznoe Obshchestvo politkatorzhan, 1929
Gali Fedorovna Chudova: poslednie pis'ma // *Gertsenka: Viatskie zapiski*. 4 (2003): 16–24.
Iuferev, V. Viatka i viatchane v vospominaniiakh uchenogo-agronoma Viacheslava Iufereva. *Gertsenka: Viatskie zapiski* 3 (2002): 149–160.
Kazanskii, P. "Bol'she bol'shevistskoi bditel'nosti." *Bor'ba klassov* 5 (1933): 122–128.
Kennan, George. *Siberia and the Exile System*. New York: Praeger, 1970.

Klements, Dmitrii. *Iz proshlogo. Vospominaniia.* Leningrad: Kolos, 1925.
Koz'min, Boris. "N. A. Charushin. O dalekom proshlom." *Pechat' i revolutsiia* 13 (1927).
Kropotkin, Petr. *Zapiski revolutsionera.* Moskva: Mysl', 1966.Levin, Shmuel. "N. A. Charushin. O dalekom proshlom." *Istorik-Marksist* 4 (1927): 242–243.
Lozhkin, N. P. "Moi vospominaniia ob izdatel'skoi rabote Viatskogo gubernskogo zemstva." *Viatka: Kraevedcheskii sbornik.* Kirov, 1972, 76–77.
Luppov, A. N. "O Viatskoi publichnoi biblioteke." *Gertsenka: Viatskie zapiski* 10 (2006): 3–13.
Novorusskii, Mikhail. *Zapiski shlissel'burzhtsa (1887–1905).* Petrograd: n/p, 1920.
Pamiatnye knizhki Viatskoi gubernii na 1895–1917 gody. Viatka, 1894–1916.
Politicheskaia katorga i ssylka. Biograficheskii spravochnik chlenov Obshchestva politkatorzhan i ssyl;no-poselentsev. Moskva: Vsesouznoe Obshchestvo politkatorzhan, 1934.
Popov, Ivan. *Minuvshee i perezhitoe. Sibir'i emigratsiia. Vospominaniia za 50 let.* Leningrad: Kolos, 1924.
———. *Zabytye stranitsy: Zapiski redaktora.* Irkutsk: Vostochno-Sibirskoe knizhnoe izdatel'stvo, 1989.
Pribylev, A. V. *Molodezh' kontsa semidesiatykh godov.* Moskva, 1928.
Protsess 193-kh. Moskva, 1906.
Revoliutsionery 1870-kh gg. Vospominaniia uchastnikov narodnicheskogo dvizheniia v Peterburge. Leningrad, 1986.
Sbornik postanovlenii Viatskogo gubernskogo zemstva za 21 god 1892–1913. Viatka, 1914.
Sergeev, Valentin. "S kompetentnost'iu i bez neterpimosti (K sporam o N.A. Charushine)." *Kraevedenie v razvitii provintsial'noi kul'tury Rossii.* Kirov, 2009.
Shishko, Leonid E. *Obshchestvennoe dvizhenie v shestidesiatykh i pervoi polovine semidesiatykh godov.* Moskva: Izdanie Russkogo bibliograficheskogo instituta Granat, 1920.
———. *S. M. Kravchinskii i kruzhok chaikovtsev (Iz vospominanii i zametok starogo narodnika).* St. Petersburg: Raspopov, 1906.
Sinegub, Sergei. *Zapiski chaikovtsa.* Moskva: Molodaia Gvardiia, 1929.
Stepniak-Kravchinskii, Sergei. *Podpol'naia Rossiia.* Petersburg, 1906.
Sukhanov, Nikolai. *Zapiski o Revoliutsii.* 3 vols. Moskva: Respublika, 1992.
"Tezisy k 50-letiiu 'Narodnoi Voli.'" *Pravda*, April 9, 1930, 4.
Tikhomirov, Lev. *Vospominaniia.* Moskva: Gosudarstvennaia publichnaia istoricheskaia biblioteka Rossii, 2003.
V podpol'e. St. Petersburg, 1907.
"Viatka mne ochen' po dushe" (Iz pisem E. V. Gogel' k A. F. Koni i N. A. Charushinu). *Gertsenka: Viatskie zapiski* 12 (2007): 12–26.
Zasulich, Vera. *Vospominaniia.* Moskva: Vsesouznoe Obshchestvo Politkatorzhan, 1931.
Zhurnaly Viatskogo gubernskogo zemskogo sobraniia. Viatka, 1892–1917.
Zinov'ev, N. A. *Otchet po revizii zemskikh uchrezhdenii Viatskoi gubernii.* Vols. 1–3. Peterburg, 1905.

SECONDARY SOURCES

Acton, Edward, Cherniaev, V. I., and Rosenberg, William G. *Critical Companion to the Russian Revolution 1914–1921.* Bloomington: Indiana University Press, 1997.
Andreev, V. M. "Nauchnaia deiatel'nost' ssyl'nykh narodnikov v Sibiri." *Ssyl'nye revoliutsionery v Sibiri.* Irkutsk: Irkutskii gosudarstvennyi universitet, 1979, 42–71.
Andreeva, E. A. *Arkhitektor Ivan Charushin.* Izhevsk: n/p, 2007.

Antonov, V. F. *Revoliutsionnoe narodnichestvo*. Moskva: Prosveshchenie, 1965.
Assmann, Aleida. "Re-framing Memory. Between Individual and Collective Forms of Constructing the Past." In *Performing the Past: Memory, History, and Identity in Modern Europe*. Edited by Karin Tilmans, Frank van Vree, and J. M Winter. Amsterdam: Amsterdam University Press, 2010.
Assmann, A., and L. Shortt, eds. *Memory and Political Change*. New York: Palgrave Macmillan, 2012.
Bachman, J. E. "Recent Soviet Historiography of Russian Revolutionary Populism." *Slavic Review* 29, no. 4 (1970): 599–612.
Badcock, Sarah. *Politics and the People in Revolutionary Russia: A Provincial History*. New Studies in European History. Cambridge: Cambridge University Press, 2007.
———. *A Prison Without Walls? Eastern Siberian Exile in the Last Years of Tsarism*. Oxford: Oxford University Press, 2016.
Bakulin, V. I. *Drama v dvukh aktakh: Viatskaia guberniia v 1917–1918 gg*. Kirov: Viatskii gosudarstvennyi gumanitarnyi universitet, 2008.
Banner, L. W. "Biography as History." *American Historical Review* 114, no. 3 (2009): 579–586.
Barber, John. *Soviet Historians in Crisis, 1928–1932*. New York: Holmes and Meier, 1981.
Beer, Daniel. *Renovating Russia: The Human Sciences and the Fate of Liberal Modernity, 1880–1930*. Ithaca, NY: Cornell University Press, 2008.
———. *The house of the dead: Siberian exile under the Tsars*. London: Allen Lane, an imprint of Penguin Books, 2016.
Berdinskikh, V. A. *Istoriia goroda Viatki*. Kirov, 2002.
Berezovaia, L. G. *Samosoznanie russkoi intelligentsii nachala 20 veka. Dissertatsiia na soiskanie uchenoi stepeni doktora istoricheskikh nauk*. Moskva: typeprint, 1994.
Biograficheskie spravki na Viatskikh namestikov i gubernatorov (1780–1917). Kirov: GAKO, 1996.
Bogucharskii, Vasilii. *Aktivnoe narodnichestvo semidesiatykh godov*. Moskva: Sabashnikovy, 1912.
Brower, Daniel. *Training the Nihilists: Education and Radicalism in Tsarist Russia*. Ithaca, NY: Cornell University Press, 1975.
Brown, K. "A Place in Biography for Oneself." *American Historical Review* 114, no. 3 (2009): 596–605.
Burbank, Jane. *Intelligentsia and Revolution: Views of Bolshevism, 1917–1922*. New York: Oxford University Press, 1989.
Canright, Chiari E. *Undoing Time: The Cultural Memory of an Italian Prison*. Oxford: Peter Lang, 2012.
Chudova, Gali F. "Nikolai Apollonich Charushin (1861–1937)." *Gertsenka: Viatskie Zapiski* 24 (2013): 73–95.
———. "N. A. Charushin-bibliograph." *Sovetskaia bibliographiia* 4 (1984): 41–45.
Confino, Alan. "Collective Memory and Cultural History: Problems of Method." *American Historical Review* 102, no. 5 (1997): 1386–1403.
Conroy, Mary S. *Emerging Democracy in Late Imperial Russia: Case Studies on Local Self-Government (the Zemstvos), State Duma Elections, the Tsarist Government, and the State Council before and During World War I*. Niwot: University Press of Colorado, 1998.
Dahlke, Sandra. *Individuum und Herrschaft im Stalinismus: Emel'jan Jaroslavskij (1878–1943)*. Munich: R. Oldenbourg, 2010.

Darevskaia, E. M., Tagarov, Zh. Z. "Kiakhtintsy Lushnikovy i ssyl'nyi narodnik D.A. Klements." *Ssyl'nye revoliutsionery v Sibiri.* Irkutsk, 1989, 118–138.

Eklof, Ben. "The Archaeology of 'Backwardness' in Russia: Assessing the Adequacy of Libraries for Rural Russian Audiences in Late Imperial Russia." In *The Space of the Book in Imperial Russia: Print Culture in the Russian Social Imagination,* edited by Miranda Remnek. Toronto: Toronto University Press, 2011.

———. *Russian Peasant Schools: Officialdom, Village Culture, and Popular Pedagogy, 1864–1914.* Berkeley: University of California Press, 1986.

Engel, Barbara A. "Women as Revolutionaries: The Russian Populists." In *Becoming Visible: Women in European History,* edited by Renate Bridenthal and Claudia Koonz. Boston: Houghton Mifflin, 1977.

———. *Breaking the Ties That Bound: The Politics of Marital Strife in Late Imperial Russia.* Ithaca, NY: Cornell University Press, 2011.

———. *Mothers and Daughters: Women of the Intelligentsia in Nineteenth-Century Russia.* Evanston, IL: Northwestern University Press.

———. "Women, the Family and Public Life." In *The Cambridge History of Russia,* edited by Dominic Lieven, vol. 3. Cambridge: Cambridge University Press, 2006.

Enteen, George M. *The Soviet Scholar-Bureaucrat: M. N. Pokrovskii and the Society of Marxist Historians.* University Park: Pennsylvania State University Press, 1978.

Erman, L. K. *Intelligentsiia v pervoi russkoi revoliutsii.* Moskva: Nauka, 1966.

Evtuhov, Catherine. *Portrait of a Russian Province: Economy, Society, and Civilization in Nineteenth-Century Nizhnii Novgorod.* Pittsburgh, PA: University of Pittsburgh Press, 2011.

Eyerman, R. "The Past in the Present: Culture and the Transmission of Memory." *Acta Sociologica* 47, no. 2 (2004): 159–161.

Figes, Orlando. *Peasant Russia, Civil War: The Volga Countryside in Revolution (1917–1921).* London: Phoenix Press, 1989.

Figes, Orlando, and Boris Kolonitskiĭ. *Interpreting the Russian Revolution: The Language and Symbols of 1917.* New Haven, CT: Yale University Press, 1999.

Fivush R., and C. A. Haden, eds. *Autobiographical Memory and the Construction of a Narrative Self: Developmental and Cultural Perspectives.* Mahwah, NJ: Lawrence Erlbaum, 2013.

Frankel, J. "Party Genealogy and the Soviet Historians (1920–1938)." *Slavic Review* 25, no. 4 (1966): 563–603.

Frierson, Cathy A. *All Russia Is Burning! A Cultural History of Fire and Arson in Late Imperial Russia.* Seattle: University of Washington Press, 2002.

———. *Peasant Icons: Representations of Rural People in Late Nineteenth Century.* New York: Oxford University Press, 1993.

Gaudin, Corinne. *Ruling Peasants: Village and State in Late Imperial Russia.* DeKalb: Northern Illinois University Press, 2007.

Geifman, Anna. *Thou Shalt Kill: Revolutionary Terrorism in Russia, 1894–1917.* Princeton, NJ: Princeton University Press, 1993.

Gerasimov, I. V. "On the Limitations of Analysis of 'Experts and Peasants' (an Attempt at the Internationalization of a Discussion in *Kritika*)." *Jarhrbucher fur Geschichte Osteuropas,* Neue Folge 52, no. 2 (2004): 261–273.

Gernet, M. N. *Istoriia tsarskoi tiur'my. 1870–1900.* Vol. 3. Moskva: Gosudarstvennoe izdatel'stvo iuridicheskoi literatury, 1952.

Ginzburg, Lidia. *O psikhologicheskoi proze*. Leningrad: Khudozhestvennaia literatura, 1977.
Gleason, Abbot. *Young Russia: The Genesis of Russian Radicalism in the 1860s*. New York: Viking, 1980.
Goffman, Erving. *The Presentation of Self in Everyday Life*. New York: Anchor, 1990.
Good, Jane E. *Babushka: The Life of the Russian Revolutionary Ekaterina K. Breshko-Breshkovskaia (1844–1934)*. Edited by David R. Jones. Newtonville, MA: Oriental Research Partners, 1991.
Hardy, Deborah. *Land and Freedom: The Origins of Russian Terrorism, 1876–1879*. New York: Greenwood Press, 1987.
Hartnett, Lynn Ann. *The Defiant Life of Vera Figner: Surviving the Revolution*. Bloomington: Indiana University Press, 2014.
Holquist, Peter. "In Accord with State Interests and the People's Wishes: The Technocratic Ideology of Imperial Russia's Resettlement Administration." *Slavic Review* 69, no. 1 (Spring 2010): 151–179.
Hoogenboom, Hilde. "Vera Figner and Revolutionary Autobiographies: The Influence of Gender on Genre." In *Women in Russia and Ukraine*, edited by Rosalind Marsh. Cambridge: Cambridge University Press, 1996.
Hundley, Helen. *George Kennan and the Russian Empire. How America's Conscience Became an Enemy of Tsarism*. Washington, DC: Woodrow Wilson Center, 2000.
Intelligentsiia i revoliutsiia. XX vek. Moskva, 1985.
Intelligentsiia i rossiiskoe obshchestvo v nachale XX v. Sbornik statei. Petersburg, 1996.
Istoriia goroda Kirova. 1374–1974. Kratkii ocherk. Kirov, 1974.
Itenberg, Boris. *Dvizhenie revoliutsionnogo narodnichestva. Narodnicheskie kruzhki I 'khozhdenie v narod' v 70-kh godakh 19 veka*. Moskva: Nauka, 1965.
———. *Rossiia i Parizhskaia Kommuna*. Moskva: Nauka, 1971.
Jelinek, Estelle C. *Women's Autobiography: Essays in Criticism*. Bloomington: Indiana University Press, 1980.
Johanson, Christine. *Women's Struggle for Higher Education in Russia, 1855–1900*. Kingston, Canada: McGill-Queen's University Press, 1987.
Junge, Mark. "Ugroza likvidatsii OPK v 1922 godu." *Vsesoiuznoe Obshchestvo politkatorzhan i ssyl'noposelentsev. Obrazovanie, razvitie, likvidatsiia. 1921–1935. Materialy mezhdunarodnoi nauchnoi konferentsii*. Moskva: Memorial—Zven'ia, 2004, 23–66.
———. *Revoliutsionery na pensii: vsesoiuznoe obshchestvo politkatorzhani ssyl'noposelentsev, 1921–1935*. Moskva: AIRO, 2015.
Keep, John L. *The Russian Revolution: A Study in Mass Mobilization, Revolutions in Modern World*. London: Weidenfeld & Nicolson, 1976.
Khodarkovsky, Michael. *Bitter Choices: Loyalty and Betrayal in the Russian Conquest of the North Caucasus*. Ithaca, NY: Cornell University Press, 2011.
Kler, L. "Kariiskaia katorga. Ee mesto i rol' v karatel'noi sisteme samoderzhaviia." *Ssyl'nye revoliutsionery v Sibiri*. Irkutsk: Irkutskii Gosudarstvennyi Universitet, 1985.
Knight, Nathaniel. "Was the Intelligentsia Part of the Nation? Visions of Society in Post-Emancipation Russia." *Kritika: Explorations in Russian and Eurasian History* 7, no. 4 (2006): 733–758.
Kolesnikova, L. A. *Istoricheskie i istoriograficheskie problemy na stranitsakh zhurnala "Katorga i ssylka."* Nizhnii Novgorod, 2001.
Kolevatov, N. A. *Orlov: Drevnie goroda Rossii*. Kirov, 1998.

Kolupaeva, V. N. "'Vse s knigami i o knigakh'. E. V. Gogel' (1864–1955) i Viatskaia gubernskaia publichnaia biblioteka im. A.I. Gertsena." *Gertsenka: Viatskie zapiski* 11 (2007): 25–36.
———. "K istorii Gertsenki (1917–1922)." *Gertsenka: Viatskie zapiski* 3 (2002): 7–16.
Korelin, A. P., ed. *Zemskoe samoupravlenie v Rossii. 1864–1918*. Moskva: Nauka, 2005.
Koroleva, N. G. *Zemstvo na perelome* (1905–1907 gg.) Moskva: IRI RAN, 1995.
Kotsonis, Yanni. *Making Peasants Backward: Agricultural Cooperatives and the Agrarian Question in Russia, 1861–1914*. New York: St. Martin's Press.
Kriegel A., and E. Hirsch. "Generational Difference: The History of an Idea." *Daedalus* 107, no. 4 (1978): 23–38.
Kurenyshev, A. A. *Krest'ianskie organizatsii v Rossii v pervoi treti XX veka*. Moskva: AIRO, 2007.
———. *Vserossiiskii krest'ianskii soiuz 1905–1930 gg. Mify i real'nost'*. Petersburg: Dmitrii Bulanin, 2004.
Leikina-Svirskaia, V. R. *Intelligentsiia v Rossii vo vtoroi polovine XIX veka*. Moskva: Mysl', 1971.
———. *Russkaia intelligentsiia 1900–1917 gg*. Moskva: Mysl', 1981.
Leonard, Carol Scott. *Agrarian Reform in Russia the Road from Serfdom*. New York: Cambridge University Press, 2011.
Liubichankovskii, S. V. "Smushchenie v tsentre gubernskoi tverdoi vlasti obostraietsia": dokumenty Kirovskoi oblasti o konflikte viatskogo gubernator S.D. Gorchakova s vitse-gubernatorom A. D. Shidlovskiim. 1907g. *Otechestvennye arkhivy* 2 (2007).
Lobanova, E. V. "K. V. Driagin: uchenyi, pedagog, lichnost'." *Gertsenka: Viatskie zapiski* 3 (2002): 175–181.
Lovell, Stephen. "From Genealogy to Generation. The Birth of Cohort Thinking in Russia." *Kritika: Explorations in Russian and Eurasian History* 9, no. 3 (2008): 567–594.
Luppov P. N. *Politicheskaia ssylka v Viatskii krai*. M.: Vsesoiuznoe Obshchestvo politkatorzhan i ssyl'noposelentsev, 1933.
Luppov, P. N. *Istoriia goroda Viatki*. Kirov, 1958.
Malia, Martin M. *Alexander Herzen and the Birth of Russian Socialism, 1812–1855*. Cambridge, MA: Harvard University Press, 1961.
Manchester, Laure. "Gender and Social Estate as National Identity: The Wives and Daughters of Orthodox Clergymen as Civilizing Agents in Imperial Russia." *Journal of Modern History* 83, no.1 (2011): 48–77.
Manheim, Karl. "Problema pokolenii." *Novoe literaturnoe obozrenie* 2 (1998): 7–47.
Mason, Mary Ann. *The Equality Trap*. New York: Simon and Schuster, 1988.
Maxwell, Margaret. *Narodniki Women: Russian Women Who Sacrificed Themselves for the Dream of Freedom*. New York: Pergamon, 1990.
Melamed, E. I. *Dzhordzh Kennan protiv tsarizma*. Moskva: Kniga, 1981.
Miller, Martin A. "Ideological Conflicts in Russian Populism: The Revolutionary Manifestoes of the Chaikovskii Circle, 1869–1875." *Slavic Review* 29, no. 1 (1970): 1–21.
Mogil'ner, Marina. *Mifologiia 'podpol'nogo cheloveka': Radikal'nyi mikrokosm v Rossii nachala 20 veka kak predmet semioticheskogo analiza*. Moskva: NLO, 1999.
Morrissey, Susan K. "Terrorism, Modernity, and the Question of Origins." *Kritika: Explorations in Russian and Eurasian History* 12, no. 1 (Winter 2011): 215–26.
Naimark, Norman M. *Terrorists and Social Democrats: The Russian Revolutionary Movement under Alexander III*. Cambridge, MA: Harvard University Press, 1983.
Nora, P. "Between Memory and History: Les Lieux de Mémoire." *Representations*. Special Issue: *Memory and Counter-Memory* 26 (1989): 7–24.

Ocherki istorii Kirovskoi oblasti. Ed. A. V. Emmauskii. Kirov, 1972.
Offord, Derek. "The Contribution of V. V. Bervi-Flerovsky to Russian Populism." *Slavonic and East European Review* 66, no. 2 (1988): 236–251.
Offord, Derek. *The Russian Revolutionary Movement in the 1880s*. Cambridge: Cambridge University Press, 1986.
Ottsy i deti. Pokolencheskii analiz sovremennoi Rossii. Biblioteka zhurnala *Neprikosnovennyi zapas*. Moskva: Novoe literaturnoe obozrenie, 2005.
Ovsianiko-Kulikovskii, Dmitrii. "Istoriia russkoi intelligentsii." *Sobranie sochinenii* 8. Petersburg: O. N. Ovsianiko-Kulikovskaiia, 1914.
Pallot, Judith. *Land Reform in Russia, 1906–1917: Peasant Responses to Stolypin's Project of Rural Transformation*. Oxford: Clarendon, 1998.
Paperno, Irina. *Chernyshevskii and the Age of Realism: A Study in the Semiotics of Behavior*. Stanford, CA: Stanford University Press, 1988.
———. *Semiotika povedeniia: Nikolai Chernyshevskii—chelovek epokhi realizma*. Moskva: NLO, 1996.
Patyk, L. E. "Remembering 'The Terrorism': Sergei Stepniak-Kravchinskii's 'Underground Russia.'" *Slavic Review* 68. no. 4 (2009): 758–781.
Petriaev, E. D. *Literaturnye nakhodki*. Kirov: Volgo-Viatskoe knizhnoe izdatel'stvo, 1966.
———. *Liudi, rukopisi, knigi*. Kirov: Volgo-Viatskoe knizhnoe izdatel'stvo, 1970.
———. *Literaturnye nakhodki: Ocherki kul'turnogo proshlogo Viatskoi zemli*. Kirov: Volgo-Viatskoe knizhnoe izdatel'stvo, 1981.
Pipes, Richard. "Narodnichestvo: A Semantic Inquiry." *Slavic Review* 23, no. 3 (1964): 441–458.
Pirumova, N. M. *Zemskaia intelligentsiia i ee rol' v obshchestvennoi bor'be do nachala XX v.* Moskva: Nauka, 1986.
———. *Zemskoe liberal'noe dvizhenie*. Moskva: Nauka, 1977.
Pomper, Philip. *The Russian Revolutionary Intelligentsia*. Europe since 1500. New York: Crowell, 1970.
Ionescu, Ghita, and Ernest Gellner, eds. *Populism: Its Meaning and National Characteristics*. London: Weideneld & Nicolson, 1969.
Popyvanova, N. D. "A. V. Pallizen (1883–1943)—zaveduiushchaia mestnym (kraevedcheskim) otdelom Viatskoi biblioteki im. Gertsena." *Gertsenka: Viatskie zapiski* 16 (2009): 127–33.
Porter, Cathy. *Fathers and Daughters: Russian Women in Revolution*. London: Virago / Quartet Books, 1976.
Porter, Thomas E. *The Zemstvo and the Emergence of Civil Society in Late Imperial Russia 1864–1917*. San Francisco: Mellen Research University Press, 1991.
Protasova, A. V. *Peshekhonov: chelovek i epokha*. Moskva: ROSSPEN, 2004.
Pujals, Sandra. "When Giants Walked the Earth: The Society of Former Political Prisoners and Exiles of the Soviet Union, 1921–1935." PhD diss., Georgetown University, 1999.
Rabinowitch, Alexander. *The Bolsheviks Come to Power: The Revolution of 1917 in Petrograd*. New York: W. W. Norton, 1976.
Rabinowitch, R. I. *Opal'nyi millioner*. Perm': Knizhnoe izdatel'stvo, 1990.
Raeff, Marc. *Origins of the Russian Intelligentsia: The Eighteenth-Century Nobility*. New York: Harcourt, 1966.
Renders Hans, Binne de Haan, and Jonne Harmsma, eds. *The Biographical Turn: Lives in History*. Abingdon: Routledge, 2017.
Retish, Aaron B. *Russia's Peasants in Revolution and Civil War: Citizenship, Identity, and the Creation of the Soviet State, 1914–1922*. Cambridge: Cambridge University Press, 2008.

Rieber, Alfred J. "The Sedimentary Society." In *Between Tsar and People: Educated Society and the Quest for Public Identity in Late Imperial Russia*, edited by E. W. Clowes. Princeton, NJ: Princeton University Press, 1991.

Rodigina, Nataliia. "*Drugaia Rossiia.*" *Obraz Sibiri v russkoi zhurnal'noi presse vtoroi poloviny XIX-nachala XX v.* Novosibirsk: Novosibirskii gosudarstvennyi pedagogicheskii universitet, 2006.

Rodigina, Nataliia, and Tatiana Saburova. "Pokolencheskoe izmerenie sotsiokul'turnoi istorii Rossii 19 veka: preemstvennost' i razryvy." *Dialog so vremenem. Al'manakh intellektual'noi istorii* 34 (2011): 138–157.

Ruane, Christine. "Subjects into Citizens: The Politics of Clothing in Imperial Russia." In *Fashioning the Body Politic: Dress, Gender, Citizenship*, edited by Wendy Parkins. Oxford: Berg, 2002.

———. *The Empire's New Clothes: A History of the Russian Fashion Industry, 1700–1917*. New Haven, CT: Yale University Press, 2009.

Saburova, Tatiana. *Russkii intellektual'nyi mir/mif. Sotsiokul'turnye predstavleniia intelligentsii v Rossii XIX v.* Omsk, 2005.

Saburova, Tatiana, and Ben Eklof. *Druzhba, Sem'ia, Revoliutsiia. Nikolai Charushin i pokolenie narodnikov 1870-kh godov.* Moskva: Novoe Literaturnoe Obozrenie, 2016.

Safronova, Iulia. *Russkoe obshchestvo v zerkale revoliutsionnogo terrora, 1879–1881 gody.* Moskva: NLO, 2014.

Scott, James C. *Seeing Like a State: How Certain Schemes to Improve the Human Condition Have Failed.* Yale Agrarian Studies. New Haven, CT: Yale University Press, 1998.

Seregny S. J. "Zemstvos, Peasants, and Citizenship: The Russian Adult Education Movement and World War I." *Slavic Review* 59, no. 2 (2000): 290–315.

Sergeev, Valentin. *Platony i Nevtony Viatskoi zemli: Istoriko-kraevedcheskie ocherki.* Kirov, 2006.

———. *Nikolai Charushin—narodnik, obshchestvennyi deiatel', izdatel', kraeved-bibliograf.* Kirov, 2004.

———. "N. A. Charushin i biblioteka imeni A.I. Gertsena." *Gertsenka: Viatskie zapiski* 1 (2000): 25–31.

———. *Raznochintsy-demokraty Viatki.* Kirov, 2003.

———. "Lishnyi shtrikh dostopamiatnoi epokhi: A. A. Charushin." *VIII Petriaevskie chteniia.* Kirov, 2005, 234–238.

Shelokhaev V.V., ed. *Modeli obshchestvennogo pereustroistva Rossii. 20 vek* Moskva: ROSSPEN, 2004.

———., ed. *Politicheskie partii Rossii, konets XIX-pervaia tret' XX veka: entsiklopediia.* Moskva: ROSSPEN, 1996.

Shumikhin, V. G. *Dlia zhizni nastoiashchei i budushchei: knizhoe delo Viatskogo zemstvo.* Kirov, 1996.

Smith, A. K. "The Shifting Place of Women in Imperial Russia's Social Order." *Cahiers du Monde Russe* 51, no. 2 (2010): 353–367.

Smith, Sidonie. *A Poetics of Women's Autobiography: Marginality and the Fictions of Self-Representation.* Bloomington: Indiana University Press, 1987.

Smith, Sidonie. *Subjectivity, Identity, and the Body: Women's Autobiographical Practices in the Twentieth Century.* Bloomington: Indiana University Press, 1993.

Solov'eva, I. A. "Nikolai Vasil'evich Chaikovskii." *Voprosy Istorii* 5 (1997): 38–48.

Startsev, V. I. *Vnutrenniaia politika vremennogo pravitel'stva.* Leningrad: Nauka, 1980.

Stites, Richard. *The Women's Liberation Movement in Russia: Feminism, Nihilism, and Bolshevism, 1860–1930*. Princeton, NJ: Princeton University Press, 1991.
Sudovikov, Mikhail S. "Iakov Poskrebyshev: Portret gorodskogo golovy." *Gertsenka* 6 (2009): 99–104.
———. "Mashkovtsevy. Kuptsy i obshchestvennye deiateli." In *Kupechestvo Viatskoe*, edited by Mikhail Sudovikov and Tamara Nikolaeva. Kirov, 1999, 15–34.
Sunderland, Willard. *The Baron's Cloak: A History of the Russian Empire in War and Revolution*. Ithaca, NY: Cornell University Press, 2014.
Suvorov, G. "Gorod Orlov v kontse XVIII-pervoi polovine XIX v." *Pamiatnaia Knizhka Kirovskoi Oblasti i Kalendar' na 2009 god*. Kirov, 2009, 267–275.
Sypchenko A.V. *Narodno-sotsialisticheskaia partiia v 1907–1917 gg*. Moskva: ROSSPEN, 1999.
Timkin, Iu. N. *Smutnoe vremia na Viatke: Obshchestvenno-politicheskoe razvitie Viatskoi gubernii vesnoi 1917-osen'iu 1918 gg*. Kirov, 1998.
Tkachenko, P. "O nekotorykh voprosakh istorii narodnichestva." *Voprosy Istorii* 5 (1956): 34–45.
Tolstoy, Leo. *L. N. Tolstoy i A. A. Tolstaia. Perepiska (1857–1903)*. Moskva: Nauka, 2011.
Trigos, Ludmilla A. *The Decembrist Myth in Russian Culture*. New York: Palgrave Macmillan, 2009.
Troitskii, Nikolai. *"Narodnaia Volia" pered tsarskim sudom (1880–1891)*. Saratov: Izdatel'stvo Saratovskogo universiteta, 1971.
———. *Bezumstvo khrabrykh. Russkie revolutsionery i karatel'naia politika tsarizma. 1866–1882*. Moskva: Mysl', 1978.
———. *Russkoe revoliutsionnoe narodnichestvo 1870-ikh godov*. Saratov: Izdatel'stvo Saratovskogo universiteta, 2003.
———. *Pervye iz blestiaschei pleiady: Bol'shoe obshchestvo propagandy 1871–1874*. Saratov: Izdatel'stvo Saratovskogo universiteta, 1991.
Turton, K. "Keeping It in the Family: Surviving Political Exile, 1870–1917." *Canadian Slavonic Papers / Revue Canadienne des Slavistes* 52, no. 3–4 (2010): 391–415.
Ulam, Alan B. *The Bolsheviks: The Intellectual and Political History of the Triumph of Communism in Russia*. New York: Macmillan, 1965.
Vakhrushev, A. A. "Viatskii Krai"—pervaia obshchestvenno-politicheskaia chastnaia gazeta." *Vestnik Viatskogo Gosudarstvennogo Universiteta*. 2 (2009): 134–139.
Venturi, Franko. *Roots of Revolution: A History of the Populist and Socialist Movements in Nineteenth Century Russia*. New York: Grosset & Dunlap, 1966.
———. "Russian Populism." In Ventury, *Studies in Free Russia*. Chicago: University of Chicago, 1982, 216–287.
Verhoeven, Claudia. *The Odd Man Karakozov: Imperial Russia, Modernity, and the Birth of Terrorism*. Ithaca, NY: Cornell University Press, 2009.
Veselovskii, Boris. *Istoriia zemstva za sorok let*. 4 Vols. S.-Peterburg: Izd-vo O.N. Popovoi, 1909–1911.
Volk, S. *"Narodnaia Volia" (1879–1882)*. Moskva, Leningrad: Nauka, 1966.
Wachtel, Andrew. *The Battle for Childhood: Creation of a Russian Myth*. Stanford, CA: Stanford University Press, 1990.
Wade, Rex A. *The Russian Revolution, 1917*. 2nd ed. New Approaches to European History. Cambridge: Cambridge University Press, 2005.
Wager, A. "Anti-Zemstvo Riots, Adult Education and the Russian Village during World War One: Stavropol' Province." *Slavonic and East European Review* 79, no. 1. (2001): 90–126.

Waldron Peter. *Governing Tsarist Russia*. European History in Perspective. New York: Palgrave Macmillan, 2007.

Walicki, Andrzej. *A History of Russian Social Thought from the Enlightenment to Marxism*. Stanford, CA: Stanford University Press, 1979.

Wcislo, Francis W. *Tales of Imperial Russia: The Life and Times of Sergei Witte, 1849–1915*. New York: Oxford University Press, 2011.

Wood, Elisabeth. "The Woman Question in Russia: Contradictions and Ambivalence." In *A Companion to Russian History*, edited by Abbott Gleason. Chichester, UK: Wiley-Blackwell, 2009.

Wortman, Richard. *The Crisis of Russian Populism*. Cambridge: Cambridge University Press, 1967.

Yarmolinsky, Avrahm. *Road to Revolution: A Century of Russian Radicalism*. Princeton: Princeton University Press, 1957.

Zelnik, Reginald. "Populists and Workers: The First Encounter between Populist Students and Industrial Workers in St. Petersburg, 1871–1874." *Soviet Studies* 24, no. 2 (1972): 251–269.

Zharavin, Vladimir. *Aleksandr Lebedev—prosvetitel' i kraeved*. Kirov, 2011.

Zhenina, L. V. "Uchastie Viatskogo zemstvo v Obshchezemskoi organizatsii (1904–1907)." *Zemskoe samoupravlenie: organizatsiia, deiatel'nost', opyt*. Materialy nauchnoi konferentsii. Kirov, 2002.

Znamenskii, O. N. *Intelligentsiia nakanune velikogo Oktiabria*. Leningrad: Nauka, 1988.

INDEX

Aksenov, Vasilii, 356, 364
Alasheev, E., 254
Alexander I, 16
Alexander II, 1, 6, 9, 26, 102, 104, 107, 138, 140, 153, 156–158, 322, 333, 366, 375
Alexander III, 376
Andreeva, Nina, 350
Antonov, Vasilii, 345, 354
Aptekman, Osip, 13–14, 327, 341
Ashenbrenner, Mikhail, 341
Assmann, Aleida, 7
Axelrod, Pavel, 55, 63, 70

Badcock, Sarah, 286, 302
Bakulin, Vladimir, 271, 286, 293, 299
Bakunin, Mikhail, 55–57, 70–71, 100, 346, 365, 373–374, 377
Baranov, Alexander, 201, 205, 223, 257–258, 265–268, 327
Basov, P. S., 288–292, 294, 304
Batuev, Avksentii, 200–201, 203–204, 218, 226–227, 229, 253, 267
Beer, Daniel, 369
Bervi-Flerovskii, Vasilii, 1, 32, 64–65
Bibergal', Ekaterina, 164
Biriukov, Dmitrii, 201, 223, 230, 255, 258, 262
Blinov, Nikolai, 22, 203, 253, 267
Bliukher, Vasilii, 297, 314, 353

Bogoslovskii, Mikhail, 271, 283, 290
Bogucharskii, Vasilii, 48, 59, 326
Borodin, Mikhail, 22, 201, 205, 223, 260, 267
Borovoi, Alexei, 327, 335–336, 379
Branovskii, N., 252
Breshko-Breshkovskaia, Ekaterina, 73, 94, 96, 109, 158, 318, 385
Brower, Daniel, 2, 34
Bulychev, Tikhon, 194–195, 225
Butin, M., 168

Chaikovskii, Nikolai, 13, 18, 30, 44, 47–48, 63, 69, 71, 140, 202, 226, 266, 276, 300, 325, 370, 373
Charushin, Apollon, 27
Charushin, Arkadii, 15, 21, 43, 134, 148, 180, 191–194, 215, 223–225, 248–249, 265, 308
Charushin, Ivan, 15, 21, 163, 182, 185, 193–196, 223–225, 248, 272, 296, 309–310, 313, 337, 352, 361
Charushin, Leonid N., 95, 190
Charushin, Leonid V., 337–338
Charushin, Vladimir, 95, 190, 246, 308, 337–338
Charushina, Lydia, 190, 248
Charushina, Lydia N., 94, 164, 181
Charushina, Yulia, 190–191, 248
Charushnikov, Alexander, 205, 226, 324
Chekhov, Anton, 163–163, 303

Chernavskii, Mikhail, 68, 125, 135, 142, 168, 325, 341
Chemodanova (Sinegub), Larisa, 77–78, 88–92, 104–106, 99, 108–110, 121, 133, 142, 146, 153, 159, 162, 164, 181, 187, 226, 259, 265, 268, 309, 339, 374
Chernyshevskii, Nikolai, 2, 29, 32, 51–53, 57, 70, 74–75, 84, 86, 90, 345
Chudnovskii, Solomon, 28, 37, 63, 70–71, 114–116, 118, 120, 123, 125, 129, 135–136, 140–142, 143–144, 222, 374, 381
Chudova, Gali, 347–349, 351–352, 354, 356–359, 364
Confino, Michael, 34

Darwin, Charles, 57
Debogorii-Mokrievich, Vladimir, 58, 71, 141, 148, 156, 183–184, 374, 381
Depreis, A. S., 283
Deutch (Deich), Lev, 96, 120, 122, 151, 155, 375
Dickens, Charles, 31
Dobroliubov, Nikolai, 52
Dostoevsky, Fedor, 34, 48, 113
Driagin, K. V., 313, 339–340
Engel, Barbara, 74, 81, 97, 107–108
Engelstein, Laura, 369
Epstein, Anna, 92
Evtuhov, Catherine, 197

Farmakovskii, 24, 29–31, 227
Figes, Orlando, 281, 302
Figner (Sazhina), Evgeniia, 99, 309, 337, 341
Figner (Stakhevich), Lidiia, 103–104, 342, 375
Figner, Vera, 4, 13–14, 18–20, 34, 50, 57, 60, 73–74, 78–80, 90, 92, 98–99, 101–105, 107, 109–110, 112, 115, 117–119, 121, 123, 125–133, 136, 160, 181, 199, 214–215, 226, 229, 273, 284–285, 298, 307–309, 317, 319–323, 325–328, 333–337, 340–343, 370, 375
Filippov, A. V., 102–104
Frolenko, Mikhail, 55, 60, 121, 317
Furmanov, Dmitrii, 328

Gerasimov, Ilia, 282
Ginzburg, Lydia, 22

Gogel', Elena, 294, 300, 305–307, 312–315, 317, 339–340, 382
Golubev, Petr, 22, 201, 203, 205, 222–223, 230, 242, 260
Gorbachev, Mikhail, 9, 349–350, 354, 357
Gorchakov, Sergei, 224, 232–234, 236, 239, 242–243, 245–248, 250, 253–257, 262–268, 283, 386
Gur'ev, A. A., 201, 203, 217, 222, 230, 260, 302
Gur'eva L. A., 260–261

Hallbachs, Maurice, 7
Hartnett, Lynn, 229, 343
Herzen, Alexander, 24, 74, 159
Holmes, Larry, x
Holquist, Peter, 204
Hoogenboom, Hilde, 19, 35–36

Iakimova, Anna, 22, 60, 71–72, 226, 309, 332, 341
Igoshin, I. I., 239, 264
Itenberg, Boris, 345–346, 354, 364
Iuferev, Ivan, 15, 27, 224
Iuferev, Viacheslav, 190–194, 198, 224
Iufereva (Charushina), Ekaterina, 15–16, 27, 43, 248

Kamyshanskii, Petr, 257–258
Kaufman, A. A., 249
Kennan, George, 8, 11, 165–167, 171, 179, 183–186, 378, 381
Kenney, Padraic, x
Kerensky, Alexander, 291
Khlusevich, S. O., 195
Khoroshavin, Ivan, 191
Klements, Dmitrii, 67, 71, 92, 109, 169, 226, 315, 382
Klingenberg, Nikolai, 204
Kliucharev, Vasilii, 190, 201, 222, 239–240, 264
Kniazev, 239
Komarov N., 347, 352–354, 357, 363
Kornilova, Luibov, 44, 98, 101, 121, 374
Kornilova, Vera, 44, 100
Kornilova-Moroz, Alexandra, 39, 44, 47, 52, 56–58, 67, 75–76, 80–82, 85, 99, 101,

108, 128, 131, 139, 226, 261, 321–323, 325, 336–337, 362, 375
Kon, Felix, 330–332
Koni, Anatolii, 307, 312, 339–340, 382
Kononovich, Vladimir, 160–164, 167, 184–185, 331
Koshkareva, Olga, 309, 339
Kovalik, Sergei, 46, 49, 55, 71, 137, 143
Koz'min, Boris, 328–329, 342
Krasnoperov, Ivan, 21, 31
Krasovskii, A. A., 31
Kravchinskaia, Fanni, 307
Kravchinskii (Stepniak), Sergei, 60, 64, 67, 72, 81, 92–94, 101, 109, 124, 157, 318, 340, 377, 380, 382
Kropotkin, Petr, 46, 49, 55–56, 69, 81, 101, 276, 325–326, 375, 382
Kugushev, Georgii, 196, 201, 217, 264
Kuskova, Ekaterina, 19
Kuvshinskaia (Charushina), Anna, 3–5, 10, 22–23, 30, 37, 60, 71, 73–74, 76–79, 83–87, 91, 94–99, 106, 108–110, 129, 132–134, 140, 146, 153, 159–160, 162–167, 172, 179–180, 182, 187, 190–191, 195, 198–199, 206, 209–210, 222, 226, 228–229, 231, 237, 243, 245–249, 254, 260–263, 265, 267–268, 324, 341, 352, 365
Kuznetsov, Alexei, 150, 167–170, 316, 376
Kviatkovskaia, 154

Lassalle, Ferdinand, 32, 57–59, 64, 71, 109
Lavrov, Petr, 2, 44, 52, 55, 57, 71, 326, 365, 376
Lazarev, Egor, 226, 307, 318, 334–335
Lebedev, Alexander, 311, 313–314, 339–340, 390
Lermontov, Mikhail, 54
Leshern, Sofia, 108
Levchenko, Alexander, 232
Levin, Shmuel, 323, 328, 345–346, 353
Lipiagov, Sergei, 255, 258
Lopatin, Alexei, 190, 218, 225, 239, 264
Lopatin, Nikolai, 34
Lovell, Stephen, 6
Lozhkin, Nikolai, 201, 205–206, 227, 264, 266–267
Lushnikov, Alexei, 171, 179

Makushin, Vladimir, 278, 288
Mashkovtsev, 30–32, 37
Meshkov, Nikolai, 195
Mezentsev, 124, 157, 378
Miakotin, Venedikt, 276
Mikhailovskii, Nikolai, 57
Mill, John Stuart, 32
Morozov, Nikolai, 96
Morrissey, Susan, 366
Myshkin, Ippolit, 139, 326

Natanson, Mark, 44, 67
Nechaev, Sergei, 34, 47–49, 167, 373, 376
Nekrasov, Nikolai, 32, 54, 74, 158–159
Nicholas II, 181, 199, 269, 273
Novorusskii, Mikhail, 116–118, 121–123, 125–126, 130, 135–136, 141–143, 341–342, 376, 382

Ogorodnikov, N. A., 206
Ovchinnikov, 229

Padarin, 258
Palkin, K. A., 305
Pallizen, Adol'fina, 312, 314, 339
Paperno, Irina, 50
Pavlenkov, Florentii, 203, 227
Perovskaia, Sofia, 57, 71, 73, 78, 81–82, 101, 300, 322, 333, 375
Peshekhonov, Alexei, 196, 226, 274, 280, 300
Petriaev, Evgenii, 347, 358
Pisarev, Dmitrii, 52, 54
Popov, Ivan, 92, 95, 100, 109–110, 147, 150, 159, 169–171, 173, 179, 181–184, 186, 226, 315–316, 324, 329–330, 332, 340–342, 376, 379, 382
Portugalov, V. O., 227
Poskrebyshev, Iakov, 195, 218, 225, 310
Potanin, Grigorii, 173–174, 186
Pribylev, Alexander, 19, 102, 196, 382
Pribyleva-Korba, Anna, 91, 101–102, 105, 109, 341
Pushkin, Alexander, 52–54

Rabinowitch, Alexander, x
Rabinowitch, Janet, x

Raeff, Mark, 34
Reiber, Alfred, 204
Retish, Aaron, 281, 286
Reva, Alexander, 351–352, 357, 359
Rochefort de, 233, 254
Rosenberg, William, 298–299
Rozhdestvenskii, Iakov, 28, 31, 55
Rudnev, N. A., 269–270

Salamatov, P. T., 276, 288–291, 293, 302
Saltykov-Shchedrin, Mikhail, 127, 257
Sazhin, Mikhail, 19, 99–100, 110, 261, 334, 337, 341–342, 377
Sedov, Mikhail, 345, 354
Semenov-Tian-Shanskii, Petr, 173, 186
Semianovskii, 154, 185
Serapikhskii, E. V., 288, 292
Serdiukov, Anatolii, 101, 326
Seregny, Scott, 282
Sergeev, Valentin, 14, 225, 346, 355–361, 364
Shebalin, Mikhail, 341, 379
Shebalina, Maria, 308, 323, 327, 329, 334, 337, 341–343
Shelgunov, Nikolai, 84
Shidlovskii, A. F., 255, 257
Shishko, Leonid, 44, 59, 64, 69, 93, 153–154, 164–165, 226, 324, 377, 382
Shubin, V. A., 218, 220, 229
Sinegub, Sergei, 41–42, 46, 63–64, 66, 68–70, 77, 84, 88–91, 95, 99, 107–110, 114, 116, 118–120, 122, 124, 126–130, 133, 135, 140–144, 146–147, 149, 153–154, 160–162, 164–165, 183–185, 226, 324, 374, 377
Sintsov, Matvei, 27, 29–30
Sokolov, N. N., 197
Spielhagen, Friedrich, 57, 90, 109
Starodumov, N. P., 252
Startsev, Vasilli, 270
Stites, Richard, 74
Stolypin, Petr, 4, 208, 222, 231, 233, 236, 239, 246, 254–258, 262
Sukhanov, Nikolai, 79, 107
Sukhodoev V., 347, 352–354, 357, 363

Tagantsev, N. S., 59, 71
Tanaevskaia, Vera, 100, 199, 223, 226, 238, 244, 264

Tikhomirov, Lev, 13, 42, 64, 68, 89, 122, 157, 184, 323, 378, 382
Timkin, Yuri, 270, 286, 299
Tkachenko, P. S., 345
Tolstoy (Tolstaia), Alexandra, 77–78, 146, 159–160, 185
Tolstoy, Leo, 20–21, 78
Treiter, V. A., 283–284, 291–294, 302–303, 305
Trepov, Fedor, 200
Troitskii, Nikolai, 47, 58, 144, 345–346, 354, 364
Trotskii, Leon, 344
Turgenev, Ivan, 29, 32, 54, 74, 86
Tyrkova-Williams, Ariadna, 267

Uspenskaia, Alexandra, 164
Uspenskii, Petr, 156, 325, 341

Veselovskii, Boris, 72, 217–218, 227, 233, 263
Vil'berg, Anna, 82
Vol'kenshtein, Ludmila, 105
Volkhovskii, Felix, 71, 222, 226

Wachtel, Andrew, 20
Wade, Rex, 282
Walicki, Andrzej, 369
Wood, Elisabeth, 75, 79

Yumashev, Leonid, 30, 195, 201–202, 217–223, 229, 236, 238–241, 252, 263–264, 272, 288–289, 291–292, 294–295, 308, 374

Zasulich, Vera, 51, 92, 98, 140, 157
Zavolzhskii, Vsevolod, 29
Zelnik, Reginald, 66
Zharavin, Vladimir, 356
Zhdanov, Andrei, 333
Zhdanov, L. I., 350–351
Zheliabov, Andrei, 300, 333
Zhuikov, 297
Znamenskii, O. N., 273
Zonov, A., 304
Zvereva (Klements), Elizaveta, 92
Zviagintsev, 243, 245–246, 254

BEN EKLOF

is Professor of History at Indiana University and author or editor of books and articles on the Russian peasantry, on Russian and Soviet-era education, and on political reform from the mid-nineteenth century to the Perestroika era.

TATIANA SABUROVA

is Visiting Professor of History at Indiana University and a Research Fellow at the Higher School of Economics in Moscow. Her books and articles focus on the Russian intelligentsia, autobiography, memory, and, recently, on the history of photography in Russia.

www.ingramcontent.com/pod-product-compliance
Lightning Source LLC
Chambersburg PA
CBHW052054300426
44117CB00013B/2125